The New Century Handbook of

LEADERS OF THE CLASSICAL WORLD

The New Century Handbook of

LEADERS OF THE CLASSICAL WORLD

edited by

Catherine B. Avery

APPLETON-CENTURY-CROFTS
Educational Division
MEREDITH CORPORATION
NEW YORK

10-30-72 Eastern 6.46

Copyright © 1972 by
MEREDITH CORPORATION

Selected from *The New Century Classical Handbook,*
edited by Catherine B. Avery
Copyright © 1962 by
APPLETON-CENTURY-CROFTS, INC.

72   73   74   75   76/10   9   8   7   6   5   4   3   2   1

61199

Library of Congress Catalog Card Number:
71-189007

#399037

PRINTED IN THE UNITED STATES OF AMERICA
(X) 390-66948-2

OK 10-26-72 DT

Preface

Hundreds of gifted and energetic leaders shaped and protected the civilization that developed over 2,500 years ago in the Mediterranean basin. There were the soldiers, who warded off enemies or conquered new lands through which the developing culture spread. There were the politicians and statesmen, who organized and governed, to produce a kind of order in which the burgeoning civilization could flourish. There were also any number of notorious figures whose influence was far from benign. In the following pages are listed the names and histories of hundreds of leaders who played important or prominent roles in the civilization that flowered in classical Greece and Rome. Generally speaking, the soldiers, statesmen, rulers, politicians, consuls, admirals, queens, princes, and influential ladies who appear in the following pages are historical figures, rather than the heroes and heroines of legend. Their deeds, and even the deeds that surrounded their names, provided vibrant examples of courage, skill, cunning perhaps, and energy for the generations that came after them.

In the belief that a biographical handbook of such outstanding characters would be useful, the entries on the following pages have been selected from *The New Century Classical Handbook,* published by Appleton-Century-Crofts in 1962. The late Professor Jotham Johnson, Head of the Department of Classics, New York University, served as Editorial Consultant for that book. Articles signed with the initials JJ were prepared by him.

The explanation of the pronunciation guide that appears after each entry name is given in the key at the bottom of facing pages.

Catherine B. Avery

——A——

Achaemenidae (ak-ē-men′i-dē). [Also: *Achaemenides, Ache-menides, Achemenids.*] Ancient royal family of Persia, founded c600 B.C. Its leading members were Achaemenes, Cyrus the Great, Cambyses (Gaumata, the Magian usurper), Darius Hystaspes, Xerxes I, Artaxerxes I, Xerxes II, Sogdianus, Darius Ochus, Artaxerxes Mnemon, Ochus, Arses, and Darius Codomannus.

Achemenides (ak-ē-men′i-dēz) or *Achemenids* (ak-ē-men′idz). See *Achaemenidae.*

Ada (ā′dạ). Sister and wife of Idrieus, ruler of Halicarnassus. When her husband died she succeeded him as ruler, but was driven out by her brother Pixodarus. Alexander the Great, having defeated the Persians at the Granicus River (334 B.C.), marched through Asia Minor, overthrowing the tyrannies established by the Persians in the Greek cities there. Ada sought his protection. He adopted her as his mother, and when he had taken Halicarnassus by force he restored Ada and made her ruler of the satrapy of Caria.

Aelius Paetus (ē′li-us pē′tus), *Sextus.* Roman jurist; fl. 2nd century B.C. He was consul in 198 B.C., censor in 193, and was the author of the *Tripartita* (or *Jus Aelianum*) containing a recension of the Twelve Tables (450 B.C.) with commentary.

Aeschines (es′ki-nēz). ["The Orator."] Athenian orator. He was born in 389 B.C., and died on the island of Samos in 314 B.C. He was a cultivated man of good family, but war had destroyed his family's fortunes and he was compelled to work. He was for a time an actor and then, through his association with Athenian statesmen, secured a post as a clerk in the public service. He yoked the legal training he received in the public service with his talents as an actor and became a

---

fat, fāte, fär, fȧll, ȧsk, fāre; net, mē, hėr; pin, pīne; not, nōte, möve, nôr; up, lūte, pull; oi, oil; ou out; (lightened) ēlect, agōny, ūnite; (obscured) errạnt, ardẹnt, actọr; ch, chip; g, go; th, thin; ᴛʜ, then; y, you; (variable) ḍ as d or j, ṣ as s or sh, ṭ as t or ch, ẓ as z or zh.

public speaker and a political figure. He was one of ten commissioners sent to make peace with Philip of Macedon (346 B.C.). Demosthenes, also one of the commissioners, alone refused to accept the peace terms which he rightly considered dangerous to Athens and accused Aeschines of treason (345 B.C.). He defended himself of the charge in a brilliant speech and was acquitted. Subsequently he was again compelled to defend himself when Demosthenes, who had become his enemy, charged that he had accepted bribes from Philip of Macedon. In the end, his enmity for Demosthenes brought his downfall. He made a speech, *Against Ctesiphon* (330 B.C.) but really aimed at Demosthenes, charging that Ctesiphon had acted illegally in proposing a golden crown for Demosthenes. Demosthenes counterattacked strongly and brought suit against him in a speech, *On the Crown.* Aechines lost the case, was compelled to pay a fine, and went into voluntary exile at Rhodes. From there he went to Samos, where he subsequently died. Three of his orations, *Against Timarchus* (an ally of Demosthenes who had joined him in the attack on Aeschines in 345 B.C.), *On the False Embassy* (a reply to an oration of the same name which Demosthenes made against him, 342 B.C.), and *Against Ctesiphon,* survive. The force and grace of the orations of Aeschines caused him to be ranked next after Demosthenes among the orators of his period.

Agariste (ag-a̯-ris′tē). Daughter of Clisthenes of Sicyon (fl. 580 B.C.). Her father invited such of the young princes and heroes of Greece as desired to do so to come to his court and sue for the hand of Agariste. Many came from the wealthiest and noblest families. They stayed in Sicyon a year, and were there put through various tests so that Clisthenes could determine the one best fitted to become his son-in-law. After a year in which the suitors endured such athletic contests as foot racing and wrestling, and such social affairs as banquets where their deportment and prowess as trenchermen were observed, the field was narrowed to the Athenians Hippoclides, son of Tisander, and Megacles, son of Alcmaeon. In the end, Hippoclides frittered away his chances by making a spectacle of himself through excessive dancing at a banquet. Agariste was given to Megacles. One of her sons was Clisthenes, the Athenian who divided the Athenians into ten tribes. Her granddaughter, another Agariste, married the Athenian nobleman Xanthippus. When she was expecting a child, she dreamed she had given birth to a lion. Soon afterwards she bore Xanthippus a son, Pericles.

Agathocles or **Agathokles** (a̯-gath′ō̯-klēz). Sicilian despot, tyrant of Syracuse (317–289 B.C.), born at Thermae, Sicily, 361 B.C.; died 289 B.C. He seized power with an army of exiles and Campanian hirelings and shortly became involved in war with Carthage, traditional enemy of the Sicilian Greeks. He made his way through the Carthaginian forces around Syracuse and crossed the Mediterranean to attack Carthage in 310 B.C., but returned to find Syracuse rumbling with incipient revolt. He thereupon made peace with the Carthaginians and put down his opposition, but died before he could renew the attack on Carthage.

Agesilaus (a̯-jes-i-lā′us) or **Agesilaos** (-os). King of Sparta (c399–c360 B.C.), born c444 B.C.; died in Libya, c360 B.C. He was a younger son of Archidamus II, of the Eurypontid line of Spartan rulers, by his second wife Eupolia. Because his older half-brother Agis was the heir, Agesilaus was not trained for kingship, but shared in the regular training of Spartan youths. Archidamus had been fined by the Spartans when he married Eupolia, because she was a small woman and would bear, they said, "not kings but kinglets." To the extent that Agesilaus was of modest stature and lame, their prophecy was carried out. He did not let his lameness interfere with his activities; rather, he was the bolder in spirit to compensate for it. When Agis died (398 B.C.) Lysander, a Spartan general and intimate of Agesilaus, promoted Agesilaus for the throne on the grounds that Leotychidas, who passed as the son of Agis, was actually the son of Alcibiades who was rumored to have had a liaison with the wife of Agis when he deserted Athens for Sparta. However, an oracle stood in the way of the accession of Agesilaus; "Bethink thee now, O Sparta, though thou art very glorious, lest from thee, sound of foot, there spring a maimed royalty . . ." Diviners said the oracle forbade Sparta to take a lame king. Lysander countered by saying the "maimed royalty" of the oracle referred to the illegitimacy of Leotychidas, who was not a true descendant of Heracles. His view prevailed and Agesilaus became king (c399 B.C.). He won the respect of the ephors by his seeming deference, and won the love of the people by the simplicity of his personal life. Having done so, he had the essence rather than the appearance of power. He showed himself honorable in dealing with his enemies and supported his friends unreservedly, even when their actions were unjust or harmful to the state. His loyalty to his friends, in fact, sometimes led to disaster. When word came that the Persians were gathering their forces, Lysander persuaded Agesilaus to march against them and to help the friends he had established in power in Asia Minor. Agesilaus, who dreamed of conquering Persia, went to Aulis to assemble his forces, following in the path of Agamemnon, "king of men." At Aulis he was advised in a vision to sacrifice to Artemis as Agamemnon had done before sailing to Troy. Agesilaus promised a sacrifice that would be pleasing to the goddess but would not imitate the cruelty of Agamemnon's sacrifice of his daughter. He ordered a hind to be garlanded and offered up by his own priests. The Thebans, enraged that a foreign priest should sacrifice on their soil without their permission, disrupted the ceremony and carried off the thighs of the victim. Agesilaus was troubled by this unfavorable circumstance, and never forgave the Thebans. He went to Ephesus where he found that Lysander, who had been in the region before and had many friends, was the center of attention and was regarded as the real commander of the expedition. Up to this time, relations between Agesilaus and Lysander had been very close. Now Agesilaus found his own ambitions hindered by the respect in which Lysander was held, and feared that if he did succeed in Asia Lysander would win all the credit. He resolved to nullify Lysander's influence. He refused his advice. Then he denied those who were recommended by Lysander and came to him for help, and aided those known to be unfriendly to Lysander. Instead of giving Lysander a military post of command, he appointed him as his official meat-carver. Lysander, appreciating the situation, asked for and received permission to depart to a region where he could be of real service to his country. Agesilaus marched through Phrygia and conquered many cities. In the spring of 395 B.C. he defeated the Persians on the plain before Sardis. He followed his victory by ravaging Phrygia, the satrapy of Pharnabazus. Pharnabazus came to parley with him. With dignity, he remonstrated with Agesilaus, saying he had been the faithful ally of Sparta in

fat, fāte, fär, fäll, ȧsk, fãre; net, mē, hėr; pin, pīne; not, nōte, möve, nôr; up, lūte, pu̇ll; oi, oil; ou out; (lightened) ẹlect, agǫny, ụnite;

her wars against Athens and now he was rewarded by having his satrapy devastated. Was this justice, he asked, or gratitude? Agesilaus answered that since he was at war with Persia, all satraps must be regarded as his enemies, and invited Pharnabazus to desert the Persian king and join him as an ally. Pharnabazus replied that while he held a post under the Persian king he would support him, and wage war against Sparta with all his power. Agesilaus admired his loyalty. He promised to leave the satrapy and to respect it in the future. Before his interview with Pharnabazus he had received word from Sparta putting him in command of the fleet which was to be assembled. This was the first time the posts of general and admiral had been united in one person. He unwisely entrusted the command of the fleet to his brother-in-law Pisander, a man of no experience, in order to please his sister. This appointment is an extreme example of the extent to which Agesilaus was at the mercy of his affections with disastrous results for Sparta. He restored order in Asia Minor and planned to pursue and capture the Persian king Artaxerxes II at Susa, in order to bring to an end the continual interference of Persia in Greek affairs, supporting now one now another of them in their internecine wars. Before he could embark on the project, he was called home to subdue the Corinthian League of Greek states that had formed an alliance against Sparta. He marched overland by the route Xerxes had taken when he invaded Greece (480 B.C.), asking permission of the tribes along the way to pass through their territory. Most gave it. One tribe, however, demanded 100 talents of silver and as many women as the price for passage through their land. Agesilaus, retorting that they must come and get it, fought and defeated them. The king of Macedonia said he must deliberate before giving permission to the Spartans to cross his land. "Let him deliberate then," said Agesilaus, "but we will march on." The Macedonian prudently refrained from interfering. The Spartans ravaged Thessaly in their passage because of ancient enmity with the Thessalians. On his homeward journey Agesilaus learned of a battle near Corinth in which some Spartans and many of their enemies had fallen. "Alas for Hellas," he groaned, "which has by her own hands destroyed so many brave men. Had they lived, they could have conquered in battle all the barbarians in the world." On orders from Sparta he invaded Boeotia. At Chaeronea there was an eclipse of the sun. The unfavorable omen was followed by news that Pisander had been thoroughly defeated off Cnidus by a fleet under the command of Conon, the Athenian admiral, and Pharnabazus (394 B.C.). All his work in Asia Minor was now undone, and the Spartan fleet was destroyed. He concealed the news from his army and marched quickly to Coronea where he met the allies—Thebes, Athens, Corinth, and Argos—arrayed against him. He was badly wounded in the battle (394 B.C.) but was awarded the victory when the Thebans asked for a burial truce. The victory was fruitless, as he dared not stay in the area but withdrew to Sparta, where he was warmly welcomed. In 391 B.C. he captured Lechaeum, one of the ports of Corinth, and the following year marched again to the Isthmus and took over the presidency of the Isthmian Games, then being celebrated. The Corinthians nullified his presidency by holding the games all over again as soon as he left. He supported the King's Peace (386 B.C.), handed down by Artaxerxes II, under which the Greek cities of Asia Minor were abandoned to Persia and the Greek states were declared autonomous. However, he violated its terms by sanctioning the seizure of the Theban citadel (382 B.C.) by Phoebidas and the government friendly to Sparta that he set up in Thebes. When the Thebans expelled the Spartans (379 B.C.) he waged war on them, leading expeditions against Thebes in 378 and 377 B.C. The expeditions accomplished nothing and Agesilaus was badly wounded. The wars against Thebes were provoked by Agesilaus more from his hatred of the city than for strategic reasons, and were an open violation of the peace. Even Xenophon, a great admirer of Agesilaus and Spartan institutions, was critical of these violations. He attributed the ultimate downfall of Sparta to retribution by the gods for her harsh and unjust actions toward other states. Agesilaus was rebuked by one of his generals, when he was wounded, who said to him, "Indeed, this is a fine tuition-fee which thou art getting from the Thebans, for teaching them how to fight when they did not wish to do it and did not even know how." The expeditions also caused discontent among the Spartan allies. In 371 B.C. an attempt was made to end the crippling warfare by the Peace of Callias. Agesilaus demanded of Epaminon-

---

fat, fāte, fär, fåll, ȧsk, fāre; net, mē, hèr; pin, pīne; not, nōte, mȯve, nôr; up, lūte, pᵾll; oi, oil; ou out; (lightened) ḙlect, agǫ̇ny, ụnite;

das, the Theban envoy, that the Boeotian cities be permitted, as independent cities, to sign the peace treaty separately. Epaminondas retorted that it would be permitted if Agesilaus acknowledged the independence of the Laconian cities. Agesilaus had no intention of so doing, and Thebes was not a party to the treaty. In the same year the Thebans, under Epaminondas, defeated the Spartans at Leuctra. The following year they invaded the Peloponnesus and pushed into Laconia itself, the first time in 600 years that its borders had been violated. Agesilaus kept the Thebans out of the city of Sparta and withstood a series of attacks, culminating in a campaign by four armies against the unwalled city (369 B.C.). The Spartans, safe within their borders for centuries, were in despair when war touched their land. They longed for peace and began to plot against Agesilaus for preventing it. He seized the plotters and put them to death without trial. He again defended the city (362 B.C.) against a Theban army, and a few days later marched at the head of a force to take part in the battle of Mantinea in which Epaminondas was slain. Afterward, Agesilaus refused to take part in the general peace settlement. His countrymen, worn out by war, no longer honored and respected him; they considered his obstinacy dangerous to his country and his friends. Now in his eighties, he put himself at the head of a band of mercenaries and set out (361 B.C.) for Egypt. He agreed to help the Egyptian Tachos in return for money that he needed to carry on Sparta's wars. The Egyptians knew of Agesilaus by reputation. When they saw the simply clad, lame old man, they mocked him, and he did not receive supreme command of their expedition as he had expected. A revolt broke out against Tachos. Agesilaus joined the conspirators against him and helped them to gain control in Egypt. They begged him to remain, but he was anxious to return to Sparta. Loaded with honors, gifts, and 230 talents for the war at home, he set sail. On the return voyage he died (c360 B.C.) at a place called the Harbor of Menelaus, on the coast of Libya. His body was enclosed in melted wax and taken to Sparta for burial. He had been a dominating figure in Sparta for over 40 years. He had witnessed his country's triumph over Athens in the Peloponnesian War, and was its king during the period of its greatest power. A story goes that a visitor marveled that Sparta, with its many enemies, had no

(obscured) errạnt, ardẹnt, actọr; ch, chip; g, go; th, thin; ŦH, then; y, you;
(variable) ḏ as d or j, ş as s or sh, ṭ as t or ch, ẓ as z or zh.

walls. Agesilaus is said to have pointed to the citizens in arms and replied, "These are the walls of Lacedaemon." He was still king when Sparta lost the rich land of Messenia and was compelled to defend its very citadel against invaders. Wrong-headed but indomitable, he made a final contribution to his country by serving as a mercenary to replenish its empty treasury.

Agis I (ā′jis). Traditionally, king of Sparta (c1032 B.C.). He was the reputed founder of the royal line known as the Agiadae, or Agidae.

Agis II. King of Sparta (c427–399 B.C.). He was the son of Archidamus II, of the Eurypontid line of Spartan kings. In 418 B.C. he defeated Athens and her allies in a great battle at Mantinea and restored the prestige to Sparta which it had lost by the surrender at Sphacteria (425 B.C.). In 413 he led an expedition that took and fortified Decelea, from which point the Spartans commanded all Attica. In 405 B.C. he moved his forces up to the walls of Athens, but finding them impregnable he withdrew. The Athenians, defeated at Aegospotami (405), asked for peace and the long Peloponnesian Wars came to an end (404 B.C.). Agis had been one of the two kings of Sparta for almost the entire duration of the wars. During the reign of Agis, Alcibiades, the Athenian general, repudiated at home, came to Sparta. Because of Alcibiades' notorious liaison with Timaea, wife of Agis, her son was not recognized by Agis as his heir on the grounds that he was actually the son of Alcibiades. However, in his last illness Agis was prevailed upon to declare this son, Leotychidas, as his legitimate heir. His earlier refusal to recognize him made it possible for Agesilaus, half-brother of Agis, to succeed him as king in place of Leotychidas.

Agis III. King of Sparta (338–331 B.C.). He was allied with Persia against Macedon. In an attempt to throw off Macedonian control, while Alexander the Great was in Asia, he was defeated by Antipater, Alexander's regent, at Megalopolis (331 B.C.), where he lost his life in battle.

Agis IV. King of Sparta (244–240 B.C.); son of Eudamidas II of the Eurypontid line of Spartan rulers. He proposed to recruit additions to the ranks of the Spartans from among the Perioeci, and advocated a redistribution of the landed property. In these measures of reform he was opposed by his colleague Leonidas II, of the royal line known as the Agidae,

fat, fāte, fär, fâll, ȧsk, fâre; net, mē, hèr; pin, pīne; not, nōte, möve, nôr; up, lūte, púll; oi, oil; ou out; (lightened) ḝlect, agǫny, ūnite;

and after some transient successes he was captured and sentenced to death by the Spartan ephors.

Agricola (a̱-grik′ō̱-la̱), *Cnaeus Julius.* Roman soldier and politician; born at Forum Julii (now Frejus, France), 40 A.D.; died at Rome, 93 A.D. He was the father-in-law of Tacitus. Quaestor in Asia (63) under Salvius Titianus; made commander (70) of the XXth Legion in Britain by Vespasian; governor of Aquitania (74-76); elected consul (77) and assigned to southern Britain, where in seven campaigns (78–84) he extended Roman law to the northern boundary of Perth and Argyll. He may have been poisoned by agents of the emperor. Tacitus' *Agricola*, an account of his life and accomplishments, is generally considered to be an outstanding example of good classical biography.

Agrippa (a̱-grip′a̱), *Marcus Vipsanius.* Roman soldier and politician, born at Rome, 63 B.C.; died in Campania, 12 B.C. He rose from a humble birth to become son-in-law, friend, and counselor to Augustus. He put down the Aquitanian revolt (38 B.C.) in Gaul, was elected consul (37) and defeated (36) Sextus Pompeius Magnus (often called Pompey the Younger) at Mylae and Naulochus. He became aedile in 33, and defeated (31) Antony's fleet at Actium. Recalled from the governorship of Syria to become (23) Augustus' chief counselor, he shared the tribuneship with Augustus (18 B.C. *et seq.*). Agrippa was married to a daughter of Octavia the niece of Augustus but when Julia, the daughter of Augustus, was widowed, Augustus persuaded Agrippa to divorce his wife, the mother of his children, and marry Julia who was young enough to be his daughter and whose reputation for immoral living was to become the scandal of Rome. Julia bore three sons, Gaius, Lucius, and Agrippa Postumus, to Agrippa, and two daughters, Julia and Agrippina the Elder. Many of the military successes of the reign of Augustus were due to the capacity of Agrippa. He is also known for his geographical writings.

Agrippina (ag-ri-pī′na̱), *Julia.* [Called *Agrippina the Younger.*] Daughter of Germanicus and Vipsania Agrippina. She was born at Oppidum Ubiorum (later named, for her, Colonia Agrippina, now Cologne), c15 A.D. She was killed near Baiae (now Baia), on the Bay of Naples, 59 A.D. She married Domitius Ahenobarbus and by him was the mother of the future emperor Nero. She later married Crispus Passienus and in 49 A.D. her uncle, the emperor Claudius, whom she poisoned (54) after excluding his son Britannicus from the throne in favor of Nero. She was influential during the early part of Nero's reign, but was eventually murdered at his orders after she threatened to support the claims of Britannicus.

Agrippina, Vipsania. [Called *Agrippina the Elder.*] Roman matron, born c13 B.C.; died at Pandataria, 33 A.D. She was known for the loftiness of her character. She was the youngest daughter of Marcus Vipsanius Agrippa and Julia, daughter of Augustus, and the wife of Germanicus and mother of Caligula. She accompanied her husband on his military campaigns and was with him at Antioch when he was poisoned (19 A.D.). She returned to Rome and publicly denounced the governor of Syria, Calpurnius Piso, as the poisoner. By implication, her accusation involved the emperor Tiberius himself. Her accusation, the popularity with which her husband had been regarded, and the popular feeling which his death aroused, promoted the jealous hatred of Tiberius and Sejanus. She was banished to the lonely island of Pandataria (Ventotene) off the Campanian coast, where she was flogged so savagely that she lost an eye. Her sons, the elder of them at least, were ordered starved to death. Agrippina, some say, starved herself to death, although Tiberius ordered her jaws pried apart for forcible feeding. But others say Tiberius himself ordered her to die by starvation.

Ahasuerus (a̱-has-ū-ē′rus). In the Old Testament, a Persian shah, mentioned as the father of Darius the Mede (Dan. ix. 1). He has been variously identified as Astyages and Cyaxares.

Ahasuerus. In the Old Testament, a great ruler of Persia, and husband of Esther, probably identical with Xerxes I. He is mentioned in Ezra, iv. 6., and throughout the Book of Esther.

Ahenobarbus (a̱-hē-no̱-bär′bus, a̱-hen-o̱-), *Cnaeus Domitius.* Roman official, fl. 104–92 B.C. He was the father of Lucius Domitius Ahenobarbus. A tribune (104 B.C.), pontifex maximus (103), consul (96), and censor (92), he framed the law, later repealed by Sulla, that priests of certain classes should be selected by the lay citizenry rather than by each other.

Ahenobarbus, Lucius Domitius. Roman official and political opportunist, fl. 54–48 B.C.; son of Cnaeus Domitius Ahenobarbus. He was a consul in 54 B.C. and Caesar's successor as governor of Gaul in 49 B.C. He opposed both Caesar and Pompey, but later attached himself to Pompey and was slain after the defeat at Pharsalus.

Alcibiades (al-si-bī′a̧-dēz). Athenian general and politician, born c450 B.C. at Athens; killed at Melissa, Phrygia, 404 B.C. His father was Clinias, who claimed descent from Eurysaces, the son of Telamonian Ajax. On his mother's side he was a member of the wealthy Alcmaeonid family. His father, who had fought bravely at Artemisium (480 B.C.), was killed (447) fighting the Boeotians and Alcibiades was brought up as a ward of Pericles, one of his kinsmen. From childhood he loved rivalry and sought preëminence. A story is told that once as a youth he was wrestling, and to prevent his opponent from gaining a fall, he bit him. His opponent accused him of biting "as women do." "Not as women do," Alcibiades retorted, "but as lions do." He pursued his studies successfully but was not a docile scholar. He refused to play the flute on the ground that it made men look ridiculous when they puffed and blew out their cheeks. He justified his refusal to play it by citing the goddess Athena, who threw the flute away in disgust when she saw how it distorted her face, and the god Apollo, who flayed the flute-player Marsyas. He consented to play the lyre, which a gentleman could play with dignity, while at the same time he could converse or sing in company with it. As he grew up he drew many prominent and able men to him with his brilliant youthful beauty, and in the fashion of the time had many who sought his company. To them he displayed unparalleled insolence, which had the effect apparently of binding them even more securely to him. Once, it is said, Anytus, one of his most ardent admirers, invited him to a banquet. Alcibiades did not attend. He spent the evening drinking with his companions; then going to the house of Anytus and, observing the gold and silver cups on the banquet table, he sent in a servant to sweep up half of them and carried them away. Anytus refused to be insulted. On the contrary, he remarked that Alcibiades had shown great kindness in taking only half of his cups. On another occasion because of a wager he struck Hipponicus, the father of Callias, with his fist. The unwarranted assault aroused great indignation in the city. The next day Alcibiades went to the house of Hipponicus, took off his cloak, and invited Hipponicus to beat him. Hipponicus forgave him, refused to scourge him and later gave him his daughter Hipparete in marriage. Hipparete was a discreet and affectionate wife and bore his children. However, Alcibiades continued to carry on scandalous and public affairs with various courtesans. Hipparete left him and finally sued for divorce. When she appeared in court, Alcibiades strode in, seized her and carried her off through the agora to his home. She lived with him until her death, which occurred not long afterward. He had a famous stable of horses and once entered seven racing chariots in the games at Olympia—the only man ever to enter so many—and won first, second, and fourth (or third) prizes. Such an extravagant display made a great stir in Athens and in the other cities as well, and Nicias cited it as an instance of the arrogance of Alcibiades. Alcibiades justified his extravagance on the ground that it glorified Athens. The people were delighted with his retort. Along with his arrogance and lawlessness, he had such brilliance and excellent native qualities that he won the devoted friendship of Socrates, the only man he respected and loved. Socrates feared that Alcibiades would be ruined by those who pandered to him and had no hesitation in pointing out to him the many areas in which he fell short of excellence, and bent his efforts—unsuccessfully as it turned out—to developing his great native talents. When Alcibiades served in the campaign against Potidaea (432–431 B.C.), Socrates shared his tent and was his companion in arms. In a fierce action Alcibiades fought bravely and was wounded. Socrates with conspicuous bravery defended his fallen comrade and saved him together with his armor. At a later time Alcibiades returned the service. When Socrates was participating in the general retreat at Delium (424 B.C.), Alcibiades came by on horseback and protected him from the encompassing enemy.

Because of his birth, wealth, and courage in battle, his many friends and followers, and his personal magnetism, it was natural that he should enter public service. Fundamentally aristocratic in his views, having stated that democracy is "acknowledged folly," he yet used the tools of democracy to further his ambitions, which were without limit. His initial appearance in public life was the occasion on which he made the first of his many large contributions to the state. He soon became a leading figure and, as leader of the radical party, he was the rival of Nicias. Hyperbolus, a "base fellow" according to Thucydides, thought to take advantage of this rivalry for his own ends. He engineered a vote of ostracism with the idea that either Alcibiades or Nicias would be ostracized. When Alcibiades became aware of it, he joined forces with Nicias and the result, astonishing to all, was that Hyperbolus himself was ostracized. However, the unity with Nicias was short-lived. Alcibiades schemed to break the peace with Sparta negotiated by Nicias (421 B.C.). He plotted with the Argives. He attacked Nicias in the assembly, accused him of treachery and raised a great outcry against him. When Spartan envoys came to negotiate, he secretly met with them, it is said, and persuaded them to say that they did not have full powers to negotiate, as in fact they had. When they then stated in the assembly that their powers were limited, Alcibiades accused them of lying. Nicias was confounded by their change and the negotiations collapsed. Alcibiades was then appointed general (420 B.C.), and urged the Athenians to extend their dominion on land, as was required by the oath young warriors took "to regard wheat, barley, the wine, and the olive as the natural boundaries of Attica." He brought the Argives, Mantineans, and Eleans into alliance with Athens and persuaded Argos and Patrae to build walls to the sea. But after the Spartan victory at Mantinea (418 B.C.) he was not reelected as general and Nicias took his place. Conservative and respectable men feared him for his influence and were indignant at his personal life, for all his public acts were accompanied, as Plutarch says, "with great luxuriousness, with wanton drunkeness and lewdness, with effeminacy in dress—he would trail long purple robes through the agora—and with prodigal expenditures." He carried a golden shield, the device of which was an Eros armed with a thunderbolt. But the people, though they feared his insolence, admired his military skill, were charmed by his discourse and looked indulgently on his excesses, excusing them as the high spirits of youth. According to Aristophanes, the public "yearns for him, and hates him too, but wants him back." (*Frogs.*)

When the Egestaeans of Sicily sent envoys to Athens (416 B.C.) and asked for aid against Selinus, Alcibiades was foremost in urging the Athenians to answer their appeal. By his

(obscured) errant, ardent, actor; ch, chip; g, go; th, thin; ᴛʜ, then; y, you;
(variable) ḏ as d or j, ṣ as s or sh, ṭ as t or ch, ẓ as z or zh.

eloquence, which even the comic poets acknowledged, he inspired the Athenians with the wildest hopes and dreams of conquest. Some say his interest was to win glory for himself, and that Sicily was to be but the stepping stone for the conquest of Carthage and Libya. Nicias and some others, among them Socrates, opposed the expedition and on good grounds. But Alcibiades fanned the enthusiasm of the young men with extravagant hopes and set their elders to dreaming of past glories. The exercise grounds were crowded with men who daily drew maps of Sicily, Carthage, and Libya in the sand. Those who considered such an expedition to be folly found it prudent to say nothing of their doubts. An expedition was voted and a great armament was prepared. Alcibiades, Nicias (against his will), and Lamachus were named generals with full powers. Two unfavorable omens marred the carnival-like atmosphere in which the fleet made ready to sail. It was discovered that many of the Hermae— square stone figures surmounted by a head of the god Hermes which stood at the entrances to temples and before private houses—had been mutilated. This act of impiety greatly aroused and disturbed the Athenians and large rewards were offered for information concerning its authors, and of any other acts of impiety to the gods. Alcibiades was implicated in a charge of having taken part in a drunken mockery of the rites of Eleusinian Demeter. The two impieties were thought to be connected and his enemies claimed that they were part of a plot by which he planned to overthrow the democracy. He demanded a trial before he set out on the expedition for he understood how perilous it was to be starting off with such suspicions hanging over him, and he wanted at once either to be cleared of the charges, or to be executed for impiety. His enemies feared he would be acquitted by the people. They claimed that some of the allies in the expedition might withdraw if Alcibiades was not the commander; therefore he should sail and stand trial on his return. He could not persuade them otherwise. The day for the departure fell on the festival of Adonia, in which small images of the dead Adonis were carried in procession and were given burial rites. This was thought to be unfavorable as foretelling that the splendid armament would fade in its glory as had the youthful beauty of Adonis. Nevertheless, in the summer of 415 B.C. the splendid fleet sailed.

---

fat, fāte, fär, fåll, åsk, fâre; net, mē, hèr; pin, pīne; not, nōte, möve, nôr; up, lūte, půll; oi, oil; ou out; (lightened) ĕlect, agǫny, ūnite;

Hardly had the expedition arrived in Sicily when a galley came from Athens bearing news of Alcibiades' recall. He went aboard willingly, but when the galley put in at Thurii he went ashore and escaped. When news of his escape reached Athens, he was tried *in absentia* on a charge of impiety. His property was confiscated, priestesses were ordered to curse his name, and he was condemned to death. When he heard the sentence in the Peloponnesus whither he had gone, he exclaimed, "I'll show them that I'm alive!" He went to Sparta, where he asked for immunity and offered his aid. The Spartans were instantly charmed by him. All were amazed to see the luxury-loving Athenian adopt the rigid Spartan ways, even to sharing the simple diet of black pudding with the soldiers. He urged the Spartans to send help to Syracuse against the faltering Athenians under Nicias. He also persuaded them to renew the war against Athens at home and lastly, and most devastating for the Athenians, he advised them to fortify Decelea. This was a mountain fortress of Attica, about 14 miles from Athens, which commanded the Attic plain and the routes to Euboea and Boeotia. The Spartans adopted his advice and effectively removed from Athenian control all the farmland that had supplied Athens with food. Although the Spartans used the advice of Alcibiades to their advantage, he ultimately lost their good will. Their leaders became jealous of him. While King Agis was away, Alcibiades seduced his wife Timaea, and the child she subsequently bore was presumed to be his. He went to Ionia on a successful mission to stir up revolt against Athens. While there, he learned that the Spartans had sent orders demanding his death. He went (412 B.C.) to the Persian satrap Tissaphernes whom he advised to be less generous in his aid to Sparta. Rather, he suggested, Tissaphernes should encourage Athens and Sparta to exhaust themselves and then they would be easy prey for the Persian king. Athens was in straitened circumstances and desired the return of Alcibiades. In 412–411 B.C. he sent secret messages to the Athenian forces at Samos, hinting at aid from Tissaphernes for Athens if the democracy was overthrown. However, he did not return to Athens when the Four Hundred seized control there in June, 411 B.C. He went to Samos and took command of a fleet. By his advice he prevented the Athenians at Samos from sailing to the

---

(obscured) errạnt, ardẹnt, actọr; ch, chip; g, go; th, thin; ŦH, then; y, you;
(variable) ḍ as d or j, ş as s or sh, ţ as t or ch, ҫ as z or zh.

Piraeus to overthrow the Four Hundred, for they would have left the Hellespont and Ionia defenseless before the Spartan fleet operating in nearby waters. When the Four Hundred were overthrown in Athens (Sept., 411 B.C.), he was invited to return. He wanted some military successes to take back with him. He defeated the Spartans at Abydos and then went to Tissaphernes, who had been his great friend. Tissaphernes, however, now feared Athens and cast him into prison. Within a month he escaped and joined the Athenians at Cardia in the Thracian Chersonese and led them to victory over the Spartan commander Mindarus at Cyzicus (410 B.C.). In the following year he routed both the Persian satrap Pharnabazus and the Spartan Hippocrates, plundered the satrapy of Pharnabazus, and captured Selymbria on the Hellespont. In 408 B.C. he took Byzantium and was now ready to return to Athens. He sailed back from Samos with a fleet decked with the trophies of his victories and was wildly acclaimed when he landed. His property was restored, he was crowned with a gold crown, and he was elected general with sole powers by land and by sea. In his prosperity he determined to celebrate the rites at Eleusis and clear away any lingering shadow as to his piety. Since the Spartans had occupied Decelea the procession had been carried to Eleusis from Athens by sea. He resolved to take it across the ancient sacred way and to protect it with his soldiers, and carried out his resolve. He became so popular that the people sought to make him their tyrant. There were others who feared him, however, and encouraged him to sail and pursue the Spartans. He assaulted Andros but failed to take the city (Oct., 408 B.C.). Plutarch says he was ruined by his own reputation for success, for when he failed it was thought he did so deliberately, and now his enemies renewed their attacks on him. But the truth was that the Athenians had voted him full power but no money, and he had to occupy himself sailing about to collect funds. While he was doing this he left the fleet at Notium in charge of Antiochus, with strict orders not to engage the Spartans. Antiochus disobeyed and was lost with the ships that went to his aid in an engagement with the Spartans at Ephesus (407 B.C.). When Alcibiades learned of it he set out against the Spartan commander Lysander but the latter refused to fight. This was held to be treachery on the part of Alcibiades.

fat, fāte, fär, fȧll, ȧsk, fãre; net, mē, hėr; pin, pīne; not, nōte, möve, nôr; up, lūte, pu̇ll; oi, oil; ou out; (lightened) ẹlect, agǫny, ūnite;

The fickle Athenians again turned against him. He fled to Thrace with some mercenaries and occupied a stronghold near Pactye. Before the battle of Aegospotami (405 B.C.) he saw the peril in which the Athenian fleet had placed itself vis-à-vis the Spartans, and rode down to the Athenian camp to warn the generals. They invited him to go away and were utterly defeated in the ensuing battle with Lysander. After the defeat of Athens, Alcibiades retired to Bithynia, then proceeded to the satrap Pharnabazus, a good friend of Sparta, and offered his services to the Persian king Artaxerxes. The Spartans sent orders to have him slain. It is said that when he was visiting the courtesan Timandra, he dreamed that he was lying in her arms and that she was robing him in women's clothing and painting his face. According to one account, when he was in his house with her, the minions of Pharnabazus set fire to his house. He rushed out unscathed to quell his attackers. But they dared not meet him hand to hand and slew him with javelins and arrows. Some say Timandra recovered his body, dressed it in her own sumptuous robes, and gave it as brilliant a burial as was possible.

Alcmaeonidae (alk-mē-on'i-dē). Noble family of Athens, a branch of the family of the Nelidae which, according to tradition, came from Pylus in Messenia to Athens about 1100 B.C. Among the more notable members of the family are Alcmaeon, an Athenian general in the Cirrhaean war; Megacles, a son of Alcmaeon and a rival of Pisistratus; Clisthenes the legislator and son of Megacles; Pericles, the celebrated Athenian statesman, great-grandson of Megacles; and the scarcely less-famous Alcibiades, cousin of Pericles. The family was banished for sacrilege about 596 B.C. on account of the action of the Alcmaeonid archon Megacles, who in 632 B.C. put to death the participants in the insurrection of Cylon while they clung for protection to the altars. They returned through an alliance with Lycurgus, carried on with varying fortunes a struggle with Pisistratus and the Pisistratidae, and were finally restored in 510 B.C.

Alexander I (al-eg-zan' dėr) (of *Epirus*). King of Epirus; died c330 B.C. He was the son of Neoptolemus and the brother of Olympias, mother of Alexander the Great. His youth was spent at the court of Philip II of Macedon who made him king of Epirus. Philip II gave him his daughter in marriage to strengthen his ties with Epirus and her king, whose sister Olympias he had recently cast aside. At the celebration of the marriage of Alexander and Philip's daughter, Philip was murdered. Alexander's aid against the barbarians of Italy was sought by Tarentum in 334 B.C. His arms met with such success in southern Italy that Rome thought it expedient to make an alliance with him. Subsequently, Tarentum came to fear the conqueror who had come to her aid, renounced her alliance with Alexander, and during a battle that ensued at Pandosia Alexander was stabbed in the back and killed.

Alexander II (of *Epirus*). King of Epirus, son of Pyrrhus and Lanassa, the daughter of Agathocles, tyrant of Syracuse. He succeeded his father in 272 B.C. He was dispossessed of Epirus and Macedonia by Demetrius, whose father, Antigonus Gonatas, had been deprived of Macedonia by Alexander. Epirus was recovered subsequently chiefly with the aid of the Acarnanians.

Alexander I (of *Macedon*). King of Macedon (c500–c454 B.C.). He was a son of Amyntas I, whom he succeeded. In the Persian Wars he was allied to Persia, both by ties of marriage and by force, for his father had given earth and water to Darius in token of his submission to the Great King. In the spring of 479 B.C. Mardonius sent him as an envoy to Athens because he was aware of Alexander's friendship for Athens. Alexander was authorized to tell the Athenians that Mardonius would forgive the wrong they had done to the Persians, restore their territory, and rebuild their temples if Athens would join an alliance with him. Alexander added his own words, as a known friend of Athens, to persuade them to make an alliance. For, he said, they could never overcome the power and might of the Persian Empire. To him the Athenians replied, "So long as the sun keeps his present course, we will never join alliance with Xerxes. Nay, we shall oppose him unceasingly." According to Herodotus, when the Greeks were encamped at Plataea, waiting favorable omens to engage Mardonius, a man rode up on horseback to their camp at night, and asked to speak to the generals, but would not give his name. He told the generals that out of friendship for Athens, and at great peril to himself, he had come to inform them that the Persians had been unable to obtain favorable omens for many days and had decided to attack without them on the next day. He also told them that

fat, fāte, fär, fâll, àsk, fāre; net, mē, hèr; pin, pīne; not, nōte, mŏve, nôr; up, lūte, půll; oi, oil; ou out; (lightened) ēlect, agǫny, ūnite;

Mardonius' supplies were running low. Then he asked them to do something for his freedom if they were successful. Finally, he announced to them that he was Alexander of Macedon, turned his horse and rode back to the Persian camp and took up the station assigned to him.

Alexander II (of *Macedon*). King of Macedon (369–368 B.C.). He was a son of Amyntas II, whom he succeeded. He was murdered by his mother's paramour, Ptolemy Alorus (368 B.C.).

Alexander III (of *Macedon*). See *Alexander the Great.*

Alexander the Great. [Also: *Alexander III* (of *Macedon.*)] Macedonian ruler and conqueror of the civilized world, born at Pella, Macedonia, 356 B.C.; died at Babylon, June 13, 323 B.C. Alexander claimed descent from Heracles and from Aeacus, the ancestor of his favorite hero, Achilles. He was the son of Philip II of Macedon and the Epirote princess Olympias, whom Philip met in Samothrace when he was initiated into the mysteries there. Some say he inherited his military ability from his father, a rough mountain king of genius, while from his mother came his mysticism and impetuousness. Before he was born there were potent omens of his future greatness: his mother dreamed a thunderbolt fell on her body from which great flames sprang, spread all about, and were then extinguished; his father dreamed he sealed up his wife's body with a seal bearing the impression of a lion, a portent that she would bear a son as courageous as a lion. On the day of his birth the great temple of Artemis at Ephesus burned—some said this was because the goddess was absent assisting at his birth—and seers mourned over the ruined temple, foretelling that the day brought forth the ruin of Asia. Philip, victorious at Potidaea, on the same day received news that his horse had won at the Olympic Games, that Parmenio, his general, had conquered the Illyrians, and that his wife had borne him a son. Born amid so many successes, Alexander was considered destined for spectacular success himself.

Among his earliest teachers was Leonidas, a kinsman of his mother who trained him for conquest. A story is told that once when the lad was preparing to sacrifice, he filled both hands with incense to pour on the altar fire. Leonidas rebuked him, advising Alexander to be more sparing of his offerings until he had conquered the lands that produced them. Later (332 B.C.), when Alexander had taken Tyre, he

---

(obscured) err**a**nt, ard**e**nt, act**o**r; ch, chip; g, go; th, thin; ᴛʜ, then; y, you;
(variable) ḍ as d or j, ş as s or sh, ţ as t or ch, ẕ as z or zh.

remembered his old tutor. He sent him 500 talents of frank-incense and 100 talents of myrrh, accompanying his gift with a message that Leonidas would no longer need to be stingy in his offerings to the gods. It is said that as a boy Alexander was unhappy when he learned of any new success won by his father for the more Philip won, the less there would be for him to conquer. Philip had a handsome horse in his stables, so high-spirited none could ride him and Philip ordered the horse destroyed. Alexander begged to be allowed to try his skill, and Philip reluctantly gave his permission. Alexander had observed that the horse was terrified by its own shadow. He turned its eyes into the sun, stroked and talked to it, succeeded in mounting, and was the first, and from there-after the only one, to ride Bucephalus. On this occasion Philip is said to have told him proudly that he must find a kingdom for himself, "For Macedonia is too small for thee." Bucephalus was the mount preferred above all others by Alexander when he went into battle. Once when the horse was captured, he threatened to put to the sword all the inhabitants of the town where Bucephalus had been taken unless his horse was restored. Bucephalus was returned and Alexander then showed great moderation to the city. When at last Bucephalus died of old age after the crossing of the Hydaspes River in India, Alexander grieved as for a dear companion and built a city on the banks of the river which he named Bucephalia in his honor.

Philip was a great admirer of the Greeks whom he had subdued, and of Greek culture, and wished to be identified with them. In 343 B.C. he sent for Aristotle to come as a tutor to Alexander. Alexander studied literature and languages with him, and learned something of medicine, but did not subscribe to the philosophy subsequently evolved by Aristotle, and in later years his affection for the philosopher cooled. He was a great reader. His favorite book was the *Iliad* which he kept under his pillow at night along with his dagger. When he had embarked on his conquests he came into possession of a magnificent jeweled casket. In it he placed his copy of the *Iliad*, the only article that he felt worthy of the precious box. Ambassadors from Greece and the East coming and going at Philip's court gave him an education in political and diplomatic affairs. When the boy was 16, Philip left him in charge of Macedonia while he was

fat, fāte, fär, fâll, ȧsk, fãre; net, mē, hėr; pin, pīne; not, nōte, mȯve, nôr; up, lūte, pu̇ll; oi, oil; ou out; (lightened) ẹlect, agͺ͜ony, ūnite;

absent. Alexander subdued the hill tribes on the northern border of the kingdom and founded the city of Alexandropolis in his father's absence. In 338 B.C. he accompanied his father in the expedition against the Greek allies and led the charge against the Sacred Band in their defeat at Chaeronea. This was the first time the Sacred Band had suffered defeat. Philip was proud of his son's bravery but intrigues in his court caused a breach between father and son. Olympias, no longer secure in the affections of Philip, sought his downfall. When Philip took another wife (the Macedonian rulers practised polygamy) Olympias encouraged Alexander to take her side against his father. In 336 B.C. Philip was murdered, perhaps at the instigation of Olympias and possibly with the knowledge of Alexander. His infant son by his new wife Cleopatra was murdered as was Alexander's cousin Amyntas, thus removing rival claimants to the throne. Supported by the army, Alexander disposed of other rivals for the throne. He became king of Macedonia and leader of the Greeks in war against the predatory Persian Empire that had never ceased to intrigue with one after another of the Greek states to bring ruin to all Greece. Alexander spent two years restoring order in his father's turbulent kingdom, first pacifying the tribes in his rear. With the death of Philip, the Greek cities he had defeated burst into rebellion. Believing Alexander to be in Macedonia, they rose up to throw off his rule. By a forced march, so rapid as to be unbelievable, he arrived at rebellious Thebes. He offered to spare Thebes the violence of attack if the city would submit. The Thebans refused. Alexander stormed the city and razed it to the ground. By his order the temples and the house of Pindar the poet were left standing. Six thousand Thebans were massacred in the city before Alexander put an end to the slaughter, and 30,000 were sold into slavery. The furious destruction of Thebes must be ascribed largely to his Phocian and Boeotian allies, who thus brought low the proud city that had lorded it over them for many years. Alexander later regretted the destruction of Thebes, and attributed whatever misfortunes later befell him to the anger of Dionysus for having ruined his city. Now, however, he was truly master of the Greece he admired so ardently. He forgave the Athenians for going into mourning and omitting the celebration of the mysteries on the fall of Thebes; he

---

(obscured) errạnt, ardẹnt, actọr; ch, chip; g, go; th, thin; ŦH, then; y, you;
(variable) ḏ as d or j, ş as s or sh, ţ as t or ch, ẓ as z or zh.

never wavered in his admiration and respect for their city, and continued to treat the Athenians with courtesy and to enrich them with gifts. Before he made his forced march from Macedonia to Thebes, Alexander had marched through Greece and had been named general of the league of Hellas to lead the invasion of Persia. In Corinth, where he had been elected general, he had his famous encounter with the Cynic philosopher Diogenes, in which the latter requested the young king and general to "stand from between me and the sun." Alexander expressed admiration for Diogenes, and said if he were not Alexander he would choose to be Diogenes. He had also gone to Delphi and sought an oracular response on a day when it was forbidden to give them. He seized the priestess to compel her, and her remark, "My son, you are invincible," was oracle enough for him.

With order restored in Macedonia and Greece submissive, he set out (334 B.C.) to reduce Persia. His highly professional army, which was devoted to him, consisted of 30,000 heavy- and light-armed infantry and 5000 cavalry, with a superior siege train, commissary, and intelligence service. Crossing the Hellespont, he stopped at Troy to visit the ancient battleground, sacrificed to Athena, and honored the heroes who had fallen in the Trojan War. He ran naked, as was the custom, around the tomb of Achilles to honor his favorite hero. From Troy he marched to the Granicus River where the Persian forces were encamped and there he defeated them (334 B.C.) Of the great spoils taken, he kept little for himself, sent some to the Athenians, and the rest to his mother. Following his victory at the Granicus many of the cities of Asia Minor, including Sardis, surrendered to him, and the object of the league, the liberation of the Greek cities of Asia Minor from Persia, was accomplished. The tyrannies favorable to Persia were overthrown and democracies were established. Halicarnassus and Miletus resisted him and were taken by force. In Caria he restored the princess Ada to the throne and adopted her as his mother. According to Plutarch, while Alexander was deliberating what to do next, a fountain in Lycia overflowed and washed up on its banks a copper plate on which was written, in ancient characters, a prophecy that the time would come when the Greeks would destroy the Persian Empire. Taking this as a

fat, fāte, fär, fâll, ȧsk, fāre; net, mē, hèr; pin, pīne; not, nōte, möve, nôr; up, lūte, pùll; oi, oil; ou out; (lightened) ĕlect, agǫny, ūnite;

sign, he marched by the sea through Cilicia and Phoenicia along the coast of Pamphylia where, some say, divine power held back the waves so that his army could make its way on the beach (others say his soldiers waded in water up to their armpits), to Phaselis, where he stopped and danced about a statue of Theodectes he found in the market-place to honor this philosopher he had once known. He subdued the Pisidians, conquered the Phrygians, and turned inland to Gordium where he was shown the famous knot on the yoke of the chariot of Gordius. Concerning the knot, an oracle had decreed that whoever untied it would rule the world. Some say Alexander looked at it and impatiently cut it through with his sword. Others say he unloosed it by withdrawing the pin in the yoke about which it was tied. He reduced Paphlagonia and Cappadocia, and now Darius III led his Persian forces against him. At Tarsus, Alexander became very ill. None of his physicians dared prescribe for him lest he die and they be accused. Alexander's friend Philip, an Acarnanian, anxious for his health, concocted a potion to cure him. Philip did not know that Alexander had received a letter which accused him of plotting against the young king's life. He took the medicinal draft to Alexander and handed it to him. Alexander drank it, then handed the letter of accusation to Philip, having already indicated his perfect trust in his friend by drinking the medicine. Whether it was by reason of Philip's medicine or of nature, Alexander was soon well again and advanced to meet Darius who had mocked his delay as cowardice. The armies met in the mountainous defiles near the town of Issus. In such cramped quarters the large armaments of the Persians could not act effectively; the terrain was of great advantage to Alexander. In the thick of the battle Alexander was wounded, some say by Darius himself, but his forces surged on and the Persians were overwhelmed. Darius saw that the battle was lost. He abandoned his war chariot and fled on horseback, leaving his mother, his wife and his children behind in his camp. When Alexander learned of their presence among his captives he sent word that they need not grieve for Darius who still lived, nor fear him, as he intended to accord them the honor and service due their royal estate. Alexander kept his promise. Though Statira, wife of Darius, was counted the most beautiful princess living, he did not seek her out but

(obscured) errant, ardent, actor; ch, chip; g, go; th, thin; ᴛʜ, then; y, you; (variable) ḍ as d or j, ş as s or sh, ṭ as t or ch, ẓ as z or zh.

had all the women of Darius' household maintained according to their customary standard. From his victory at Issus (333 B.C.), he took great spoils, the largest share of which he gave to his Thessalian horsemen because they had fought most gallantly. After Issus he resolved to render the Persian fleet harmless by winning control of the ports on the coast. He conquered Phoenicia, except for Tyre. Without a fleet, it seemed an impossible task to conquer Tyre, a city on an island. Alexander accomplished it by building a mole from the mainland to the island and after a siege of seven months the city fell (332 B.C.). He scattered its inhabitants, selling vast numbers of them into slavery. He took Gaza after a siege, and went on to Egypt (332 B.C.), where he was welcomed as a deliverer of the Egyptians from Persian tyranny. In Egypt he founded the city of Alexandria on the mainland opposite the island of Pharos, a site chosen, it is said, because of a dream in which Homer appeared to him and named Pharos. Alexandria was the first of 70 communities founded by him which became powerful forces for the Hellenization of the non-Greek world. While the city was being erected he made the difficult and dangerous journey across the desert to the oracle of Ammon in Libya, though seers advised him not to go. On the way the gods protected him, it was said, by sending rain so that his band would not perish of thirst, and by sending ravens to lead him when he was lost in the desert. The priest of Ammon addressed him as the son of Zeus and predicted that he would conquer the world. His circle encouraged him to believe he was the son of a god and it appeared that he was frequently willing to do so.

With the eastern coasts of the Mediterranean now in his possession he turned inland (331 B.C.). Darius had earlier sent word to him asking that he be allowed to ransom his family, and offering to partition his empire with him, ceding to Alexander all the lands west of the Euphrates. Parmenio, a general in his army who had served under Philip, said if he were Alexander, he would accept the offer of Darius. Alexander replied, "So would I, if I were Parmenio." But being Alexander, he wrote Darius a letter worthy of a conqueror, informing him that if Darius would come and surrender himself, he would be treated with every courtesy. Otherwise, Alexander was prepared to go and fetch him. Darius could not accept such terms and prepared to march

fat, fāte, fär, fåll, àsk, fãre; net, mē, hėr; pin, pīne; not, nōte, möve, nôr; up, lūte, pùll; oi, oil; ou out; (lightened) ēlect, agǫny, ūnite;

against him. When the Macedonians arrived before the camp of Darius at Gaugamela (for the battle sometimes called the Battle of Arbela, 331 B.C.), the fires from the Persian camp at night gave stunning evidence of the vast forces Darius had arrayed against them. Alexander's generals advised that the attack be made at night when darkness would conceal the dangers of the battle. Alexander answered that he would not "steal a victory," went to bed, and slept so soundly he had to be awakened when it was time to muster his army. Dressed in spectacularly rich armor and mounted on Bucephalus, he charged the enemy at the head of his cavalry, the phalanx of foot soldiers following. The Persians were overwhelmed. Again Darius left his chariot and fled on horseback. Alexander would have pursued, but Parmenio sent a message calling for help in his sector. Alexander went to his aid, but from that time on he suspected Parmenio, now an old man, if not of treachery, at least of incompetence. After the victory at Issus Alexander was proclaimed king of all Asia. Of the rich spoils taken he sent some to Greece, some to the Greek cities of Italy, and with the rest he rewarded his friends and followers. He now proceeded into the heart of the Persian empire, first putting to the sword the many prisoners who were an encumbrance. At Susa he found fabulous treasure. Going on to Persepolis, the royal city, he found untold riches and sat upon the Great King's throne. Some say that at a banquet in the Persian king's palace his generals and their mistresses were present. Thais, the Athenian mistress of his general Ptolemy, when the company was flushed with wine, proposed that the palace be burned in revenge for the burning of Athens by Xerxes (480 B.C.). Alexander gave his permission, and the diners with heads garlanded paraded through the palace putting it to the torch. But soon Alexander regretted the wanton destruction and ordered the fire quenched. From Persepolis, having subdued Persia, Alexander set out after Darius. He pursued him through Media, where he left Parmenio to guard the treasures taken at the Median capital Ecbatana. With a small band, by a series of tireless marches, he chased Darius past the Caspian Gates and overtook him near Thara south of the Caspian Sea. The Persian nobles accompanying Darius, chief of whom was his cousin Bessus, stabbed him when he refused to continue the flight and deserted him. When Alexander arrived, Darius had just died (330 B.C.). In pity, some say, Alexander threw his own cloak over the body of the Great King, and later sent it with great pomp to the dead king's mother for burial with his ancestors.

From here he took his army through Parthia, south to Seistan in Drangiana (modern Iran), swung north and passed through Arachosia and Bactria to Maracanda (Samarkand) in Sogdiana, fighting and conquering all the way. The wealth he won and distributed to his friends began to have its effect on them. Some of them soon acquired a taste for luxury and extravagant living. He feared they would become soft and vulnerable. "Have you not yet learned," he asked, "that the end and perfection of our victories is to avoid the vices and weaknesses of those we conquer?" For himself, he kept in good physical condition by violent sports and hunting. He ate with moderation and, contrary to legend, he rarely drank but did enjoy sitting long over the wine in conversation with his friends. His mother wrote to scold him for enriching his companions for, as she said, if they became the equal of kings in wealth, they might attack his own kingship. He showed the letters to his dear friend Hephaestion and then ensured the latter's silence on these matters by placing his seal ring against Hephaestion's lips. He continued to send his mother rich presents from his spoils, but did not let her advice interfere with his plans. When he went through Parthia, he adopted Persian dress, and it seemed to his men that he wished to be honored as a god. More and more he adopted barbarian (Persian) customs, but at the same time he attempted to introduce Greek ways. He had 30,000 Persian boys chosen to be educated in the Greek tongue and the Macedonian military discipline. He married Roxana, a Bactrian princess, some say to make a stronger bond between the Macedonians and the Persians. The changes in his personal life and habits made his Macedonians uneasy. Of his dearest friends, Hephaestion followed Alexander in adopting barbarian ways, and was used as his emissary in dealing with them. Craterus kept to the Macedonian customs. Alexander was said to have had affection for Hephaestion, whom he called "Alexander's friend," and to have respected Craterus, whom he named "the king's friend." Wealth and luxury brought enmity and

fat, fāte, fär, fåll, àsk, fāre; net, mē, hėr; pin, pīne; not, nōte, möve, nôr; up, lūte, pùll; oi, oil; ou out; (lightened) ēlect, agǫny, ūnite;

envy in its train. Philotas, son of Parmenio, became arrogant in his display of riches. His father advised him to be "less great," for he knew Alexander had received complaints of him. Philotas took no heed, and boasted that it was he and his father who had won the great victories for which Alexander claimed the credit. His boasts were repeated to Alexander who at first disregarded them. But when an abortive plot to kill Alexander was wrongly ascribed to Philotas, Alexander had him tortured and put to death. Afterward, he sent men to kill his father Parmenio who had faithfully served Philip as well as himself. Now many of his friends began to fear him. The Macedonians resented what they considered to be Persian domination over him. Clitus, one of his companions, during a long evening in Maracanda (Samarkand) in which much wine was drunk, accused Alexander of preferring the Persians who bowed the knee to him to the company of free-born men who dared to speak their minds. Clitus had saved his life in battle at the Granicus and reminded Alexander of it. Friends of both at the gathering tried to quiet Clitus. Alexander himself tried to change the subject. But the resentment he had stored up drove Clitus on. When he was hustled out of the room by guards, he returned through another entrance and shouted a verse from Euripides' *Andromache:* "In Greece, alas! how ill things ordered are." The lines that follow in the play (which Clitus did not speak) contained the insult:

"When trophies rise for victories in war,
Men count the praise not theirs who did the deed,
But to the one commander give the meed;
Who, sharing with ten thousand more the fight,
For one man's service takes the general right."

Infuriated, Alexander seized a spear and ran Clitus through. Instantly he came to his senses, drew the spear from the body of his friend, and would have killed himself but for the intervention of his guards. He mourned for days, but his grief was at last eased by the self-made philosopher Anaxarchus, who told him, "Zeus is represented to have Justice and Law on either hand, to signify that all the actions of a conqueror are lawful and just." Alexander was able to convince himself with this, that his acts as ruler were just, thus doing irreparable damage to the qualities of moderation and justice he had formerly possessed. He became convinced that

(obscured) errạnt, ardẹnt, actọr; ch, chip; g, go; th, thin; ŦH, then; y, you;
(variable) ḍ as d or j, ş as s or sh, ţ as t or ch, ẓ as z or zh.

Callisthenes, a philosopher in his train who had been brought up in Aristotle's household, was in a plot against him. He seized Callisthenes, and with no grounds at all cast him into prison. There he died (327 B.C.) or as some say, was killed by Alexander's order.

His march of conquest now carried him from Maracanda north to Tashkent, across the Jaxartes River. He then turned south again, went through Bactria and on to the Indus River, which he crossed, and entered India (326 B.C.). He marched to the Hydaspes River where he defeated King Porus. Porus, badly wounded, fell into his hands. When Alexander asked Porus how he expected to be treated, he replied, "Like a king," and he was treated so. Proceeding from the Hydaspes, the Macedonians rebelled at the proposal to cross the Ganges, and he was compelled to turn back. He returned by way of the Indus valley and at the mouth of the Indus sent his admiral Nearchus on a voyage to the mouth of the Euphrates. Part of his own overland journey was made through deserts with great privation, and his forces were enormously reduced by lack of supplies. On the way he was harassed by hostile tribes and impeded by the necessity of subduing their cities. At one city of the Malli he performed an exploit of personal valor and recklessness that was typical of him. He climbed the wall of the town with a few companions in his impatience to take the place, and leaped in among the hostile forces. He was badly wounded before his army could gain entrance to the city and rescue him. At Carmania he came upon abundance again and spent days feasting and resting his army. Nearchus had met him at Gedrosia and gave such reports of his voyage that Alexander resolved to make one himself, but various parts of his empire were in revolt. Olympias had seized Epirus and Cleopatra had taken control in Macedonia. Returning through Persepolis, he married Statira, a daughter of Darius III, at Susa, as well as a second Persian wife, and gave the noblest of the Persian ladies to his friends. These marriages were intended to cement the ties between the Persians and Macedonians. Great feasts and celebrations attended the weddings. His friends grieved, however, to see him become Persianized. In 324 B.C. an open rebellion broke out in his army when he discharged some of his Macedonian veterans. In the end he quelled it by the force of his personality and his threat to

take a Persian guard. Then he forgave the dissidents, rewarded the veterans too old for combat and sent them
home. When Hephaestion died of a fever at Ecbatana (324
B.C.), he ordered the manes and tails of all his horses and
mules cropped in mourning, destroyed the fortifications of
neighboring cities, crucified the physician who attended Hephaestion, and forbade the playing of music until at last
word came from the oracle of Ammon in Libya instructing
him to make sacrifices to Hephaestion and to worship him
as a hero. He fell upon the Cossaeans and put the whole
tribe to the sword, some say as a sacrifice to Hephaestion.
Proposing to go to Babylon, he was told by Nearchus that
Chaldean diviners ordered him not to go there. He ignored
the warnings, but as he proceeded unfavorable omens oc-
cured in rapid succession: a tame ass kicked the finest lion
he had and killed it; a man appeared, clad in the king's
clothes, and seated himself on the king's throne, saying he
was sent by Serapis. Alexander had him put to death, but the
incident depressed him. Embassies from all over the world
came to Babylon to honor him as the acknowledged conqueror. He planned and prepared a voyage to explore a
route from Babylonia around Arabia to Egypt. All was in
readiness, and on the approach of the departure, Alexander
and one of his favorites drank deep to celebrate the departure for two days and nights. On the third day he was
afflicted with a fever which he at first disregarded, but it
persisted and with the elapse of ten more days he had succumbed and lost his speech. The Macedonians were led
through his tent to say farewell to their king and commander. The next day (June 13, 323 B.C.), not yet 33 years
of age, weakened by his old wounds and disease, he died at
Babylon. Napoleon called him the greatest general in history. Alexander strongly believed in the fusion of races; all
his wives were eastern princesses. His life altered the course
of history, for he created a new world-society based on a
common Greek culture. He became after his death a legendary figure to medieval Europe and to the Orient of all periods.

Alyattes (al-i-at′ēz). Son of Sadyattes, whom he succeeded as
king of Lydia, c617 B.C., and reigned until 560 B.C. He
waged war on the Medes under Cyaxares, drove the Cimmerians out of Asia, and extended the conquests of the

(obscured) errạnt, ardẹnt, actǫr; ch, chip; g, go; th, thin; ᵮн, then; y, you;
(variable) ḍ as d or j, ş as s or sh, ţ as t or ch, ẓ as z or zh.

Lydian kings on the coast of Asia Minor by conquering Smyrna, a colony of Colophon, and attacking Clazomenae. He attempted to extend his empire by taking Miletus. Twice he defeated the Milesians in battle but did not take the strongly walled city which commanded the sea. Since siege under these circumstances was hopeless, each year he marched through the country surrounding the walled city and burned the standing crops but spared the houses of the farmers, as he wanted them to return and plant more crops for him to plunder. The sixth year that he did this flames from the burning grain were carried by a high wind to the temple of Athena Assesia and burned it to the ground. The army of Alyattes withdrew to Sardis and there, in a short while, Alyattes fell sick. As his illness could not be cured he sent messengers to Delphi for information but his messengers were told that no answer would be given him until he rebuilt the temple of Athena at Assesus. Alyattes now sought a truce that would give him time to rebuild the temple. But Thrasybulus, tyrant of Miletus, had been informed of the oracle by his friend Periander of Corinth and prepared a trick by which he hoped to bring the war to an end. He ordered all the meager supply of grain to be brought to the market-place, commanded the Milesians to dress in their finery and gather there, and to be ready at a signal to fall to feasting and revelry. When the herald of Alyattes arrived he found the Milesians feasting and making merry as if they had not a care in the world. On his return he reported the prosperity of the city to Alyattes who was astonished, for he had hoped to starve the city into submission by burning the crops. The news brought by the herald convinced Alyattes that it was fruitless to prosecute a war against a city that seemed to thrive on it. He made an alliance of friendship with Miletus and brought the war to an end. He then built two temples of Athena at Assesus to replace the one he had burned and shortly afterward recovered from his illness. Alyattes was the father of Croesus who succeeded him as king. The tomb of Alyattes north of Sardis, his capital, was an outstanding monument of antiquity.

Amasis II (ạ-mā′sis). [Also: *Amosis, Aahmes, Ahmes.*] Egyptian king, the fifth of the XXVIth dynasty, fl. c569–525 B.C. According to Herodotus, Amasis was sent by Apries, king of Egypt, to quell a rebellion of the soldiers after they had been

---

fat, fāte, fär, fåll, ȧsk, fãre; net, mē, hėr; pin, pīne; not, nōte, möve, nôr; up, lūte, pùll; oi, oil; ou out; (lightened) ĕlect, agǫny, ụnite;

defeated by the Cyrenaeans. As Amasis was exhorting the soldiers one came up behind him and placed a helmet on his head, saying he thereby crowned him king. The soldiers acclaimed him and instead of quashing the revolt in the army, Amasis marched at the head of it to seize power from Apries. Apries sent a man of high rank to go and bring Amasis back with him. The envoy soon saw what Amasis planned and hastened back to tell Apries. But the latter was so enraged with his envoy for returning without Amasis that he cut off his ears and nose. This barbarous act to a man of high rank caused the Egyptians, who up to now had supported Apries, to go over to the side of Amasis to whom they now offered their aid. Apries, at the head of a force of mercenaries, marched against Amasis and was defeated. Amasis took Apries captive and returned with him to Saïs, where he took over the palace of Apries. He treated Apries kindly until criticism of his kindness to an enemy caused him to turn Apries over to his former subjects, who strangled him. Amasis now became king. At first he was somewhat despised by his subjects because he had been a mere private citizen before seizing the throne but he won their respect by diplomacy rather than force. He caused a golden vessel in which he had habitually washed his feet to be melted down. From this he made a golden image of one of the gods and set it up in the city. The Egyptians immediately began to worship it. Amasis called his people together and revealed that the image had been made of a vessel formerly used for bathing the king's feet yet now it was given unquestioning worship. He compared himself to the vessel. Once he had been a private person and nobody paid much attention to him; now he was king and he ordered them to honor and obey him. His lesson was not lost on his subjects. Herodotus says of Amasis that from dawn to noon he carried on the public business with great earnestness. But from noon on he joked, feasted, and drank wine, enjoying himself as much as he might. Criticized for his light-hearted manner after carrying on affairs of state all morning, Amasis replied with an analogy. Bowmen, he said, string and bend their bows when they want to shoot; when shooting is over, they unstring the bows for if the bow was kept always tautly strung it would break and in time of need would fail the bowman. For the same reason, he divided his own time between business and pleasure. It is said that before Amasis became king he was in the habit of stealing when he needed funds to carry on his pleasures. When discovered on various occasions if he denied that he was a thief he was brought before the nearest oracle. Sometimes the oracle would say he was guilty, sometimes it would declare he was not a thief. When he became king, he neglected the temples of the oracles that had pronounced him innocent of his thefts because he judged them to be utterly unreliable and worthless. But those that had rightly judged him guilty he honored with great reverence.

Amasis had treaties of alliance and friendship with Polycrates of Samos and with Croesus, king of Lydia. He extended his kingdom by conquering Cyprus and he exerted great influence in Cyrene. Egypt was immensely prosperous during his reign. He erected many monuments and made gifts to the temples. He built a gateway to the temple of Isis at Saïs, added a number of colossal statues and sphinxes and a recumbent colossus. At Memphis also he gave a recumbent colossus to the temple and built a temple of Isis. Remains of his monuments still exist. He welcomed Greeks to his kingdom (Solon was one of his visitors), established them in the port city of Naucratis and allowed them to set up temples and altars to their gods. He contributed the very large sum of 1000 talents to the rebuilding of the temple of Delphi that had burned in 548 B.C.; and also gave rich gifts to the temple of Athena in Cyrene, the home of his wife Ladice, daughter of King Battus; to the temple of Athena at Lindus in Rhodes, because the daughters of Danaus stopped there on their flight from Egypt; and to the temple of Hera at Samos, because he was a bond friend of Polycrates, tyrant of Samos. Later Amasis dissolved the bond of friendship with Polycrates because, according to Herodotus, Polycrates enjoyed too good fortune. Amasis said he knew that such uninterrupted good fortune would surely bring down the envy and wrath of the gods on Polycrates. He therefore no longer wished to be his bond friend so that he would not be obliged to grieve on his account when the inevitable doom overtook him. This is the story Herodotus gives for the dissolution of the alliance between Amasis and Polycrates. Others, however, say that the alliance may have been weakened when Amasis learned that Polycrates was intriguing with the Persians against Egypt when Cambyses, son of

Cyrus, proposed a campaign against Egypt. It was supposedly because of anger against Amasis that Cambyses resolved to make war on Egypt, but by the time Cambyses
reached Egypt with his army Amasis had died and been
succeeded by his son Psammenitus (Psammetichus III), 525
B.C. When he came to Saïs, Cambyses ordered that the body
of Amasis should be brought from its tomb. His tomb was
in the sacred precinct of Isis at Saïs near the tomb of the king
he had deposed. Cambyses commanded his soldiers to stab
Amasis' body and pull out the hair, but since the body had
been embalmed it did not fall apart under this treatment and
Cambyses ordered it to be burned, an act of the most frightful impiety to the Egyptians. But some say that Amasis,
having been warned by an oracle of what would happen to
him after his death, had given orders for his body to be
entombed in a secret place in the sanctuary and another
body substituted in his tomb so that Cambyses did not, after
all, defile his body. However, Herodotus, who tells this
story, does not believe it and thinks the Egyptians made it
up to preserve the dignity of their king.

Ambiorix (am-bī'ō-riks). Gallic chief; fl. 1st century B.C., leader
of the Eburones. He is famous for his campaigns against the
Romans (54–53 B.C.), in which he twice defeated them in
what is now Belgium, but fled across the Rhine at the approach of Julius Caesar.

Amestris (a̱-mes'tris). Daughter of Otanes, according to
Herodotus, but daughter of Onophas, according to Ctesias,
and the favorite wife of Xerxes, to whom she bore at least
five children. Her crimes and cruelties are related by Ctesias
at some length, and are mentioned by Herodotus. She is
believed by some to be the Vashti of the Book of Esther.

Amyntas I (a̱-min'ta̱s). King of Macedonia; died c498 B.C. He
was a son of Alcetas and fifth in descent from Perdiccas, the
founder of the dynasty. He presented earth and water as a
token of his submission to the Persian commander Megabazus, whom Darius, on returning to Persia, had left at the
head of 80,000 men in Europe.

Amyntas II. King of Macedonia (394–370 B.C.); nephew of
Perdiccas II. He obtained the crown of Macedonia proper in
394 B.C. by the murder of Pausanias, son of the usurper
Aëropus. He was forced to flee from his kingdom (385 B.C.)
when Argaeus, the son of Pausanias and supported by the

(obscured) erra̱nt, arde̱nt, actor; ch, chip; g, go; th, thin; ᴛʜ, then; y, you;
(variable) d̪ as d or j, s̱ as s or sh, t̪ as t or ch, ẕ as z or zh.
61199

Illyrians, invaded it. He left the southern districts of Macedonia and the cities on the Thermaic Gulf to the Chalcidian League, a federation of some of the cities of Chalcidice under the leadership of Olynthus. When he was restored to his throne by the Thessalians with whom he had taken refuge, Olynthus refused to give up the cities he had handed over. Amyntas asked the aid of Sparta. The Spartans answered his appeal, defeated the Olynthians, broke up the Chalcidian League, and restored his coastal cities to Amyntas. Amyntas died in 370 B.C. and was succeeded by his son Alexander II, the oldest brother of Philip II.

Amyntas III. King of Macedonia (360–359 B.C.); died 336 B.C. He was the grandson of Amyntas II. He was an infant at the death of his father in 360 B.C., and was excluded (359) from the throne by the regent, his uncle Philip of Macedon, at whose court he was brought up and whose daughter he married. He was executed by Alexander the Great for a conspiracy against the king's life (336 B.C.).

Anacharsis (an-a-kär′sis). Scythian prince, brother of Saulius, king of Thrace, active c600 B.C., and a contemporary of Solon. He traveled widely and visited Athens, where he obtained a great reputation for wisdom. By some he was reckoned among the legendary seven great sages of ancient times. On his way back to Thrace he stopped at Cyzicus. There he found the inhabitants celebrating a festival to Cybele, the Great Mother. He was so impressed by the magnificence of the festival that he vowed to create a similar festival if he returned safely to his homeland. On his arrival in Thrace he went to a sequestered place and performed the rites. Some Scythians, who observed him in the course of the ritual, informed his brother, King Saulius, of what they had seen and Saulius went to see for himself. Such was the hatred of the Scythians for foreign customs and rituals that when he beheld Anacharsis carrying out the rites for Cybele, Saulis shot Anacharsis with an arrow and killed him.

Anaxilaus (a-nak-si-lā′us) or *Anaxilas* (-nak′si-las). Tyrant of Rhegium (494–476 B.C.); died 476 B.C. He won control of Zancle, which thereafter was known as Messana (Messina), and thus controlled both sides of the straits between Sicily and Italy.

Andocides (an-dos′i-dēz). Athenian orator and politican, born c440 B.C. at Athens; died c390 B.C. He was a member of a

fat, fāte, fär, fåll, ȧsk, fāre; net, mē, hėr; pin, pīne; not, nōte, möve, nôr; up, lūte, pùll; oi, oil; ou out; (lightened) ęlect, agǫny, ūnite;

distinguished aristocratic family. In 415 B.C. he was accused
of mutilating the statues of Hermes. The defacing of the
sacred images before the start of the Athenian expedition to
Sicily caused a near panic in Athens. Three hundred people
were denounced for the act of impiety, which was probably
committed in a spirit of skepticism and youthful exuberance
(see *Alcibiades*). To save himself and others who might be
innocent, Andocides agreed to give information about his
aristocratic accomplices under a promise of amnesty. In
spite of the promise he was deprived of some of his civic
rights. He went to Cyprus and became a trader, in which
occupation he made many shrewd deals for the benefit of
Athens to show his patriotism. Twice he sought to have his
status restored, and at last in 403 B.C., he was readmitted to
Athens under a general amnesty which followed the establishment of the democracy. On his return he was active in
public life, successfully defending himself against charges of
impiety based on the old scandal of 415 B.C. In 391 B.C. he
was sent as an ambassador to negotiate peace with Sparta.
One of his orations, still extant, was made in behalf of the
treaty he brought back on this occasion. The treaty was
rejected and he went into exile. Of two other orations which
are preserved, *About Returning Home* pleaded for the restoration of his status as an Athenian, and was made in 410 B.C.
In another he defended himself again against the old
charges of impiety which were resurrected in 399 B.C.

Androtion (an-drō'shi-on). Athenian orator, fl. c350 B.C., a
contemporary of Demosthenes and pupil of Isocrates. He
was a chronicler of Attica, whose work was probably contained in ten books, only fragments of which survive. He is
known chiefly as a subject of attack by Demosthenes in one
of his early orations.

Antalcidas (an-tal'si-das). Spartan diplomat, politican, and
warrior; fl. in the first half of the 4th century B.C. He was
sent (c393 B.C.) to undermine Athenian relations with the
Persian satrap in Asia Minor. He proceeded (388 B.C.) to the
Persian court, where aid against Athens was finally obtained,
and shortly thereafter he defeated the Athenian fleet near
the Hellespont. He prevented the grain ships from reaching
Athens and was thus able to compel Athens to accept the
"Peace of Antalcidas" (or "King's Peace") in 386 B.C., which
provided that all of Asia Minor as well as Cyprus and

(obscured) errant, ardent, actor; ch, chip; g, go; th, thin; ꜰʜ, then; y, you;
(variable) ḍ as d or j, ṣ as s or sh, ṭ as t or ch, ẓ as z or zh.

Clazomenae would be abandoned to Persia, while all remaining Greek city-states would be independent except for Imbrus, Lemnos, and Scyrus, which remained Athenian.

Antigonidae (an-ti-gon'i-dē). The descendants of Antigonus I of Macedonia (died 301 B.C.), one of the generals of Alexander the Great. The principal members of the family were Demetrius I (Poliorcetes), king of Macedonia (died 283 B.C.), son of Antigonus I; Antigonus II (Gonatas), king of Macedonia (died 239), son of Demetrius I; Demetrius of Cyrene (died 250), son of Demetrius I; Demetrius II, king of Macedonia (died 229), son of Antigonus II; Antigonus III (Doson), king of Macedonia (died 221), son of Demetrius of Cyrene; Philip V, king of Macedonia (died 179 B.C.), son of Demetrius II; and Perseus, king of Macedonia, conquered by the Romans in 168 B.C.

Antigonus I (an-tig'ō-nus) (of *Macedonia*). [Surnamed *Cyclops* or *Monophthalmos,* meaning the "One-Eyed."] King of Macedonia (306–301 B.C.), born c382 B.C.; killed at the battle of Ipsus, 301 B.C. He was one of the generals of Alexander the Great. After the latter's death he received the provinces of Greater Phrygia, Lycia, and Pamphylia. He carried on war against Perdiccas and Eumenes, made extensive conquests in Asia, assumed the title of king in 306 B.C., and was overthrown at Ipsus in Phrygia by a coalition of his enemies.

Antigonus II (of *Macedonia*). [Called *Antigonus Gonatas.*] King of Macedonia (283–239 B.C.), son of Demetrius Poliorcetes, born c320 B.C.; died 239 B.C. He assumed the title in 283, after the death of his father, but did not actually reign until 276. He suppressed the Celtic invasion and was temporarily driven from his land by Pyrrhus in 273 B.C.

Antigonus III (of *Macedonia*). [Called *Antigonus Doson.*] King of Macedonia (229–221 B.C.), newphew of Antigonus II and a great-grandson of Antigonus I, Alexander's general. He died 221 B.C. He was appointed guardian of Philip, son of Demetrius II, and on the death of Demetrius (229 B.C.) he married his widow and ascended the throne. He successfully supported Aratus and the Achaean League against Cleomenes, king of Sparta, and the Aetolians, and defeated the former at Sellasia in 222 B.C. He is said to have been dubbed "Doson" because "he was always about to give, and never did."

Antiochus (an-tī′ō̞-kus). Athenian sea captain; died 407 B.C. He chanced to be in the assembly at Athens when contributions were being made to the state. Alcibiades, passing by, heard the applause and inquired the reason for it. When he was told, he entered the assembly and offered a large contribution himself. In the applause that followed he forgot that he was carrying a quail in his cloak. The bird escaped, and all took part in the scramble to retrieve it. Antiochus caught it and restored it to Alcibiades. Henceforth he became a great favorite with Alcibiades and served loyally under him. In 407 B.C. when Alcibiades, general in command on land and sea, sailed to collect money for his operations, he left the main body of the fleet at Notium under the command of Antiochus with strict orders not to engage the Spartan fleet under Lysander at Ephesus. Antiochus disobeyed his orders, sailed out and taunted the Spartans. Lysander sailed out against him and destroyed his ship and the Athenian ships that had come to his aid. Fifteen ships were lost in all.

Antiochus I (of *Syria*). [Called *Antiochus I Soter*.] King of Syria (280–261 B.C.), born 324 B.C.; killed c261 B.C. He was a son of Seleucus I Nicator. It is said that when he fell sick from love of Stratonice, the young wife of his father, Seleucus, on the advice of the physician Erasistratus, allowed Stratonice to marry his son, and invested him with the government of Upper Asia giving him the title of king. On the death of his father Antiochus succeeded to all his dominions, but relinquished his claims to Macedonia on the marriage of Antigonus II of Macedonia to Phila, the daughter of Seleucus and Stratonice. He was the greatest founder of cities after Alexander the Great.

Antiochus II (of *Syria*). [Called *Antiochus II Theos*.] King of Syria; killed 247 B.C. He was the second son of Antiochus I, whom he succeeded in 261 B.C. He became involved in a ruinous war with Ptolemy Philadelphus, king of Egypt, during which Syria was further weakened by the revolt of the provinces of Parthia and Bactria, Arsaces establishing the Parthian empire in c250 B.C., and Theodotus the independent kingdom of Bactria about the same time. Peace was concluded with Egypt in 250 B.C. Antiochus was obliged to reject his wife Laodice and to marry Berenice, the daughter of Ptolemy. On the death of Ptolemy (247 B.C.), he recalled Laodice (who, it is thought, caused Ptolemy's murder) and

(obscured) errạnt, ardẹnt, actọr; ch, chip; g, go; th, thin; ₮H, then; y, you; (variable) ḍ as d or j, ṣ as s or sh, ṭ as t or ch, ẓ as z or zh.

also Berenice and her son. The connection between Syria and Egypt is referred to in Daniel, xi. 6.

Antiochus III (of *Syria*). [Called *Antiochus the Great.*] King of Syria (223–187 B.C.), the most famous of the Seleucidae. He was born c241 B.C.; died 187 B.C. He was the second son of Seleucus II and grandson of Antiochus II, and succeeded his brother Seleucus Ceraunus at the age of 15. His epithet "the Great" was earned by the magnitude of his enterprises rather than by what he accomplished. He subdued (220 B.C.) his rebellious brothers Molo and Alexander, satraps of Media and Persia, and was forced (after having undertaken an aggressive war against Ptolemy Philopator) by the battle of Raphia, near Gaza, to relinquish (217 B.C.) his claims to Coele-Syria and Palestine. He defeated and killed (214) Achaeus, the rebellious governor of Asia Minor; attempted (212–205 B.C.) to regain the former provinces Parthia and Bactria; and was compelled to recognize (205) the independence of Parthia. The victory of Paneas (198) gave him back the Egyptian provinces of Coele-Syria and Palestine. He made peace, however, with Ptolemy Epiphanes to whom he betrothed his daughter Cleopatra, promising Coele-Syria and Palestine as a dowry. He conquered (196 B.C.) the Thracian Chersonese from Macedonia; received (195) Hannibal at his court; carried on (192–189) a war with the Romans who demanded the restoration of the Egyptian provinces and the Thracian Chersonese; was defeated at Thermopylae in 191, and at Magnesia in 190; and sustained naval losses at Chios (191) and at Myonnesus (190 B.C.). He purchased peace by consenting to the surrender of all his European possessions, and his Asiatic possessions as far as the Taurus, and the surrender of Hannibal, who escaped, and by giving up his elephants and ships of war. Antiochus was killed by his subjects in an attempt to plunder the rich temple of Elymaïs in order to pay the Romans, an event which, like his defeat by the Romans, is supposed by some to be referred to in Daniel, xi. 18, 19.

Antiochus IV (of *Syria*). [Called *Antiochus IV Epiphanes.*] King of Syria (175–c163 B.C.); third son of Antiochus III; died 163 B.C. He reconquered Armenia, which had been lost by his father, and made war on Egypt in the period 171–168 B.C., recovering Coele-Syria and Palestine. His policy of destroying the Jewish religion, in pursuance of which he took

---

fat, fāte, fär, fâll, ásk, fāre; net, mē, hėr; pin, pīne; not, nōte, mȯve, nôr; up, lūte, p·ull; oi, oil; ou out; (lightened) ēlect, agǫny, ūnite;

Jerusalem by storm in 170 B.C. (when he desecrated the temple) and again in 168, led to the successful revolt under Mattathias, the father of the Maccabees (167 B.C.).

Antiochus V (of *Syria*). [Called *Antiochus V Eupator.*] King of Syria (163–162 B.C.); son of Antiochus IV, whom he succeeded at the age of nine years, under the guardianship of Lysias. He was born c173 B.C.; died 162 B.C. He concluded a peace with the Jews who had revolted under his father, and was defeated and killed by Demetrius Soter (the son of Seleucus Philopator) who laid claim to the throne.

Antiochus VII (of *Syria*). [Called *Antiochus VII Sidetes.*] King of Syria (c139–c129 B.C.); born c159 B.C.; died c129 B.C. He was the second son of Demetrius Soter. He carried on war with the Jews, taking Jerusalem in 133 B.C., after which he concluded peace with them on favorable terms. He was killed in a war with the Parthians.

Antipater (an-tip′a̱-tėr). Macedonian general and diplomat, born c398 B.C.; died 319 B.C. He was one of the ablest and most trusted of the ministers of Philip II of Macedon. Philip sent him (346 B.C.) to Athens as an ambassador to receive the oaths by which the Athenians accepted the peace imposed by Philip after the fall of Olynthus. He also acted in the peace negotiations after the defeat of the Athenians and Thebans at Chaeronea (338 B.C.). After the death of Philip, Antipater served Alexander the Great as regent of Macedonia while the king was in Asia. As regent he suppressed a Spartan revolt under Agis III through a victory at Megalopolis (330 B.C.). Olympias, mother of Alexander, constantly sent letters of accusation against Antipater to her son. In his turn he constantly complained to Alexander of her intrigues. On Alexander's death (323 B.C.) the partition of the empire left Macedonia under Antipater's control as joint ruler with Craterus; he defeated a Greek attempt (322 B.C.) to throw off Macedonian rule in the Lamian war. As conditions for peace with Athens following this war, he ordered modifications in the democratic constitution, placed a Macedonian garrison in Munychia at the Piraeus, and demanded the surrender of Demosthenes and Hyperides, the orators who agitated for revolt against Macedonia. Demosthenes fled to Calauria and committed suicide. Hyperides fled to the temple of Aeacus in Aegina. He was captured, taken to Antipater, and put to death. Antipater is said by

(obscured) errạnt, ardẹnt, actọr; ch, chip; g, go; th, thin; ᵺн, then; y, you; (variable) ḍ as d or j, ş as s or sh, ṭ as t or ch, ẕ as z or zh.

some authors to have died of illness and by others to have been killed in battle.

Antiphon (an'ti-fon). Athenian orator and politician, the oldest of the "ten Attic orators." He was born at Rhamnus, Attica, c480 B.C. He taught political eloquence in his own school of rhetoric and also prepared speeches which he sold to others to deliver. He trained his aristocratic friends for legal practice in the democracy with exercises in speech-craft. His method was to take an imaginary case and prepare two speeches for the prosecution and two speeches for the defense. Three of these so-called tetralogies are extant. In addition, there are three extant speeches which were delivered in actual murder cases. These, though written by Antiphon, were delivered by others. As a member of the aristocratic party, he was brought to trial (411 B.C.) for his share in establishing government by the Four Hundred. This revolution was the death-blow to the democracy. He had spent all his life preparing for this revolution to restore the aristocrats and an oligarchy, and the speech he made in defense of his actions (the only instance of his delivering publicly one of his own speeches) was considered by Thucydides to be the best defense made by a man accused of such a charge up to his own time. In spite of it he was condemned to death and executed (411 B.C.).

Antony (an'tō-ni), **Mark.** [Also: **Marc Antony;** Latin, **Marcus Antonius.**] Roman triumvir and general, born c82 B.C.; died at Alexandria, in August, 30 B.C. He was the grandson of Marcus Antonius the orator. He served in Palestine and Egypt; was quaestor in 52 and tribune in 49 B.C. He became a prominent adherent of Caesar, and when he was expelled from Rome he fled to Caesar, who thereupon commenced the civil war. He commanded the left wing at the battle of Pharsalus, was master of the horse in 47 and became consul in 44 B.C. He engaged in intrigues after Caesar's death, and was denounced by Cicero. After having fled from Rome, he formed with Octavian (the future Augustus) and Lepidus the Second Triumvirate in 43. He defeated Brutus and Cassius at Philippi in 42 B.C., summoned Cleopatra to Asia and later followed her to Alexandria, and renewed the triumvirate in 40 and 37 B.C. From c40 B.C. he lived chiefly at Alexandria with Cleopatra, abandoning his wife Octavia, the sister of Octavian. He conducted an unsuccessful expedition against

Parthia in 36. He was defeated by Octavian at Actium in 31 B.C., returned to Egypt and committed suicide before Octavian's entry into Alexandria.

Anytus (a'ni-tus). Athenian politician; fl. end of the 5th century B.C. He was an ardent admirer of Alcibiades who treated him with the utmost insolence. He was a democrat and fled to Thebes when the government of Athens was in the control of the Thirty Tyrants (404 B.C.). With Thrasybulus and other exiles from Athens he seized the fortress of Phyle in Attica and took part in the overthrow of the Tyrants, 403 B.C. Anytus was among those who brought the charge of impiety against Socrates that resulted in the death of the aged philosopher. Part of the charge against Socrates was that he corrupted the young men by his teachings. Some say this was a particular reference to the influence of Socrates on Alcibiades, who had been a pupil and friend of the philosopher and had insulted Anytus, and who had brought disaster to Athens by his military advice to Sparta.

Aratus of Sicyon (a̧-rā'tus; sish'i-on, sis'i-). Greek general, born at Sicyon, near Corinth, Greece, 271; died 213 B.C. He was the leader of the second Achaean League. He liberated (251 B.C.) Sicyon from the usurper Nicocles and set up a democracy; elected (245 B.C.) strategus (military leader) of the Achaean League, he took the citadel of Corinth in 243 B.C., and brought Athens and Argos into the League. Defeated in a succession of campaigns by the Spartans under Cleomenes III, he formed an alliance with Antigonus III of Macedonia (Antigonus Doson), who defeated Cleomenes at the battle of Sellasia near the city of Sparta in 222 B.C., but thus brought the League under Macedonian domination. He carried on an unsuccessful defensive war (221–219 B.C.) against the Aetolians.

Arcesilaus (är-ses-i-lā'us) or *Arcesilas* (är-ses'i-la̧s). Name of several kings of Cyrene, of the Battiadae dynasty. Arcesilaus I (590–574 B.C.) was the son of Battus, founder of the Greek city of Cyrene and of the dynasty. In the reign of Arcesilaus II (c560–c550 B.C.), grandson of Arcesilaus I, the city of Barca was founded by dissidents from Cyrene. A black-figure cup of Cyrene shows Arcesilaus II overseeing the weighing out and packing of silphion, a medicinal plant. The sale of the plant, which was widely exported, was the

(obscured) erra̧nt, ardȩnt, acto̧r; ch, chip; g, go; th, thin; ŦH, then; y, you; (variable) ḍ as d or j, ş as s or sh, ṭ as t or ch, z̧ as z or zh.

monopoly of the king and brought him great wealth. See *Battiadae.*

Archelaus (är-ke̯-lā′us) (of *Cappadocia*). Cappadocian general under Mithridates VI; fl. in the 1st century B.C. He served in Mithridates' wars against Rome. Sent to Greece (87 B.C.) with a large force, he made Athens his headquarters, occupied Piraeus, and stirred up revolt against Rome in the other Greek states. Sulla came from Rome to command the war against Mithridates, and defeated Archelaus at Chaeronea (86) and at Orchomenus (85 B.C.). Mithridates came to distrust Archelaus who then deserted to the Romans (81 B.C.).

Archelaus (of *Cappadocia*). King of Cappadocia, c34 B.C.–17 A.D.; a grandson of Archelaus (of Egypt). He owed his elevation to Mark Antony, who was captivated by the charms of Archelaus' mother, Glaphyra. He sided with Antony in the war with Octavian (Augustus), but was permitted after the defeat of Antony to retain his kingdom, to which was subsequently added part of Cilicia and Lesser Armenia. He was finally summoned to Rome by Tiberius, where he was held prisoner until his death. Cappadocia became, after his death, a Roman province.

Archelaus (of *Egypt*). King of Egypt in 56 B.C.; a son of the general Archelaus (of Cappadocia). He became high priest at Comana in 63 B.C., and secured the hand of Berenice, queen of Egypt, by representing himself to be the son of Mithridates VI Eupator. He was defeated and slain by the Romans after a reign of six months.

Archelaus (of *Macedonia*). King of Macedonia (c413–399 B.C.); son of Perdiccas II. He was a patron of Hellenic art and literature, and attracted to his court Zeuxis, Euripides, and Agathon, and invited Socrates who declined.

Archidamus I (är-ki-dā′mus). King of Sparta, of the Eurypontid house of Spartan kings, who reigned after the close of the Second Messenian War (7th century B.C.).

Archidamus II. King of Sparta, of the Eurypontid house of Spartan kings, who reigned c476–c427 B.C. He was the son of Zeuxidamus, who did not reign, and the grandson of Leotychides, the hero of Mycale (479 B.C.). He was a friend of Pericles. Early in his reign (c471 B.C.) he defeated the Arcadian League at Dipaea. In 432 B.C. when the allies of Sparta asked her to declare war on Athens for having broken

the Thirty Years Peace by aiding Corcyra against Corinth, by
the seizure of Potidaea, and more immediately, by assisting
the Plataeans against Thebes, Archidamus prudently counseled moderation. He advised the Spartans to delay, on the
ground that Sparta was not financially prepared for war and
lacked a fleet. He was over-ruled. In the ensuing war he
fought so bravely and well that the early years of the Peloponnesian War (431–421 B.C.) are called the Archidamean
War. In the spring of 431 B.C. he led a large part of the
Peloponnesian forces in an invasion of Attica, first however,
sending an envoy from the Isthmus to make one last attempt
to settle the disputes between Athens and the Peloponnesians. His envoy was not received. Archidamus besieged the
fortress of Oenoë on Mount Cithaeron but could not take
it. He marched to the plain of Eleusis and devastated it,
crossed the plain of the Cephissus and encamped under
Mount Parnes, from where he could see the Acropolis of
Athens. Before this threat the populace poured for refuge
into the city. The following year he invaded Attica again and
ravaged the area south of the city. But the Athenians had a
worse enemy inside their walls. Plague broke out. Among
those who succumbed to it was Pericles. In 429 B.C. Archidamus led his forces against Plataea. The Plataeans appealed to him to refrain from violating their territory in the
name of the heroes who had fallen there in the Persian War,
among whom were many Spartans whose memories were
annually honored by the Plataeans. Archidamus replied that
he would so refrain if the Plataeans detached themselves
from Athens and remained neutral. This the Plataeans were
unwilling to do, and were besieged. In 428 B.C. Archidamus
and the allies invaded Attica for the third time, destroyed
the standing crops and, having used up the supplies they
brought with them, retired.

Archidamus III. King of Sparta, of the Eurypontid line of Spartan kings. He reigned from 360/359 to 338 B.C. He was the
son of Agesilaus II, whom he succeeded. After the defeat of
the Spartans at Leuctra (371 B.C.) he was made commander
of a Spartan force sent to the relief of the survivors of that
battle. He defeated the Arcadians, Messenians, and Argives
in 368 B.C. in a fight called "the Tearless Battle," because
although great loss was suffered by the Arcadians and their
allies, not one Spartan lost his life. In 364 B.C. he occupied

(obscured) errạnt, ardẹnt, actọr; ch, chip; g, go; th, thin; ŦH, then; y, you;
(variable) ḍ as d or j, ş as s or sh, ṭ as t or ch, ẓ as z or zh.

the fortress of Cromnon, between Megalopolis and Messenia. The garrison he placed there was besieged by the Arcadians and their allies, and when he sought to relieve it he was driven off with losses. He fought bravely to defend Sparta from the attacks of Epaminondas and the Thebans in 362. In 356 B.C. he supported the Phocians in their Sacred War to seize Delphi. In 343 B.C. he answered an appeal from Taras (Tarentum) in Italy for aid against the Italian tribes. Leading a band of mercenaries he sailed to Italy, waged inconclusive war there for some years and was killed (338 B.C.) at Manduria.

Ariovistus (ar″i-ō-vis′tus). Germanic leader, active from c71–58 B.C. He was a chief of the Suevi, who crossed the Rhenus (Rhine) and invaded Gaul c71 B.C.to aid the Sequani, conquering the Aedui in 61 B.C. He was made an ally of Rome by Julius Caesar, but on an appeal by the Gauls Caesar engaged him in battle at Vesontio (now Besançon, France) and finally defeated him near what is now Mulhouse, France, in 58 B.C.

Aristagoras (ar-is-tag′ō-ras). Tyrant of Miletus (fl. c500 B.C.). He was the nephew and son-in-law of Histiaeus, former tyrant of Miletus who was, under the guise of friendship, kept a virtual prisoner at the court of Darius at Susa. Aristagoras thought to enrich himself by restoring some exiled leaders to Naxos, and secured the aid of the Persian satrap for this venture by proposing to him the conquest of the Cyclades and Euboea, with the capture of Naxos as the first step in this program. He assured the Persian that such a conquest would be easy and on gaining the consent of Darius for his expedition, he set out at its head to carry through his purpose. But the expedition was a complete failure. On the way Aristagoras quarreled with the Persian admiral who was sent to help him, and as a result of the quarrel the admiral warned the Naxians of the coming attack. Thus forewarned, they made preparations and were able to withstand Aristagoras and his forces. After four months of an expensive and useless siege he was compelled to retire. Rather than winning the island and the plaudits of the Persians he had wasted their money, and incurred the distrust of the Persian satrap and the enmity of the Persian admiral. To recoup his fortunes he resolved to foment a revolt of the Ionian cities which were already seething with

fat, fāte, fär, fåll, àsk, fāre; net, mē, hèr; pin, pīne; not, nōte, möve, nôr; up, lūte, pùll; oi, oil; ou out; (lightened) ēlect, agǫny, ūnite;

unrest under the tyrants the Persians had placed over them. At this point, according to Herodotus, a messenger came to him from his uncle Histiaeus in Susa. The only message he bore was a request that the courier's head be shaved. Aristagoras did so, and on the messenger's scalp was pricked a command from Histiaeus to raise revolt in Ionia. This fitted in with the plans of Aristagoras to save himself from the wrath of the Persians because of the failure of the Naxian venture. He stirred the Ionians to revolt, and to make them the more eager to throw off the Persian yoke he called on the cities to throw off their tyrants, and he himself stepped down as tyrant of Miletus. He journeyed to Sparta to ask the help of Cleomenes. He showed Cleomenes a map of the world engraved on bronze, the first map Cleomenes had ever seen, and pointed out to him the rich Persian empire it would be so easy for him to conquer. But when Cleomenes asked him how long a journey it was from Ionia to Susa and heard that it was three months, he told Aristagoras to quit Sparta before sunset. Aristagoras did not give up. He returned as a suppliant to Cleomenes' house and attempted to bribe him. As Herodotus tells the story, Cleomenes listened as Aristagoras raised the bribe from ten to 50 talents. At that point the nine-year-old daughter of Cleomenes appealed to her father to send the stranger away before he was corrupted, and so Aristagoras lost again. He went next to Athens and Eretria, where he was more successful and won some support. But Aristagoras had neither the courage nor the ability to weld the Ionians into a united fighting force. The Persians gathered their forces and began to win systematically. In the face of their successes Aristagoras gathered his leaders together and discussed with them whether it would be wise to flee to Sardinia and establish a colony there, or to carry on his operations in Thrace. In the end he went to Thrace and was killed while besieging a city there (497 B.C.).

Aristides (ar-is-tī′dēz). [Also: *Aristeides;* surnamed *the Just.*] Athenian statesman and general, born c530 B.C.; died probably at Athens, c468 B.C. He was the son of Lysimachus, a man of modest circumstances of the tribe of Antiochus in Athens. As a great admirer of Lycurgus the Spartan lawgiver and, after the expulsion of the Pisistratidae from Athens, a particular friend of Clisthenes, grandson of the tyrant of

Sicyon, he had a leaning toward aristocracy. A conservative and an advocate of Athens as a land power, he was continually opposed by Themistocles. Some say they had been rivals from boyhood. He came to oppose Themistocles almost as a matter of principle for, he said, the good of Athens. He was aware that he made this a practice. Once he successfully opposed Themistocles in a matter that was really advantageous to the public, and remarked, "The affairs of the Athenians will never prosper unless they throw Themistocles and myself in the Barathron (a deep pit into which condemned persons were hurled)." He was appointed public treasurer and found that the public funds had been mishandled, especially by Themistocles. The latter raised a hue and cry against him and, some say, would have had him condemned but the court (the Areopagus) was so aroused that they not only caused the charge to be dropped but got Aristides reëlected chief treasurer. Aristides now pretended he had been too strict and closed his eyes, apparently, to those who pilfered the public money. Those who profited thereby praised him and urged that he be reëlected. He now came before the people and said that when, as an honest man, he did right and looked out for their interests, he was abused and condemned, but when he let robbers steal the public monies he was praised. He added, "I am more ashamed of the present honor than I was of the former disgrace, and it is with indignation and concern that I see you esteem it more meritorious to oblige bad men than to take proper care of the public revenue."

Aristides was one of the ten generals sent by the Athenians to repel the Persians at Marathon (490 B.C.), and there fought with valor. The practice, some say, was to rotate the command among the ten generals, so that each commanded a day in turn. Some say that realizing the ability of Miltiades, when his day came to command Aristides voluntarily yielded it to Miltiades, and by his example caused the other generals to do the same.

He was chosen archon eponymus in 489 B.C. The people admired him most for his justice, and gave him the name "the Just." This name made him first loved, and then envied. Because he was so much in demand as a mediator, Themistocles accused him of usurping judicial power and sought to have him ostracized. (Ostracism was a means of removing from the city, for a stated time, any man who seemed to be becoming too powerful or who appeared capable of causing disorder in the state; it was not a punishment for crimes. According to the system, 6000 votes must be cast or the total voting was void. Of the 6000, the man whose name was written on the greatest number of *ostraka*—a tile or broken piece of pottery—was banished for ten years.) When the day for voting arrived, Aristides was in the marketplace where the votes were cast and counted. An illiterate citizen, unaware who he was, approached him and asked him to write the name Aristides on his *ostrakon*. He was asked whether Aristides had ever injured him in any way. "No," said the citizen, "I don't even know him, but I'm tired of hearing everyone call him 'the Just'." Aristides made no reply, but took the shell and wrote his own name on it as requested. He received the most votes and was banished (483 B.C.). A number of *ostraka* inscribed with Aristides' name, ballots used in this voting, have been found in the Agora excavations.

Themistocles also wished him banished because Aristides did not agree with his policy of building up the Athenian fleet. When he was leaving Athens he prayed that the people of his state would never see the day when they would be forced to remember him. When Xerxes marched into Greece (480 B.C.) all who had been banished by ostracism were recalled. Aristides did all he could to encourage resistance to the Persians, contrary to the fears of some who thought that since he had been ill-treated by the Athenians he might go over to the Persians. After the burning of Athens the Greek forces withdrew to Salamis. There Themistocles wished them to make a fight with their fleet, as the advantage in the narrow strait would lie with the Greek ships, as against the Persian ships. But the Spartans wished to withdraw to the isthmus and make a stand there. While they debated the Persians surrounded Salamis. Aristides, at great peril, sailed through the Persian fleet to Salamis and called Themistocles from the council. He urged that they forget their personal quarrel in the face of the common danger and told him there was now no question of withdrawing to the isthmus, as the Greeks were surrounded. In the battle that followed, he took a force to the island of Psyttalia and wiped out the Persian garrison there. After the Greek success at Salamis (480 B.C.) he opposed sailing to the Hellespont to cut off the Persian retreat. On the contrary, he was eager to carry the war against the enemy vigorously to the end that the Persians would the sooner be driven out of Greece, rather than to destroy their means of exit and force them to ravage Greece. Xerxes left at once to return to Persia. Mardonius was left in command of a vast land force of Persians and their allies. He sought to separate the Athenians from their allies by bribes. The Spartans heard of this and sent urgent envoys to Athens, offering in their turn what amounted to bribes if the Athenians would stay in the war and help them to resist the Persians. Aristides was grieved that the Spartans would think the Athenians capable of such deeds. To their envoys he said, "The people of Athens would not, for all the gold either above or under the ground, barter the liberties of Greece." As for the envoys of Mardonius, he pointed to the sun and said, "As long as this luminary shines, so long will the Athenians carry on war with the Persians, for their country which has been laid waste and for their temples which have been profaned and burned."

At the battle of Plataea (479 B.C.), he commanded 8000 Athenian foot soldiers. In drawing up the battle line both the Tegeans and the Athenians claimed the honor of the left wing and hot words were uttered by both in defense of their claims. Aristides addressed Pausanias, the Spartan general in command, "The post neither gives valor nor takes it away, and whatever post you assign us, we will endeavor to do honor to it, and take care to reflect no disgrace upon our former achievements. For we are come hither not to quarrel with our allies, but to fight with our enemies." His words restored calm and Pausanias awarded the left wing to the Athenians. After Plataea, he was a commander at Byzantium (c479 B.C.) and succeeded Pausanias as admiral after the Ionian revolt. After the Persian war he won the friendship and support of the Greek allies of Athens through his mildness and fair treatment. He was sent to assess the tax that the members must pay to support the Delian League, and won the gratitude of all by the fairness of his assessments. He drew up the articles of alliance between the Greek states, and confirmed them for Athens with an oath. But he yielded to expediency later on the occasion of transferring the treasure of the League from Delos to Athens, though this was contrary to the treaties. In agreeing to the change he said, "It is not just, but it is expedient."

To the end of his days he enjoyed honor and though he wielded vast power, especially in financial matters, he spent his life in relative poverty. The circumstances and whereabouts of his death are obscure. A monument was erected to him at the public expense at Phalerum. Athens continued to honor him by giving dowries for his two daughters and a sum of money, a pension, and land to his son. He was noted for his moderation, his steady service to the state, and for his justice. He was neither elated with honors nor unduly cast down by failures. He refused to seek support by granting favors, and he treated his enemies with justice. Once, it is said, he prosecuted a man and the judges, influenced because it was Aristides who prosecuted, were about to pass sentence without giving the accused a hearing. Aristides sprang up and insisted that he be heard before sentence was passed. Another time he was the mediator between two citizens. One of them sought to influence him by saying the other had done many injuries to Aristides. He replied, "Don't speak of that, but tell me what injury he has done you, for it is your cause that I am judging, not my own." The following verses are from *The Seven Against Thebes,* the tragedy by Aeschylus:

"To be and not to seem, is this man's choice;
Reaping the fruits that in a rich mind grow,
Whence sage advice and noble actions flow."

When they were recited upon the stage everyone in the audience looked at Aristides as being the man whose reputation for justice and service best exemplified the sentiments of the verses. According to Plutarch, "Plato, among all that were accounted great and illustrious men in Athens, judges none but Aristides worthy of real esteem."

Aristodemus (ạ-ris-tọ-dē′mus). Messenian king, 8th century B.C. (c731–724 B.C.), and traditional hero of the First Messenian war with Sparta which, according to tradition, lasted 20 years and ended 724 B.C. An oracle told the Messenians they would be successful if a father willingly sacrificed his virgin daughter. Aristodemus offered his daughter, but she was betrothed, and her young prospective husband, wild with grief at the thought of losing her, first claimed Aristodemus no longer had authority to offer her up for Messenia. Since she was to be his wife he alone could make such a decision. His claim being denied he then declared that she was not a virgin but was about to become a mother. Aristodemus was enraged at this accusation; he killed his daughter and opened her body to prove that she was not pregnant. His impious rage offended the gods, and her death did not satisfy the oracles. Grief-stricken in his turn, Aristodemus was haunted by evil dreams, despaired of defeating the Spartans, and at length committed suicide on his daughter's tomb.

Aristomenes (ar-is-tom′ē̆-nēz). Messenian national hero of the Second War against Sparta, which took place in the first half of the 7th century B.C. He was the son of Nicomedes, or, as some say, of a god who assumed the shape of a serpent when he embraced Aristomenes' mother. In the years following the end of the First Messenian War against Sparta, Aristomenes urged the defeated Messenians to revolt, with such success that they gathered a force and waged war on Sparta. Aristomenes, noted for his daring, went secretly at night to the temple of Athena of the Bronze House, in Sparta, and fixed thereon a shield. This shield, a goad to the Spartans, was inscribed that it was a gift to the goddess from Aristomenes, and was a shield he had taken from the Spartans. In the battle which the Spartans waged against the Messenians Aristomenes fought like a whirlwind and threw the Spartans into such confusion that they broke and fled. Before the battle Aristomenes was warned by a seer not to pass a certain pear tree where the Dioscuri, protectors of Sparta, were sitting. In his ardor to pursue the Spartans he forgot the seer's warning and lost his shield for disobeying the seer. While he looked for it the Spartans escaped. Later he recovered his shield and took it to Lebadia, where he dedicated it at the shrine of Trophonius. When he returned to Messenia he was received with the wildest acclaim. He made a successful cattle raid on Laconia, and though wounded drove the stolen cattle back to Messenia, but when he made an attack on Sparta at night he was deterred by the appearance of Helen and the Dioscuri. In the continuing war, he was taken prisoner in a sanctuary but escaped during the night. The Arcadians were allies of the Messenians, but Aristocrates, their leader, accepted a bribe to betray the Messenians. In the midst of a battle Aristocrates, without letting his people know he had been bribed, ordered his men to retreat. He led them through the thick of the battling Messenian forces, throwing them into utter confusion, so that the Spartans cut them to pieces. Aristomenes collected the survivors and took them to Mount Eira. There they withstood siege for 11 years, plundering the countryside to maintain themselves. In a sharp engagement with the Spartans Aristomenes was struck on the head by a stone, and while stunned was set upon by the enemy and taken prisoner with about 50 of his followers. The Spartans resolved to kill them all by hurling them into a jagged chasm that had no outlet, but when Aristomenes was hurled forth an eagle swooped down and rescued him, and deposited him unharmed in the bottom of the pit. As he could not escape he prepared himself for death, but soon observed a fox scavenging on the dead bodies of his comrades who had been cast into the pit. Aristomenes realized that there must be some entrance to the pit by which the fox had come in. He seized the animal and followed it to a hole just large enough for the fox, but he enlarged it, escaped, and returned to Mount Eira and resumed his command of the Messenians. He attacked and slew a force of Corinthians on their way to the aid of Sparta, and the Spartans asked for a truce. During the truce Aristomenes was careless and was seized by some Cretan archers in Spartan employ. They were elated with his capture and sent messengers to tell the Spartans, while they took their captive to a farmhouse for safe-keeping. But there he was freed by a maiden of the house, in accordance with a dream she had had. He gave her to his son for a wife. An oracle now foretold the destruction of Messenia. According to the oracle, when a he-goat drank of the waters of the Neda, Messenia would fall. The seer who related this oracle to Aristomenes, in secret, said that a wild fig tree which grew on the banks of the Neda was now leaning over the bank to such an extent that its branches were in the water. The Messenians used the same word for the fig tree as for he-goat and Aristomenes realized that the end was at hand, but did not tell the Messenians. He took certain secret things and buried them in a secret place at Ithome, calling on Zeus as he did so to honor the pledge, for an oracle had said that if these things were preserved the Messenians would recover their country. After this he exhorted his followers to defend themselves on the acropolis at Mount Eira. But their citadel was betrayed by an adulterous woman. In a violent storm the Spartans attacked with ladders, and the Messenians could not hold out much longer. The seer who knew of the oracles told Aristomenes to lead out as many Messenians as he could, and to save them and himself, while a few brave Messenians held up the Spartans to cover their retreat. Aristomenes followed his advice and took his Messenians to Arcadia. There he and his followers were cordially received, for the Arcadians had never learned that their king betrayed the Messenians for money. Now he prepared to betray them again, but was discovered and stoned to death by the Arcadians themselves. Aristomenes went to Rhodes on his way to Persia, but died while at Rhodes, and was honored by a splendid tomb built for him by the Rhodians.

Arminius (är-min′i-us). [Latinized name of *Armin;* German, **Hermann.**] German chieftain of the Cherusci (near modern Hanover); born c17 B.C.; assassinated 21 A.D. He was immortalized as the liberator of the Germans from Roman rule. He entered the Roman military service in 1 A.D. and became a Roman citizen of the equestrian order, but on his return to Germany he found his people oppressed by Roman rule and secretly organized a revolt of the Cherusci. He surprised Quintilius Varus, the Roman governor, in the Teutoburgian Forest in 9 A.D. and destroyed him and three complete legions of Roman troops. The news of this disaster caused a near panic at Rome. The massacre of the three legions by Arminius forced the withdrawal of the Roman frontier from the Elbe to the Rhine. This was the worst disaster suffered by Roman arms during the rule of Augustus, and he never ceased to mourn it. Germanicus Caesar defeated him in 16 A.D., and captured his wife, but he still maintained the independence of the right bank of the Rhine. The victory of Germanicus had been so costly that he was recalled and the frontier on the Elbe was abandoned. Arminius overthrew Maroboduus, head of the Marcomanni, but was killed in a feud among rival chiefs.

Arrhidaeus (ạr-i-dē′us). Macedonian soldier; half brother of Alexander the Great; killed 317 B.C. He was one of the military leaders who disputed the empire after Alexander's death in 323 B.C., being elected by the soldiers under his

fat, fāte, fär, fâll, ásk, fāre; net, mē, hėr; pin, pīne; not, nōte, mŏve, nôr; up, lūte, pùll; oi, oil; ou out; (lightened) ēlect, agǫny, ūnite;

command in Babylonia. He was put to death by order of
Olympias, mother of Alexander.

Artabanus (är-ta̧-bā′nus). Brother of Darius the Great (king of
Persia, 521–c485 B.C.). When Xerxes, son of Darius, decides
to wage war on the Greeks Artabanus reminds him that he
advised his father not to make war on the Scythians. Darius
ignored his advice and so lost many good men before making a safe retreat from Scythia. The Greeks, he says, are
much more valiant than the Scythians, and are bold fighters
on sea and land. He advises Xerxes of the dangers that so
nearly befell Darius in crossing the Hellespont, and warns
him of the worse dangers an invasion of Greece would present. But at least, he urges Xerxes to withdraw from the
council that is discussing war against the Greeks and think
well what course he should follow before he makes up his
mind to go to war, as his other chiefs advise; or to refrain
from war, as Artabanus advises. He reminds Xerxes that the
gods knock down the tallest trees in the forest with the
lightning, for the gods love to cut down all things and men
that stand above their fellows, and thus a great host (the
Persians) can, by the will of the gods, be destroyed by a small
force (the Greeks). Artabanus chides Mardonius, a counselor who strongly advises war, for belittling the Greeks and
stirring up Xerxes' will to war. He suggests that if war is
determined on Xerxes should remain in Persia. He proposes
that he and Mardonius put up their sons as pledges, that
Mardonius march at the head of as large an army as he feels
is necessary to defeat the Greeks. If Mardonius is successful,
Artabanus and his sons must perish, but if he is not successful Mardonius and his sons must be slain. This advice from
Artabanus infuriates Xerxes. He commands Artabanus to
remain at home with the women and decides in favor of war.
Later Xerxes thinks it over and decides that Artabanus has
given good advice. He makes up his mind to abandon the
war. In the night he dreams a man appears to him and tells
him not to abandon his plans for war. He pays no attention
to the dream, and next day calls his chiefs together and
acknowledges that Artabanus is right, and he will not make
war. The Persians are delighted. That night Xerxes has the
same dream; the figure that appears to him threatens that
unless he makes war he will be brought low. Xerxes sends
for Artabanus and tells him the dream. If, as he thinks, the

(obscured) errạnt, ardẹnt, actọr; ch, chip; g, go; th, thin; ᴛʜ, then; y, you;
(variable) ḏ as d or j, ş as s or sh, ţ as t or ch, ᴢ̧ as z or zh.

dream was sent by the gods it will be sent to Artabanus too, if only Artabanus clothes himself in Xerxes' raiment and sleeps in his bed. Artabanus tries to soothe him, saying man is likely to dream of what is uppermost in his mind, and the war against the Greeks had occupied them above all else for many days. However, if the dream was really sent by the gods it will come to him too. Although, he tells Xerxes, the dream will not be so simple-minded as to be fooled by the disguise of Xerxes clothes. Yet he agrees to put them on. He sits on the throne, dons Xerxes' garments, and lies down on Xerxes' bed to sleep, thinking that thus he will prove Xerxes is mistaken. But the same dream comes to him, and threatens him for advising Xerxes not to make war. Artabanus springs up and hurries to Xerxes. He agrees that the dream has come from the gods, who desire the war against the Greeks, and he now gives it his support. Xerxes makes preparations for the war. After four years a host is assembled at the Hellespont. Artabanus now expresses his fears about two things: land and sea. For the army is too great to live off the land and the fleet is too vast to find harbor in case of storms. Xerxes upbraids him for his fears. If a man were to consider every possible hazard before he acted he would never act at all. He tells Artabanus Persia would never have grown so great if his predecessors had been so afraid of taking a chance as Artabanus. Xerxes, taking the three sons of Artabanus with him as captains, leaves his sceptre and his empire in Artabanus' hands and sends him back to Susa as he leaves for the invasion of Greece. Subsequent events proved that Artabanus was correct in all his fears, that the gods could indeed cut down the mighty forces of Persia.

Artaphernes (är-tạ-fèr′nēz). Persian general; fl. c500 B.C. He was a brother of Darius the Great (of Persia), by whom he was appointed satrap of Sardis. He interfered ineffectually in behalf of Hippias, the expelled tyrant of Athens, and took part in suppressing the revolt (499–498 B.C.) of the Ionians against Persian rule.

Artaphernes. Persian general; son of the foregoing Persian general of the same name. He commanded, with Datis, the Persian army which invaded (490 B.C.) Greece and was defeated at Marathon, and led the Lydians in the expedition of Xerxes I against Greece ten years later which ended in the defeat of the Persians.

Artaxerxes I. (är-tȧ-zẽrk′sēz). [Surnamed ***Longimanus,*** meaning "the Long-handed"; name in the Old Testament, *Artach-shast.*] King of Persia (464–425 B.C.). He was a younger son of Xerxes I. Aided by the vizier who had murdered his father, he ascended the throne (464 B.C.). When, some time later, he discovered this vizier was his father's murderer and the author of other crimes, Artaxerxes killed him and his sons in a hand-to-hand struggle in the palace. According to ancient writers he was handsome, brave, of a mild disposition, and greatly influenced by his mother and his wife. Early in his reign he was forced to put down the rebellion of one of his satraps. Following this the Libyan Inarus raised a rebellion in Egypt and called in the Athenians to help him. After a long struggle (460–454 B.C.) in which the Athenians sailed up the Nile and took possession of most of Memphis (459), Egypt was subdued. The forces of Artaxerxes were defeated (449 B.C.) on sea and land in a double action at Salamis in Cyprus by the Athenians. That same year peace was concluded with the Athenians under which the Persians agreed not to invade the Aegean, while the Athenians abandoned their interest in Cyprus and pledged to honor the coasts of the Persian Empire. This peace, known as the Peace of Callias, ended the great struggles with Persia for over a hundred years. Artaxerxes is presumed to have instigated the mission of Ezra and Nehemiah (his cup-bearer) to Jerusalem, thus furthering Judaism. He won the epithet "Longimanus" because of the excessive length of his right hand.

Artaxerxes II. [Surnamed ***Mnemon.***] King of Persia (404–358 B.C.). He was the son of Darius II and Parysatis, and succeeded his father on the throne of Persia (404 B.C.). His mother, who had great influence over him, preferred to see her younger son, her favorite Cyrus, as king, and plotted unsuccessfully to secure the throne for him. Cyrus, with a band of Greek mercenaries that included Xenophon and a body of Asiatic troops, took the field and prepared to seize the throne from Artaxerxes. He marched across Asia Minor, along the Euphrates, and into Babylonia. At the village of Cunaxa, outside Babylon, Artaxerxes came out to oppose him. Cyrus was killed (401 B.C.), his Asiatic troops fled, and Artaxerxes retained his throne. He willingly gave the Greek mercenaries permission to depart, after which they made the

(obscured) errạnt, ardẹnt, actọr; ch, chip; g, go; th, thin; ᴛʜ, then; y, you;
(variable) ḍ as d or j, ş as s or sh, ṭ as t or ch, ẓ as z or zh.

famous march to the sea celebrated in Xenophon's *Anabasis*
At the beginning of the 4th century B.C. a Peloponnesian
force under the Spartan king Agesilaus II invaded the coasts
of Asia Minor and temporarily freed the Greek cities there
(396). The Spartan triumphs were short-lived, as Agesilaus
was called home to fight the Greek enemies of Sparta. In 388
B.C. the Spartan Antalcidas journeyed to Susa to make peace
with Artaxerxes. By the terms of the peace, concluded in 386
B.C. and called the "King's Peace," the cities of Asia Minor
and Cyprus fell to Persia, and the other Greek cities were
declared autonomous, except Lemnos, Imbrus, and Scyrus
which continued to belong to Athens. Having concluded
peace with Sparta Artaxerxes was compelled to turn his
attention to the series of rebellions within his empire. Satraps in the provinces from the Hellespont to the Nile rose
up against him; Egypt freed herself from Persian domination. In his last years Artaxerxes had given himself up to the
pleasures of the harem, had put his three eldest sons to
death as a result of the intrigues of their brother Ochus, but
by the time of his death (358 B.C.), thanks largely to the
jealousy and intrigues of the various revolting satraps
against each other, the king's authority over the empire had
been restored.

Artaxerxes III. [Surnamed *Ochus.*] King of Persia (385–338
B.C.). He was the son of Artaxerxes II, and cleared his path
to the throne by inducing his father to put to death the three
older brothers who stood in his way. He succeeded to the
throne on the death of Artaxerxes (358 B.C.). On his accession he put to death most of his relatives who might have
contested his right to rule. He energetically and harshly
asserted his power over his satraps, compelled them to dis-
band their mercenary armies, and succeeded (343 B.C.) in
conquering Egypt which he thereupon treated with great
cruelty. He was poisoned (338 B.C.), along with his older
sons, by his favorite, the eunuch Bagoas, who had come to
have great power.

Artemisia (är-tẹ-miz′i-ạ, -mish′i-ạ). A daughter of Lygdamis
who succeeded to the throne of Halicarnassus on the death
of her husband, and ruled over the Dorian cities of Halicarnassus, Cos, Nisyrus, and Calydna. As a vassal of Persia she
furnished five triremes to Xerxes I in the Second Persian
War. Her ships, says Herodotus, were the most famous o

the fleet after those of the Sidonians. She acted as a counselor to Xerxes and stood high in his favor. She advised Xerxes not to risk a sea fight with the Greeks after he had taken Athens, because she considered the Greeks superior at sea and besides, he had accomplished what he set out to do—made himself master of Athens. In her opinion the Greeks who had gathered on Salamis would not be able to hold out against him, cut off as they were from supplies, and she did not think it likely that they would do battle on behalf of Athens. Thus a sea fight was unnecessary in her view. She expressed the fear that if he undertook such a battle and was unsuccessful at sea great harm would come to his land forces. In addition, she had no very high opinion of some of the allies on whom he would be forced to rely in a sea fight. Xerxes was delighted that Artemisia, who had fought bravely at Euboea, dared to differ from his other captains in her advice which, however, he did not take. The fleet was ordered to Salamis and the army began to march towards the Peloponnesus. The Athenians were so indignant that a woman dared appear in arms against them that they offered a reward of 10,000 drachmas to whoever could capture her. The reward was never claimed. At the Battle of Salamis (480 B.C.) the Persian fleet was in confusion. Artemisia's ship was pursued by an Athenian trireme. In the press of ships which choked the escape route Atemisia rammed a Calydnian ship, one of the Persian allies, and sank it without a trace. This act of destroying one of her allies brought her luck from two sides. The Athenian ship, seeing her sink the Calydnian, thought she was a Greek ship or a Persian deserter and gave up pursuit, thus saving her life. Xerxes, watching the battle, saw her sink a ship and thought it was a Greek ship, as his advisers assured him it was. He is said to have remarked, "My men have behaved like women and my women like men." Since there were no survivors of the Calydnian ship there was no one to expose her. After the Persian defeat at Salamis Xerxes again asked advice of Artemisia: whether to return to Persia and leave Mardonius behind with a land army, as Mardonius wished. She advised Xerxes to go home, so that the Persians would still have their master. What happened to Mardonius was unimportant, she thought. If he were successful it would redound to the credit of Xerxes; if he failed it would be the loss only of a slave. This time

Xerxes took her advice and, entrusting certain of his children to Artemisia, he departed for Persia.

Artemisia (of *Caria*). Queen of Caria, in Asia Minor, 352–c350 B.C.; fl. middle of 4th century B.C. In memory of her husband Mausolus, she built at Halicarnassus a tomb, the Mausoleum, which was regarded by the ancients as one of the seven wonders of the world. To give further proof of her affection she is said to have mixed her husband's ashes with a precious liquid and to have drunk the potion so prepared.

Aspasia (as-pā′zhạ). Greek courtesan, born at Miletus, in Ionia; fl. c440 B.C. She was renowned for her wisdom, beauty, and wit. She was for many years the mistress of Pericles, who was so attracted to her that he left his wife and would have married her except for his own law of 451 B.C., which forbade Athenians to take foreign wives. Her brilliance made her house a center of Athenian literary and philosophical life. According to some accounts, she advised Pericles on public policy and helped him write his speeches. Accused of impiety, she was saved from death by Pericles' eloquence; her son, by Pericles, was legitimized under his father's name by a special Athenian decree after the death of Pericles' two sons by his first wife.

Astyages (as-tī′ạ-jēz). Son of Cyaxares, king of the Medes. According to Herodotus, who is the source of the following information, he married a daughter of Alyattes, king of Lydia, and thus was the brother-in-law of Croesus, who later became king of Lydia. Astyages succeeded his father as king of the Medes and reigned in the period 584–c549 B.C. He had a daughter Mandane, of whom he dreamed that such a flood of water flowed from her that it covered all Asia. The interpretation which the Magi put on this dream terrified him. As a consequence, he married his daughter to a Persian nobleman, Cambyses, who was of the royal race of the Persians and their hereditary monarch, but since at that time the Persians were subject to the Medes he was looked on as inferior as a husband to a Mede of a lower class. After Mandane was married to Cambyses and had gone to his home in Persia, Astyages dreamed again. This time it seemed that from his daughter's womb grew a tree which overshadowed all of Asia. The Magi interpreted this to mean that Mandane's offspring would become king if he lived long enough. Astyages sent to Persia and ordered Mandane brought back to his court. He gave orders that the child she was about to bear should be destroyed as soon as it was born. Soon afterward Cyrus was born. He was given into the hands of Harpagus, a trusted aid of Astyages, to be destroyed. As it happened the orders of Astyages were not carried out—the shepherd to whom Harpagus gave the task brought up the child as his own son—but Astyages and Harpagus were unaware of this. Years later a boy was brought before Astyages on the complaint of a Median noble, who accused the lad of playing the king and insulting the son of the nobleman. Astyages was struck by the appearance of the boy, and soon learned that is was his own grandson, whom he thought had been slain. He sent the child, Cyrus, to his mother in Persia, having been assured that his dream was fulfilled because Cyrus had acted as king among his playmates. But Harpagus he punished for his disobedience by slaying his son, cutting the body in pieces, and serving it to Harpagus at a banquet. At the end of the banquet he asked Harpagus how he had enjoyed it. When Harpagus answered that he had enjoyed it very much, Astyages ordered his servants to bring in the hands, feet, and head of Harpagus' son, that the father might know on what flesh he had feasted. (This story appears in various myths, as in the story of Atreus and Thyestes.) Harpagus maintained his composure, saying that whatever pleased the king pleased him, but thenceforth he determined on revenge. He enlisted the interest of some powerful Median nobles who chafed under the harsh rule of Astyages. When Cyrus grew to manhood Harpagus sent messages to him, urging him to lead the Persians in a revolt against Astyages, and assuring him of the coöperation of the Median nobles and himself. The Persians had long been anxious to throw off the Median yoke, thus when Cyrus proposed that they revolt they accepted him as their leader with enthusiasm. Astyages got wind of the plot and summoned Cyrus into his presence. When Cyrus came it was at the head of an army. Astyages, forgetting the cruelty he had earlier inflicted on Harpagus, sent out an army against Cyrus that was commanded by Harpagus and, according to plan, this army was quickly put to flight. When Astyages learned of the defeat of his army he sent for the Magi who had advised him to send Cyrus to his parents in Persia, because the dream had been fulfilled, and impaled them. Then at the head of a hastily gathered force he marched out against Cyrus and was utterly defeated by him in battle (c549 B.C.). Astyages had ruled for 35 years when he was defeated by Cyrus and his people passed under the dominion of Persia. Astyages spent the remainder of his days in the court of Cyrus, where he was courteously treated. Later he encountered Harpagus, who taunted him with having lost his kingdom and bragged that he had engineered the revolt. Astyages answered him that if it was true he was powerful enough to stir up the revolt then he was a fool not to have led it himself and made himself sovereign; and moreover, he had done an evil service to his own countrymen, the Medes, by helping to set a Persian over them.

Athenion (a̤-thē′ni-on). Leader in the second slave insurrection in Sicily, 103–99 B.C. He is said to have been the commander of bandits in Cilicia, where he was captured and sold as a slave into Sicily. He was chosen leader of the insurgents in the western part of the island, made an unsuccessful attack on Lilybaeum, joined Tryphon (Salvius), king of the rebels, by whom he was for a time thrown into prison, fought under Tryphon in the battle with Lucius Licinius Lucullus, and on the death of Tryphon became king. He was slain in battle by the hand of Marcus Aquillius who put down the revolt.

Atossa (a̤-tos′a̤). Queen of Persia in the 6th century B.C. She was a daughter of Cyrus the Great and Cassandane, and the full sister of Cambyses. The latter fell in love with her and since it was not the custom for Persians to marry their own sisters he asked the Persian judges if there was any law which permitted the king to marry his sister. The judges said there was no such law but, on the other hand, there was a law which permitted the king of Persia to do whatever he chose. In this way the judges allowed Cambyses to do what he planned to do and at the same time to save their own skins. Cambyses married Atossa. She did not accompany him on his expedition to Egypt, for by that time he had fallen in love with another of his sisters and took her with him to Egypt. On the death of Cambyses Atossa became the wife of his successor, the False Smerdis, as it was the custom for the successor to inherit wives as well as throne. When the False Smerdis was exposed and slain by a group of conspirators who set Darius on the throne in his place, Atossa married Darius. She bore him four sons, the eldest of whom was Xerxes. Such was her power and influence over Darius that, although he had older sons by a woman he had married before he became king, Atossa was able to persuade him to appoint her son Xerxes as his heir. She survived Darius and lived to see her son Xerxes I return from Greece defeated.

Attalus (at'ạ-lus). [Also: *Attalos*.] Macedonian general; died c336 B.C. He was a general under Philip II of Macedon. Philip cast aside his wife Olympias to marry Cleopatra, daughter or niece of Attalus. At the wedding feast, Attalus urged those present to pray for a legitimate heir, thus impugning the virtue of Olympias, who had borne Alexander to Philip. Alexander, who was present, flung a wine-cup into the face of Attalus. Attalus was sent to Asia with other generals to prepare for Philip's planned attack on the Persian Empire. When Philip was murdered, he supported the claims of Cleopatra's infant son to the throne, thus incurring again Alexander's hatred. At the latter's order he was murdered in Asia (c336 B.C.).

Attalus I. [Also: *Attalos;* surnamed *Soter*.] King of Pergamum (241–197 B.C.); born 269 B.C.; died 197 B.C. He carried on war with the Galatians, with Syria, and with Macedonia, and was allied with Rome against Macedonia in the latter part of his reign. Votive groups were set up by him on the Acropolis at Athens in honor of his victory over the Gauls. These groups of figures of about half life-size, depicted a battle of the gods and giants, combat between Athenians and Amazons, the victory of Marathon, and destruction of the Gauls by Attalus. Four figures from these groups were acquired by the National Museum at Naples: a fallen giant, a dead Amazon, a fallen Persian, and a dying bearded Gaul. Attalus was an outstanding patron of literature, philosophy, and the arts. He presented Delphi with a colonnade (stoa) for the shelter of pilgrims. His successors, Eumenes II and Attalus II, presented similar stoas to Athens.

Attalus II. [Also: *Attalos;* surnamed *Philadelphus*.] King of Pergamum (c159–138 B.C.); born 220 B.C.; died 138 B.C. He was a son of Attalus I and successor to his brother Eumenes II. He was an ally of Rome. Like all the Attalids he was interested in letters and the arts. He presented Athens with a stoa which bears his name. Restoration of the Stoa of Attalus in the Agora was completed in 1956 by the American School of Classical Studies.

Attalus III. [Also: **Attalos;** surnamed **Philometor.**] King of Pergamum (138–133 B.C.); born 171 B.C.; died 133 B.C. He was a nephew of Attalus II. By his will he left his kingdom to the Romans. He is of some interest to historians of science for his studies in botany and, more narrowly, in agriculture (a treatise by him in this field was used by Pliny). However, his interests in these fields seem to have had a very practical motive not unrelated to the political hazards of his day: his chief interest was in poisonous plants, and he prepared and experimented with a number of poisons.

Augustus (ô-gus′tus). [Original name, **Caius Octavius;** called later **Caius Julius Caesar Octavianus.**] The first Roman emperor. He was the son of a wealthy knight, Caius Octavius, and Atia, the niece of Julius Caesar. He was born just before sunrise, on Sept. 23, 63 B.C.; died August 19, 14 A.D. Some say he was born in the Palatine district in Rome, and the room in which he was said to have been born became a shrine after his death. But the people of Velitrae, the home of his father and his ancestors, insisted that Octavius was born there in a small room on his father's estate. Later, it was forbidden to enter this room before ceremonies of purification had been performed. Numerous legends have been preserved concerning his birth and predictions of his future greatness. In ancient times part of the wall of Velitrae had been struck by lightning. Seers foretold that a native of the city would become ruler of the world. On the night that Octavius was born, a seer, on learning the hour of his birth, prophesied that the ruler of the world had been born. Later, Octavius consulted the priests of Dionysus in Thrace concerning his son's future. When the priests poured wine for the sacrifice over the altar, a pillar of flame rose from it. This same sign had appeared when Alexander the Great sacrificed at the same altar. That night Caius Octavius dreamed that his son appeared, armed like Jupiter with the thunderbolt, crowned, and riding in a chariot decked with laurel branches. Other dreams and omens confirmed that he would wield supreme power. At the ceremonies in honor of his coming of age, the gown of a senator that Caesar permitted him to wear, split apart and fell about his feet. This was interpreted as a sign that the Senate itself would one day be brought to his feet.

---

fat, fāte, fär, fåll, åsk, fãre; net, mē, hėr; pin, pīne; not, nōte, möve, nôr; up, lūte, pủll; oi, oil; ou out; (lightened) ĕlect, agǫny, ūnite;

Before he was legally entitled to them, he was given many honors. At the age of 18 he followed Caesar to Munda in Spain to help him against the sons of Pompey. At Munda, Caesar noticed a palm tree and ordered his men not to cut it down as the palm was a symbol of victory. The tree suddenly put out a new shoot that grew so fast it overshadowed the original stock. Doves nested in it. Some say that this omen confirmed Caesar in his intention to name Octavius as his heir. In the following year Octavius was in Apollonia, in Illyria. While he was there news of Caesar's death reached him (44 B.C.). He returned to Rome at once. Having learned that Caesar had adopted him and made him his heir, he took the name Caius Julius Caesar Octavianus, and was henceforth known as Octavian. He took command of the army and assumed the reins of government.

In Rome he was at first scorned by Mark Antony, who ridiculed his pretensions; Brutus and Cassius, the chief conspirators against Caesar, thought him beneath their notice and retired to their estates. But Octavian maneuvered shrewdly. He gained the influence of Cicero, the Senate, and the people against Mark Antony. After defeating Mark Antony at Mutina (43 B.C.), he became reconciled with him, and in the same year formed the Second Triumvirate with him and Marcus Lepidus. The three members divided the western provinces between them. Brutus and Cassius held the eastern provinces in the name of the Republic. The triumvirs consoldiated their power by proscribing a large number of citizens and confiscating their estates as well as the territories of many cities, which they handed over to their soldiers. Those citizens of republican complexion who escaped the proscription went to Brutus and Cassius in the east. In 42 B.C. Octavian and Mark Antony pursued them. It is said that on his way to Philippi, Octavius met a Thessalian who assured him that he had met the ghost of Julius Caesar on the road and that the ghost foretold the victory of Octavian over the forces of Brutus and Cassius. In his first encounter with the enemy at Philippi, he was unsuccessful, and was forced to flee to the camp of Mark Antony. It was said that he escaped death only by the intervention of a friend's dream. The dream caused him to leave his tent, which was afterwards surrounded by an enemy party that cut the tent to ribbons under the impression that Octavian was in it. In

(obscured) errạnt, ardẹnt, actọr; ch, chip; g, go; th, thin; ꟻH, then; y, you;
(variable) ḍ as d or j, ṣ as s or sh, ṭ as t or ch, ẓ as z or zh.

the second engagement at Philippi he defeated Brutus and Cassius (42 B.C.). Both the conspirators committed suicide. Some say that Octavian cut off the head of Brutus and sent it to Rome to be flung at the feet of Caesar's divine image as proof that he had avenged Caesar's death. After the success at Philippi, Octavian and Mark Antony, whose friendship had never been strong, quarreled. Lucius, brother of Antony, raised a revolt at Perusia. Octavian proceeded to the city and laid siege to it. It is said that one day as he was sacrificing before the walls, a party of the enemy raided his camp and carried off the sacrificial vessels as well as the carcasses of the victims. Soothsayers foretold that the dangers threatened by the omens, which had been unpropitious on the victims, would now fall on those who had carried them off. Octavian forced the city to capitulate. Some say that after its fall he chose 300 prisoners from the upper ranks of citizens and offered them as human sacrifices on the Ides of March to the god Julius (Caesar). In 40 B.C. Octavian and Mark Antony were again reconciled. Antony married Octavia, the sister of Octavian, and departed to rule the eastern half of the empire. Lepidus was given 20 legions and command of one province in Africa. Sextus Pompey, son of Pompey the Great, had control of Sicily and was constantly threatening to cut off the grain supply on which Rome depended. Octavian waged war on him (43–35 B.C.). Two stories are told of propitious omens in connection with the battle against Sextus. One, that when he was walking near the shore before a naval battle off Sicily, a fish leaped out of the water and fell at his feet. The other, that he met a peasant driving a donkey and asked him his name. The peasant answered that his name was Eutychus *(Prosperous)* and his donkey's name was Nicon *(Victory)*. In spite of these favorable omens, the war dragged on; Antony at first refused to send assistance. Octavian lost two fleets in violent storms, but raged that he would win this war "whatever Neptune may do." Antony finally did send some help and the war ended in victory for Octavian. He was greatly aided by the services of his good friend and admiral, Marcus Vipsanius Agrippa, to whom he gave his daughter Julia in marriage, despite the fact that Agrippa was already married and that Julia was very much younger and already becoming well known for her vices. Sextus Pompey fled to Asia and per-

fat, fāte, fär, fâll, ȧsk, fāre; net, mē, hėr; pin, pīne; not, nōte, mŏve, nôr; up, lūte, pu̇ll; oi, oil; ou out; (lightened) ḙlect, agǫny, ūnite;

ished there soon afterwards. Lepidus, whose ideas of his own importance had become highly exaggerated, demanded the leading place in the government and was expelled from the triumvirate for his presumption, and went into permanent exile (36 B.C.). For the next five years Octavian and Antony shared power, but whereas Antony accomplished little in the East except for promoting his liaison with Cleopatra, Octavian consolidated his power in the West. When Antony cast aside Octavia, the sister of Octavian, and when it was discovered that in his will he had made his children by Cleopatra his heirs, Octavian had a proper reason for declaring war on him and eliminating the only serious rival who opposed him. He met Antony at Actium in Epirus, and defeated him decisively (31 B.C.). After the battle he was compelled to go to Brundisium and put down a mutiny, which he did with dispatch. He then pursued Antony to Alexandria, besieged the city, and forced Antony to sue for peace. As a condition of the peace he compelled Antony to promise to commit suicide, and saw that he had carried out the promise by inspecting the corpse. He was so anxious to have Cleopatra in the triumphal procession that would follow this victory that, some say, he tried to have her restored by sending a snake charmer to suck out the poison of the asp that she had allowed to bite her. This was a failure, and with some magnanimity Octavian permitted Antony and Cleopatra to be buried in the same tomb. But he dragged Antony's son by Fulvia from the image of the god Julius whither he had fled for sanctuary and had him slain. He also sought out and killed Caesarion, Cleopatra's son by Caesar. But the children of Antony and Cleopatra he brought up with as much care as if they had been members of his own family. In memory of his victory at Actium he founded the city of Nicopolis *(City of Victory)* near the scene of the battle, and instituted public games to be held every five years there.

With the defeat of Antony, Octavian became sole ruler of the Roman dominion, and remained sole ruler for the next 44 years. In 28 B.C. he was made *princeps senatus* (First senator). On Jan. 17 of the following year he received the title of Augustus, by which title he is best known in history. Augustus preserved the republican forms, but united in his own person the consular, tribunician, proconsular, and other powers. His generals carried on various wars in Spain,

Africa, Germany and elsewhere, but the Roman advance in the last-named country received a definite setback through the defeat of Varus by Arminius in 9 A.D. The loss of Varus and three legions with all their officers and men was a blow from which Augustus never completely recovered. It was said that when he heard the news, he went into a state of depression, and let his hair and his beard grow, and that he was often observed to beat his head on a door while he shouted, "Quintilius Varus, give me back my legions!" The anniversary of the loss was observed as a day of mourning. Yet Augustus preferred to avoid war if he could. During his reign the gates of the Temple of Janus on the Quirinal, which were open during times of war, were closed three times, signifying that the country was at peace. From the founding of Rome up to his time, they had been closed only twice before. Augustus was a strict disciplinarian over the army, did not encourage the creation of new citizens lest he dilute Roman blood, built libraries, and beautified the city. He boasted that he had found Rome a city "of sun-dried brick and left it clothed in marble." Among the structures for which he was responsible were the Forum, a temple of Apollo on the Palatine, and a temple of Jupiter the Thunderer on the Capitoline. He also urged such Romans as could afford it to raise new temples and public monuments and to restore such of the existing ones as stood in need of it. He revived ancient religious rites and customs; restored the calendar, which had been allowed to lapse, and named one month (formerly Sextilis) for himself; he tidied up the civil and administrative forms that had fallen into disorder during the years of civil war; he provided the most elaborate public spectacles ever to be presented to the Roman public; and he encouraged the growth of an indigenous Roman literature, which under him reached its greatest point. Above all, he consolidated the empire and brought peace to it. He was in fact, supreme ruler and emperor. Twice he thought of restoring the republican constitution, but was persuaded that the time was not ripe to do so. He rejected divine honors as well as the title "Father of his Country."

Augustus married first, Claudia, stepdaughter of Antony, for reasons of state, but divorced her when he quarreled with her mother. His second wife was Scribonia, who bore him a daughter, his only child, Julia. Julia caused him great

fat, fāte, fär, fåll, àsk, fâre; net, mē, hèr; pin, pīne; not, nōte, möve, nôr; up, lūte, pùll; oi, oil; ou out; (lightened) ĕlect, agǫny, ūnite;

sorrow, for though he attempted to raise the moral tone of Roman life, the activities of Julia his daughter and Julia his granddaughter were a public scandal. When he learned what all Rome knew, he had them both banished and refused all pleas to forgive them, or to lessen the severity of their punishment. He adopted his grandsons, the children of Julia and Agrippa, Caius, Lucius, and Agrippa Postumus. Caius and Lucius died in young manhood. Agrippa Postumus was accused of plotting against him, was banished, and died under mysterious circumstances. The third wife of Augustus was Livia Drusilla, whom he took from her husband Tiberius Nero, though she was pregnant at the time. He adopted her son Tiberius and, having lost the heirs of his body, made him his heir. There is no doubt that Livia Drusilla was a strong character and that she exerted great influence on Augustus. Some say that her constant aim in the exercise of her influence was to strengthen the office of emperor and to see to it that her son Tiberius eventually filled it. Whether, as is sometimes hinted, she hastened the end of Augustus by the judicious use of poison, can probably never be proved. Omens foretold his death: lightning struck his name on one of his statutes, for example. On Aug. 19, 14 A.D., after a very brief illness, he died in the same room at Nola where his father had died. His body was burned and the ashes placed in the mausoleum on the Tiber that he had built for himself and his family. By a decree of the Senate, Augustus was named one of the gods to be worshiped by the Romans. He had prepared an official biography, the *Res Gestae Divi Augusti* or *Index Rerum Gestarum,* containing lists of his public honors, of his public benefactions from his private purse, and of the military successes of the Romans during his principate, and a statement of his attitude toward and position in the Roman state. In accordance with his wishes this was engraved on two bronze tablets and placed on his mausoleum. Copies, in Latin and in an official translation, have been found at Ancyra (Ankara) in Galatia, and at Apollonia and Antioch in Pisidia, the most nearly complete of which, inscribed on the walls of the temple of Rome and Augustus at Ancyra, is known as the *Monumentum Ancyranum,* a term consequently sometimes used synonymously for the official title.

——B——

Bacchiadae (ba-kī′a-dē). Ruling family of Corinth. They were descendants of Heracles, and took their name from Bacchis, said to have been king of Corinth in the period 926–891 B.C. As members of the ruling class they intermarried, lived luxuriously, and displayed the utmost arrogance toward the people. They were deposed by Cypselus, 657 B.C., and many of them fled to other parts of Greece and to Italy.

Bagoas (ba-gō′as). Egyptian eunuch, originally in the service of Artaxerxes III of Persia. For a short time he virtually usurped the sovereignty of the empire. He put to death Artaxerxes (338 B.C.) and his son Arses (336 B.C.), but was himself compelled to drink poison (336 B.C.), which he had intended for Arses' successor, Darius III.

Battiadae (ba-tī′a-dē). Dynasty of Greek rulers in Cyrene in N Africa, which reigned from the 7th to the 5th century B.C. They have been classified as follows: Battus I (630–590 B.C.), founder of the city; Arcesilaus I (590–574 B.C., his son); Battus II (the Happy, his son, 574–c560 B.C.); Arcesilaus II (the Ill-tempered, his son, c560–c550 B.C.); Battus III (the Lame, his son, c550–c530 B.C.); Arcesilaus III (his son, c530–c510 B.C.); Pheretima, regent c515–c514 B.C.; Battus IV (the Fair, son of Arcesilaus III, c510–c470 B.C.); Arcesilaus IV (his son) ascended the throne c470 B.C., gained a Pythian victory in 462, and lived until c450 B.C. With his death the dynasty ended and a popular government was established.

Bessus (bes′us). Persian soldier and satrap of Bactria, fl. 331–330 B.C. He commanded the left wing of the Persian army at the battle of Gaugamela (Arbela), 331 B.C., and when the Persians were overwhelmed there by Alexander the Great, he fled with Darius III, king of Persia. In the flight of Darius and his noble companions through Media and past the Caspian Gates, Bessus and the rest refused to halt when Darius wanted to stand and make another fight against Alexander. With the consent of the other nobles, Bessus plotted against

---

fat, fāte, fär, fäll, àsk, fãre; net, mē, hèr; pin, pīne; not, nōte, möve, nôr; up, lūte, pùll; oi, oil; ou out; (lightened) ẹlect, agǫny, ūnite;

Darius to make himself king of the Persians in his place. Darius became virtually a prisoner of his companions. When Alexander, hotly pursuing Darius, now that he had subdued the lands behind him, drew near, Bessus stabbed Darius (330 B.C.), and fled to Bactra where he assumed the title "Great King" of the Persians under the name Artaxerxes. In 328 B.C., having secured his rear, Alexander pursued Bessus, whose cavalry now deserted him, across the Oxus River into Sogdiana. The people there had no desire to endure warfare for the benefit of Bessus, and sent word to Alexander offering to surrender him. He was brought to Alexander's camp and placed naked and in chains, by Alexander's order, by the side of the road as the army marched by. When Alexander came up to him and asked why he had murdered Darius, he replied that he had done it to win Alexander's favor. This did not please Alexander, for having made himself by conquest the successor of Darius, he held that Darius was under his protection. He ordered Bessus to be scourged. He was then sent to Bactra, tried for the murder of Darius, and found guilty. He was sentenced to have his ears and nose cut off and was afterward crucified.

Bibulus (bib′ū̄-lus), *Marcus Calpurnius.* Roman politician. He was Julius Caesar's colleague as aedile and praetor. In 59 B.C. he was consul with Julius Caesar, after having been elected through the efforts of the aristocratic party. After an ineffectual attempt to oppose Caesar's agrarian law, he shut himself up in his own house, whence he issued edicts against Caesar's measures. Pompey appointed him commander of the fleet in the Ionian Sea in 49 B.C. to prevent Caesar from crossing over into Greece. His vigilance was, however, eluded by the latter in January of the following year, and Bibulus died in the same year (48 B.C.) near Corcyra (now Corfu).

Boges (bō′jēz). Persian governor of Eion, a fortress at the mouth of the Strymon River. He was besieged by the Athenians under the command of Cimon (476–475 B.C.). Cimon offered him terms to withdraw and return to Persia, but Boges refused, rather than appear as a coward who would surrender his trust to save his own life. Instead he held out. When all supplies were exhausted, he caused a huge funeral pyre to be erected, slew his wife, children, and all those attached to his household, and threw their bodies on the

(obscured) errant, ardent, actor; ch, chip; g, go; th, thin; ᴛʜ, then; y, you;
(variable) ḍ as d or j, ş as s or sh, ṭ as t or ch, ẓ as z or zh.

blazing pyre. Then he collected all the treasures of gold and silver in the fortress and hurled them into the Strymon River, beyond the reach of the Athenians. When all this was accomplished, he flung himself onto the funeral pyre. Though Eion was taken by Cimon, the Persians long honored Boges for his bravery.

Bomilcar (bō-mil'kȧr). Carthaginian general; fl. at the end of the 4th century B.C. He commanded (310 B.C.) the Carthaginians against Agathocles, the tyrant of Syracuse. Possibly impressed by the example of Agathocles, he conspired in 308 B.C. to make himself tyrant of Carthage with the aid of 500 citizens and a number of mercenaries, but was captured and crucified.

Brasidas (bras'i-dȧs). Spartan general; killed at Amphipolis, Macedonia, 422 B.C. He was the son of Tellis, and was noted for his incomparable bravery, eloquence, simple honesty, justice, moderation, and for his frank and winning manner. In 431 B.C., at the outbreak of the Peloponnesian War, the Athenians sent 100 ships around the Peloponnesus and attacked Methone on the coast of Messenia. Brasidas commanded a defense force in the area. When he learned of the attack, he rushed to the relief of Methone with a hundred heavy infantry. The Athenians, attacking the wall of the city, were completely surprised when he appeared from behind them. He and his men made their way through the enemy with small loss and entered the city. By his daring raid he saved Methone and was publicly thanked by Sparta for his exploit, the first to win such an honor in the war. In the Spartan attack (425 B.C.) on Pylus in Messenia, which had been taken and fortified by the Athenians, Brasidas distinguished himself by his bravery. It was difficult and hazardous to bring the Spartan ships in against the defenders. Brasidas, observing the reluctance to risk their vessels, shouted to the Spartan captains that "they must never allow the enemy to fortify himself in their country for the sake of saving timber, but must wreck their vessels and force a landing." He ordered his own steersman to run his ship aground. In the landing he received many wounds, fainted, and lost his shield in the water. It was afterward found by the Athenians and set up in the victory trophy they erected. The following year he hurried from the northeast of the Peloponnesus to relieve Megara, which was under Athenian

fat, fāte, fär, fâll, ȧsk, fāre; net, mē, hėr; pin, pīne; not, nōte, möve, nôr; up, lūte, půll; oi, oil; ou out; (lightened) ē̯lect, agǭny, ūnite;

attack, and the Athenians withdrew. Next (424 B.C.) he marched through Thessaly to Acanthus, on the Chalcidian peninsula, and by his eloquence and personality persuaded Acanthus to detach herself from the Athenian Confederacy. The burden of his plea to the Acanthians, who admitted him alone to present his case, was that the Spartans "were taking up arms to protect the liberties of Hellas against Athens." Stagira and Argilus in the same area followed Acanthus, and enabled Brasidas to capture Amphipolis, one of the most important cities of the Athenian empire. In the following year, with the aid of traitors, he captured Torone, on the Sithonian peninsula of Chalcidice, and completed his highly successful campaign against the Athenian cities in the region. His successes were not viewed with unmixed admiration by the Spartans themselves; rather, they aroused jealousy of the brilliant commander. Scione, on the Pallene peninsula of Chalcidice, revolted against Athens, put herself in his hands (423 B.C.), put a golden crown on his head as the liberator of Hellas, and wreathed him with garlands of victory. Such adulation, and his acceptance of it, made the Spartans uneasy and spurred his own ambitions. A one-year truce between Athens and Sparta had meanwhile been concluded. Nevertheless, when Mende, a neighbor of Scione, also revolted, Brasidas accepted the offer of an alliance with Sparta and continued his activities in the area. At the expiration of the truce (422 B.C.) the Athenians sent a fleet against Scione. Brasidas was unable to arrive in time to save it and withdrew to Amphipolis. Hither the Athenians under Cleon followed, but decided not to engage him and began to withdraw. Brasidas rushed out after them. Cleon was slain in the battle. Brasidas received a mortal wound. He was carried into the city and expired. The people of Amphipolis gave him the honors of a hero. They removed all the monuments of the actual founder of their city, the Athenian Hagnon, and named Brasidas their founder. Sacrifices were offered to him, and games were celebrated annually in his honor. He was the outstanding general of the first ten years of the Peloponnesian War.

Brennus (bren'us). Roman name for a leader of the Gauls who marched on Rome early in the 4th century B.C., and sacked it. Brennus first marched his forces into Italy and laid siege to the Etruscan city of Clusium. The Romans sent ambassadors to treat with him, to see if they could persuade him to withdraw. When asked what his purpose was, Brennus is said to have replied that his purpose was the same as that of the Romans: to take land from people who had so much they could not till it and give it to his own people who needed it. As the Romans made war to satisfy their needs, so did the Gauls, said Brennus. The Roman ambassadors, seeing they could accomplish nothing, withdrew into Clusium. In a subsequent engagement the Gauls attacked Clusium and one of the Roman ambassadors took part on the side of Clusium. He was recognized by the Gauls, who demanded his surrender. For it was against all the rules of war, they said, for an ambassador to take part in a battle. The Romans refused to surrender their envoy. At once the Gauls marched on Rome. They did no damage to the country they passed through, for, they said, their quarrel was with Rome because of the violation of the laws concerning ambassadors. When they arrived at Rome they found the gates of the city open and unguarded, and the city almost abandoned, so terrified were the Romans at news of their coming. A small force under Marcus Manlius had withdrawn to the citadel on the Capitoline Hill, and a few priests and magistrates sat quietly in the Forum, having refused to abandon their city. The Gauls suspected a trap, but as they proceeded into the city, they found there was no resistance. They came upon the speechless, unarmed men in the Forum, who neither looked up nor moved at their approach. One of the barbarians approached a seated Roman and gently stroked his long beard. The Roman took up his staff and brought it down heavily on the barbarian's head. The Gaul at once drew his sword and killed him. Following this, the Gauls, who had up to this point done no damage, killed the rest of the men in the Forum, plundered the city, and put all those they found in it to the sword. But they could not take the Capitol, which was defended by Marcus Manlius. Brennus kept part of his forces in Rome, having burned most of the city, to keep up the siege of the Capitol. After seven months, those on the Capitol were weakened by lack of supplies, and the Gauls in the ruined city were weakened by disease. Brennus agreed to withdraw his forces in return for 1000 pounds of gold. The defenders in the Capitol brought the gold to him to be weighed. As Brennus was weighing it, the Romans saw that he was tipping the scales and cheating them. When they protested, he laughed, took off his sword and belt, and flung them on the scales. They asked what this meant and he mocked them, saying, "Vae victis!" (that is, "Woe to the vanquished," conveying approximately the same meaning as, in modern times, "to the victor belong the spoils"). However, Brennus was not to be victor after all. While the weighing of the gold was proceeding, Camillus entered with a force he had gathered, took up the gold and gave it to an attendant, and gave the scales back to Brennus, to whom he said that Rome was accustomed to delivering herself with iron, not with gold. Brennus withdrew to a camp outside the city. The next day Camillus fell upon him and routed his forces with great slaughter.

Brennus. A leader of the Gauls. Attracted by the weakness of the Greeks and the wealth of their sanctuaries, he led an attack against them, 279 B.C. His army, or part of it, eluded the Greeks and swam across the Spercheus River, using their shields as rafts. They plundered the country around Thermopylae but were defeated by the Greeks, with the aid of ships from Athens, at Thermopylae. The Gauls would now have retired in discouragement, but Brennus rallied them. He sent part of his forces into Aetolia to draw off the Aetolians, and they sacked and murderously ravaged the town of Callium. As Brennus had expected, the Aetolians rushed back from Thermopylae to protect their cities. Some Greeks at Thermopylae who, according to Pausanias, were not so much traitors as they were anxious to get rid of the Gauls, led Brennus and a large part of his force around the pass at Thermopylae, even as the armies of Xerxes had been led around it 200 years earlier. From there Brennus began his march to Delphi to plunder the rich sancturay there. But again, they say, the god Apollo came to protect his own, as he had done in the time of the Persian War. When the Gauls drew near, the ground shook with earthquakes; thunder and lightning assaulted the Gauls, rock slides fell on them, and lastly, during the night snow fell. The Greeks attacked them at sunrise, surprising them from the rear. Brennus was wounded. The same night Pan came to aid the Greeks by spreading panic among the barbarians. They thought they heard the sound of horses galloping, and rushed to arms and fell on each other, under the delusion they were fighting

(obscured) errạnt, ardẹnt, actọr; ch, chip; g, go; th, thin; ᴛʜ, then; y, you; (variable) ḍ as d or j, ş as s or sh, ṭ as t or ch, ẕ as z or zh.

off enemies. The Greeks, beholding this, attacked them relentlessly and drove them off. Brennus, seeing that all was lost, committed suicide. According to legend, he brought his life to a close by drinking undiluted wine.

Britannicus (bri-tan'i-kus). [Original name. *Claudius Tiberius Germanicus.*] Roman noble, born c41 A.D.; died at Rome, 55 A.D. He was the son of the emperor Claudius and Messalina, and was heir apparent to the throne until the intrigues of his stepmother, Agrippina, and her paramour, the freedman Pallas, secured from Claudius the precedence for Nero, Agrippina's son by a former marriage. He is thought to have been poisoned at a banquet by Nero, whose mother had sought to work upon the fears of her rebellious son by threatening to bring the claims of Britannicus before the soldiery. The name *Britannicus* was given to him by the Senate because of the conquest of Britain about the time of his birth.

Brutus (brö'tus), **Decimus Junius.** [Surnamed *Gallaecus* or *Callaicus.*] Roman consul and military leader; fl. 138 B.C. The surname Gallaecus (Callaicus) derived from his conquest of the Gallaeci (Callaïei), a people of NW Spain. He also repulsed the forays of the Lusitanians into the Roman colonies in Spain. He was consul in 138 B.C. He is remembered not only as a soldier, but also as a patron of poets, especially of Accius.

Brutus, Decimus Junius. [Surnamed *Albinus.*] Roman general; executed 43 B.C. He was one of the assassins of Julius Caesar. He was put to death by order of Mark Antony, with whom he disputed the province of Cisalpine Gaul. At the time of his death, Brutus was consul-designate. He is not to be confused with Marcus Junius Brutus, Caesar's chief assassin.

Brutus, Lucius Junius. Roman consul in 509 B.C., known as "The Founder of the Roman Republic." According to legend, he feigned idiocy (whence the name *Brutus* "stupid"; probably an erroneous etymology) to avoid exciting the fear and enmity of his uncle Tarquin the Proud (Tarquinius Superbus), who had put to death the father and the elder brother of Brutus to possess himself of their wealth. Tarquin, alarmed at the prodigy of a serpent appearing in the royal palace, sent his sons Titus and Aruns to consult the oracle at Delphi. They took with them for amusement

---

fat, fāte, fär, fåll, åsk, fåre; net, mē, hėr; pin, pīne; not, nōte, möve, nôr; up, lūte, půll; oi, oil; ou out; (lightened) ēlect, agǫny, ūnite;

Brutus, who propitiated the priestess with a hollow staff filled with gold. When the oracle in response to an inquiry of Titus and Aruns as to who should succeed to the throne, replied, "He who first kisses his mother," Brutus stumbled to the ground and kissed mother earth. When Tarquin seized and violated Lucretia, wife of Tarquinius Collatinus (whose father was a cousin of Tarquin the Proud), she called her husband and her father to her house. Brutus was one of several prominent Romans who accompanied Tarquinius Collatinus. Lucretia told them all that had happened, begged them to punish her ravisher, and then, in spite of their pleas, she took up a dagger and plunged it into her breast. Brutus, casting aside forever his pretense of idiocy, took up the blood-stained dagger, held it before them all, and swore by Lucretia's blood, once so pure, that he would "pursue Tarquin the Proud, his wicked wife and their children, with fire and sword: nor will I ever suffer any of that family, or any other whatsoever, to reign at Rome." He called the gods to witness his oath, then gave the dagger to the other men present and asked them to swear the same oath. With the aid of Publius Valerius, Brutus drove Tarquin out. The people immediately wanted to choose a new leader, but with the memory of the tyranny of Tarquin before them, they decided to divide the rule between two consuls. Brutus and Tarquinius Collatinus, as the man most implacably the enemy of Tarquin, were chosen consuls (509 B.C.), and established the Roman Republic.

On the understanding that he would give up his attempts to regain the throne and reëstablish the kingship, envoys of Tarquin were allowed to reënter Rome to collect his personal treasure and belongings. While in the city, they plotted with two of the leading families of Rome to kill the consuls and restore Tarquin. Two young sons of Brutus were involved in the conspiracy. When the plotters were discovered, brought before the consuls and accused, they made no defense, since the proof against them was incontrovertible. They stood in silence. In the stillness Brutus addressed his sons, "You, Titus, and you, Tiberius, why don't you defend yourselves of this charge?" As they made no answer, Brutus turned to the lictors and delivered his sons into their hands. The lictors flogged them, then stretched them on the ground and cut off their heads. The others present averted their eyes before the scene, the humiliation of Brutus, but he sternly watched to see that justice was done for the crime against Rome. Some said his face showed neither grief nor pity, but others said that to the dignity of his expression was added a look of fatherly anguish. When his sons were dead, he left the Forum. Immediately afterward, Publius Valerius and Tarquinius Collatinus began to dispute as to what should be done with the other conspirators, some of whom were related to Collatinus. Valerius called for Brutus. He returned to the Forum and informed them that, he having pronounced judgment on his own sons, it was up to the people to pronounce judgment on the other traitors. The matter was put to a vote, and the conspirators were condemned to death and at once beheaded. But Tarquin had not given up his determination to regain power at Rome. He sought aid from the Etruscans and marched with a great force against Rome. Brutus and his new colleague as consul, Publius Valerius, led the Roman troops against them. Aruns, the son of Tarquin, met Brutus on the field. They charged head-long at each other and killed each other.

Brutus, Marcus Junius. [Adoptive name, **Quintus Caepio Brutus.**] Roman politician and general, born c85 B.C.; died near Philippi, Macedonia, 42 B.C. Of a prominent Roman family, on his father's side he claimed descent from Lucius Junius Brutus who expelled the Tarquins from Rome. His mother was Servilia, a sister of Cato the Younger. She was a descendant of Servilius Ahala, who slew Spurius Maelius (439 B.C.) for plotting to usurp power in Rome. Thus, on both sides of his family, Brutus had a heritage of hatred of tyrants. He was well educated, and was particularly devoted to the philosophy of Plato. In the disturbances that shook Rome before Caesar won control, he was noted for his conspicuous devotion to the ideals of the republic and for the fact that he was impervious to bribery and flattery. Pompey was responsible for the death of his father, and though on this account he would not even speak to Pompey, when the struggle for power between Pompey and Caesar erupted, Brutus unhesitatingly chose to ally himself with Pompey who had legality on his side. He voluntarily joined Pompey in Macedonia before the battle of Pharsalus. It is said that when Caesar learned that Brutus was in the enemy camp, he gave particular orders to his men not to harm him in the fighting; if possible, he was to be taken prisoner, but if he refused to give up, Caesar ordered his men to leave him. Some say Caesar did this out of regard for Brutus' mother Servilia, who was the woman most loved by Caesar. And some say that Brutus was Caesar's son by Servilia. At all events, Brutus was not harmed in the battle of Pharsalus (48 B.C.), which ended in the defeat of Pompey. Brutus then wrote to Caesar, who forgave him and made him one of his companions. Caesar appointed him governor of Cisalpine Gaul (46 B.C.), where he won the devotion of the province by his wise rule and by his refusal to enrich himself by plundering it. In 44 B.C. Caesar made him first praetor *(praetor urbanus)*, and it appeared that there was no limit to his future in Rome. But there were many in Rome who hated and feared Caesar on personal or public grounds. For there was no doubt that under him the ancient liberties of the republic had vanished. Cassius, married to Brutus' sister Junia, was continually warning of the dangerous power Caesar held. Others who felt the same turned to Brutus because of his incorruptible spirit and because his name and heritage made him a natural choice to pull down tyranny. Urged on by Cassius and others, Brutus at last agreed to a plan to kill Caesar for the good of the republic. Some of the most prominent men in Rome joined the conspiracy, and it was decided that the deed would be committed at a meeting of the Senate which Caesar was expected to attend on the Ides of March (March 15, 44 B.C.). On that day the conspirators met at the Portico of Pompey. For various reasons, among them the omens of disaster that came to his wife Calpurnia, Caesar delayed his coming to the meeting, and the conspirators felt alarm that the plot might have been exposed. At last, however, Caesar arrived. As the conspirators gathered about him, Cassius turned his eyes to the statue of Pompey as if to invoke his spirit. Casca was first to strike at Caesar with his dagger. He hit him a glancing blow. Others approached and he fended them off, but when he saw Brutus threatening him, Caesar murmured "Et tu, Brute?" *(You, too, Brutus?)*, covered his head with his robe, and ceased to defend himself. The thrust of Brutus went home. It was said that of the 23 wounds that struck Caesar on that day it was the second one, that inflicted by Brutus, that caused his

(obscured) err*ạ*nt, ard*ẹ*nt, act*ọ*r; ch, chip; g, go; th, thin; ᵮH, then; y, you; (variable) *ḍ* as d or j, *ṣ* as s or sh, *ṭ* as t or ch, *ẓ* as z or zh.

death. When Caesar was dead, the senators fled. The conspirators had wanted to kill Antony also, but Brutus forbade it as they had agreed not to kill anyone else. Following the assassination, Brutus made a speech on the Capitol, exhorting the Romans to take back their liberties. There was no immediate outcry against the conspirators. On the contrary, Brutus was taken to the Forum with an escort of honor, but when Cinna, one of the conspirators, began to revile Caesar, the crowd murmured against him. The next day the Senate met and voted not only to give amnesty to the conspirators but also to honor them. Brutus was entertained by Lepidus. The following day the Senate met again and distributed the provinces, awarding Crete to Brutus. Mark Antony, who had fled in disguise after the murder of Caesar, returned and proposed that Caesar be given a public funeral. Cassius opposed him, but Brutus gave permission for it and also for a public reading of Caesar's will. When the will, bequeathing largesse to the citizens, was read, the crowd was moved by sympathy and affection for Caesar. Antony, aware of the tide of opinion that was rising, inflamed the crowd, praising Caesar, and holding up the blood-stained robe in which he died. His speech precipitated a riot, and Brutus and the other conspirators withdrew from the city.

Brutus went to Greece, where he was honored and welcomed, and from there to Asia, where he began to gather money and men to fight against Octavian (heir of Caesar) and Antony, who had temporarily given up the struggle between themselves for control in order to unite against Brutus. At Sardis, Brutus met Cassius, who had also by this time collected a large force. Before he left Asia, Brutus was sitting alone in his tent, late at night, meditating on the forces that he was about to set in motion. He thought he heard someone enter his tent, and looking up saw a phantom of monstrous shape. "Who of gods or men are you?" he asked, "and what is your errand with me?" "I am your evil genius, Brutus," the phantom answered, "and you will see me at Philippi." Turning back to his work, Brutus said, "I shall see you." There were other evil omens: when the armies of Brutus and Cassius embarked on their ships, two eagles perched on the leading standards and went with them, but flew off the day before the battle; at the sacrifices performed before battle was joined at Philippi, there were

so many unfavorable omens that even the skeptic Cassius
became alarmed. In a discussion before the battle Brutus
and Cassius agreed that in case of failure they would commit
suicide. In the first battle of Philippi (42 B.C.), Brutus was
victorious over Octavian, who barely escaped with his life,
but the forces of Cassius were overwhelmed by Antony.
Cassius did not know that Brutus had been successful and
he committed suicide. Twenty days later the forces of Brutus
again met those of Octavian. The night before, the monstrous shape that had come to Brutus in Asia appeared in his
tent again, but departed without saying a word. Next day the
battle began in the afternoon. The army of Brutus was surrounded. He escaped with some friends and hid in a cave.
He asked his companions to hold his sword, that he might
fall upon it, but they refused. He then grasped the hilt of his
naked sword with both hands and fell upon it (42 B.C.).
According to Plutarch, when Antony found the body of
Brutus, he wrapped it in one of his own costly robes for
burial and sent the ashes of Brutus to his mother Servilia.
But others say the head of Brutus was cut off and sent to
Rome, where it was flung at the feet of a statue of Caesar.

Burrus or **Burrhus** (bur′us), **Sextus Afranius.** Roman officer;
died 62 A.D. He was appointed sole praetorian prefect by
Claudius in 51 A.D., and was, together with Seneca, entrusted with the education of Nero. By his influence with the
praetorian guards he secured the undisputed succession of
his pupil in 54. He is thought to have been put to death by
poison, probably for having offended Nero.

Caelius (sē′li-us). [Full name, **Marcus Caelius Rufus.**] Roman
politician, born at Puteoli, Italy, May 2, 82 B.C. died 48 B.C.
He was a friend and correspondent of Cicero. It is said that
his education was supervised by Crassus and Cicero, and he
was an especially close friend of the latter during the great
orator's public career. He was also for a time intimate with
Catiline, but according to Cicero was not involved in the

latter's conspiracy, and in fact he exposed the part played by C. Antonius in that intrigue. In 56 B.C. his mistress Clodia, the sister of Publius Clodius and the *Lesbia* of the poems of Catullus, charged him with an attempt on her life, but he was acquitted with the aid of Cicero, whose oration in his defense, *Pro Caelio,* is one of the latter's most famous efforts. A tribune in 52 B.C. and an aedile in 50, Caelius supported Julius Caesar against Pompey in 49 B.C. Caesar appointed him *praetor peregrinus* (that is, judge of legal actions between persons at least one of whom was not a Roman citizen). But whether from a resentful feeling that this reward was insufficient to his services, or from impatience with what he considered the slow pace of Caesar's measures to cancel debts (of which Caelius had many), Caelius joined in a foredoomed conspiracy against Caesar's rising power. In 48 B.C. he was killed by soldiers whom he was attempting to win over to his rebellious plans.

Caesar (sē′zar). In ancient Rome, a patrician family of the Julian gens, of which the origin was fancifully traced to a legendary Julius, son of Aeneas, and hence claimed descent from the goddess Venus. The first Caesar actually to be noted in the annals was Sextus Julius, who was a praetor in 208 B.C. Lucius Julius Caesar, consul in 90 B.C., had an important part in shaping Roman institutions by securing the enactment of the law granting Roman citizenship to such of the Italian allies as had not fought against Rome in the Social War or who had laid down their arms at once. Lucius Julius Caesar was killed in 87 B.C., during the civil war, and with him his brother Caius Julius Caesar Strabo Vopiscus, whom Cicero numbered among the Roman orators. A son of Lucius Julius Caesar, bearing the same name, served in Gaul under that other Caius Julius Caesar (c100–44 B.C.) who made the family name one of the most noted in history. This younger Lucius Julius Caesar accompanied his great relative in the campaign which secured for the latter mastery of the Roman world, and after his assassination, joined the avenging forces of Mark Antony, whose mother, Julia, was a sister of Lucius. He quarrelled with Antony, however, and was saved from proscription only by Julia's intervention.

Caesar (sē-zar), *Caius Julius*. Roman general, statesman, orator, and writer, born July 12, 100 B.C. (according to Theodor Mommsen, 102 B.C.); killed at Rome, March 15, 44 B.C. It is

fat, fāte, fär, fåll, åsk, fāre; net, mē, hėr; pin, pīne; not, nōte, mŏve; nôr; up, lūte, pull; oi, oil; ou out; (lightened) ĕlect, agǫny, ūnite said that Caesar had a charger, each of whose hoofs was cloven into five parts, resembling toes. Soothsayers foretold that the master of the horse would one day rule the world. Caesar reared it carefully, was the first and only man ever to ride it, and eventually raised a statue of it before the Temple of Venus. Early in his career Caesar made an enemy of the dictator Sulla, who stripped him of his office as a priest of Jupiter and forced him to go into hiding. Sulla ceased to hound him at the plea of influential members of the aristocratic party, but when he did so, he warned them never to forget that the man they pleaded for would one day cause the ruin of their party. Caesar served in Mytilene in 80 B.C., and was awarded a crown of oak-leaves for saving a soldier's life there. While on the way to Rhodes (76 B.C.) he was captured by pirates and held for ransom. He sent his staff to procure it and swore to the pirates that as soon as he was free, he would capture and crucify them. On the arrival of the ransom he sailed off, raised a fleet, and pursued, captured, and crucified the pirates as he had sworn to do. In 68 B.C. he was appointed quaestor and went to Spain. There, at Gades (now Càdiz), he saw a statue of Alexander the Great in the Temple of Hercules, and is said to have sighed because at an age when Alexander had already conquered the world, he had accomplished nothing. He returned to Rome and was made curule aedile (65 B.C.) and began his program of winning the commons to his side with public spectacles, wild beast hunts, gladiatorial combats, and plays. By bribery he succeeded in getting himself elected pontifex maximus (63 B.C.). The following year he became praetor, and the year after that, propraetor in Spain. Successful in Spain, he returned to Rome, was elected consul, and formed the "First Triumvirate" with Pompey and Crassus in 60 B.C. By this maneuver he associated himself with the popularity and influence of Pompey and won access to the wealth of Crassus. He was named proconsul in Gaul and Illyricum in 58 B.C.; defeated the Helvetii and Ariovistus in 58, and the Belgae in 57; invaded Britain in 55 and 54; was the first Roman to build a military bridge across the Rhenus (Rhine), crossed it in 55 and 53 B.C., inflicting heavy losses on the Germans; and defeated Vercingetorix in 52 B.C.

His extraordinary military successes did not allay the fears of those who suspected him of plotting against the aristocratic party and the Republic. The consul in Rome proposed that since the Gallic War was over, Caesar should be recalled, his armies disbanded, and a new commander appointed to take his place. It was further proposed that he should not be allowed to stand for the consulship unless he was present in Rome, for this was the law. In the meantime, Caesar had won many to his side, with bribes, gifts, public spectacles, triumphs and their accompanying holidays. He now crossed into Cisalpine Gaul and came to Ravenna. The choice before him was to return to Rome as a private citizen and stand trial for all manner of alleged crimes and irregularities before a hostile court, or to march on Rome at the head of his loyal army and embroil it in civil war. He advanced to the river Rubicon, the boundary between Gaul and Italy. It is said that when he was considering whether to cross the Rubicon and bring on civil war, an apparition of great size and beauty was observed sitting on the bank of the river and playing a pipe. Shepherds gathered to listen and were joined by some soldiers from Caesar's army. When the soldiers neared, the apparition seized a trumpet from one of them, ran to the river, stopped there, blew a blast on the trumpet, and then crossed over. Caesar cried out this was a sign from the gods that they should cross over too. "The die is cast," he said, led his army across (49 B.C.) and began the civil war. In this he was eminently successful. Pompey, for the defense of the Republic, led an army opposed to him. Caesar defeated him (48 B.C.) at Pharsalus in Greece, and pursued him to Alexandria in Egypt. There he found that Ptolemy had murdered him. Ptolemy having drowned while attempting to escape after being defeated by Caesar in the Battle of the Nile, Caesar gave the rule of Egypt to Cleopatra and her younger brother. (Cleopatra lived with Caesar at Rome, 46–44 B.C., and bore him a son, Caesarion.) He went next to the Near East and defeated Pharnaces at Zela in 47 B.C. In the triumph for Zela at Rome, one of the chariots carried the inscription, "Veni, vidi, vici." (I came, I saw, I conquered.) He defeated the followers of Pompey at Thapsus in 46 B.C. and at Munda in 45 B.C. He reformed the calendar in 46 B.C., brought the Senate up to strength, beautified the city, set about codifying the laws, and proposed many great public works, as the draining of the Pontine Marshes and Lake Fucinus.

Caesar first married Cornelia, daughter of the consul Cinna. She bore him a daughter, Julia. His second wife was Pompeia, a granddaughter of Sulla. He divorced her because she was implicated in an impiety with Publius Clodius, who, disguised as a woman, invaded the feast of the Bona Dea, a sacred festival from which men were excluded. The charge was never proved, nor was an accusation against her of infidelity with Publius Clodius. Caesar divorced her, he said, because "Caesar's wife must be above suspicion." His third wife was Calpurnia, daughter of the consul Lucius Piso.

Caesar was a persuasive and cogent orator, and a lucid writer. The *Commentaries* (or Memoirs), the only one of his literary works extant, contain the history of the first seven years of the Gallic War in seven books, and three books of the Civil War. As a brilliant military leader he was idolized by his soldiers. He had played brilliantly on the caprices of the people and won their entire support. The crown was offered to him on several occasions, the last of these being Feb. 15, 44 B.C., when he refused it as he had done before. However, as his power increased, he made powerful enemies, some of whom feared for the Republic and others who had personal reasons for enmity. He also lost some of the support of the people with his infringement of their ancient liberties. A plot was hatched to assassinate him. According to tradition, many omens, signs, and auguries foretold his death. Veterans who had been sent to colonize in Capua unearthed the tomb of Capys, the legendary founder of the city. With it was a bronze tablet bearing an inscription in Greek warning that if any disturbed the bones of Capys "a man of Trojan stock will be murdered by his kinsmen, and later avenged at a great cost to Rome." (Caesar claimed descent from Venus and Aeneas, hence his "Trojan stock.") An augur warned him that he would not be safe until the Ides of March had passed. The night before he was assassinated his wife Calpurnia dreamed that a temple-like gable, voted in his honor, had collapsed, and that he lay stabbed in her arms. Some say that before he went to the Senate on his last day, he was handed a note describing the plot, but he saved it to read later. Victims sacrificed before he went to the Senate were unfavorable. He saw the augur who had made the prediction about the Ides of March and taunted him, saying, "The Ides of March have come." The augur answered, "Yes, they have come, but they have not gone." He entered the Senate and was immediately surrounded by a ring of daggers. About 60 men were in the plot. The first dagger thrust wounded him, but he parried it. When he saw Marcus Brutus, who had defected from Pompey and become one of Caesar's lieutenants, preparing to make the second thrust, he sorrowfully murmured, "You, too, Brutus?" before he received the wound. Then he drew the top of his robe over his face and ceased to defend himself. Some say that of the 23 wounds he received, only the second was mortal. At news of his death great lamentation rose throughout the city. The conspirators dared not seize control. The blood-stained robe in which Caesar died was placed on an ivory funeral couch and set in a gilded shrine. At his funeral, a dispute arose as to whether his body should be cremated at the Temple of Capitoline Jupiter or in Pompey's Assembly Hall. According to one account, suddenly two divine beings appeared, armed with spear and sword, and set fire to the couch on which his body rested. The crowd of mourners added branches to the flames; those in the funeral procession who were wearing the robes he himself had worn at his triumphs, tore them to pieces and flung them on the flames. Women tossed on their jewelry, the soldiers contributed their weapons. As soon as the funeral was over, the crowd snatched brands from the pyre and ran to burn the houses of Brutus and Cassius, the two chief conspirators, but were prevented from doing so. Later a column of Numidian marble was raised in the Forum. Inscribed on it were the words, "To the Father of his Country." It became the custom to offer sacrifices at the foot of this column, to make vows there, and to settle disputes by taking oaths in Caesar's name. He was deified immediately by the Senate. At the games given by Augustus in honor of Caesar the god, a comet appeared, and shone thereafter for seven days in a row. This was said to be Caesar's soul, taken up to heaven, and in his honor a star was placed above the forehead of his divine image. The hall where he was murdered was closed. The Ides of March were henceforth known as "The Day of Parricide." The name *Caesar* was assumed by all male members of the Julian dynasty, and after them by the successive emperors, as inseparable from the imperial dignity. It thus became the source of the German *Kaiser* and the Russian *Tsar* or *Czar*. After the death of Hadrian the title *Caesar* was specifically assigned to those who were designated by the emperors as their successors and associated with them in the government.

Caesar, Drusus. See **Drusus Caesar.**

Caesarion (sē-zār'i-ọn). Egyptian ruler, son of Cleopatra and (probably) Julius Caesar; born 47 B.C.; died 30 B.C. He was executed by order of Octavian. As Ptolemy XV he was, with his mother, a nominal ruler of Egypt from c44 B.C. to the time of his death.

Caius Caesar (kā'us, kī'us; sē-zạr). See **Caligula.**

Caligula (kạ-lig'ū-lạ). [Original name, **Caius Julius Caesar Germanicus.**] The third emperor of Rome (37–41 A.D.); born at Antium, Italy, Aug. 31, 12 A.D.; killed at Rome, Jan. 24, 41 A.D. He was the youngest son of Germanicus and Agrippina the Elder. As a child he was a great pet with his father's troops and wore a miniature uniform of the private soldiers, even including the half-boot *(caliga)*, whence the name Caligula, "Little Boot," given him by the soldiers. His popularity with the troops was such that when they rioted on hearing of the death of Augustus, the threat to remove Caligula to safety calmed them. He accompanied his father on his expedition to the East (18 A.D.), and after the death of Germanicus (19 A.D.), lived at Rome with his mother until she was banished (29 A.D.) by Tiberius, after which he lived with his grandmother Livia. At the age of 19 he went to Capreae at the request of Tiberius. There he behaved with such obsequiousness that he escaped the fate of his relatives, most of whom had been murdered by Tiberius. He refused to be tricked into making any complaint against the emperor, either in behalf of his relatives or on any other grounds, and in general behaved so slavishly that it was said of him, "Never was there a better slave, or a worse master." It is said that his unnatural obsession with brutality and his addiction to scandalous living manifested themselves early. Tiberius is said to have remarked of him, "I am nursing a viper in Rome's bosom. I am rearing a Phaëthon who will mishandle the fiery chariot of the sun and burn up the world." He succeeded Tiberius (37 A.D.), whose death he had caused or accelerated. Some say he caused Tiberius to be poisoned, and that before the emperor died, an attempt was made to remove the imperial ring from his finger. Tiberius would not let it go and he was smothered with a pillow. When Caligula became emperor, he was warmly regarded by the Romans, who had adored his father Germanicus. The Senate gave him absolute power and ignored Tiberius' will, by which his other grandson, Tiberius Gemellus, was named coheir. The Romans were so pleased at the accession of Caligula that, so it is said, 160,000 victims were sacrificed in thanksgiving. Among his first acts was to give the funeral oration in honor of Tiberius, shedding copious tears as he did so, and to give him a splendid funeral. He then recovered the bones of his mother and his brother Nero and returned them to Rome with great solemnity in proof of his devotion. He awarded honors in memory of his father and gave his grandmother Antonia—whose death he afterward hastened by his indifference and cruelty—all the honors once awarded to Livia, and, at first, he demanded that his sisters, Agrippina, Drusilla, and Livilla, be honored in Rome as himself. He recalled political exiles, dismissed long-standing criminal charges, published the imperial budget, restored the authority of the magistrates, carried out the bequests in Tiberius' will, and performed many other acts which won him great popularity. So great was the initial enthusiasm for him that the festival of Parilia, which commemorated the birth of Rome, was changed to the day when he became emperor, as if Rome had been born again. Among his public works was the completion of the Temple of Augustus and Pompey's Theater, begun by Tiberius, the commencement of an aqueduct to bring water to Rome, the rebuilding of the walls and temples of Syracuse, and the completion of the Temple of Didymaean Apollo at Ephesus. He ardently wished to cut a canal through the Isthmus of Corinth, but the project was abandoned. He was consul four times, in 37, 39, 40, and 41 A.D.

The moderation with which his reign began did not last long. Suetonius says he had suffered from epilepsy as a child, and that this caused mental as well as physical illness and perhaps accounts for his cruelty and his profligacy. He soon gave up the pretense that he was the ruler of a republic. Not only did he wish to be regarded as emperor; he wished to be treated as a god. He sent for the most famous statues of the Greek gods, including that of Zeus of Olympia, had

fat, fāte, fär, fåll, åsk, fāre; net, mē, hėr; pin, pīne; not, nōte, möve, nôr; up, lūte, pull; oi, oil; ou out; (lightened) ēlect, agǫny, ūnite;

their heads removed and his own head put in their places. He established a shrine to himself with priests, costly sacrifices, and a life-sized golden image. His reign was marked by wholesale killings of extreme brutality and by personal licentiousness little short of madness. On every occasion he showed his contempt for the people, and is said once to have exclaimed in a fit of vexation, "Would that the Roman people had only one head!" with the clear implication that this would considerably simplify their beheading. He was not content merely with the extermination of his enemies, real or imagined, but wanted them slain in the most cruel and lingering fashion. "Make him feel that he is dying," was a frequent order with him. He built a marble stable and an ivory manger for his horse Incitatus, and had the stable furnished with luxurious appointments for the occasions when guests had been invited in the name of Incitatus. Some say he planned to make the horse a consul. He made a fruitless expedition into Gaul in 40 A.D., and advanced to the English Channel where he ordered his men to pick up sea shells as spoils of the sea for Rome. On his return he demanded a triumph, but it was postponed. His extravagance, licentiousness, and savageries had the expected results. Plots against his life were discovered. There were omens that his life was drawing to a close. One was that when his men were preparing to move the statue of Olympian Zeus from the temple at Olympia, the statue burst into a roar of laughter and frightened the workmen away. An oracle warned him to "beware of Cassius." Thinking the governor of Asia was meant, he ordered the murder of Cassius Longinus. On Jan. 24, 41 A.D., as he left the Palatine Games to go for luncheon, he was set upon by Cassius Chaerea, tribune of a praetorian cohort, and murdered in the passageway that led from the theater he had just left. Cassius, so some say, asked him the password, and when he replied, "Jupiter," Cassius shouted "So be it!" and plunged his dagger into Caligula's throat. Caligula had married Junia Claudilla, daughter of a senator. She died in childbirth. He is said to have had incestuous relations with his sisters, one of whom, Drusilla, he treated publicly as his wife. Many other women had suffered his attentions. Some say he loved best Caesonia, who was wildly extravagant and notoriously promiscuous. She seemed to love him too, and he threatened to

obscured) errạnt, ardẹnt, actọr; ch, chip; g, go; th, thin; ꞓH, then; y, you;
variable) ḑ as d or j, ş as s or sh, ṭ as t or ch, ẓ as z or zh.

torture her to find out why she loved him. After Caesonia had borne him a daughter, Julia Drusilla, Caligula married her. Both Caesonia and Julia Drusilla were murdered following his own murder.

Callias (kal'i-as). Athenian statesman, 5th century B.C. He is known to have fought in the battle of Marathon (490 B.C.). A member of one of the oldest Attic families, he was in his time the wealthiest citizen of Athens. It seems certain that he undertook an embassy to Artaxerxes I of Persia in 449 B.C. and secured that monarch's promise to refrain from attacks upon the Delian League and from sending Persian war vessels into Greek waters, in return for Athenian acceptance of Persian hegemony in Asia Minor. Many authorities, however, doubt that there ever was a "Treaty of Callias" in the form of a written agreement of this sort, and the story that upon his return to Athens he was accused of treason and fined 50 talents is also open to doubt. The agreement, however formal or informal, was beneficial to the cities of the Delian League, for it freed them from Persian interference for several decades. The "Treaty of Callias" is sometimes referred to as the "Peace of Callias," by confusion with a pact proposed many years later and in very different circumstances by another Callias, the grandson of the Callias here referred to.

Callias Athenian soldier (died 370 B.C.) and leading citizen; grandson of Callias (5th century B.C.). A wealthy man, he was ridiculed in some of the plays of Aristophanes for his profligacy and ostentation. In 392 B.C., he commanded the Athenian hoplites in the victory over Sparta at Corinth. His name is associated with the so-called Peace of Callias, which was a proposal put forward by him at a conference in Sparta (371 B.C.). This, however, was disrupted by a quarrel between Sparta and Thebes. Callias was a friend of Xenophon and of Plato.

Callicratidas (ka″li-krat'i-das). Spartan admiral; killed in battle, 406 B.C. He was named navarch (admiral) in 406 B.C. to succeed Lysander, whose one-year term was up. Some say that out of enmity to him Lysander purposely sowed disaffection among the men of the fleet. At first Callicratidas was successful: the Spartan fleet took the fortified place of Delphinium on the island of Chios and the town of Methymna in Lesbos, and blockaded part of the Athenian fleet at Mytilene. Callicratidas left part of his fleet to maintain the blockade and sailed to Arginusae, a group of small islands south of Lesbos, to engage the remainder of the Athenian fleet. A great battle was fought at Arginusae (406 B.C.). Callicratidas was slain and the Athenians were victorious.

Calpurnia (kal-pėr'ni-ạ). Daughter of Lucius Calpurnius Piso Caesoninus. She was the third and last wife of Julius Caesar. On the night before he was murdered, she dreamed that a temple-like gable dedicated in his honor fell from its place and was smashed, and that Caesar lay dying in her arms.

Cambyses (I) (kam-bī'sēz). [Old Persian, *Ka(m)bujiya.*] Persian king whose historical character is doubtful. In the genealogy of Xerxes, as given by Herodotus, both he and his son Cyrus are omitted, and Diodorus, where he gives this name, seems to mean the father of Cyrus the Great. On the other hand, a Cambyses is mentioned whose sister was the ancestress in the fourth degree of one of the seven conspirators who put Darius on the throne. Possibly Cambyses I was one of the sons of Theispes (on the cuneiform monuments Chishpaish), and grandson of Achaemenes.

Cambyses II (or *I*). Persian ruler, c600 B.C.; the son and successor of Cyrus I, and the father of Cyrus II, called "Cyrus the Great." According to Herodotus he was merely a Persian nobleman. Astyages, king of the Medes, had a wondrous dream about his daughter Mandane which seemed to warn him that her son would dethrone him. He accordingly gave her not to a Median nobleman, but to Cambyses, a Persian nobleman of a conquered race. Their son, Cyrus the Great, did in fact dethrone Astyages. But Xenophon states that Cambyses was king of Persia, and his statement is confirmed by native records. In those chronologies which do not recognize the historically dubious Cambyses covered by the entry immediately preceding this one, he is shown as Cambyses I.

Cambyses III (or *II*). The son of Cyrus the Great and Cassandane. He succeeded Cyrus and reigned 529–521 B.C. According to some accounts, he suffered from the "sacred disease," epilepsy, and this accounted for his mad periods; others ascribed his eventual madness to the many impieties he committed. He conceived the idea of subjugating Egypt and prepared to march against that country (c525 B.C.), taking Ionian and Aeolian Greeks, vassals of his father, with

him. Amasis was king of Egypt at the time. Having crossed
the Arabian desert safely he mounted the attack. By this time
Amasis had died; his successor was his son Psammenitus
(Psammetichus). In the battle at Pelusium (525 B.C.) the
Egyptians, after stubborn resistance, were forced to retreat.
They retired to Memphis whither Cambyses pursued them,
besieged the city, compelled its surrender, and incorporated
Egypt in the Persian Empire. The Libyans bordering Egypt,
the Cyreneans, and the Barcans surrendered to Cambyses
without a struggle. He went to Saïs, ordered the body of
Amasis to be brought to him, desecrated it, and finally or-
dered it burned. This was the most impious act he could
commit, according to the laws of both the Persians and
Egyptians, for the Persians looked upon fire as a god that
they would not desecrate by burning bodies, whereas the
Egyptians regarded fire as an animal which devours whatever it can. By his act of ordering the body of Amasis to be
burned Cambyses set at nought the most deeply felt of the
Egyptian religious convictions. He planned a conquest of
Carthage, but gave it up when his Phoenician allies, the
backbone of his fleet, refused to attack Carthage. He then
set out, without proper provisioning for his forces, to conquer Ethiopia. On the way he detached a large body of his
troops and sent them to attack the Ammonians, and to burn
the oracle of Zeus there. Before he had proceeded one-fifth
of the distance to Ethiopia the supplies for his army were
exhausted. Nevertheless Cambyses, madman that he was,
persisted in going on. It was only when he learned his men
had resorted to cannibalism that he gave up his plan for the
conquest of Ethiopia and returned to Egypt, having lost
great numbers of his men through starvation, according to
Herodotus. The troops which he had sent against the Ammonians never reached their destination and never returned
to Egypt. Some say they were buried in a sandstorm.

Returned to Memphis, Cambyses committed many out-
rages against the Egyptians as well as against members of his
own entourage. According to Herodotus, he opened the
ancient tombs, insulted the images in the temples, went into
the most sacred enclosures and burned the statues, and in
every way outraged the religious laws and feelings of the
Egyptians, to no purpose. While he was in Agbatana, in
Syria, heralds reported that Smerdis had seized his throne

in Persia. His instant reaction was that Prexaspes, whom he had ordered to slay Smerdis, had betrayed him and had not slain his brother. Prexaspes convinced him that the Smerdis who had seized the throne was an imposter. Cambyses determined to proceed at once to Susa and expose the false Smerdis. In leaping to his horse he pierced his thigh. The wound did not heal, and when he realized he was in Agbatana in Syria he recalled an old oracle that foretold his death in Agbatana. When he first heard the oracle he assumed that it meant Agbatana in Persia. Now he realized that his end had come. He called his chiefs before him, told them he was dying, revealed that his brother Smerdis had been slain at his command, and urged them with the threat of unending curses, to regain the throne for the Persians. Shortly thereafter he died (521 B.C.), having reigned about seven and a half years, and leaving no son to succeed him.

Camillus (kạ-mil'us), **Marcus Furius.** [Called "The Second Founder of Rome."] Roman general and statesman; died 365 B.C. The traditional accounts of his career probably contain many embellishments to suit the purposes of various authors. In his early years he served with distinction in a war against the Aequi and Volscians (429 B.C.), in which he was wounded in the thigh by an enemy javelin, but he plucked it out and continued to fight. He was made censor and in this important post one of his acts was to compel bachelors to marry, for there were many widows in Rome as a result of the frequent wars. In 396 B.C. he was appointed tribune, and then dictator, to bring an end to the siege of Veii. The Romans had been besieging that Etruscan city for seven years, and were getting discouraged. He renewed their flagging spirits, vowed games to the gods, and promised to consecrate the temple of Mater Matuta if he was victorious. After defeating the Faliscans, he went to Veii, mined the walls, and took the city which he allowed his troops to plunder. As he stood on the citadel of Veii, he wept and prayed that if the gods must send a misfortune to balance the good fortune of the Romans in taking the city, such misfortune would fall on him personally and not on the Roman people. Finishing his prayer, he turned, stumbled, and fell. His associates were alarmed, but Camillus was delighted. The trifling inconvenience to him, he said, was the misfortune that balanced the good fortune of Rome. He

(obscured) errạnt, ardẹnt, actọr; ch, chip; g, go; th, thin; �, then; y, you; (variable) ḍ as d or j, ṣ as s or sh, ṭ as t or ch, ẓ as z or zh.

resolved to carry the image of Juno in Veii to Rome, and prayed to her, inviting her to take up her abode in Rome. According to legend, the image replied softly that she was ready and willing to go to Rome. For his capture of Veii (c396 B.C.) he was honored with a triumph, but incurred the displeasure of the Romans by riding into the city in a chariot drawn by white horses, which no commander had ever done before, as white horses were used only to draw images of Jupiter. The ungrateful citizens were also angered because he, with other leading citizens, thought it would be harmful to Rome if half her people were removed to Veii, as they wished to do in order to relieve the overpopulation of Rome, and he opposed it. In addition, they were irate because he had not carried out his vow to give one-tenth of the plunder of Veii to Apollo. It was decided to make a golden bowl and dedicate it at Delphi, and when it was found that there was not enough gold in Rome for the purpose, the ladies of the leading families contributed their golden ornaments. In a war with the Falisci, Camillus was again tribune and laid siege to Falerii. The Falerians felt so secure within their walls that life was carried on as usual. A schoolmaster of Falerian boys resolved to betray the city. He led his charges outside the walls and into the camp of Camillus, where he presented them as hostages to the Romans. Camillus was incensed at the treachery. "War," he said, "is indeed a grievous thing, and is waged with much injustice and violence; but even war has certain laws which good and brave men will respect . . . the great general will wage war relying on his own native valor, not on the baseness of other men." So saying, he gave the Falerian schoolboys rods and ordered them to flog their schoolmaster back into the city. The Falerians were so struck with his honor in this instance that they surrendered to him. Camillus exacted an indemnity from the Falerians and made an alliance with them. His solidiers were disappointed because they were not allowed to plunder the city, and brought a charge of fraud against him, saying he had taken booty for himself. When he found that he could not be acquitted of the charge, he chose to go into exile (389 B.C.). On reaching the gates of Rome, he prayed that if he had been driven out unjustly, the Romans would quickly repent of it and express to the world their need of him.

His prayer was swiftly answered. The Gauls, under Brennus, attacked and defeated the Romans at Allia (389 B.C.). They marched on the city, which had been almost abandoned by the terrified Romans, plundered and burned it, and put all who were taken captive to the sword. Only a handful, under Marcus Manlius, resisted them successfully on the Capitol. Camillus, living in exile at Ardea, rallied the young men there. Brennus had divided his forces and sent half of them to ravage the country, while the others remained in Rome. Part of the barbarians were encamped outside the walls of Ardea. In the night Camillus led out the Ardeans and killed the barbarians in their camp while they slept. News of his victory came to the Romans, who were forced to remember and long for him. They named him dictator, but he would not accept the office until he was properly appointed by the citizens of Rome on the Capitol. This posed a great difficulty, since the Capitol was surrounded by the forces of Brennus. Pontius Cominius volunteered to go through the enemy lines to the Capitol to secure the appointment, and he was successful. Camillus collected a great force and prepared to free Rome. In the meantime, the citizens on the Capitol were suffering from lack of provisions; the Gauls were suffering from the unaccustomed heat and from disease. Brennus agreed to withdraw on recept of 1000 pounds of gold. As the gold was being weighed out, Camillus entered with his forces. He took the gold from the scales and gave it to an aide, saying to Brennus that Rome was accustomed to deliver herself with iron, not with gold. He was dictator, he announced, and agreements made with any other were invalid. After a skirmish Brennus withdrew and made camp outside the city. The next day Camillus and his Romans, now full of courage, attacked and routed the forces of Brennus with great slaughter. Camillus was honored with a triumph, made sacrifices to the gods, purified the city, restored the temples, and raised a temple of Aius Locutius. He set the Romans to rebuilding the city, but they were discouraged by the overwhelming task, and talked again of Veii. They wished to occupy that city and abandon the ruins of Rome. Their clamor was so great that Camillus brought up the subject for debate in the Senate. In the silence before the vote was taken on whether or not Rome should be abandoned, the voice of a centurion outside the chamber was heard. He commanded the standard bearer of his squad to halt, "for this is the best place to settle down and stay." The senators interpreted this as divine intervention and all voted to stay in Rome. Now the Romans fell to rebuilding their city with new courage and hope. They built feverishly and without plan, so that the city was honeycombed with narrow lanes, crooked passages, and winding streets; nevertheless, the city was raised again within a year, and Camillus was named "The Second Founder of Rome." Before the city was completely restored, the Aequians, Volscians, and Latins rose against Rome. Camillus was appointed dictator again and defeated them. When he was quite an aged man, the Volscians rose against Rome again, and Camillus was made tribune for the sixth time, although he at first refused the post because of his age and ill health. He defeated the Volscians and returned to the city with great booty. He took Tusculum and gave its people Roman citizenship. Word now came that the Gauls were on the move. Camillus was again appointed dictator, although he was nearly 80 years old, and defeated them at Anio. Shortly thereafter, plague struck Rome. Many citizens succumbed to it, including Camillus, but he was, as Plutarch says, "full ripe for death, if any man ever was, considering his years and the completeness of his life." In the time of Camillus the selection of consuls was changed so that thereafter one of them was chosen from the plebeians. Camillus himself, though he was tribune six times, dictator five times, and celebrated four triumphs, never served as consul.

Campaspe (kam-pas′pē). [Also: *Pancaste, Pacate.*] Favorite concubine of Alexander the Great. She is said to have been the model for the picture Venus Anadyomene of Apelles.

Candaules (kan-dô′lēz) or *Myrsilus* (mėr-sī′lus). King of Lydia in the 8th or 7th century B.C. He was the last Heraclid king of that country. According to Herodotus, he compelled his aide and friend Gyges to spy on his beautiful wife. When she discovered that Gyges had watched her with Candaules' consent, she forced Gyges to murder Candaules, to marry her, and to succeed Candaules on the throne.

Carbo (kär′bō), *Cnaeus Papirius.* Roman plebeian leader, soldier and consul; born c130 B.C.; died 82 B.C. A member of one of the most prominent of the plebeian families, Carbo

fat, fāte, fär, fâll, àsk, fãre; net, mē, hėr; pin, pīne; not, nōte, möve, nôr; up, lūte, pùll; oi, oil; ou out; (lightened) ę̄lect, agǫny, ūnite;

vigorously supported Marius and fought in the Marian forces against Sulla. In 85 B.C. he became consul with Cinna and remained as sole consul after Cinna's murder. In 82 B.C. he checked Sulla near Clusium (modern Chiusi), but suffered disastrous defeat at the hands of Metellus Pius, one of Sulla's lieutenants, near Faventia (modern Faenza). Carbo fled abroad but was taken by Pompey on the island of Pantelleria near Sicily and was put to death.

Casca (kas'kạ), **Publius Servilius.** Roman politician; died after 42 B.C. He was one of the conspirators against Caesar (44 B.C.), and was the first of them to strike Caesar with his dagger at the base of Pompey's statue in the Senate house.

Cassander (kạ-san'dẻr). King of Macedonia; born 358 B.C.; died 297 B.C. He was the eldest son of Antipater, who had been made regent of Macedonia while Alexander the Great was engaged on his Asiatic campaigns. Olympias, mother of Alexander, was constantly sending accusations against Antipater to her son. Cassander went to Babylonia to meet Alexander and defend his father. On the death of Antipater (319 B.C.), Cassander waged war on the successors of Alexander, especially on Polysperchon, who had been appointed regent of Macedonia by Antipater. Ptolemy Soter and Antigonus were in alliance with him, and most of the Greek states, including Athens, came under his dominion. He made an alliance with Eurydice, wife of Philip Arrhidaeus of Macedon, but Olympias soon had them slain. Cassander then marched against Olympias, compelled her to surrender at Pydna, and put her to death (316 B.C.). In 311 B.C. he was made regent for Alexander IV, the young son of Roxana and Alexander the Great. In the same or the following year, he had them both slain. After the battle of Ipsus (301 B.C.) and the death of Antigonus, he was recognized as king of Macedonia and ruler of Greece. He married Thessalonica, sister of Alexander the Great, restored Thebes, which had been destroyed by Alexander, changed the name of Therma to Thessalonica, and rebuilt Potidaea, which was thereafter known as Cassandrea.

Cassius Longinus (kash'us long-jī'nus), **Caius.** Roman general and politician, who died near Philippi, Macedonia, 42 B.C. He was distinguished in the Parthian war of the period 53–51 B.C. A participant in the battle of Pharsalus, he was subsequently pardoned by Caesar. Nevertheless, in 44 B.C.

(obscured) errạnt, ardẹnt, actọr; ch, chip; g, go; th, thin; ₮H, then; y, you; (variable) ḏ as d or j, ş as s or sh, ṭ as t or ch, ẕ as z or zh.

he was one of the leading conspirators against Caesar. A commander in Syria and Asia (44–42 B.C.), he was defeated by Antony at Philippi in 42 B.C. and killed himself.

Cassius Longinus, Quintus. Roman politician; died 45 B.C. Although he was accused of corruption during his tenure of the quaestorship in Spain in 54 B.C., he became a tribune, and with his colleague in that office, Mark Antony, in 49 B.C. vetoed a decision of the Senate to order Julius Caesar to relinquish command of his army. When the Senate nevertheless persisted in its purpose, Cassius and Antony joined Caesar, who thereupon crossed the Rubicon and began the campaign which made him master of Rome. In 47 B.C. Cassius was given a command in Spain, and presently was faced with a rebellion which he was unable to handle, so that Caesar had to come to his rescue.

Cassius Viscellinus (vis-ẹ-lī'nus), **Spurius.** Roman reformer; died c485 B.C. There is little doubt that Spurius Cassius Viscellinus was a historic person, though so much legend has gathered about him as to give him an almost mythical character. He appears to have held the consulship several times, and is named as the negotiator in 493 B.C. of treaties between Rome and the cities of Latium. Trouble between the Roman patricians and the lower orders had long been festering because of the continual arrogation of public lands by the patricians. Cassius, while consul in 486 B.C., proposed a redistribution of lands, but the patricians accused him of courting popular support with the object of becoming king, and brought about his death in the following year.

Catiline (kat'i-līn). [Full name, **Lucius Sergius Catilina.**] Roman politician and conspirator, born c108 B.C.; killed at Pistoia, Italy, 62 B.C. He was of an old but impoverished patrician family. As a partisan of Sulla he rendered himself infamous by his complicity in the horrors of the proscription, destroying with his own hand his brother-in-law, Q. Caecilius. He was praetor in 68 B.C. and governor of Africa in 67 B.C. After an abortive attempt, in conjunction with P. Autronius, to murder the consuls-elect for 65 B.C., with a view to seizing power, and after an unsuccessful candidacy in the consular elections of 64 B.C., he organized a widespread conspiracy against the republic, whose object is said to have been the cancellation of debts, the proscription of the wealthy, and the distribution among the conspirators of all offices of honor and emolument. It was defeated by the vigilance and eloquence of Cicero, who was then consul. The rebellion having broken out in Etruria on Oct. 27, Cicero pronounced in the Senate on Nov. 8, his first oration against Catiline, which caused the latter to leave the city. On Nov. 9 Cicero delivered in the Forum his second Catilinian oration in which he acquainted the people with the events in the Senate and the departure of Catiline from Rome. On Dec. 3 documentary evidence of the conspiracy was obtained from an embassy of Allobroges, which had been tampered with by the Catilinians, and in the evening Cicero delivered in the Forum his third oration, in which he acquainted the people with the events of the day and the seizure of the conspirators remaining at Rome. On Dec. 5 Cicero delivered in the Senate his fourth oration, which was followed by the execution in prison of some of the conspirators. Meanwhile Catiline had assumed command of the revolutionary force, which amounted to about two legions, but was overtaken by the army of the Senate as he was attempting to escape into Gaul, and was defeated and slain in the battle which ensued.

Cato (kā′tō), **Marcus Porcius.** [Called **Cato the Elder** and **Cato the Censor;** surnamed Priscus.] Roman statesman, general, and writer, born at Tusculum, Italy, 234 B.C.; died 149 B.C. He was quaestor under Scipio in 204 B.C., served as consul in 195, served in Spain in 194 and against Antiochus in 191, was censor in 184, and was ambassador to Carthage in 157 or 153 B.C. He sought to restore the integrity of morals and the simplicity of manners prevalent in the early days of the Republic, his severity as a censor earning him the epithet "Censorius." The prosperity of Rome's old enemy Carthage led him to advocate a third Punic war. In his effort to initiate this war, for years he closed every speech in the Senate with the words, "Ceterum censeo Carthaginem esse delendam" ("Furthermore, I am of the opinion that Carthage ought to be destroyed."). He wrote voluminously; his *De Agri Cultura* survives, but of his historical *Origines,* in seven books, and his speeches, letters, and essays, only fragments have reached us.

Cato, Marcus Porcius. [Called **Cato the Younger;** surnamed **Uticensis,** meaning "Of Utica."] Roman patriot and Stoic philosopher; great-grandson of Marcus Porcius Cato (234–149 B.C.), born at Rome, 95 B.C.; committed suicide at Utica,

North Africa, 46 B.C. He fought under Gellius Publicola against Spartacus in 72 B.C., served as military tribune in Macedonia in 67, and was quaestor in 65, tribune of the people in 62, and praetor in 54 B.C. He supported Cicero against the faction of Catiline, and sided with Pompey against Caesar on the outbreak of the civil war in 49 B.C. After the battle of Pharsalus he retired to Utica, where he put himself to death on receiving intelligence of the victory of Caesar at Thapsus. He had a reputation for scrupulous fairness and honor, and his death was considered noble and courageous.

Catulus (kat'ū-lus), **Caius Lutatius.** Roman general; fl. 3rd century B.C. He was chosen consul for the year 242 B.C. When he entered office, the First Punic War had been waged since 264 B.C. and the Senate, discouraged by numerous losses, had abandoned the war at sea. He obtained command of a fleet built by wealthy patriots at Rome, and in 241 B.C. gained the decisive victory at the Aegadian Islands which resulted in a treaty of peace favorable to Rome.

Catulus, Quintus Lutatius. Roman general; born c152 B.C.; died 87 B.C.; father of Quintus Lutatius Catulus (died 60 B.C.). He was consul with Marius in 102 B.C., and was associated with him in the victory over the Cimbri at Vercellae in 101 B.C. He joined Sulla in the civil war and, having in consequence been proscribed by Marius, he is said to have committed suicide in 87 B.C.

Catulus, Quintus Latatius. Roman politician; died 60 B.C.; son of Quintus Lutatius Catulus (c152–87 B.C.). Consul in 78 B.C. and censor in 65 B.C., he was a strong supporter of Cicero against the conspiracy of Catiline in 63 B.C.

Cethegus (sē-thē'gus), **Marcus Cornelius.** Roman general; died 196 B.C. He was curule aedile (213 B.C.), praetor (211), censor (209), and consul (204 B.C.). In the following year he commanded as proconsul in Cisalpine Gaul, where, with the aid of the praetor Quintilius Varus, he defeated the Carthaginian general Mago, brother of Hannibal.

Chabrias (kā'bri-as). Athenian general; fl. 388–357 B.C.; killed near Chios, 357 B.C. In 388 B.C. he was sent to the assistance of Evagoras, king of Cyprus, against the Persians. On the way he landed at the island of Aegina, which the Spartans were using as a base, and by an ambush defeated the Spartans in battle and seized and killed Gorgopas, the Spartan commander. In 378 B.C., in a campaign against Agesilaus, he acquired great celebrity by the adoption of a new maneuver, which consisted in receiving the enemy's attack on one knee with spears presented and shields resting on the ground. In 376 B.C. the island of Naxos revolted against the reconstituted Athenian Confederacy. Chabrias sailed against the island to put down the revolt. The Spartans sent a fleet to the relief of Naxos. Chabrias engaged their fleet and utterly defeated the Spartans. Eleven Spartan ships were allowed to escape while Chabrias, mindful of the fate of the Athenian victors at Arginusae (406 B.C.), stopped to rescue from the water his men whose ships had been wrecked. Thus the Spartan fleet was not completely destroyed, but the victory was impressive. Chabrias sailed about the Aegean and enrolled new members in the Athenian Confederacy. He acted as military adviser to the king of Egypt (c373 B.C.). The island of Ceos revolted from the Confederacy (364 B.C.), and was subdued by Chabrias in the same year. On the outbreak of the Social War (357 B.C.) he was placed in command of the Athenian fleet, which coöperated with the army under Chares. Chios revolted. He was sent to put down the revolt and was killed at the siege of the island (357 B.C.).

Chares (kā'rēz, kār'ēz). Athenian general; died after 332 B.C. In 357 B.C. he captured Sestus in the Chersonesus, put the inhabitants to the sword, and regained the Chersonesus for Athens. In the same year he was sent to put down a revolt of the Athenian ally Chios with Chabrias as his co-general. Chabrias was killed in attempting to force a landing. Chares withdrew but later returned, sharing the command with two admirals. They refused to support his plan for attacking Chios. He attacked without them and was driven off with loss. He accused them of treachery; they were tried on a charge of bribery and Chares was vindicated. As sole commander, he now went to Asia Minor to subdue the revolting Athenian allies. In Asia he helped a rebellious satrap of the Persian king to a brilliant victory (355 B.C.) and was rewarded by the grateful satrap with the money he urgently needed to maintain his army. But the Persian king made strong representations against the Athenians for helping his satrap in a rebellion. Peace was made (354 B.C.) between Athens and her revolting allies, and Chares was recalled. He went next (349 B.C.), to help the Phocians against Philip II of Macedon, but accomplished little. In 340 B.C. he was sent to aid Byzantium to resist a siege by Philip. The Byzantines, mindful of his ruthlessness at Sestus, refused to receive him in their city. He was one of three Athenian commanders at the Battle of Chaeronea (338 B.C.) in which the Greeks were overwhelmed by Philip. After Alexander the Great conquered Thebes, he demanded the surrender of Chares, but the latter fled to the east and, some say, entered the service of the Persian king, Darius III.

Charidemus (ka-ri-dē′mus). Greek mercenary captain; executed 333 B.C. He served under the Athenian general Timotheus in an unsuccessful attempt to recapture the city of Amphipolis (364–362 B.C.). After being dismissed by Timotheus, he went over to the Thracian king Cotys, one of whose daughters he married, and opposed the Athenians. After the murder of Cotys, he became the chief minister of his son, Cersobleptes, and defeated an Athenian fleet that was sent to take over the Chersonesus (c359 B.C.). When the Chersonesus was at length retaken by the Athenians (357 B.C.). Charidemus was able so to twist the appearance of his activities that the Athenians not only again invited him to serve them but honored him as well. In following years he commanded Athenians against Philip II of Macedon, who had now won control over large parts of Thrace, but without great success. He was one of those whose surrender Alexander the Great demanded after his capture and destruction of Thebes. He escaped and fled to Darius III, king of Persia, whom he served as a mercenary. According to some accounts, he was put to death by the Persians (333 B.C.) for insubordination concerning the preparation Darius was making to meet Alexander the Great before the battle of Issus.

Cicero (sis′ē-rō), *Marcus Tullius.* [Formerly called *Tully.*] Roman orator, philosopher, and statesman; born at Arpinum, Italy, Jan. 3, 106 B.C.; assassinated near Formiae, Italy, Dec. 7, 43 B.C. He was the son of Marcus Tullius Cicero and Helvia. His father, a member of the equestrian order and a man of comfortable means, wished to give his sons a sound education, and to that end took young Marcus and his younger brother Quintus Tullius (102–43 B.C.) to Rome. There Cicero came into contact with some of the foremost intellects of the time: the poet Archius of Antioch who,

---

fat, fāte, fär, fåll, àsk, fãre; net, mē, hėr; pin, pīne; not, nōte, möve, nôr; up, lūte, pùll; oi, oil; ou out; (lightened) ēlect, agǫny, ūnite;

according to Cicero, gave him a love for literature; the celebrated orators Lucius Licinius Crassus (140–91 B.C.) and Marcus Antonius (143–87 B.C., grandfather of the triumvir), who interested him in oratory and a legal career; the noted jurists Quintus Mucius Scaevola the Augur (c159–c88 B.C.) and Quintus Mucius Scaevola the Pontifex Maximus (died 82 B.C.); the philosophers Diodotus the Stoic, Phaedrus the Epicurean, and Philo of Larissa, who was head of the Academy; and the rhetorician Molo of Rhodes. In the course of a two-year journey (79–77 B.C.) which he took for his never robust health, he went to Athens where he attended the lectures of Antiochus of Ascalon, to Rhodes, where he heard Posidonius the Stoic, and once more studied with Molo. That master chided him for his florid style. Cicero took his comments to heart, pruned the excesses of which Molo complained, and thereafter assiduously cultivated the style that made his the classic pattern of oratory. Before returning to Rome he visited Asia Minor, where he heard the lectures of the Greek rhetorician and historian, Dionysus of Magnesia, and those of Menippus of Stratonicea, the Cynic. Some time before 68 B.C. he met Pomponius Atticus who became his lifelong friend and confidant, and the recipient of many revealing letters.

Earlier, Cicero had fulfilled his military service in the Marsic War (89 B.C.), under Pompeius Strabo and Sulla. He had also delivered (81) his earliest extant oration, *Pro Quinctio* (For Quinctius). In 80 he had defended Sextus Roscius *(Pro Sextus Roscio)* on a trumped-up charge of murdering his father. To defend Roscius and oppose Chrysogonus (a favorite of Sulla) took courage on Cicero's part, as Sulla was dictator at the time. He won his case and shortly after (79) went on the journey for his health, not entirely, as it was sometimes said, to escape Sulla's possibly wrathful notice. When he returned to Rome (77) he married Terentia, a strong-willed woman who subsequently bore him his beloved daughter Tullia (c76–45 B.C.) and a son Marcus (born 65 B.C.). In 75 he went to Lilybaeum in Sicily as quaestor and won admiration there for honest and conscientious administration of his office—a rare experience for Sicilians under Roman officials. The following year he entered the Senate and energetically embarked on his legal career in Rome. In 70 he was asked to lead the prosecution of Verres, who as governor of Sicily had ravaged that province for three years. Hortensius, the most famous orator in Rome at the time, defended Verres. Cicero marchaled such testimony in the first action *(In Verrem)* against Verres that the latter decided to go into voluntary exile. The material prepared for the second action against Verres was not delivered, but was subsequently published in five parts by Cicero. He was curule aedile (69) and praetor (66). As praetor he favored *(De Lege Manilia,* For the Manilian Law), the proposal by the tribune Caius Manilius to give Pompey vast power as general in command of the Mithridatic War. His argument dealt less with the constitutional questions posed in awarding such great power to one man than with the virtues and qualities of Pompey, among which he named the good luck with which Pompey seemed to be blessed.

Devoted to the principles of the Republic and the maintenance of order, Cicero's natural sympathies were with the *optimates* (the aristocratic and conservative party). However, he was regarded with some hostility by them as a "new man," and had won influence with the *populares* (popular party) by his victory in the presecution of Verres. Seeking the consulship, he wavered for a time between the two, but when, with the help of the optimates he defeated Catiline and became consul (63), his loyalty to the optimates never thereafter failed. As consul he was at the height of his power and influence. But in this turbulent period between civil wars the cause for which he lived, and ultimately died, was already almost lost. The great days of the Republic, which in any event existed only in an idealized version in his mind, were irretrievably lost. He delivered three speeches, *Contra Rullum* (Against Rullus) or *De Lege Agraria* (On the Agrarian Law), against a proposal by the tribune Servilius Rullus, who sought to win popularity by a distribution of land to the poor. The proposal lost, and Cicero lost favor with the populares. He defended the aged Rabirius *(Pro Rabirio),* who was charged with having illegally put to death Saturninus in 100 B.C. This old charge was revived to warn those in authority against dealing summarily, as Rabirius had done, with suspected rebels. Rabirius was not acquitted, but after some complicated maneuvering went free, and Cicero shortly proceeded to ignore the warning presented by the charge against Rabirius. The most dramatic episode of his consulship was his discovery, energetic exposure, and suppression of the Catilinarian conspiracy. Catiline, a renegade aristocrat, plotted to overthrow the government, and kill the most prominent men of Rome, including Cicero. The night of Nov. 7, 63, was fixed for the murder of Cicero. He learned of the plot, as he had of other intrigues by Catiline, and took steps to protect himself. On Nov. 8 he rose in the Senate, in the presence of Catiline himself, and delivered the first of four orations *In Catilinam* (Against Catiline). He accused him, and urged him and his followers to withdraw, that Rome might be relieved of the fear that had gripped it since Catiline first organized his band of rebels and rumors of his intentions had got abroad. Cicero noted that it was once considered virtuous for patriotic men to punish a traitorous citizen even more harshly than a foreign foe. However, he sought the withdrawal of Catiline with his followers lest the well-deserved execution of the latter leave embers which his supporters, if still in the city, might fan to a conflagration of revolt at a later time. Catiline fled to Etruria that same night. On Nov. 9 Cicero delivered the second oration to a tremendous gathering, in order to quiet the fears which the flight of Catiline to his camp outside Rome had aroused. On Dec. 2 it was learned from the Allobroges, with whom Catiline was conspiring to attack Rome, that Catiline meant to strike on Dec. 19. The third oration, in which these plans were exposed, was delivered, Dec. 3, to another huge crowd. Some of the conspirators, not including Catiline, were seized. The fourth oration, in which Cicero favored the death penalty for the conspirators, was delivered before the Senate on Dec. 5. Subsequently, they were put to death without trial, and early in the next year Catiline and his followers were destroyed in battle. Although he was given the title *pater patriae* for his services, on leaving the consulship Cicero was increasingly subject to attack. He prosecuted (61) Clodius Pulcher on a charge of impiety: that of invading the ceremony of the *Bona Dea* (a sacred festival from which men were excluded) disguised as a woman. Clodius was acquitted and became Cicero's mortal enemy. Amid rising disorder, Caesar and Pompey approached him and invited him to join a secret coalition to control Rome. After great hesitation, he refused (Dec., 60) and opposed them. In 58 Clodius, who was tribune, pro-

(obscured) errant, ardent, actor; ch, chip; g, go; th, thin; ₮H, then; y, you;
(variable) d̪ as d or j, ş as s or sh, t̪ as t or ch, z̧ as z or zh.

posed a law that any Roman who had put citizens to death without trial should be outlawed. This was directly aimed at Cicero, for his part in the death of the Catilinarian conspirators. Having put himself at odds with Pompey and Caesar, they now left him to his fate at Clodius' hands, and he went into exile at Thessalonica. His property in Rome was seized and destroyed; the site of his house was consecrated to Liberty by Clodius. The next year he was recalled to Rome and was greatly honored. However, he was out of favor with the Triumvirate (formed 60 B.C., by Caesar, Pompey, and Crassus), and so played small part in political affairs. Instead, he occupied himself with his legal career and with literary pursuits. In 53 he was elected augur; in 51 he was made proconsul of Cilicia. Although he had not wanted a province, he carried out his office efficiently and honestly, put down a revolt in Cappadocia, and waged successful war on the tribes of Mount Amanus. By 50, when he returned to Rome the differences between Caesar and Pompey made civil war inevitable. After great vacillation, for Cicero recognized the vigor and qualities of Caesar, he elected to join Pompey in Greece. Following the latter's defeat by Caesar at Pharsalus (48), Cicero, who had not taken part in the battle because of illness, abandoned Pompey and went to Brundisium, where he waited a year for Caesar's forgiveness. When it came he returned to Rome, was generously treated by Caesar but kept apart from public affairs. Private sorrows occupied him. He divorced Terentia (46), made a disastrous marriage with his young and wealthy ward, and lost his beloved daughter Tullia (45). In this period he consoled himself with literary work and the study of philosophy.

The murder of Caesar (March 15, 44 B.C.) brought him once more from retirement. His great aim was to restore order and to bring about a reconciliation between the rival factions. To this end he secured an amnesty for the conspirators. However, the intrigues of Caesar's partisans caused him to leave Rome. He was recalled, and began to express his intense hostility to Mark Antony in the first of the 14 *Philippicae* (Philippics). Cicero put his hopes in Octavian (Caesar's heir), who had always shown him the greatest respect, and while Octavian struggled to enter into his inheritance Cicero became the acting head of state, although he held no office. In his optimism, he thought he could influence Octavian to restore the Republic. He realized to what extent he had deluded himself when Octavian formed the Second Triumvirate (43) with Antony and Lepidus. Cicero, who had shown unrelenting hostility to the last two, prepared to fly. His ship was driven back by contrary winds, he was seized by agents of the triumvirs (but against the wishes of Octavian, it is said), and put to death near Formiae, Dec. 7, 43 B.C. His head and right hand were cut off and sent to Rome, where Antony caused them to be nailed to the rostra.

For all his great activity in public affairs, Cicero could not shape the time in which he lived. His monument rests in the contributions he made as the greatest enricher and stylist of the Latin language that Rome had ever produced. His contributions and example were consciously employed in the next 15 centuries to shape literary and linguistic expression. Aside from some early attempts at verse-writing and the translations from the Greek which he made from time to time throughout his life, his literary output may be divided into four groups. *The Orations,* of which 58 survive, in whole or in part: *Pro Quinctio* (81); *Pro Sextus Roscio* (80); *Pro Roscio Comoedo* (77); *Pro Tullio* (71?); *In Caecilium Divinatio, In Verrem* (The First Action against Verres, the Second Action against Verres, six speeches altogether) (70); *Pro Fonteio, Pro Caecina* (69); *Pro Lege Manilia, Pro Cluentio* (66); *Contra Rullum* (three speeches), *In Catilinam* (four speeches), *Pro Murena* (63); *Pro Sulla, Pro Archia* (62); *Pro Flacco* (59); *Post Reditum ad Quirites, Post Reditum in Senatu, De Doma Sua* (57); *De Haruspicum Responso, Pro Sestio, In Vatinium, Pro Caelio, De Provinciis Consularibus, Pro Balbo* (56); *In Pisonem* (55); *Pro Plancio, Pro Rabirio Postumo* (54); *Pro Milone* (52); *Pro Marcello, Pro Ligario* (46); *Pro Rege Deiotaro* (45); *Philippicae* I-XIV (44–43). In *Pro Fonteio* he defended Marcus Fonteius, former governor of Gaul, on charges similar to those on which he had secured the conviction of Verres the year before. *Pro Cluentio* was notable for the clever handling of a highly equivocal case in behalf of a client for whom Cicero had little use. The two speeches, *Post Reditum ad Quirites* and *Post Reditum in Senatu,* were addressed to the Roman people and Senate on his recall from exile. *De Doma Sua* was a plea for the restoration of his house, and *De Haruspicum Responso* was a dissertation on an Etruscan soothsayer's interpretation of an earthquake, which Clodius had taken to mean disapproval of the restoration of Cicero's property. In *Pro Caelio* he defended Marcus Caelius Rufus who was charged, among other things, with an intention to poison Clodia, sister of Clodius Pulcher, and with having bought the poison with gold given to him by Clodia herself. In the speech Cicero defended the sowing of wild oats by the young man and castigated Clodia for her morals and manner of living. With the two speeches *De Provinciis Consularibus* and *Pro Balbo*, Cicero made his peace with Caesar and Pompey; in the first he dealt with the command in Gaul, and in the second he upheld the claim to citizenship of Pompey's protégé Lucius Cornelius Balbus. The published speech *Pro Milone* is not the same as that delivered in defense of Titus Annius Milo, accused of slaying Cicero's old enemy Clodius Pulcher. Milo was condemned and went into exile. *Pro Marcello*, *Pro Ligario*, and *Pro Rege Deiotaro* were addressed to Caesar in behalf of former supporters of Pompey.

Rhetoric: *De Inventione* (84); *De Oratore (55)*; *Oratoriae Partitiones (c54)*; *De Optimo Genere Oratorum* (52); *Brutus* or *De Claris Oratoribus* (46); *Orator* (46); and *Topica* (44), which last was an adaptation and exposition of a work by Aristotle. These works form a compendium of Circero's ideas and conclusions on the subject of oratory. They include observations on style, the arrangement of subject-matter, use of language, manner of delivery, the qualities the orator himself must have, and a form of history of oratory in Greece and Rome.

Philosophy. Through Cicero Greek philosophy passed to western Europe. He did not claim to be an original thinker. On the contrary, he said of his philosophical writings that they were just copies; that he supplied nothing but the words, of which he had plenty. "Supplying the words" may be taken quite literally, for Latin, lacking a philosophical tradition, also lacked the words with which to express philosophical concepts. Cicero provided them, as well as clear, simple expositions of the concepts themselves. In periods of political inactivity he turned to philosophy. *De Republica* (54), in six books, is a blueprint for the best constitution for Rome, and ends with the famous "Dream of Scipio." *De Legibus* (of which three books survive) discusses the function of law and sets forth laws as he thinks they should be. *Hortensius* (45?) and *De Consolatione* (45) have been lost. The first concerned the orator Hortensius and is said to have caused St. Augustine to study philosophy. The second is Cicero's consolation to himself on the death of his daughter. *Paradoxa Stoicorum* (46?) deals with certain Stoic maxims. *Academica* (45) in two books, is an exposition of the Academic school, descended from Plato, which most nearly coincided with Cicero's own conclusions. *De Finibus Bonorum et Malorum* (45?) discusses Epicureanism and Stoicism in the first four books and ends, in the fifth book, with statements of Academic ideas. *Tusculanarum Quaestionum* (45?), in five books, treats fear of death, pain, grief, other disturbances of the soul, and virtue, which last is declared to be sufficient for happiness; the whole is ornamented with many quotations from Greek and Roman writers and with many examples. In the three books of *De Natura Deorum* (45?) the Epicurean, Stoic, and Academic precepts are again set forth. *De Divinatione*, in two books, argues the validity of oracles; *De Fato* discusses whether man's fate and actions are predestined. *Cato Major* or *De Senectute* is an essay in which Cicero has Cato the Elder describing the advantages and comforts of old age to Laelius and the younger Scipio. The work was dedicated to Cicero's friend Atticus. *Laelius* or *De Amicitia* (44) is concerned with friendship. For his son Marcus, who stood in need of it, Cicero wrote *De Officiis* (44), in three books, on duties.

Letters. Cicero was a tireless letter writer. Thirty-seven books of his letters are extant, and represent only a part of the letters known to antiquity. From those that have been preserved, especially those to such intimates as Atticus, emerges a vivid picture of turbulent Rome, and a portrait in death of the hopes and fears, weaknesses and strength, of its most articulate citizen.

Cimon (sī'mon). Son of Miltiades, who gained the victory at Marathon, and Hegesipyle, daughter of Olorus, prince of Thrace. It is said that he led a gay and irresponsible life as a young man, but when Aristides recognized his latent ability and encouraged him to enter public life, he gained popularity quickly with his generosity and his honesty, and added to it with his military victories. One of his first acts was to pay the 50 talents his father had been fined for having deceived the Athenians about the use he intended to make of the 70 ships they had granted him some time after his victory at Marathon. Payment of this sum was a heavy financial burden, but Cimon managed it. He served under Aristides in the Athenian fleet and later (477 B.C.) was made head of the Confederacy of Delos to carry on the war against Persia. He commanded a squadron sent out by the Athenians against Pausanias, the Spartan hero of Plataea, who at this time seemed ready to betray his counry to the Persians. Cimon seized Sestos on the Hellespont and drove him out of Byzantium (476 B.C.). He captured Eion (476–5 B.C.), a fortress at the mouth of the Strymon River, from its Persian governor, Boges, and wrested all the cities of the seaboard of Thrace, except Doriscus, from the Persians. After the battle of Marathon, in which the image of Theseus was said to have aided the Athenians, the priestess of Delphi had ordered that the bones of Theseus be recovered from the island of Scyrus and brought to Athens. Scyrus was infested with Dolophian pirates, who continually preyed on Athenian commerce, and the Athenians were warned that the raids would continue so long as the bones of the Athenian hero remained in Scyrus. Cimon led an expedition against Scyrus (c474 B.C.), cleared the pirates from the island, and reduced the natives to slavery. But the inhabitants would not tell him where Theseus was buried. According to tradition, Cimon saw an eagle tearing at the earth with its talons. He regarded this as a sign from heaven, went to the spot, and dug in the hole started by the eagle. A stone coffin was revealed, in which rested the bones of a very tall man and a bronze spear and sword. As the bones of Theseus, these were reverently carried back to Athens and reburied with a great public ceremony in the sanctuary of Theseus. The recovery of the bones of Theseus added greatly to the popularity of the already popular general. As a final blow at Persian power he led an expedition against the Persians in southern waters off Asia Minor, in which he delivered the Greek towns of Caria from Persian rule, brought the Lycian cities into the Confederacy of Delos, and overcame the Persian land and sea forces at the battle of the Eurymedon (468 B.C.). Plunder taken in the expedition was used to rebuild the walls of the Acropolis at Athens. About 463 B.C. he put down a revolt on the island of Thasus and forced the inhabitants to pull down their walls, surrender their ships, and pay tribute to Athens. After the death of Themistocles and Aristides, Cimon had become

fat, fāte, fär, fâll, ȧsk, fãre; net, mē, hėr; pin, pīne; not, nōte, möve, nôr; up, lūte, pùll; oi, oil; ou out; (lightened) ĕlect, agŏny, ūnite;

the dominant figure in Athens and was elected general of the Confederacy year after year. He was a noble and, conservative in his views, did not forward the democracy that was developing in Athens, although by his victories he helped to make it possible. With the rise of Pericles his influence was threatened. He was accused of having accepted a bribe from the Macedonians, but was acquitted. When he led a force to aid Sparta to put down a revolt of the helots, the Athenians were rebuffed by Sparta, who feared the rising power of Athens, and Cimon's policy of friendship with Sparta was repudiated by the Spartans themselves. In his absence from Athens, Pericles and Ephialtes, his political enemies, made many democratic and popular reforms. When Cimon returned, his Spartan policy discredited and Athens insulted, he was denounced as a lover of Sparta and was ostracized (461 B.C.). At the battle of Tanagra (457 B.C.), Cimon appeared at the Athenian camp and asked permission to fight for his country against Sparta, but permission was denied. Nevertheless, his supporters fought so stubbornly that although Athens was defeated, the Spartans were forced to withdraw. Cimon's action in this case prepared the way for his recall. Athens was exhausted by the long war with Sparta and wanted a truce; Cimon was recalled to bring it about (451 B.C.), after which he retired to a place outside Athens. Later he was recalled by Pericles to command an expedition against Persia. At the head of a large fleet he sailed to Cyprus to attack the Phoenician fleet gathered there to keep Cyprus under Persian control. He died at Citium in Cyprus (c450 B.C.) and was buried in Athens. The main points of Cimon's policy were to prosecute the war against Persia, which he did successfully, and to remain on friendly terms with Sparta, for with Athens as a great sea power and Sparta a great land power, a united Greece would be invulnerable. Because of Sparta's fear of the growing power of Athens, this part of Cimon's policy was a failure. One of the main effects of his dominance in Athens was the change in the voluntary nature of the Confederacy of Delos; it became an organization in which membership was compulsory. Carystus, Naxos, and Thasus were forced to pay tribute to it. This marked the emergence of Athens as an empire.

Cincinnatus (sin-si-nā'tus, -nat'us), **Lucius Quinctius.** Roman hero, to whose life later writers have added embellishments, born c519 B.C.; fl. 1st half of the 5th century B.C. He was consul suffectus in 460 B.C. and distinguished himself as an opponent of the plebeians in the struggle between them and the patricians in the period 462–454 B.C. In 458 B.C. a Roman army under Lucius Minucius having been surrounded by the Aequi in a defile of Mount Algidus, he was named dictator by the Senate whose deputies, dispatched to inform him of his appointment, found him digging in the field on his farm beyond the Tiber. He gained a complete victory over the Aequi, and laid down the dictatorship after the lapse of only 16 days, then returning to his farm. In 439 B.C., at the age of 80, he was appointed dictator to opose the traitor Spurius Melius, who was defeated and slain. The details of his story vary; the story of the first dictatorship is probably legendary embellishment on a factual basis; that of the second dictatorship is probably wholly false.

Cinna (sin'ạ), **Caius Helvius.** Roman tribune and poet; a friend of Catullus. On the occasion of the funeral of Julius Caesar (44 B.C.), he was slain by the populace, who mistook him for Lucius Cornelius Cinna (fl. 44 B.C.).

Cinna, Lucius Cornelius. Roman general and statesman; slain in a mutiny at Brundisium, Italy, 84 B.C. He was celebrated as a leader of the popular party and an opponent of Sullà; father of Lucius Cornelius Cinna (fl. 44 B.C.). He was consul with Octavius in 87 B.C., with Marius in 86 B.C., and was also consul in the period 85–84 B.C. During his first consulship he took advantage of Sulla's absence from Rome to recall Marius and attempted to pass a voting bill in opposition to Sulla's partisans. Cinna was defeated in his attempt and was removed as consul. He raised a force and besieged the city. A massacre of Sulla's supporters took place after Marius' return. Cinna's daughter Cornelia was Julius Caesar's first wife.

Cinna, Lucius Cornelius. Roman politican; active 44 B.C. He was the son of Lucius Cornelius Cinna (d. 84 B.C.) and brother-in-law of Julius Caesar. He was praetor in 44 B.C. He sided with the conspirators against Caesar.

Claudius I (klô'di-us). [Full name, **Tiberius Claudius Drusus Nero;** surnamed **Germanicus.**] Emperor of Rome in the period 41–54 A.D. He was born at Lugdunum in Gaul, Aug. 1,

fat, fāte, fär, fâll, ȧsk, fãre; net, mē, hėr; pin, pīne; not, nōte, mŏve, nôr; up, lūte, pŭll; oi, oil; ou out; (lightened) ĕlect, agǫny, ūnite;

10 B.C.; died 54 A.D. He was the grandson of Tiberius Claudius Nero and Livia Drusilla, who afterward became the third wife of Augustus, and son of Drusus Germanicus (sometimes called Drusus Senior) and Antonia, the daughter of Mark Antony. He was excluded from public affairs by Caligula, his predecessor, although the empty honor of consulship was bestowed on him in 37 by his nephew Caligula, on whose murder in 41 he was proclaimed emperor by the praetorian guards. Because Claudius was naturally of a mild and amiable disposition, his accession was signalized by acts of clemency and justice, which, however, under the influence of his third wife, Valeria Messalina, and his favorites, the freedmen Narcissus, Pallas, and others, were subsequently obscured by cruelty and bloodshed. He visited Britain in 43. In 49, after the execution of Messalina, who, during Claudius' absence at Ostia, had contracted a public marriage with Caius Silius, he married his niece Agrippina the younger. She persuaded him to set aside his own son Britannicus, and to adopt her son by a former marriage, Lucius Domitius, as his successor. When he repented of this step soon after, he is thought to have been poisoned by Agrippina, and Lucius Domitius ascended the throne under the name of Nero. The Claudian aqueduct at Rome was built during his reign and named for him. Claudius was noted for his writing, but none of his works is extant.

Claudius, Appius. [Surnamed *Sabinus Inregillensis* or *Regillensis*.] Original name, Attus or Attius Clausus. Roman consul. Coming from Regillum in the Sabine country to Rome c504 B.C., with others of the Claudian family, of whom some were patricians and some plebeians, he seems to have gathered a number of families into a tribe which evidently was a force to be reckoned with, for he was admitted to the ranks of the patricians, at that time taking the name Appius Claudius, and was elected consul in 495 B.C. In that office he applied the laws concerning debts with a severity which caused the plebeians to take refuge on the sacred mount.

Claudius, Appius. [Surnamed *Crassus.*] Roman consul (471, 451 B.C.). In 451 B.C. he was a decemvir (one of ten magistrates) appointed to draw up a new code of laws. These decemvirs held virtually complete ruling powers during their time in office. In 450 B.C. the group was reconstituted, and Appius Claudius became its leading member, popular with patricians and plebeians alike, although his suggested legislation favoring plebeians roused considerable opposition. He remained in office until the group resigned in 449 B.C. Legend connects Claudius with Virginia, a young woman supposedly killed by her father, Virginius, to save her from being possessed by Appius Claudius, and advances this story as the cause for the public indignation that brought about the fall of the decemvirs. In fact, however, there may not be any connection at all.

Claudius, Appius. [Surnamed *Caecus,* meaning "the Blind."] Roman statesman, who died after 280 B.C. He was censor in the period 312–c308 B.C., and consul in 307 and 296 B.C. He advised the Romans not to make an alliance with King Pyrrhus of Epirus. He commenced the Appian Way and completed the Appian aqueduct, the first at Rome. He abolished the limitation of the full right of citizenship to landed proprietors.

Claudius, Appius. [Surnamed *Pulcher.*] Roman politician; brother of Clodius (Publius Clodius Pulcher); died in Euboea, c48 B.C. Before serving as governor in Sardinia he had been praetor in 57 B.C. He was consul in 54, proconsul in Cilicia from 53 to 51, and censor in 50 B.C. In 49 B.C. he was a follower of Pompey.

Claudius, Publius. [Surnamed *Pulcher.*] Roman consul of the 3rd century B.C.; son of the consul Appius Claudius (surnamed Caecus). While consul in 249 B.C., he commanded the Roman fleet in the course of the First Punic War, and was disastrously defeated at Drepanum. It was believed that this disaster resulted from an impious act by Claudius. Just before the Roman and Carthaginian fleets clashed, the sacred chickens carried on the Roman ships are said to have refused to eat. This act was an alarming omen. Claudius said, "If they will not eat, let them drink," and ordered them thrown overboard. For this and certain other acts, he was accused of treason and heavily fined. It is thought that he died in 246 B.C. or earlier, probably a suicide.

Clearchus (klē-är′kus). Lacedaemonian general, born at Sparta; executed by Artaxerxes II, 401 B.C. He fought at the battle of Cyzicus in 410 B.C. when the Spartan fleet was destroyed by Alcibiades. In 408 B.C. his tyrannous conduct as governor of Byzantium during the siege by the Athenians led to the surrender of the city by the inhabitants during his absence

fat, fāte, fär, fåll, åsk, fāre; net, mē, hėr; pin, pīne; not, nōte, möve, nôr; up, lūte, pùll; oi, oil; ou out; (lightened) ĕlect, agǫny, ūnite;

in Asia, whither he had gone to collect a force to raise the siege. In 406 he fought under Callicratidas at the naval battle of Arginusae, where the Spartans again were defeated, this time by Conon. After the Peloponnesian War he persuaded the *ephors* (magistrates) to send him as general to Thrace to protect the Greeks against the natives. Having proceeded thither in spite of an order for his recall which overtook him on the way, he was condemned to death. Defeated by a force sent against him, he fled to Cyrus the Younger, who was seeking to wrest the Persian throne from his brother Artaxeres II. Clearchus offered him his services and raised a force of over 13,000 Greek mercenaries to fight in his cause. A young Athenian officer, Xenophon, later known for his writings, was one of the Greek volunteers in the force. Clearchus, alone of the Greeks, knew that the object of the expedition which now set out under command of Cyrus was Babylon, where Artaxerxes II maintained his forces. When it became apparent to the Greeks that they were on the way to Babylon, a three months' march from the sea, they rebelled. Clearchus, a strict disciplinarian, attempted to put down the rebellion by force, but was unsuccessful. He resorted to a trick. The forces by this time had marched from Celaenae in Phrygia to Tarsus. They were a long way from home. Clearchus called his soldiers together, and then stood before them and wept before he spoke. Then he told them that their rebellion had placed him in an extremely difficult position: either he must break his pledged word to Cyrus or desert the Greeks. What, he asked his men, did they propose to do? They must decide, since he would not command them and could not pay them. They decided to go on as soldiers of Cyrus. Arrived, after a long march, before Babylon, Clearchus refused to adopt the wise plan of battle outlined by Cyrus, but Cyrus did not insist. In the battle against the forces of Artaxerxes II the Greeks were successful, but Cyrus, in his eagerness to slay his hated brother, was slain when he was on the point of victory; his forces fled in confusion. Thus the Greeks found themselves alone in the midst of enemies, and a long march from the sea. Artaxerxes was delighted to get rid of them and let them go. They were to be guided by the Persian satrap Tissaphernes, who marched with his forces ahead of them. On the way the suspicion and hostility between the two forces became so sharp that Clearchus sought a conference with Tissaphernes. Tissaphernes advised him to meet in his tent and to bring the leading Greek generals with him. Clearchus went to the Persian satrap's tent with his principal generals. They were all treacherously seized by Tissaphernes, bound in fetters, and sent to the court of Artaxerxes, where they were executed. The surviving Greeks chose new generals and accomplished the famous retreat known as the "Retreat of the Ten Thousand," the story of which is told in Xenophon's *Anabasis.*

Cleisthenes (klĭs'thē-nēz). See *Clisthenes.*

Cleobulus (klē-ọ̄-bū'lus, klẹ̄-ob'ụ̄-lus). Tyrant of Lindus, born at Lindus, Rhodes, and flourished in the 6th century B.C. He was one of the Seven Sages of Greece. The reputed author of various riddles, he is credited with having formulated the first literary riddle. His daughter Cleobulina shares his reputed skill in riddles, being credited with inventing the riddle on the year: "A father has 12 children, each has 30 daughters, white on one side, black on the other; all are immortal, yet they die."

Cleombrotus (klẹ̄-om'brọ̄-tus). Regent of Sparta early in the 5th century B.C. He was the son of Anaxandridas, king of Sparta. Anaxandridas was married to his niece, whom he loved dearly, but as she bore him no children, the Spartan ephors and elders asked him to put her aside and take another wife that he might have an heir to the throne. Anaxandridas refused to give up the wife he loved. He agreed, however, to act on a suggestion of the ephors and elders, which was to take an additional wife, while he continued to love and honor his first wife as before. As a result of this advice he had two wives and lived with them in two separate houses; this was quite contrary to Spartan custom. The new wife bore him Cleomenes, who became his legitimate heir. Then the first wife produced, in rapid succession, Dorieus, Leonidas (the hero of Thermopylae), and Cleombrotus. Cleombrotus was regent of Sparta during the Persian War and commanded the forces that gathered at the Isthmus of Corinth after the death of Leonidas and built a wall across the Isthmus to keep the Persians out of the Peloponnesus. When the wall was built, Cleombrotus sacrificed victims to learn whether he should march against the Persians. As he was offering the sacrifices, the face of the sun was darkened in mid-sky. Cleombrotus interpreted this as a warning and marched his army back to Sparta, where shortly thereafter he died. The prodigy of the darkened sun was a partial eclipse which occurred October 2, 480 B.C.

Cleombrotus I. King of Sparta, 380–371 B.C.; killed at Leuctra, 371 B.C. He was co-king with Agesilaus, and was sent to Boeotia (378 B.C.) when the pro-Spartan rulers of Thebes were slain and the Spartan garrison expelled from the city as the result of a plot by the Theban patriot Pelopidas. Various maneuvers carried on by Cleombrotus in the vicinity were fruitless. He could not enter Boeotia because the mountain passes of Cithaeron were securely held by the Thebans. In 371 B.C. he led an army from Phocis against Thebes, to free the Boeotian cities from the Boeotian Confederacy which some had joined under compulsion. This march was a distinct violation of the Peace of Callias, concluded in the same year, by which all the signatories, Sparta among them, agreed to bring their armies home and remove their garrisons from foreign cities. Cleombrotus went first to the port of Creusis on the Gulf of Corinth, seized it and captured some Theban ships at anchor there. He then proceeded toward Thebes. The Thebans under Epaminondas marched out against him and barred his way at Leuctra. The Thebans took up position on the hills on one side of the Asopus River; the Spartans ranged themselves on the hills across the stream. When the opposing forces moved down the hills and engaged, the army of Cleombrotus was shattered by the impact of the Thebans, spearheaded by the Sacred Band. Cleombrotus was slain in the fighting and his army admitted defeat by asking for a truce to bury their dead (371 B.C.). This defeat marked the end of Spartan leadership in Greece that had been unquestioned since the end of the Peloponnesian Wars (404 B.C.).

Cleomenes I (klē-om'ē-nēz). King of Sparta from c519–487 B.C. He was the son of Anaxandridas, king of Sparta, and half-brother to Cleombrotus (q.v.), Dorieus, and Leonidas. He succeeded his father as king. Maeandrius, a man of Samos, fled to Sparta to seek aid against the Persians. He sought to bribe Cleomenes, but the latter refused to accept the bribe and advised the Spartan ephors to send Maeandrius away, lest he succeed in bribing someone else to give aid to Samos. Aristagoras also sought his aid when he was stirring up the

Ionian revolt against the Persians. He painted a glowing picture of the ease with which Cleomenes could overcome the Persians and of the treasures he would gain thereby. Cleomenes, on learning that the Persian capital was a three-month march from the sea, refused to consider fighting the Persians and ordered Aristagoras to leave Sparta before sunset. Aristagoras persisted. He took an olive branch and went as a suppliant to Cleomenes' house. He offered him ten talents if he would bring Sparta to the aid of the Ionians. Cleomenes shook his head. Aristagoras raised the offer, and continued to raise it each time Cleomenes shook his head. At last Gorgo, the eight or nine year old daughter of Cleomenes who was present at this interview, interrupted and advised her father to send the stranger away before he was corrupted. Cleomenes thought her advice was good and sent Aristagoras away. At the same time, he again proved his own honesty. In 510 B.C., as a consequence of repeated reminders from the oracle at Delphi to free the Athenians from the tyrannical Pisistratidae, Cleomenes led a force of Spartans against Athens and drove Hippias out of the city. He interfered in a struggle for control of Athens by ordering Clisthenes (one of two men who sought to rule the city) and his followers to leave Athens. He also sent 700 Athenian families into exile at the request of Isagoras and established the latter as ruler of Athens. But when he attempted to dissolve the Athenian council, the council resisted and, supported by the rest of the Athenians, compelled Cleomenes to withdraw. Thus was the oracle fulfilled, for when Cleomenes first went to the citadel of Athens and attempted to enter the temple, the priestess rose up and told him to withdraw. At the time Cleomenes ignored her command but in the end he was forced to withdraw from the city. Cleomenes felt that the Athenians had insulted him and resolved to punish them. He gathered a large force and invaded Eleusis, where he cut down the sacred grove of the goddess. The Athenians marched to Eleusis to engage him but as the two forces were about to go into battle, the Corinthian allies of Cleomenes withdrew. Demaratus, co-king of Sparta with Cleomenes, withdrew his forces also, and the other allies, seeing that the kings were not agreed, also withdrew. Cleomenes was compelled to retire. After this, Cleomenes contrived the removal of Demaratus as co-king

fat, fāte, fär, fâll, ȧsk, fãre; net, mē, hėr; pin, pīne; not, nōte, mȯve, nôr; up, lūte, pu̇ll; oi, oil; ou out; (lightened) ḝlect, agǫny, ụnite

(491 B.C.), on the grounds that Demaratus was not the true son of Ariston, king of Sparta. Cleomenes achieved success in this matter by bribing the priestess at Delphi to say that Demaratus was not the true son of Ariston. After this Leotychides, son of Menares, became co-king with Cleomenes. When the Spartans learned of the bribe, Cleomenes was forced to flee, first to Thessaly, and then to Arcadia. Then he stirred up the Arcadians against Sparta. The Spartans learned of his activities, and fearing that he might raise a war against them, invited him to return to Sparta and be king as before. On his return Cleomenes, who according to Herodotus had never been of very sound mind, was overcome by outright madness. This was caused, according to the Spartans, because of his habit of drinking wine unmixed with water. He struck every Spartan he met on the face with his scepter. The Spartans saw that he was mad and put him in prison, binding him in stocks. From a frightened helot he secured a knife and so gashed himself that he died of the wounds. The Greeks in general thought he had become mad for seducing the priestess of Delphi, but the Athenians considered that his horrible end was a punishment for destroying the sacred grove at Eleusis. The Argives had another account of his end. Once he had thought the oracle at Delphi told him he could take Argos. He led a force of Spartans to the Erasinus River to cross over to Argos. At the banks of the river he offered sacrifices but the victims were not favorable. He therefore embarked his forces on ships and went to Nauplia. The Argives marched to meet him and were defeated. Many of them sought refuge in the sacred grove of Argus. Cleomenes called for the leading Argive warriors by name, one at a time, pretending he had received their ransoms. When they came out of the grove, he treacherously killed them. His treachery being discovered, no more Argives came forth when he called their names. He now ordered his helots to set the grove afire, and some 6000 Argives who had taken refuge therein perished. When he learned that the grove was sacred to Argus, he felt that the oracle that told him he would take Argos had deceived him, and that now the oracle was fulfilled. The Argives said his end at his own hands was caused by his violation of the sacred grove and by his later blasphemy at the temple of Hera in Argos. As he had no son, only the one daughter

Gorgo, Cleomenes was succeeded by his half-brother Leoni
das, the older half-brother Dorieus having died.

Cleomenes III. King of Sparta, c225–c220 B.C., who died c219
B.C. He abolished the ephorate (a magistracy controlling the
kings) in 225 B.C., waged war with the Achaean League and
Macedonia in the period 225–222 B.C., and was defeated a
Sellasia in 222 B.C.

Cleon (klē′on). Athenian demagogue, killed at Amphipolis
Macedonia, 422 B.C. He was the son of Cleaenetus, a tanner
and was one of a new class of leaders who came to the
forefront in Athens during the Peloponnesian Wars. He was
of the people as distinguished from the former leaders who
had come from the aristocratic class, and won his place b′
his eloquence, shrewdness, daring, and ability. As unofficia
leader of the Athenian Assembly, he was an opponent o
Pericles whom he accused of maladministration. After the
death of Pericles (429 B.C.) he became one of the foremos
men in Athenian public life. He was an imperialist, whose
policy it was to keep a tight rein on the Athenian allies and
to maintain Athenian power by force. In furtherance of hi
policy he belonged to the war party that urged and sup
ported continuation of the war against Sparta. In 428 B.C
Mytilene, a free ally of Athens, revolted. The revolt was pu
down after a siege in 427 B.C. Cleon used his influence in the
Athenian Assembly to demand death for all the adult male
of Mytilene and enslavement of the women and children. He
argued that to be a strong state and rule an empire strong
measures must be used to crush opposition. The sentenc
he urged was so voted, but a reaction immediately set in and
the sentence was reconsidered and revoked the next day. In
succeeding years Cleon opposed Nicias, one of the chie
military leaders of Athens and the head of the aristocrati
party, who advocated peace with Sparta and the conclusio
of the Peloponnesian War. As leader of the democratic part
he called himself "the people's watch-dog" and oppose
those whom he suspected of undermining the democracy
Under his leadership the pay of jurors was increased, partl
to help the citizens impoverished by the war, the tribut
required of the allies was greatly increased, and the templ
treasuries were depleted of some of their treasures "bo
rowed" to help defray the costs of the war. When the Spar
tans occupied Pylus in Messenia, they were attacked by th

---

fat, fāte, fär, fåll, åsk, fāre; net, mē, hėr; pin, pīne; not, nōte, mȯv
nôr; up, lūte, pu̇ll; oi, oil; ou out; (lightened) e̤lect, ago̤ny, ūnit

Athenians, driven to the island of Sphacteria lying off the shore of Pylus, and blockaded by an Athenian fleet. They asked for a truce and sent an embassy to Athens proposing peace terms that would allow the Athenians to keep the advantages they had won owing, as the Spartans said, to Spartan "misfortunes." Cleon countered with such terms as he knew the Spartans could not accept. The Spartan embassy returned to Sphacteria and the garrison there submitted to siege (425 B.C.). As the weeks passed and the Spartan garrison continued to withstand the siege, Cleon suffered some loss of popularity because he had prevented peace. He expressed impatience with the delay in taking the island. He criticized the generals in Athens for not going to Pylus and taking charge of the siege themselves, and ended by saying that if he were commander, he would go and capture the Spartan garrison himself. Nicias, the commander, offered to give Cleon whatever forces he required and to send him there. As described by Thucydides, when Cleon saw that Nicias was in earnest, he tried to back out, saying that Nicias, not he, was the general. But Nicias formally gave him the command in the presence of the Assembly. Cleon tried again to withdraw, but the more he shrank from the undertaking, the more the people called on him to head the expedition. Finding himself boxed in by his own words, he asked for certain troops and promised either to take the Spartan garrison on Sphacteria alive or kill them on the spot, and within 20 days. These bold words evoked laughter from the Athenians, for it was well-known that Spartans were never taken alive. In Thucydides' words, "sensible men comforted themselves with the reflection that they must gain in either circumstance; either they would be rid of Cleon, which they rather hoped, or if disappointed in this expectation, would reduce the Lacedaemonians." As it turned out, the latter circumstance was fulfilled. Contrary to all expectations, Cleon brought about the surrender of the Spartan garrison within the promised 20 days, largely, to be sure, through the skill of his colleague, the Athenian general Demosthenes. Two hundred ninety-two Lacedaemonians were taken alive to Athens. Nothing that had happened in the war surprised the Greeks as much as this, for such was the reputation of the Spartans for fighting either to victory or death that it was impossible to believe that Cleon, a man

•bscured) errant, ardent, actor; ch, chip; g, go; th, thin; ᵵн, then; y, you; ariable) ḍ as d or j, ş as s or sh, ţ as t or ch, ẓ as z or zh.

of no military experience, had compelled them to surrender
The victory completely vindicated Cleon, reëstablished hi:
popularity, and gave him immense advantage over his politi
cal rivals. In the spring of 422 B.C. Cleon sailed as com
mander of an expedition to recover Amphipolis ii
Macedonia, which had been taken by the Spartans in 424
B.C. He marched toward Amphipolis, but on observing the
Spartan commander Brasidas sacrificing in the city, and not
ing what seemed to be large forces, he ordered his men to
retreat without engaging in battle. Noting the retreat, Brasi
das sallied out and fell on the Athenians. They were thrown
into confusion by the onslaught and fled. Cleon joined then
in panic-stricken flight, and was killed by the enemy as he
fled. Cleon was satirized by Aristophanes in the *Acharnians*
the *Wasps,* and especially in the *Knights* (424 B.C.), in which
Aristophanes himself was forced to play Cleon, as none o
the players dared to take the role that showed the popula
hero in an unfavorable light. However, Aristophanes' pic
ture of Cleon was colored by the fact that the latter had
hailed him before the courts because of an earlier comedy
Thucydides too, who gives an unfavorable portrayal o
Cleon in his history of the Peloponnesian Wars, was un
doubtedly prejudiced by the fact that Cleon had caused him
to be exiled after the loss of Amphipolis (424 B.C.).

Cleopatra (klē̦-ō̦-pā′tra̧, -pat′ra̧). Wife of Philip II of Macedon
died c335 B.C. She was the niece of Attalus, one of Philip'
generals. Philip divorced his wife Olympias, the mother o
Alexander, to marry her. After the murder of Philip (33(
B.C.), Cleopatra's father was murdered, her infant was slain
in her arms, and she was forced to hang herself. These
murders were brought about by Olympias in revenge fo
being cast aside by Philip. They also removed a possible
rival of Alexander for the throne and those who might con
test his right to it.

Cleopatra. [In the chronology of Egyptian queens, *Cleopatr
VII.*] Last Macedonian queen of Egypt, born at Alexandria
Egypt, 69 B.C.; died there, 30 B.C. She was the daughter o
Ptolemy XII, called Ptolemy Auletes. In accordance with
Egyptian tradition, she was wife of and joint ruler with he
brother Ptolemy XIII from 51 to 49 B.C., when she wa
expelled by him. Her reinstatement in 48 B.C. by Caesa
gave rise to war between Caesar and Ptolemy. The latter wa

fat, fāte, fär, fȧll, ȧsk, fãre; net, mē, hèr; pin, pīne; not, nōte, mȯv
nôr; up, lūte, pu̇ll; oi, oil; ou out; (lightened) ḛlect, agǫny, ūnit

defeated and drowned as he tried to escape, and his younger brother, Ptolemy XIV, was elevated to the throne in his stead and married to her. Cleopatra lived with Caesar at Rome from 46 to 44 B.C., and had by him a son, Ptolemy XV, usually known as Caesarion because of his father; the child was afterward put to death by Augustus. She returned to Egypt after the murder of Caesar, and in the civil war which ensued sided with the Triumvirate (Octavian, Antony, and Lepidus). Mark Antony having been appointed ruler of Asia and the East, she visited him at Tarsus in Cilicia in 41 B.C., making a voyage of extraordinary splendor and magnificence up the Cydnus. She gained by her charms a complete ascendancy over him. On her account he divorced his wife Octavia, the sister of Octavian, in 32 B.C. Octavian declared war against her in 31 B.C. The fleet of Antony and Cleopatra was defeated in the same year as the battle of Actium, which was decided by the flight of Cleopatra's ships, Antony being forced to follow. After the death of Antony, who killed himself on hearing a false report of her death (according to some, a report deliberately spread by her in an attempt to win Octavian's favor by causing his death), she poisoned herself to avoid being exhibited at Rome at the triumph of Octavian, but not until she had made an attempt to charm Octavian as she had Caesar and Antony. According to the popular belief, she applied to her bosom an asp that had been secretly conveyed to her in a basket of figs. Ocatvian was so anxious to have her in his triumphal procession that, some say, he sent a snake charmer to try to revive her by sucking out the poison. Cleopatra had three children by Antony. Besides extraordinary charms of person, she possessed an active and cultivated mind, and is said to have been able to converse in seven languages. Her reputed personality and the events of the latter part of her reign, as described by Plutarch, form the basis of Shakespeare's *Antony and Cleopatra.*

Cleophon (klē′ō-fon). Athenian demagogue; executed 404 B.C. He was a lyremaker, and was said to be of Thracian origin. He came to the forefront in the last years of the Peloponnesian War. He favored a strong imperialist policy, was a leader of the war party, and opposed the oligarchical party. As a popular leader he instituted the "two-obol" payment, which is thought to have been a kind of dole to those whose

livelihoods had been destroyed by the long war with Sparta,
and he provided employment for the impoverished Athenians by a program of public works, among them being the
completion of the Erechtheum. After the Athenian victory
over the Peloponnesian fleet at Cyzicus (410 B.C.), Sparta
made peace offers to Athens which would have ended the
war in a draw. Cleophon opposed the terms and they were
rejected. Again, in 406 B.C., following the Athenian victory
at Arginusae, Sparta proposed peace and again Cleophon
used his considerable influence to oppose it. A year later the
Spartans defeated the Athenians at Aegospotami and followed up their victory by blockading Athens. Athens was
now compelled to seek peace. Cleophon, who had twice
prevented the conclusion of an honorable peace, now prevented the acceptance of terms that were humiliating. However, the Athenians, blockaded and starving, had no longer
any choice. In a wave of feeling against him, Cleophon was
sentenced to death in 404 B.C. by the Athenian council and
executed.

Clinias (klī'ni-as). Athenian commander; killed at the battle of
Coronea, 447 B.C. He was the father of Alcibiades. In the
Persian War he furnished a vessel and provided 200 men at
his own expense. He served with distinction at the battle of
Artemisium in 480 B.C.

Clisthenes (klīs'thē-nēz) or *Cleisthenes* (klis'-). Tyrant of Sicyon
a city in the Peloponnesus, early in the 6th century B.C. (fl
580 B.C.). He was leader of the Ionian part of the population
who turned upon the conquering Dorians and subjected and
humiliated them. When he was at war with Argos, a Dorian
city, he decreed an end to the contests of the rhapsodists a
Sicyon because Argos and the Argives figured so promi
nently in the Homeric poems. He also sought to extinguish
the worship of the Argive hero Adrastus in Sicyon. Clis
thenes consulted the oracle at Delphi on this matter. The
priestess said to him, "Adrastus is the Sicyonians' king, but
you are only a robber." After this discouraging reply Clis
thenes dared not use direct means to expel Adrastus, and
sought to end his worship by establishing a shrine of Mela
nippus in Sicyon. Melanippus was a Theban hero and a great
enemy of Adrastus, having slain his brother and his son-in
law Tydeus. Once Clisthenes had established the shrine of
Melanippus he took away all the honors formerly bestowed

fat, fāte, fär, fâll, åsk, fāre; net, mē, hėr; pin, pīne; not, nōte, mōve
nôr; up, lūte, pùll; oi, oil; ou out; (lightened) ėlect, agǫny, ūnite

on Adrastus and accorded them to Melanippus. He also renamed the Sicyonian tribes so that they would not have the same names as the Argive tribes. He had a daughter, Agariste, for whom he wished to find the best husband in Greece. At the Olympic Games, at which he won the chariot race, he had a proclamation made in which he invited all who considered themselves worthy to be his son-in-law to come and visit him for a year in Sicyon, at the end of which time he would choose one of them for his daughter. Many nobles from all over the Greek world accepted his invitation. They assembled from Italy, Aetolia, all over the Peloponnesus, Athens, Euboea, and Thessaly. Clisthenes prepared athletic grounds to test their prowess. In the year following their arrival the suitors were observed and tested as to their backgrounds, characters, accomplishments, and above all, their social accomplishments, and for this reason many hours were spent over the banquet table. During the year Clisthenes watched them closely, and found that the two who pleased him most were Hippoclides and Megacles, both of Athens; and of the two he preferred Hippoclides. When the time came for him to announce the successful suitor, he sacrificed 100 oxen and gave a great feast. The suitors entertained with speech and song. Hippoclides called to the flute players for a dance, whereupon he himself got up and began to dance. Clisthenes observed him with misgiving. Then Hippoclides called for a table, leaped upon it and continued to dance wildly. As Clisthenes watched with growing disgust, Hippoclides stood on his head on the table and made his feet do a jig in the air. Clisthenes lost all patience with him and called out, "You have danced your wife away." But Hippoclides was besotted with his own dancing and replied, "What does Hippoclides care?" From then on his reply became proverbial. Clisthenes now announced that the Alcmaeonid Megacles was his choice for a son-in-law. He gave rich presents and many compliments to the unsuccessful suitors and sent them back to their homes. Among the famous descendants of Clisthenes from this marriage were Clisthenes of Athens and Pericles. Clisthenes supported the Amphictyonic League in defending Delphi in the First Sacred War (590 B.C.). The men of Crisa (Cirrha), in whose territory the oracle of Apollo had been founded at Delphi, claimed control of it and levied toll on all visitors passing through their land to Delphi. The Delphian priests wished to be masters of their oracle and sought help from the Amphictyonic League, to which Clisthenes also gave his aid for the holy war in defense of the oracle. Crisa was taken after a struggle and destroyed. The land around the city was dedicated to the god, and the gulf formerly called Crisaean was henceforth known as the Gulf of Corinth. From this time the priests at Delphi became independent, and from this dates the period of the ascendancy of the Delphic oracle. The Pythian Games were splendidly reorganized, and Clisthenes won in the first chariot-race of the reorganized games. Valiant and able in war, Clisthenes was reputed a wise and humane ruler.

Clisthenes or ***Cleisthenes.*** Athenian politician of the 6th century B.C. He was the son of Megacles and the grandson of Clisthenes, tyrant of Sicyon, and was the most prominent of the Alcmaeonidae, the noble family important in Athenian politics at that period. Clisthenes and Isagoras struggled for control of Athens after the Pisistratid tyrants had been expelled with the aid of Cleomenes the Spartan (510 B.C.). Clisthenes won the advantage. He developed in a democratic spirit the constitution of Solon (adopted 594 B.C.) by substituting ten new for four old tribes, with a view to breaking up the influence of the landowning aristocracy, the new tribes being composed not of contiguous *demes* (local administrative communities), but of demes scattered through the area and interspersed with those of other tribes. The new tribes, which he named for native Athenian heroes, included new classes of free inhabitants and, with an enlarged council of 500, formed the basis of a popular government. Clisthenes, his followers, and 700 families who supported him were expelled in 507 B.C. by Isagoras, leader of the aristocratic party, aided by a Spartan army under Cleomenes, but he was recalled in the same year by the populace, which compelled the Spartans to withdraw and sent Isagoras into exile. On regaining his power he feared the Spartans, and sent envoys to King Darius in Susa to ask a treaty of alliance with the Persians. Darius agreed to an alliance provided the Athenians would give him earth and water as tokens of their submission to the Persians. The envoys agreed to this, but when they returned to Athens, they were disgraced for their submission to Darius and the

fat, fāte, fär, fåll, åsk, fāre; net, mē, hėr; pin, pīne; not, nōte, mȯve, nôr; up, lūte, pu̇ll; oi, oil; ou out; (lightened) ėlect, agǫny, ūnite;

treaty of alliance was abandoned. According to tradition, Clisthenes established ostracism, the power of the sovereign popular assembly, the *ecclesia,* to decree, by means of a secret ballot, the banishment of any citizen who endangered the public liberty.

Clitus (klī′tus). [Also: *Cleitus;* surnamed *Melas,* meaning "the Black."] Macedonian general died at Maracanda (Samarkand), Sogdiana, 328 B.C. He was the friend and foster brother, so-called, of Alexander the Great, and accompanied him on the campaigns in Asia. At the battle of the Granicus River (334 B.C.) he saved Alexander's life. As Alexander increased his conquests and penetrated deeper into Asia, he adopted Oriental customs which were greatly resented by many of his Macedonian friends. At Maracanda Alexander summoned his friends, Clitus among them, to a feast. In former years Alexander had been most temperate in his habits, but on the march through Media and into the depths of Asia he and his men became accustomed to drinking the strong wine of the country as the only means of quenching their thirst; since the water in many places was not fit to drink. On this, as on other evenings, much wine flowed. The poets and musicians who accompanied the army sang the praises of Alexander, comparing him to the Dioscuri in whose honor the feast was given. Clitus, having drunk deep, suddenly leaped up and accused the singers of blasphemy. Inflamed by wine and deep resentment, he accused Alexander of preferring the conquered barbarians, who bowed the knee to him, to the company of free-born Greeks who dared speak their minds. Friends of both tried to quiet Clitus, but he insisted on pouring out his grievances and complaints against Alexander and went so far as to imply that Alexander unjustly took credit for victories his friends had won. Elders in the company removed Alexander's sword, but when Clitus reminded Alexander that he had saved his life and recited some verses of Euripides with an implied insult, Alexander seized a spear and ran it through his old friend's body. Although he instantly came to his senses and would have killed himself in his remorse for the death of his friend, the slaying of Clitus by Alexander in a drunken brawl marks the beginning of a definite change, for the worse, in Alexander's relation to his own Macedonians and in his ideas of kingship.

(obscured) errạnt, ardẹnt, actọr; ch, chip; g, go; th, thin; ᴛʜ, then; y, you; (variable) ḍ as d or j, ṣ as s or sh, ṭ as t or ch, ẓ as z or zh.

Clodia (klō'di-ạ). Roman woman of patrician family; fl. 1st century B.C. The sister of Appius Claudius and of Publius Clodius (both surnamed Pulcher), she was reputedly of great beauty, intelligence, ambition, and extremely unconventional morals. Among her several lovers was Catullus, in whose poems she appears under the name of Lesbia. She was accused of murdering her husband Q. Caecilius Metellus Celer, and on her part she alleged that one of her lovers, M. Caelius Rufus, tried to murder her.

Clodius (klō'di-us), *Publius.* [Also: *Claudius;* surnamed *Pulcher.*] Roman adventurer and demagogue, born c93 B.C.; died Jan. 20, 52 B.C. He was the brother of Appius Claudius (also surnamed Pulcher) and of Clodia. He fought in the Third Mithridatic War, and when his services were not as well rewarded by Lucullus as he wished, he instigated a revolt, beginning the career of violence which made him notorious. In 62 B.C., disguising himself as a woman, he got admitted to the house of Julius Caesar during the observance of the Bona Dea ceremonies which were for women only. This caused a great scandal; one result was that Caesar divorced his wife Pompeia, who was said to have aided Clodius to gain entrance to the ceremonies. Another result was that Cicero prosecuted Clodius, who won acquital by bribery and became Cicero's relentless enemy. Clodius, a member of a patrician family, arranged to be adopted by a plebeian so that he might qualify for the office of tribune, which offered the maximum opportunity for demagoguery. He was elected tribune in 58 B.C. and brought about the exile of Cicero and of Cato the Younger, causing Cicero's property, moreover, to be confiscated. Determined to dominate Rome, Clodius not only wooed public favor by demagogic means, but also organized gangs of strong-armed men to assault his enemies. Pompey and Milo organized a rival mob, and Rome was terrorized by the violent conflicts of these opposing forces until Clodius was killed by Milo's adherents. The disorders promoted by Clodius prepared the way for the civil war between Pompey and Caesar.

Cnaeus (or *Cneius*) *Pompeius Magnus* (nē'us pom-pē'us mag'nus). See *Pompey.*

Codomannus (kọ-dọ-man'us), *Darius.* See *Darius III* (of *Persia*).

Codrus (kod'rus). Son of Melanthus, Messenian king who was driven from his land and became king of Athens. Codrus succeeded him and was the last king of Athens. He reigned (according to tradition) c1068 B.C. One legend is that Dorian invaders of Attica were assured by the Delphic oracle that success would come to that side whose king died. Codrus, having heard of this prophecy, disguised himself, and in unrecognizable, humble garb provoked a quarrel with some Dorian soldiers, taunting them until they killed him. This destroyed the premise by which the Dorians hoped to win, and Codrus thus saved his country by his own death. No one was considered worthy to succeed such a king. The archonship was established in Athens thenceforth, and Medon, son of Codrus, was appointed archon. But some say Codrus fell in battle. The sons of Codrus were the supposed founders of various Ionian cities, and thus connected Attica with Ionia. Among his sons was Neleus (or Nileus), named for the father of Nestor. He was said to have founded Miletus in Asia Minor. Other sons, and the cities they founded in Ionia, were Androclus (Ephesus), Damasichthon (Colophon), Andraemon (Lebedus), Damasus (Teos), Cyarethus (Myus), Cleopus (Erythrae), Promethus, and Naoclus.

Coes (kō′ēz). A Mytilenean general, contemporary with Darius the Great. He led the Mytileneans as allies of Darius when the latter bridged the Ister (Danube) and attacked Scythia. Coes advised Darius not to destroy the bridge after the crossing of the army as he had proposed to do, but to leave a detachment to guard it so that it would provide a means of return. Darius was so pleased by his advice that he promised to give Coes any boon he asked. On the return of the Persians from Scythia Coes asked to be made king of Mytilene. Darius remembered his promise and granted his request. Coes was later stoned to death by the Mytileneans when Ionia revolted against Darius.

Collatinus (kol-a̯-tī′nus), *Tarquinius*. Roman nobleman, fl. end of the 6th century B.C. His wife Lucretia was ravished by Tarquinius Sextus, son of the king Tarquinius Superbus. Collatinus, with others, vowed to punish the Tarquins whose harsh rule had made them very unpopular, and with Brutus and others he drove the Tarquins out of Rome. He was chosen (509 B.C.) with Brutus to be one of the two consuls who were to rule Rome in the place of the kings, and thus to transform it into a republic. Collatinus, though a nobleman and a relative of the Tarquins, was chosen because he would have the greatest reason for enmity to the Tarquins. However, when a plot by members of the Aquilii and Vitelii families to kill the consuls and restore Tarquin was exposed, Collatinus would have allowed the plotters, many of whom were related to him, to leave the city. In this he was opposed by Publicola and the conspirators were slain. Collatinus, who showed himself less hostile to the Tarquins than he was expected to be, resigned as consul and withdrew from the city.

Cominius (kō̱-min′i-us), *Pontius.* Roman hero who volunteered to go through the enemy forces of the Gauls who had sacked and occupied Rome (389 B.C.), to the Capitol, which still held out under the command of Marcus Manlius. His mission was to secure an appointment as dictator for Camillus who would not accept the post until he was legally appointed by the citizens on the Capitol. Cominius took a number of pieces of cork and set out. When he came to the Tiber, he tied the cork about his body, leaped into the river, and propelled himself across. He made his way to the Capitoline Hill and up the lower slopes, using the bushes and shrubs to pull himself up. When he came to the steepest part of the hill, he called to the citizens on top. They hauled him up, gave him the appointment Camillus desired, and he returned the same way he had come.

Conon (kō′non). Athenian commander in the Peloponnesian War. He succeeded to command of the Athenian fleet, 407 B.C., and shortly thereafter lost 30 of his 70 ships in an engagement with the Spartans at Mytilene. The Athenians melted down the gold and silver offerings that had been dedicated in the temples of the Acropolis and bought a new fleet with which (406 B.C.) he defeated the Spartans at Arginusae, south of Lesbos. Following the battle a fierce wind sprang up, and the Athenians did not rescue the crews of 25 of their own wrecked ships. When news of the loss of these men reached Athens, the city went into mourning, and a great hue and cry arose; the Athenian commanders were accused of negligence or worse, were tried, condemned to death, and six of them were executed. Conon, however, was not included in the charges and no blame was attached to him. In 405 B.C. the Athenian fleet under his command was disastrously defeated at Aegospotami by the Spartans. Conon prudently decided not to return to Athens on the heels of such a disaster. He went to Salamis in Cyprus with part of the fleet and made plans and preparation to avenge the defeat. He won the support of the king of Salamis and also at length received ships and money from the Persian court to wage war on the Spartans. With such Persian aid he met an inferior Spartan fleet off Cnidus (394 B.C.), destroyed it and Spartan sea power, and avenged the disaster of Aegospotami. He returned to Athens, rebuilt the Long Walls, and raised a temple to Cnidian Aphrodite at the Piraeus as a memorial of his victory. In 392 B.C. Conon went as an envoy to parley with a Persian satrap friendly to Sparta. The satrap treacherously imprisoned him. He was released when the satrap was recalled and removed from power. Conon went to Cyprus where he died soon afterward in the same year.

Corbulo (kôr'bū-lō), *Cnaeus Domitius.* Roman soldier and administrator, died 67 A.D. As legate under Claudius he governed Lower Germany, and caused a canal to be dug between the Rhenus (Rhine) and the Mosa (Meuse) which is still in service. Given command of Roman forces in the East, he waged successful campaigns against the Parthians and Armenians; but Nero, succeeding Claudius as emperor, seems to have suspected Corbulo of conspiracy, recalled him in 67 A.D., and compelled him to take his own life.

Cornelia (kôr-nēl'yạ). Roman matron of the 2nd century B.C. She was the daughter of the elder Scipio Africanus, wife of Tiberius Sempronius Gracchus, and mother of the Gracchi, the tribunes Tiberius and Caius Gracchus. She was celebrated for her accomplishments and virtues as a mother. After the death of her husband, she refused to marry again but devoted her life to her children. The story is told of her answering the boasts of another Roman matron about her jewels with the simple "These are my jewels," and pointing to her children.

Cotys (kot'is). Any of several kings of Thrace, but especially one who reigned between 382 and 358 B.C. One of his daughters married the Athenian commander Iphicrates; another married the mercenary captain Charidemus. Cotys was an enemy of the Athenians and succeeded in wresting Sestos and also all of the Thracian Chersonesus from them. He was murdered in 358 B.C., and his kingdom was divided between his three sons.

Crassus (kras'us), *Marcus Licinius.* [Surnamed *Dives,* meaning "the Rich."] Roman general and politican, born probably c112 B.C.; died 53 B.C. His father had been a censor and praetor, and he was reared modestly. His habits of life were temperate in the main. He married his brother's widow, entertained frugally, studied history and philosophy, and by cultivating the art of oratory made himself one of the most powerful public speakers in Rome. He was generous to strangers and educated his slaves for greater usefulness. But all his good qualities were obscured as he grew older by his great vice of avarice. He fattened on public calamities. It was said that when there was a fire in Rome, as often happened, he rushed to buy the burning property and then put out the fire with his own private fire brigade. The disorders of war and civil war afforded him opportunities to increase his wealth. Yet the men he most despised were those whom he deemed guilty of avarice. Besides the great amount of real estate he owned in Rome he was the owner of silver mines, of valuable lands outside Rome, and of great numbers of slaves.

In the civil wars his father opposed Marius and finally committed suicide (87 B.C.) to avoid falling into his hands. The brother of Crassus also perished in the civil war. Crassus fled to Spain with some of his retinue to escape the proscriptions of Cinna, and hid in a cave for eight months. An acquaintance his father had made when he served as praetor in Spain sent food and other necessities and comforts of life to him during the whole period, but never allowed himself to see Crassus. When Crassus learned of the death of Cinna, he ventured out of the cave, gathered a band of followers, and marched about Spain. Some say he plundered Malaca (Malaga), but he denied it. He went to Africa and joined Metellus Pius, but failed to reach an accord with him and went over to Sulla, under whom he served in the campaigns of 83–82 B.C. During the proscriptions by which Sulla got rid of his enemies and seized their property Crassus enriched himself, profiting by the liberality of his chief and by the opportunities which the war offered for speculations in confiscated property. He became the richest man in Rome and used his colossal fortune to further his political ambitions. His great rival was Pompey, whom Sulla honored for his military victories. Since he could not equal Pompey in war, he turned to politics. He headed a moderate party between the aristocratic conservative party of Pompey and the radical party of Julius Caesar. Yet, says Plutarch, he was "neither a steadfast friend nor an implacable enemy, but readily abandoned both his favors and his resentments at the dictates of his interests." It is thought that he had some connection with the conspiracy of Catiline, and that for a time he secretly supported Publius Clodius, the enemy of Cicero. He won influence by the favors he granted and by the fear which the power of his wealth inspired. In 72 B.C. he was appointed by the Senate to put down the revolt of the gladiators under Spartacus, which two consuls had been unable to quell and which spreading rapidly posed a great threat to Rome. In the course of fighting Spartacus one of his lieutenants disobeyed his orders, engaged Spartacus, was defeated, and fled with his men. Crassus chose 500 of those who had shown cowardice, divided them into 50 groups of ten men each, took one man from each group by lot and had him put to death as an example. He then pursued Spartacus to Rhegium and defeated a large part of his forces. In a succeeding engagement Spartacus was killed and the revolt was put down, but Pompey shared in the credit for the victory because he came upon those of the rebels who were fleeing from Crassus and killed them. Pompey was given a triumph, and Crassus had to be content with the knowledge that he had done his job well. This added to the jealousy he felt for Pompey and when, 70 B.C., he became consul with Pompey, he publicly disagreed with him on all matters. In 65 B.C. he was made censor but quarreled with his colleague and resigned. Caesar, who needed the military prestige of Pompey and the wealth of Crassus, succeeded in reconciling them and in winning their support. The three formed the First Triumvirate in 60 B.C., but when Caesar left for Gaul, the quarrels between Pompey and Crassus broke out anew. In 56 B.C. Caesar summoned them to Luca and again reconciled them, and urged them to run for the consulship again. There was some objection to this in Rome because they had accomplished so little when they earlier shared the consulship, but with liberal bribery, threats, and promises, as well as some juggling of the laws, they were elected (55 B.C.). In the division of spheres Crassus was awarded the province of Syria, Pompey got Spain, and Caesar was named proconsul of Gaul. Crassus was delighted. He meant to make war on the Parthians and win at last the military triumphs that would make him the equal of Pompey. Because there was no ground for a war against the Parthians his program was unpopular, and one of the tribunes of the people tried to prevent him from leaving Rome. The tribune was unsuccessful. Crassus sailed from Brundisium (54 B.C.) for the East. On the way he lost many vessels in a storm at sea. In the East he marched to the Euphrates River, crossed it, and took several cities in Mesopotamia. At Zenodotia 100 of his soldiers were slain. He captured the place, plundered and sacked it, and sold the inhabitants into slavery. He then went into winter quarters in Syria, plundered the temple at Jerusalem, and devoted himself to adding up the wealth he had taken. In the meantime the Parthians, thoroughly warned of his approach, made their preparations to resist him. A story is told that at a temple of Venus in Syria, Publius, the son of Crassus, stumbled and his father fell over him. He ignored the dire warning. His soldiers were terrified at the news they had of the Parthians, but Crassus was determined to proceed. His path was strewn with unfavorable omens. When he was crossing the Euphrates at Zeugma, a strange thunderstorm broke; the place where he intended to make camp was struck by two thunderbolts; the first Roman eagle set up turned around of its own accord and faced in the opposite direction; when rations were distributed to the men, lentils and salt, offerings customarily made to the dead, were offered them first. But most unfavorable of all was the combination in Crassus of military inexperience and unbridled ambition. He allowed himself to be duped by a barbarian chieftain pretending to be his friend into leaving the friendly valley of the Euphrates and striking out across the desert. The Parthians waited for him. When he was practically at a stand in the desert, his men weary from marching in sand and from thirst, the Parthians attacked. Publius, the son of Crassus, fought bravely. Crassus learned that he was in danger and rushed to his aid. But in the meantime Publius was wounded, and rather than submit to capture, he ordered his shield-bearer to kill him with his sword. When Crassus came up to aid him, he was met by the Parthians waving his son's head on the point of a spear. The battle was carried on furiously all day. Crassus suffered heavy losses. At night he retreated to Carrhae (modern Haran) in Mesopotamia, leaving his wounded behind to the mercy of the Parthians, who killed them all. After some days a message came to him in Carrhae, inviting him to a peace parley with the Parthians. He accepted the invitation and was treacherously slain. From the beginning to the end of the campaign, Crassus had displayed the utmost ignorance of military affairs and an obstinacy that resulted in disaster. Some 20,000 Romans are said to have lost their lives in the expedition that was undertaken to satisfy his ambition. According to Plutarch, the Parthians cut off his head and his hand, and carried the head to the pavilion of the Parthian king. The king was presiding over a banquet, at which a tragic actor was singing the lines of Euripides' tragedy, *The Bacchae.* As he came to the lines describing the frenzied Agave entering with the head of her own son, the head of Crassus was flung in and presented to the king.

Craterus (krat'ėr-us). Macedonian general, killed in Cappadocia, 321 B.C. He served Alexander the Great with distinction on the campaigns in Asia. He was one of Alexander's ablest and most trusted generals, and was often given the position of second in command as at Tyre (332 B.C.), Gaugamela (331 B.C.), and at the Hydaspes River (326 B.C.). Craterus built two cities—Bucephalia and Nicaea—on the banks of the Hydaspes while Alexander went on to the Indus River and into India. Craterus also prepared a fleet for transporting the army down the Hydaspes to the Indus and to the ocean when Alexander returned from India. From the mouth of the Indus Craterus marched inland on the homeward journey, to Arachosia to quell a revolt there and continued through Drangiana and Carmania, where he rejoined Alexander. In Asia Alexander increasingly adopted barbarian (Persian) customs to the dismay and resentment of his Macedonian veterans and friends. Craterus did not follow his commander in this, but maintained his Macedonian ways, and though he was highly respected by Alexander for his capacity, he did not enjoy the intimate affection with him that was shared by others. Nevertheless, on the occasion of a quarrel between Craterus and Hephaestion, Alexander rebuked them both, told them they were the two men he loved most in the world, but if such a quarrel ever arose again, he would kill them both, or, at least, the aggressor.

In 324 B.C. Craterus was one of the leaders of the group of veterans Alexander sent home with rich rewards. Following the death of Alexander (323 B.C.) he became co-ruler with Antipater of his empire. The Greek states rebelled when they learned of Alexander's death. Craterus marched into Thessaly and defeated them at Crannon (322 B.C.). The next year he was killed in Cappadocia (321 B.C.).

Creticus (krē'ti-kus), *Metellus.* See *Metellus, Quintus Caecilius* (d. c56 B.C.).

Critias (krish'i-as, krit'i-as). Athenian orator and politician, disciple of Socrates, and distinguished poet and orator. He was one of the Thirty Tyrants who governed Athens, opposed the revolution of 411 B.C., and proposed the recall of Alcibiades. He fell with the Tyrants in 403 B.C., perishing in the battle for the citadel of Piraeus. His reputation as a cruel, rapacious, and dissolute man may be unjust, as Plato seemed to admire him and introduced him in a dialogue which bears his name. He wrote on historical and political subjects, and was the author of several tragedies. Fragments of his political elegies survive.

Croesus (krē'sus). King of Lydia in the 6th century B.C. He was the son of Alyattes, whom he succeeded in 560 B.C. He subjugated the Ionian, Aeolian, and other neighboring peoples, and at the close of his reign ruled over the region extending from the N and W coasts of Asia Minor to the Halys River (modern Kizil Irmak) on the E and the Taurus Mountains on the S. According to Herodotus, he was visited at the height of his power by Solon, to whom he exhibited his innumerable treasures. He asked Solon who, of all the men he had seen, he considered the most happy. Solon answered that Tellus of Athens was the happiest. Croesus, incensed because he had expected Solon to name him, a rich lord of many lands, asked why he had named Tellus. Solon replied that Tellus lived at a time when his country was flourishing, had fine sons whom he saw grow up and produce children of their own, and in the end perished gloriously fighting for his country. On being pressed to name the second happiest of mortals, Solon named Cleobis and Biton. Croesus was still not satisfied; he thought surely Solon would have named him at the least as the second happiest of mortals, but he had to accept this dictum concerning happiness from Solon, "Account no man happy before his death." "It is the end that counts," said Solon, "for man is often given a gleam of happiness by the gods before being plunged into ruin." Almost immediately Croesus learned the truth of Solon's words. Of his two sons, one was a mute, the other, the apple of his eye, was accidentally slain in a hunting party. Croesus, deceived by a reponse of the oracle at Delphi to the effect that, if he marched against the Persians, he would overthrow a great empire, made war in 546 B.C. upon Cyrus, by whom he was defeated in the same year near Sardis and taken prisoner. He was, according to Herodotus, doomed to be burned alive, but as he was upon the pyre he recalled the words of Solon, and exclaimed "Solon! Solon! Solon!" Desired by Cyrus to state upon whom he was calling, he related the story of Solon, which moved Cyrus to countermand the order for his execution. He ordered his men to quench the fire which had already been lighted, but the flames were too hot and the men failed to check them. Thereupon Croesus, fettered to the pyre, called on Apollo to save him and the day, which had been bright, suddenly darkened; a torrential rain fell and extinguished the flames. Cyrus was full of wonder at this and had Croesus brought to his side. As Croesus sat near him, watching the Persians plundering Sardis, he turned to Cyrus and asked if he might speak. Cyrus gave his permission. Croesus asked him what the Persians were doing. "Plundering your city," Cyrus replied, "and carrying off your riches." Croesus corrected him. It was not any longer his city nor his riches, he said; the Persians were plundering a city that now belonged to Cyrus and were carrying off riches that also now belonged to him. Cyrus was so impressed by the wisdom of this view that he kept Croesus henceforward in his train and bestowed upon him distinguished marks of favor. In return he often received valuable advice on military and other matters from Croesus. Later Croesus sent messengers and reproached the oracle at Delphi which had deceived him with a response that encouraged him to go to war against Cyrus. The oracle replied that though Apollo had tried to prevent the fall of Sardis in the lifetime of Croesus, not even a god could delay or deny the course of fate, and that Croesus had been punished, as he was fated to be, for the sins of his ancestors of five generations before. Moreover, said the oracle, Croesus had not taken the trouble to find out what the oracle meant. It had spoken truly in prophesying that a great empire would be destroyed. The empire of Croesus was destroyed and he had only himself to blame. On hearing this from the oracle Croesus humbly acknowledged the justice of it.

Curio (kū′ri-ō), *Caius Scribonius.* Roman general and politician; died 53 B.C. He fought with Sulla against Mithridates II of Parthia, was tribune (90 B.C.), consul (76), proconsul in Macedonia (75–73), and became pontifex maximus, the chief priest of the state religion, in 57 B.C. He was the first Roman general to reach the Danube in Moesia, c73 B.C. He was an opponent of Julius Caesar.

Curio, Caius Scribonius. Son of Caius Scribonius Curio (d. 53 B.C.); a partisan of Caesar in the civil war. After struggling in Roman politics to prevent any action by the Senate against Caesar, he took the field as leader of military forces, taking Sicily and besieging a Pompeian force in Utica, in Africa, where he was killed, 49 B.C.

Cyaxares (sī-ak′sạ-rēz). King of the Medes (625–584 B.C.). In the cuneiform inscriptions his name is Uvakshtra. He was the son and successor of Phraortes, and may be considered as the founder of Media's power and greatness. According to Herodotus, he was a capable and ambitious ruler. He organized his Asiatic forces into separate divisions of spearmen, archers, and cavalry. At the head of his forces and accompanied by his allies, he marched against Nineveh, where his father had been slain in an attempt to take the Assyrian capital. He had made a successful attack and settled down to besiege the city when Media was overrun by hordes of Scythian invaders. After some years the Scythians were driven out. According to Herodotus, Cyaxares and his chiefs invited a great number of the Scyths to a banquet, got them drunk, and slew them. In any case, having driven them out, he captured Nineveh (608 B.C.), in alliance with Nabopolassar, viceroy of Babylonia, and destroyed the Assyrian empire. Toward the W Cyaxares conquered Armenia, and thus extended his dominion as far as the river Halys in Asia Minor. Herodotus says that Cyaxares received some Scythian suppliants and treated them kindly. He came to respect them and gave the care of a number of Median boys into their hands with instructions to teach them to shoot with the bow. Every day the Scythians went hunting, and every day they brought back game. One day they returned empty handed. In a rage, Cyaxares insulted them. They were so deeply offended that they resolved to punish him. They took one of the Median boys under their care, slew him, and dressed his flesh as if it were game. They cooked it and served it to Cyaxares and his guests and then fled to Sardis, to the court of the Lydian king Alyattes. Cyaxares demanded that Alyattes surrender them. He refused, and this, according to Herodotus, was the reason for the war between the Lydians and the Medians. Fighting continued for five years during which fortune favored first one side then the other. In the sixth year another battle took place. As the struggle waxed hot, suddenly day was turned to night by an eclipse of the sun (May 28, 585 B.C.). The phenomenon had been foretold by Thales of Miletus, the first man who had learned enough about the stars in their courses to predict such an occurrence. However, the Lydians and the Medians were both so terrified by the portent that they immediately laid down their arms and agreed to a peace. According to the terms of it, the daughter of Alyattes married the son of Cyaxares. This son was Astyages, who became the grandfather of Cyrus the Great.

Cylon (sī'lon). An Athenian noble of the 7th century B.C. He was married to the daughter of Theagenes, tyrant of Megara. With the advice and help of Theagenes Cylon plotted to make himself master of Athens. He was instructed by the oracle of Delphi to seize the Acropolis on "the greatest festival of Zeus." Accordingly, with the aid of a few Athenian nobles and some Megarian soldiers, Cylon seized the Acropolis (c632 B.C.) at the time of the Olympic festival, which, since he had been an Olympic victor himself, he considered "the greatest festival of Zeus." He and his alien supporters were trapped in the citadel by the Athenians. During a long siege Cylon escaped, but his followers, weakened by failing supplies, sought refuge in the temple of Athena, and finally agreed to surrender under a guarantee of safe conduct. Megacles the archon persuaded the Athenians to ignore their promise to spare the lives of the conspirators, and they were put to death. Cylon was later informed by the oracle that he had misinterpreted the oracle: that "the greatest festival of Zeus" referred to the *Diasia,* which took place in March and was celebrated outside the city. Because

(obscured) errạnt, ardẹnt, actọr; ch, chip; g, go; th, thin; ᵺH, then; y, you;
(variable) ḍ as d or j, ṣ as s or sh, ṭ as t or ch, ẓ as z or zh.

he interpreted the oracle falsely his attempt failed and Cylon and his descendants were banished forever from Athens. But Athens had put itself under a curse by breaking the pledge and insulting Athena, in whose temple the conspirators had taken sanctuary. The Alcmaeonids, of whom Megacles was a member, were tried for sacrilege, their property was confiscated, and they and their descendants were banished forever. The city was finally purged by Epimenides (596 B.C.) but the curse on the Alcmaeonids, who in the course of time returned to Athens, plagued Pericles, a descendant of Megacles, some 200 years after the murder of the followers of Cylon.

Cynaegirus (sin-ē-jī'rus). Athenian soldier; brother of Aeschylus. He distinguished himself at the battle of Marathon in 490 B.C., in which, according to Herodotus, he pursued the Persians to the sea and, having seized one of their triremes to prevent its putting off, fell with his right hand severed. Later writers add that, having lost both his hands, he seized the vessel with his teeth.

Cypselus (sip'se̜-lus). Tyrant of Corinth, c655–625 B.C. He was the son of Eëtion, a descendant of the Lapiths, and Labda, a member of the Bacchiadae of Corinth. Before he was born, the oracle of Delphi foretold to Eëtion that the son his wife was about to bear would be a rock on which the Bacchiadae, the ruling oligarchy of Corinth, would founder. This oracle coming to their ears, the Bacchiadae resolved to kill the son of Eëtion. They went to his house and asked to see the child. Labda, thinking there was no harm in it, brought the infant and laid it in the arms of the man nearest her. The plan was for whoever received the child to dash it to its death at once, the infant smiled at the man who received him and so moved him that he could not bear to murder it. Instead he passed the child on to the next man. So the child was passed from hand to hand and none of the ten men there had the heart to murder it. They left the house without accomplishing their purpose. Once outside, they began to dispute together, blaming each other for the failure to kill the child. Labda overheard them and thus learned the purpose of their visit. Lest they return, she hid her baby in a corn-bin. The men did return, but having searched the house in vain for the child, they again took their departure. Because the baby had been hidden in a corn-bin, *cypsele,* he was given the name

Cypselus. When Cypselus grew up, he went to the oracle at Delphi and heard the following response:

"See there comes to my dwelling a man much favored of fortune,

Cypselus, son of Eëtion, and king of the glorious Corinth,

He and his children too, but not his children's children."

This encouraged him to attack the Bacchiadae and gain the throne of Corinth. Successful in this, he enjoyed a prosperous reign of 30 years and was succeeded by his son Periander, thus fulfilling the first part of the oracle.

Cyrus (sī'rus). [Called *Cyrus the Great;* name in the Old Testament, *Koresh;* in the cuneiform inscriptions, *Kurush, Kurshu;* Old Persian, *Kurush.*] The founder of the Persian Empire, who died 529 B.C. All accounts of his birth and early youth are heavily encrusted by legends, among which is the following account given by Herodotus. Before Cyrus was born, his grandfather Astyages, the king of the Medes, dreamed that the child his daughter Mandane was about to bear to her husband, the Persian Cambyses, would be a king if he did not die too soon. Astyages, fearing his grandson would usurp his throne, gave orders for the child to be destroyed as soon as it was born. The man to whom he gave the orders, one Harpagus, did not wish to commit the murder himself. When Cyrus was born, Harpagus gave him into the hands of a herdsman, Mitradates. He instructed Mitradates to expose the child on the mountains, and when he was sure it was dead to send word to him. Mitradates took the infant to his house. There he found that his wife, who was awaiting the birth of her first child, had produced a still-born son. She begged Mitradates not to expose the healthy child given into their hands, and they decided to dress their own dead child in the robes worn by Cyrus and to lay him in a thicket in the mountains and to keep Cyrus as their own son. After a few days Mitradates sent for Harpagus and led him to the dead child. Harpagus duly reported to Astyages that the child was dead, and the cowherd's son was given a magnificent funeral, which pleased its parents. Cyrus, brought up with loving care by Mitradates and his wife, grew into a handsome, intelligent, manly child. When he was ten years old, he was chosen to be their king by a group of his playmates. One of the boys objected bitterly to being ordered about by the son of a cowherd, refused to do as he was bid, and was

(obscured) errạnt, ardẹnt, actọr; ch, chip; g, go; th, thin; ᵮн, then; y, you; (variable) ḍ as d or j, ş as s or sh, ţ as t or ch, ẕ as z or zh.

whipped by Cyrus for his insubordination. The boy complained to his father, who in turn complained to Astyages. Astyages sent for the cowherd and his son. In his own defense the boy said the others had voluntarily chosen him as king, and therefore bound themselves to obey his orders. When this one boy refused, he invited the punishment he received. Astyages was much struck by this speech, but more than that, a suspicion grew in his mind that this was his grandson, whom he had ordered destroyed. He sent Cyrus out of the room and questioned Mitradates until, by his threats, he forced the truth from him. Astyages now bethought him of his old dream and of the interpretation the Magi had put on it. He summoned them to learn what he should do, now that his grandson was found to be alive. The Magi listened to the whole story and concluded that the oracle had been fulfilled in a very harmless way; that as his comrades had chosen him as their king, Cyrus had already been king and his grandfather need have no further worry on that account. The omens, the Magi assured Astyages, were sometimes fulfilled in most inconsequential ways. Hereodotus adds, in connection with the birth of Cyrus, that the report that he was suckled by a bitch was circulated by his parents when they recovered him after the events related above, because Cyrus talked continually of the goodness of Cyno, his foster mother. Cyno means "bitch." However, much information of some historical repute concerning his lineage has been obtained from the inscriptions, among them a cylinder belonging to Cyrus himself, discovered in the ruins of Babylon and Sepharvaim (Sippar), combined with the accounts of the Greek historians (Herodotus, Xenophon, and Ctesiphon). On his cylinder he calls himself the son of Cambyses, grandson of Cyrus and great-grandson of Shishpish (Theispes), who were all "Kings of Anshan." Anshan is evidently identical with Anzan, the plain of Susa, and stands for Elam, which was conquered by Theispes, the son of Achaemenes, founder of the dynasty. But the Magi had been right in their original interpretation of the dream of Astyages. In 549 B.C., Cyrus, after conquering Ecbatana or Agbatana (modern Hamadan), encouraged by Harpagus, who had spared his life, led a revolt of the Persians against their Median rulers. He completely defeated the army Astyages sent against him, and made himself master of the

Medes and the Persians. He then directed his arms against
the Lydian kingdom of Croesus (q.v.), who made an offensive and defensive alliance with Nabonidus, king of Babylonia, and the reigning pharaoh of Egypt. Croesus consulted
the oracle at Delphi several times as he prepared for war
against Cyrus, and received what he considered to be most
reassuring answers, although in the event it developed that
they were equivocal. He asked the oracle if he should attack
Persia. The priestess replied that if he attacked the Persians
he would destroy a great empire. He further asked if his
kingdom would long endure. The priestess replied:

"Wait till the time shall come when a mule is monarch of
    Media;
Then, thou delicate Lydian, away to the pebbles of Her-
    mus;
Haste, oh! haste thee away, nor blush to behave like a
    coward."

This was most reassuring to Croesus, for he doubted that a
mule would ever be king of the Medes. In the war that he
now waged against the Persians Cyrus disastrously defeated
him (546 B.C.), captured him, and plundered his capital,
Sardis. But Croesus had no complaint against the oracle
when the matter was explained to him, for Cyrus, the son of
a Median mother and a Persian father, was the mule to which
the oracle referred. Cyrus kept Croesus, miraculously saved
from the pyre on which Cyrus had meant to burn him, at his
side in his court. He treated him with the utmost courtesy
and consideration, and often, according to Herodotus,
turned to him for advice or accepted suggestions he volunteered. After the conquest of Lydia by Cyrus, the Ionian and
Aeolian Greeks sent envoys to Cyrus and asked him to accept them on the same terms they had enjoyed when they
were subject to Croesus. Cyrus listened carefully to their
plea, then replied with a parable. Once a piper walking by
the sea chanced to see fish swimming in the waters. He took
out his pipes and played sweetly to them, hoping they would
come out on land in response to his music, but the fish
ignored him. Then he took a net, cast it in the sea, netted
the fish, and brought them to land. Hereupon the fish began
to leap and dance. Then the piper told the fishes they could
cease their dancing, as they had not chosen to dance when
he piped to them. And so it was with Ionians and Aeolians:

(obscured) errant, ardent, actor; ch, chip; g, go; th, thin; ŦH, then; y, you;
(variable) ḏ as d or j, ṣ as s or sh, ṭ as t or ch, ẓ as z or zh.

when Cyrus urged them to revolt, before his war with Croesus, they had ignored him, probably on the assumption that Cyrus would never overcome Croesus. Now that he was successful they offered him their allegiance on the old terms, but as his position was now different, he was a conqueror, so would his treatment of the Ionians and Aeolians be different. As it turned out, he was a very mild ruler over them. In the years following the conquest of Lydia, Cyrus consolidated his power in the conquered countries. In 538 B.C he marched with a great army into Babylonia. Sepharvaim (Sippar) was captured without fighting, Nabonidus, who defended it, fled, and two days afterward Babylon itself, which was held by Nabonidus' son Belshazzar, fell into the hands of the conqueror, likewise "without battle and fight," as he records. According to Eusebius, Nabonidus after the fall of Babylon fortified himself in Borsippa; the city was besieged by Cyrus, and after it had capitulated he treated it and Nabonidus himself with mercy, allowing the latter to make his residence in Carmania (modern Kerman). It is certain that he showed great generosity and consideration to the conquered capital Babylon, sparing its inhabitants and their religious feelings; he even represented himself as having been called by Merodach (Marduk), the god of the city, to avenge his neglect at the hands of the preceding kings. Cyrus' attitude toward the Jewish exiles in Babylonia is well known from the Old Testament (Ezra, i.). He permitted them to return to their own country (thus ending the Babylonian Exile), to rebuild Jerusalem, and to restore the temple, and even returned to them the vessels of the temple which had been carried away by Nebuchadnezzar. According to Herodotus, because of his firm, just, and kindly qualities, he was known to the Persians as "father." His death, like his birth, is shrouded in legend. The most common view is that he fell in battle with the Massagetae, on the river Jaxartes (modern Syr Darya); in this connection, see *Tomyris.* The tomb of Cyrus was at Pasargadae, a city founded by him near the site where he had defeated his grandfather Astyages, king of the Medes. The tomb was inscribed,

> "O man, whosoever thou art, and from whencesoever thou comest (for I know thou wilt come), I am Cyrus, the founder of the Persian Empire; do not grudge me this little earth which covers my body."

fat, fāte, fär, fȧll, ȧsk, fãre; net, mē, hėr; pin, pīne; not, nōte, möve, nôr; up, lūte, pùll; oi, oil; ou out; (lightened) ĕlect, agǫny, ūnite;

His plea was ignored; the officers Alexander the Great left at Pasargadae, 330 B.C., allowed the tomb to be plundered. When Alexander returned and learned that the tomb had been opened and plundered, he put the guardians of the tomb to torture but could not learn who had committed the sacrilege and outrage.

Cyrus the Younger. Persian satrap; killed at Cunaxa in Babylonia, 401 B.C. He was the son of Darius II, king of Persia, and Parysatis. He was sent to Sardis by his father, to be satrap with dominion over Cappadocia, Phrygia, and Lydia, and proved himself an able administrator. There he met the Spartan admiral Lysander, who won his confidence by his personal incorruptibility and his refusal to accept gifts from Cyrus. His contact with Lysander's Spartans gave him great respect for the fighting qualities of the Greeks. He promised money to Lysander to prosecute the war against the Athenians, and left Lysander, whom he trusted more than the Persian nobles, in charge of his satrapy when he was called back to the Persian court to attend his dying father. On the death of Darius his mother intrigued unsuccessfully to secure the throne for him in place of the legitimate heir, Artaxerxes II. Cyrus resolved to win the throne and began to collect a force of Greek mercenaries for the purpose. As finally gathered, the army of Cyrus included about 100,000 Asiatic troops and 13,000 Greeks, among whom was the Athenian Xenophon. Without telling the troops their precise destination, Cyrus led forth his army from Sardis in the spring of 401 B.C. The path wound acrosss Asia Minor, through Lycaonia, the Cilician Gates, the Pass of Beilan, and along the Euphrates River to Babylonia. At the village of Cunaxa outside Babylon, Artaxerxes marched out against him. The two hosts engaged. The forces of Cyrus were immediately successful, and Cyrus was already receiving congratulations when he suddenly spied his hated brother. With a few followers he urged his horse forward intent on killing Artaxerxes with his own hand, and did wound him slightly. But the bodyguard surrounding Artaxerxes wounded him in the eye; he fell from his horse and was instantly slain. As soon as news of his death reached his Asiatic troops, they fled in terror; the victory so quickly won was more quickly turned into a rout. Only the Greek mercenaries stood fast. They did not surrender to Artaxerxes but were allowed to depart and made the famous return described in Xenophon's *Anabasis*.

—D—

Damocles (dam'ọ-klēz). Syracusan, fl. in the first half of the 4th century B.C., a courtier of Dionysius the Elder. Cicero relates that Damocles, having extolled the good fortune of Dionysius, was invited by the tyrant to taste this royal felicity, and that, in the midst of a splendid banquet and all the luxury of the court, on looking up he beheld above his head a sword suspended by a single horsehair.

Damon and Pythias (dā'mọn; pith'i-ạs). Pythagorean philosophers of Syracuse; fl. in the first half of the 4th century B.C. They were celebrated for their friendship. Pythias (or Phintias) plotted against the life of Dionysius I of Syracuse, and was condemned to die. As Pythias wished to arrange his affairs, Damon offered to place himself in the tyrant's hands as his substitute, and to die in his stead should he not return on the appointed day. At the last moment Pythias came back, and Dionysius was so struck by the fidelity of the friends that he pardoned the offender and begged to be admitted into their fellowship.

Darius I (of *Persia*) (dạ-rī'us). [Called **Darius the Great**: also known as **Darius Hystaspes**.] King of Persia, born c558 B.C.; died 486 B.C. He was a son of Hystaspes; his brothers were Artaphernes, Artabanus, and Artanes; and he was fifth in the descent from Achaemenes. He succeeded (521 B.C.) Cambyses on the Persian throne, after defeating the magian Gaumata, who claimed to be Bardiya (the Greek Smerdis), brother of Cambyses and son of Cyrus. According to Herodotus, he won the throne in the following manner: While Cambyses was on his campaign in Egypt, the Median magus Patizeithes, whom he had left in charge of his household, plotted with his brother Bardiya to seize the throne of Persia. He set up Bardiya, pretending that he was Smerdis, the brother of Cambyses and son of Cyrus, and had

fat, fāte, fär, fâll, àsk, fâre; net, mē, hèr; pin, pīne; not, nōte, mŏve, nôr; up, lūte, pùll; oi, oil; ou out; (lightened) ẹlect, agọny, ụnite;

him proclaimed king. He felt safe in doing this as he knew the real Smerdis had been secretly slain at Cambyses' order. Cambyses died before he could return to Susa and expose the False Smerdis. There were several Persian nobles who suspected, and finally proved to their own satisfaction, that the reigning Smerdis was not the son of Cyrus but an imposter. Six of these nobles took Darius into their confidence, proposing to overthrow the False Smerdis, who was a Mede, and regain the throne for a Persian. Darius had also suspected that this Smerdis was an impostor and now urged instant action. He threatened the other six nobles—Otanes, Gobryas, Intaphernes, Megabyzus, Aspathines, and Hydarnes—that he would reveal their plot to Smerdis himself unless they acted at once. He would do so to protect himself, before the knowledge that he had been discovered reached the ears of Smerdis and caused him to take action against them. Darius convinced them, and they set off to the palace, planning to enter and slay the False Smerdis. On the way news reached them that Smerdis had been disclosed as an impostor by Prexaspes, the man who at Cambyses' order had secretly slain the real Smerdis. The conspirators now hesitated, and considered whether they should not delay a bit while the capital was in such a ferment. Darius again insisted on immediate action. As they discussed the matter, two pairs of vultures, pursued by seven pairs of hawks, flew by. The hawks overtook the vultures and tore them to pieces. At this omen the seven agreed to proceed at once. When they came to the palace the guards let them enter the courtyard without question. Eunuchs inside tried to stop them from entering the palace, but they were slain and the conspirators pushed on to the apartments of the king. The two magi heard the clamor and rose to defend themselves. One was instantly slain. The other rushed to an inner room. Darius and Gobryas followed. In the darkness Gobryas seized the magus but Darius, unable to see, hesitated. Gobryas asked why he hesitated and, hearing that Darius feared to strike lest he wound Gobryas, told him to strike anyway, even if both were killed by his blow. Darius obeyed and fortunately killed only the magus. After the slaying of the two magi, the seven nobles rushed from the palace, shouting what they had done and killing every magus they could lay their hands on.

(obscured) errạnt, ardẹnt, actọr; ch, chip; g, go; th, thin; ŦH, then; y, you; (variable) ḍ as d or j, ş as s or sh, ţ as t or ch, ẓ as z or zh.

Some days later they met to decide what they should do. After some discussion of the various merits of a monarchy, oligarchy, and democracy, they decided to restore the monarchy and choose one of their own number as king. They agreed to ride out of the city together the next morning, and that he whose horse was first to neigh after sunrise should become king. Darius was determined that the choice fall to him. He took his groom into his confidence, and was assured by him that if the choice depended on the neighing of the horse, Darius could cease to worry, as with the help of a mare he would cause Darius' stallion to neigh first. The next day the nobles, all except Otanes who favored a democracy and did not wish to become king, rode out as planned. As they rode along, they came to the spot where the groom had tethered a mare the night before. Darius' stallion leaped forward and neighed. At the same time there was a flash of lightning followed by a clap of thunder. The five other nobles leaped from their horses, knelt before Darius, and acknowledged him as their king. Thus he became ruler of all that was then known as Asia except the part occupied by the Arabians. In his own record of his reign, as set forth in the inscriptions of Behistun in three languages (Old Persian, Elamite, and Accadian), Darius caused the following to be inscribed: "Darius, son of Hystaspes, by aid of his good horse and his good groom Oebares, got himself the kingdom of the Persians." Darius, who was already married to a daughter of Gobryas, now married Atossa, daughter of Cyrus, who had been the wife of her brother Cambyses and then of the False Smerdis; she had great influence with him. He also married Phaedima, daughter of Otanes, who had proved that Smerdis was an impostor; Artystone, said to have been his favorite, another daughter of Cyrus; and Parmys, a granddaughter of Cyrus; and Phratagune, the daughter of his brother Artanes. Among the sons produced by these wives were: Artabazanes and Ariabignes, by the daughter of Otanes; Xerxes (his heir), Achaemenes, Hystaspes, and Masistes, by Atossa; Arsames and Gobryas, by Artystone; Ariomardus, by Parmys; Abrocomes and Hyperanthes (both of whom fell at Thermopylae, 480 B.C.), by Phratagune.

After gaining the throne, Darius turned his attention to putting down the revolts which broke out all over Persia following the unmasking of the impostor Smerdis. This was followed by two uprisings in Babylonia, led by Nidintu-Bel and Arachus, who made claim to be Nebuchadnezzar, son of Nabonidus. He marched to Babylon and besieged the city. But the Babylonians had taken thorough measures to prepare for a siege, and jeered at the Persians, saying their city would not fall until mules foaled. More than a year and a half passed, and still the city held out. In the twentieth month from the beginning of the siege a mule belonging to Zopyrus (son of that Megabazus who had helped to overthrow the False Smerdis), gave birth to a foal. With a stratagem worked out by Zopyrus, Darius now won entrance into the city and took it a second time. He destroyed the walls of the city and crucified 3000 of the leading citizens. He honored Zopyrus by making him governor of the city for life, free from tribute. The other countries under Persian dominion revolted in turn, but at last were brought to submission. He besieged and took Samos and gave it to Syloson to repay him for an act of generosity Syloson had shown toward him when he was a mere member of Cambyses' bodyguard with no prospects of ever becoming king. After restoring order in the empire, Darius turned his attention to reorganization and reforms of the administration. He divided the whole land into 20 satrapies, each ruled by a governor, introduced regular taxation and uniformity of coinage, constructed roads, and founded a kind of postal system by placing stations and relays with saddled horses at regular intervals on the road between Susa and Sardis. To the capitals Susa in Elam, Ecbatana in Media, and Babylon, he added Persepolis in Persia proper, which was destroyed by Alexander the Great, but the imposing ruins of which have survived. On account of his attention to trade, taxes, and industry he was called "the Huckster." He sent an expedition to explore the Indus River, and to sail to its mouth; he dug a canal from the Nile to Suez, and compelled North Africa to pay him tribute. He also explored the shores of Sicily and Italy (Magna Graecia); Herodotus relates that this was a spying trip in preparation for war on Greece, and that the idea for it was proposed by Atossa to honor her promise to Democedes, a physician of Crotona, to secure his return to his homeland.

Throughout his empire he encouraged and promoted the

native religions and priests. For this reason the oracles of Asia Minor supported the side of the Persians, and in Egypt he was regarded as a great benefactor. He is referred to in the Old Testament in connection with the building of the temple of Zerubbabel. In the second year of his reign he allowed the resumption of the building, and in the sixth it was completed (Ezra, vi. 15). In 512 B.C., over the protests of his brother Artabanus, who felt the rewards of the undertaking were not worth its difficulties, he prepared an expedition against Scythia with the idea of securing the northern boundaries of his empire. At the head of a great host he marched to the Thracian Bosporus, leaving inscribed pillars along the way to commemorate his passage. He caused the Bosporus to be bridged and passed over it into Europe. On the advice of Ceos of Lesbos he did not destroy the bridge, as he had intended to do, but left it to secure his return or possible retreat. Histiaeus, tyrant of Miletus, was left in charge of the Ionians who guarded the bridge, and fulfilled his charge well. Both Ceos and Histiaeus were richly rewarded by Darius, who never lost his gratitude to them. Now that they were in Europe, the Scythians refused to meet the hosts of Darius in open battle. Instead they kept always one day's march ahead of Darius, destroying the lands through which they passed and leading the Persians deep into Europe, to the lower steppes of Russia. Darius was exasperated with this manner of fighting and did not know which way to turn. According to the account given in Herodotus, he sent messengers to the Scythian chiefs, and asked them if they were afraid to stand and fight why they did not surrender. The Scythians sent back a bird, a mouse, a frog, and five arrows, but the Persians did not immediately understand the meaning of these tokens. After Darius had received these gifts, a part of the Scythian force was drawn up in battle array against the Persians as if to engage in battle. Suddenly a hare ran in front of their ranks. The Scyths broke their formation and went in loud pursuit of the hare. Darius, observing their action, asked what they were doing. When he was told the Scythians were pursuing a hare, he decided that these strange people were making sport of him, that they neither feared him nor would fight him. The interpretation now put on the tokens sent by the Scythians was that unless the Persians became birds and could fly off into the sky, or mice and burrowed in the ground, or frogs and sought refuge in the marshes, they would never escape the Scythians but would die of their arrows. Darius decided to withdraw. He returned to the bridge and, leaving a part of his force in Europe to subdue Thrace, crossed safely back into Asia. Now Histiaeus, who had maintained the bridge in safety against the Scyths, was brought to Susa to become the king's counselor and friend, but he longed to return to Miletus where he had been tyrant. He sent secret messages to his nephew and son-in-law Aristagoras, and urged him to stir up the Ionian cities to revolt, assuring Aristagoras that Darius would send him, Histiaeus, to put down the revolt, and thus get him away from Susa. Aritagoras busied himself in this pursuit, and soon all Ionia was in open rebellion. The Athenians and Eretrians went to the aid of the Ionians, seized Sardis and burned it. When Darius heard of this, he shot an arrow into the air and prayed that he might be allowed to avenge the burning of Sardis. He commanded his servant to remind him each day to "Remember the Athenians." The revolt of the Ionians was put down, city by city. Histiaeus, whom Darius never suspected, fled when he realized that Artaphernes knew of his part in the revolt. He was ultimately captured and beheaded by a group of Persians, who killed him because they feared if he were returned to Darius, the king would forgive and restore him. And in fact, Darius was angry when he knew what they had done. He dressed the head of Histiaeus, which had been sent to him, and buried it with all the honor befitting one who had been a benefactor to himself and to Persia, because he had saved the bridge by which the Persians withdrew from Scythia. On many occasions Darius showed great magnanimity to his fallen enemies. After the revolts in Ionia had been quelled, he sent his son-in-law, Mardonius, to rehabilitate Ionia, and the latter deposed the tyrants and restored the governments to the people. Darius sent heralds to Greece demanding earth and water from the different states as tokens of submission. Many sent him the required tokens, but the Athenians threw the heralds who came to them into a pit, and the Spartans hurled their heralds into a well and told them to fetch their own earth and water. Reminded every day by his servant to "Remember the Athenians," constantly urged by the exiled sons of Pisistratus, who had fled to him, to seize

Attica, and now inflamed by the outrage to his heralds, he
sent Mardonius into Greece (492 B.C.) but the latter was
unsuccessful and was relieved of his command. In his place
Datis and Artaphernes, guided by the Athenian Hippias,
went with a host to Marathon. There the Persians suffered
a great defeat in one of the decisive battles of history (490
B.C.) at Marathon, and withdrew. Darius was now more avid
than ever to conquer the Athenians. He set about preparing
a great expedition against Greece, and at the same time, an
expedition to put down a revolt that had broken out in
Egypt. Before he could put his forces in motion he died (486
B.C.). His reign had lasted 36 years. On his death he was
succeeded by Xerxes, his son by Atossa. The tomb of Darius
is hewn in the rock at a place called Naksh-i-Rustam, near
Persepolis, and is adorned with sculptures and inscriptions
complementing those of Behistun.

Darius II (of *Persia*). [Original name, **Ochus;** Greek surname
Nothus, meaning "Bastard."] Persian king from c423 to 405
B.C.; son of Artaxerxes I. Through his son Cyrus the
Younger, and Tissaphernes and Artabazus, satraps in Asia
Minor, he pushed the plan to conquer the Athenian power
allying himself with Sparta, about 412 B.C., in the Pelo
ponnesian Wars.

Darius III (of *Persia*). [Surnamed **Codomannus.**] Last king of
Persia, died 330 B.C. He reigned 336–330 B.C., when he was
dethroned by Alexander the Great. Fearing that Alexander
might cross into Asia, he offered money to the Greeks to
wage war against him. This maneuver failed. Alexander
came to Asia and Darius met him at Issus. In the battle of
Issus (333 B.C.) Alexander directed his attack at the spot
where Darius, standing in his war chariot and surrounded by
a guard of Persian nobles, was located. Alexander broke
through; Darius wheeled his chariot and fled. Although his
cavalry was successful on the other side of the river, when
they heard the king was fleeing their line broke, they wav
ered and then fled. Darius abandoned his wife Statira and
his mother in the camp at Issus, and when he had outdis
tanced his pursuers he abandoned his chariot, his armor
and his royal cloak, and continued his flight on horseback.
Alexander gave up his pursuit of Darius at nightfall, re
turned to the Persian camp, and dined in the Great King'
tent. He heard the wailing of women nearby and on inquiry

learned that it proceeded from the abandoned family of Darius. Alexander sent word to them that Darius still lived, and that he would accord his royal captives all the respect due to royalty. Darius wrote Alexander from beyond the Euphrates, calling him an aggressor, asking that the royal captives be restored and proposing that a treaty of friendship and alliance be concluded between them (333 B.C.). Among other things, Alexander wrote the following in reply. "Your ancestors invaded Macedonia and the rest of Greece, and without provocation inflicted wrongs upon us. I was appointed leader of the Greeks, and crossed over into Asia for the purpose of avenging those wrongs; for you were the first aggressors. . . . I have overcome in battle, first your generals and satraps, and now yourself and your host, and possess your land, through the grace of the gods. . . . I am lord of all Asia, and therefore do thou come to me. . . . You have only to come to me to ask and receive your mother and wife and children, and whatever else you may desire. And for the future, whenever you send, send to me as to the Great King of Asia, and do not write as to an equal, but tell me what your need is, as to one who is lord of all that is yours. Otherwise I will deal with you as an offender. But if you dispute the kingdom, then wait and fight for it again, and do not flee; for I will march against you wherever you may be." Darius could not bring himself to submit to this arrogant, but perhaps justified, demand, and prepared to oppose Alexander. The forces met at Gaugamela (331 B.C.) for the battle often called the Battle of Arbela, from a town 60 miles away. Before the battle a eunuch from the train of Statira escaped from Alexander's camp and came to inform Darius that his wife had died in childbirth. Darius is said to have sighed that perhaps her death ended dishonor for her and for him at Alexander's hands, but the eunuch assured him that Alexander had never abused any of the women from Darius' household. On the contrary, he had treated them with great honor for, added the eunuch, "Alexander is as gentle after victory as he is terrible in the field." Convinced of the noble and honorable treatment Alexander had shown his wife, Darius, according to Plutarch, prayed to his gods that he might be allowed to restore the fortunes of Persia, but if fate decreed that Persia must be conquered, he prayed that Alexander would be the conqueror. In the battle

of Guagamela the forces of Alexander completely overwhelmed the superior numbers in Darius' army. Once again
Darius fled before the onslaught. Again he abandoned his
war car, and again on horseback, he galloped to the mountains of Media. Accompanied by a group of Persian nobles,
he went deep into Asia past the Caspian Gates. Alexander
consolidated his gains before pursuing him; then, true to his
letter, took up the pursuit. Darius fell under the domination
of his nobles, especially his cousin Bessus, and as Alexander,
by a series of unbelievably swift rides with a small band,
began to overtake him, Bessus urged Darius to mount again
and flee. Darius refused; Bessus and the other Persians
stabbed him (330 B.C.) at a place near Thara, south of the
Caspian Sea, and deserted him. Plutarch says the dying king
expressed his trust in Alexander and signified it by saying
to his friend or servant, "I give him my right hand." But
when Alexander arrived, the king had just died. In pity, he
is said to have thrown his own cloak over the corpse, which
he sent, with great pomp, to the dead king's mother for
burial.

Darius the Mede (mēd). In the Bible, king of Chaldea or Babylonia after the overthrow and death of Belshazzar; 6th century B.C. He is said to have been a son of Ahasuerus (see
Daniel, v. 31; vi. 28; ix. 1; xi. 1; and other passages). Some
historians identify him with Cyaxares, son of Astyages, and
uncle to Cyrus the Great.

Datis (dā'tis). Median general, who with Artaphernes, commanded the army that Darius I sent to punish the Eretrians
and the Athenians for their interference in the Ionian revolt
(c499 B.C.), and the burning of Sardis. On the way to Greece
the Persian fleet stopped at Naxos and burned the temples
and houses of the town, which had been abandoned by the
Naxians in terror. The Delians, informed of the approach of
Datis, fled to Tenos. Datis anchored at Rhenia, a tiny island
lying near Delos, and sent a message to the Delians, asking
why they had fled, and assuring them that he would not
harm the country that gave birth to the two gods (Apollo
and Artemis). He offered a valuable sacrifice on the altar at
Delos and sailed away to Eretria. There he besieged the city
for six days, at the end of which time it was betrayed, according to Herodotus, by two citizens, and fell to the Persians,
who plundered and burned the temples and the town to
avenge the burning of Sardis, and carried off the inhabitants.

fat, fāte, fär, fâll, àsk, fāre; net, mē, hėr; pin, pīne; not, nōte, mŏve,
nôr; up, lūte, pùll; oi, oil; ou out; (lightened) ēlect, agǫny, ūnite;

as captives. The Persians then proceeded toward Athens. They drew up their forces on the plain of Marathon and suffered overwhelming defeat (490 B.C.) at the hands of the Athenians and Plataeans. Datis sailed back to Persia. On the way, when he reached Rhenia, he was visited by a vision in a dream. The next day he caused a search to be made throughout the ships. When a golden image of Apollo was found abroad a Phoenician vessel in his fleet, he sailed to Delos and placed it in the temple there.

Deïoces (dē′yō̱-sēz). According to some accounts, the founder (reigned c700–647 B.C.) of the Median dynasty who led the Medes in revolt against Assyria and freed them. According to Herodotus, Deïoces achieved his ambition of supreme power over his fellow-countrymen by the use of intelligence and psychology. In his own village he became so noted for his just dealings that his fellow townsmen made him mediator in their disputes. At this time the Medes lived in scattered villages and lacked the discipline of law. The reputation of Deïoces for justice spread and it became the practice for disputants in other villages to come to him to settle their affairs. As he was increasingly sought out to pronounce judgments, he suddenly gave notice that he would no longer occupy himself with securing justice for others because, by spending his whole day in regulating other men's affairs, he was neglecting his own. When he withdrew from his acknowledged position as judge, robbery and lawlessness broke out and so harried the Medes that they met together and decided to invite Deïoces to become their king and restore order. He agreed to do so on condition that he be given a personal bodyguard and that the Medes build him a palace suitable to his new rank. Moreover, he demanded that they build him a new capital city. This was the city of Ecbatana. Surrounding the city on a hill was a series of seven encircling walls. According to Herodotus, the walls were coated, beginning with the outer one, in white, black, scarlet, blue, and orange colors, and the two innermost walls were coated respectively with silver and gold. Inside this fastness Deïoces had his palace and treasury. He retreated into it and thenceforth became a power remote from the eyes of the people, for, says Herodotus, if those who had been brought up with him and considered themselves his equals saw him often, they would become jealous of the power he had acquired, though he was no better than they, and might conspire against him. Therefore he decreed that no one could come into his presence. Petitions from his subjects were communicated to him by messengers. When he had secured his bodyguard, his palace fortress, and his city, Deïoces continued to dispense justice as before, but whereas in former times he had been freely sought out as an arbiter, now his judgments were imposed from above, and a complex spy system kept him informed of the affairs of his kingdom. Some say that Deïoces was in fact probably a local chieftain named Dayukku whose grandson Cyaxares founded the Median empire in 625 B.C. and whose name was included in the list of Median kings as a matter of policy.

Deïotarus (dē-yot′a-rus). Tetrarch and king of Galatia, and an ally of the Romans; died 40 B.C. He was defended before Caesar by Cicero in 45 B.C. on a charge of plotting to assassinate Caesar. Throughout the Roman struggle for power he kept his throne, siding successively with Pompey, Caesar, Brutus, and the triumvirate of Octavian, Antony, and Lepidus.

Demades (dem′a-dēz). Athenian orator, born c350 B.C.; died 319 B.C. By his eloquence and complete lack of scruples he rose to a position of prominence in Athens. He was a member of the peace party and opposed Demosthenes, who urged war on Philip of Macedon. Demosthenes' policy prevailed. At the battle of Chaeronea (338 B.C.) Philip inflicted a disastrous defeat on the Greeks. Demades was one of 2000 captives taken. According to one story Philip celebrated his victory by drinking much wine, and after a drunken carousal went to the place where the prisoners were under guard. He mocked them and sneered at the great Demosthenes, who had fled. Demades rebuked him, saying, "O King, fortune has given you the role of Agamemnon, and you play the part of Thersites." Philip was immediately sobered by the rebuke, freed Demades, and sent him as one of the envoys to make peace with Athens, the terms of which were remarkably lenient in comparison with his treatment of Thebes at the same time. After the death of Philip (336 B.C.) Thebes revolted against his successor, Alexander the Great. Athens prepared to help Thebes, but Alexander swooped down from the north, completely defeated Thebes, and destroyed the city. Alexander demanded the surrender of the leaders

fat, fāte, fär, fåll, åsk, fãre; net, mē, hėr; pin, pīne; not, nōte, möve, nôr; up, lūte, půll; oi, oil; ou out; (lightened) ḝlect, agǫny, ūnite of the war party at Athens, including Demosthenes. Demades, who had proposed that an embassy from Athens, be sent to congratulate Alexander on his victory at Thebes, was sent as a peacemaker from Athens, and persuaded Alexander to let Athens deal with the offenders. From this time on Demades supported Phocion (q.v.), the Athenian general who played a large part in guiding Athens away from her rash desire to wage war on Macedonia. Along with Phocion, and even Demosthenes, he persuaded the Athenians not to help the Spartan king Agis in a war against Macedonia (331 B.C.), and he continued to support the peace policy of Phocion in the 12 years between the fall of Thebes (335 B.C.) and the death of Alexander (323 B.C.). At the same time that he supported the Macedonian party, he accepted bribes from their opponents, was discovered, and was several times fined. Nevertheless, he maintained his position. When news of Alexander's death reached Athens, men could scarcely believe it. Demades declared, "If he were indeed dead, the whole world would have been filled with the stench of his corpse." Nevertheless, he was indeed dead. Athens rose again in rebellion, spurred on by Demosthenes, and was defeated at Crannon, 322 B.C., by the Macedonians under Antipater. Again Demades acted as a peace envoy, but this time the terms were not so lenient, for Antipater did not share the admiration and respect for Athenian culture held by Philip and Alexander. From this time Demades conducted affairs at Athens so as to please Antipater, and excused his servile conduct on the ground that he was "in command of a shipwrecked state." According to Plutarch, his life and administration were so outrageous that Antipater said of him, when he was an old man, that he was like a victim when the sacrifice was over: nothing left but tongue and guts. Antipater also said he had two friends at Athens: Phocion, whom he could not persuade to take anything, and Demades, to whom he could never give enough. After the death of Antipater (319 B.C.) Demades went to Cassander, his son, to plead for relief from the payment Athens had agreed to make after the battle of Crannon. Cassander had found a letter written by Demades to Perdiccas, which was a betrayal of Antipater. He had Demades slain for his ingratitude and his treachery (319 B.C.).

Demaratus (dem-a̧-rā′tus). A son of Ariston and co-king of

Sparta with Cleomenes; fl. c510-480 B.C., and shared the throne with Cleomenes from 510-491 B.C. He shared with Cleomenes the command of the army sent in 510 B.C. to assist the Athenians in expelling Hippias. In 506 B.C. when Cleomenes sought to restore Hippias, Demaratus withdrew at the moment when battle was to be joined. Demaratus later brought charges against Cleomenes for a war he was waging against the Aeginetans, and when he returned from the war, Cleomenes sought to drive Demaratus from his office as king and adopted the following means to do so: He claimed that Demaratus was not the true son of Ariston, because he was born to the third wife of Ariston, the latter, on reckoning the time he had been married, exclaimed an oath that this could not be his son. Ariston later became convinced that Demaratus was truly the son he had prayed for and forgot all about the matter. But Cleomenes revived the early incident. The oracle at Delphi was consulted. To make sure that a favorable answer was given, Cleomenes sent bribes to the oracle, which thereupon declared Demaratus was not the son of Ariston and therefore not rightfully a king of Sparta. Demaratus, on losing the throne (491 B.C.), sacrificed an ox to Zeus and questioned his mother. He begged her to tell him the truth. If he were not the son of Ariston but the offspring of a groom, as some claimed, he would forgive her as such an eventuality might come to anyone, but he wanted to know the truth of his origin. His mother told him that an apparition had come to her in the appearance of Ariston, embraced her, and placed garlands on her head. The same night Ariston came, again as she thought, and asked where the garlands had come from. To her reply that he himself had placed them there, he made strong denials. The conclusion, on consultation of the priests, was that he who placed the garlands on her head and embraced her was the spirit of a hero whose shrine was nearby. His mother ended her story by telling Demaratus that he was either the son of that hero or of Ariston; which, she did not know. Demaratus now fled from Sparta, pursued by the Spartans, and sought asylum with King Darius in Susa. The bribery of the oracle was later disclosed and the priestess was removed, and when Cleomenes' part became known, he was forced to flee. Demaratus, meanwhile, was received as a guest in King Darius' court, and afterward became the bond-

friend of his son and successor Xerxes. He accompanied
Xerxes when the latter invaded Greece. After the Persians
had crossed into Europe, Xerxes called Demaratus and
asked him whether he thought the Greeks would resist the
onslaught of his mighty army. Demaratus replied that even
if all the other Greeks submitted, the Spartans would not
submit to the slavery Xerxes proposed to subject them to;
and if there were only 1000 Spartans, they would resist, no
matter what the size of the Persian host. Xerxes scoffed at
what he considered a ridiculous estimate of the bravery of
the Spartans. Demaratus insisted. He said the Spartans, as
free men who submitted voluntarily to the discipline of law,
were the bravest men in the world, for the law forbade them
to flee in battle, but commanded them to stand firm and
conquer or die. Xerxes laughed. Just before the battle of
Thermopylae, when Xerxes was opposed by 1000 Greeks,
Spartans and Thespians, he again questioned Demaratus,
and received the reply that if he could subdue the Spartans
at Thermopylae and those in Lacedaemonia, he would have
all Greece at his feet. After the battle of Thermopylae
Xerxes was compelled to admit that Demaratus had not lied
about the bravery of the Spartans. He asked his advice how
to conquer those still in Lacedaemonia. Demaratus advised
him to attack them directly by sea. Xerxes ignored his advice, saying at the same time that he knew Demaratus meant
it for his good but in this instance he was mistaken. But some
say that Demaratus had sent a message warning the Spartans
of what the Persians intended before they ever left Susa.

Demetrius I (dē-mē'tri-us). [Surnamed **Poliorcetes,** meaning
"Taker of Cities" or "Besieger."] King of Macedonia (294–
288 B.C.); born 336 B.C.; died at Apamea, in ancient Syria,
283 B.C. He was a son of Antigonus I, who was called Antigonus Cyclops. He liberated Athens and Megara in 307
B.C., defeated Ptolemy I in 306, unsuccessfully besieged
Rhodes (305–304), and was defeated at Ipsus in 301 B.C. He
was chosen king by the army in 294 B.C., gained control
(293–289 B.C.) of Greece, and invaded Asia, which Antigonus had held, with an inferior force in 287 B.C. He surrendered to Seleucus I in 285 B.C. and drank himself to
death.

Demetrius II. King of Macedonia; born c276 B.C.; died 229 B.C.
He was a son of Antigonus II Gonatus, whom he succeeded

(obscured) errănt, ardĕnt, actǫr; ch, chip; g, go; th, thin; ŦH, then; y, you;
(variable) ḍ as d or j, ş as s or sh, ţ as t or ch, ẕ as z or zh.

c239 B.C. During his reign the Macedonians fought to preserve their territory; the Demetrian War, so called, was fought against the Aetolian League and the Achaeans, but Demetrius was defeated in the north. Philip V of Macedon was his son by his second wife Phthia (or Chryseis).

Demetrius I (of *Syria*). [Surnamed *Soter,* meaning "Savior."] King of Syria from 162 B.C.; born 187 B.C.; killed 150 B.C. He was a grandson of Antiochus the Great. After living as a captive in Rome while his uncle, Antiochus IV, and his cousin, Antiochus V, sat on the throne, he escaped (162 B.C.), killed his cousin, and became king himself. He suppressed the revolt of Timarchus in Babylon and put down the Maccabee uprising in Palestine. But Alexander Balas, a pretender, claimed the throne, and, with the help of the Maccabees, Egyptians, and others, overthrew Demetrius.

Demetrius II (of *Syria*). [Surnamed *Nicator.*] King of Syria (145–141 and 129–126 B.C.); son of Demetrius I. He was born c161 B.C.; died near Tyre, 126 B.C. He overthrew Alexander Balas, the usurper, with the aid of Ptolemy VI (Ptolemy Philometor), obtaining both the throne and Ptolemy's daughter, Cleopatra Thea, wife of Alexander Balas. He defeated the attempt (145–142 B.C.) to place Antiochus VI, son of Alexander Balas, on the throne. In 141 B.C. he was captured by the Parthians and remained their prisoner for about ten years, his brother Antiochus VII occupying the throne in his absence and marrying Cleopatra, Demetrius' wife. Demetrius regained the throne in 129 B.C. but was soon after killed in a civil war. He was succeeded by his sons Seleucus V and Antiochus VIII.

Demetrius III (of *Syria*). [Surnamed *Euergetes* and *Philometor.*] King of Syria 94–88 B.C.; son of Antiochus VIII Grypus. He struggled for the throne with his cousin Antiochus X and his brother Philip; he was defeated, captured, and held prisoner by the Parthians until his death.

Demetrius Phalereus (fạ-lē′rös, fạ-lir′ē-us). Athenian statesman and orator; born at Phalerum, in Attica, 345 B.C.; died in Upper Egypt, 283 B.C. He entered public life c325 B.C. as a supporter of Phocion, and in 317 B.C. was placed by Phocion's successor, Cassander, at the head of the administration of Athens. Expelled from Athens in 307 B.C. by Demetrius I of Macedonia (Demetrius Poliorcetes), he retired to the court of Ptolemy Lagus at Alexandria, where he devoted himself wholly to literary pursuits. He was exiled by Ptolemy's successor of Upper Egypt, where he is said to have died of the bite of a snake.

Demochares (dē-mok′a̱-rēz). Athenian orator; fl. 322–280 B.C. He was a nephew of Demosthenes. He came forward in 322 B.C. as an orator of the anti-Macedonian party, and after the restoration of democracy by Demetrius I of Macedonia (Demetrius Poliorcetes) in 307 B.C. became the leader of the popular party. He was several times expelled by the anti-democratic party, returning the last time in 287 or 286. He was sent as ambassador to Lysimachus c282, and disappears from view in 280 B.C.

Demosthenes (dē-mos′thē-nēz). Athenian general in the Peloponnesian War. He died at Syracuse, 413 B.C. He led an expedition (426 B.C.) against the Aetolians which ended in failure. He did not dare return to Athens with the news that he had lost 120 Athenian hoplites to the Aetolian javelins. Instead he went to Naupactus, where he drove off an attack by the Spartans, and followed this up by defeating the Ambracians, Spartan allies. In 425 B.C., sailing to the relief of the people of Corcyra, Demosthenes put in at Pylus, on the western coast of the Peloponnesus, and fortified it, in defiance of the jeers of his fellow commanders who thought it a forsaken, useless spot. He remained at Pylus with five of his ships when the rest of the fleet sailed on. The Spartans hurried to Pylus to destroy a fortress that the enemy had raised on their own soil. For a time they blockaded the Athenians under Demosthenes at Pylus. Then they occupied the island of Sphacteria in the mouth of the bay, but the Athenians destroyed the ships by which the Spartans had landed and in turn blockaded them on the island. The siege went on longer than was expected and the Athenians at home became impatient. They sent Cleon, who had boasted that he would take the Spartans alive or kill them on the spot, with enlarged forces to end the siege. He arrived at Pylus and with Demosthenes, who had worked out a plan of attack, as his co-commander, did succeed in bringing about the surrender of the Spartans on Sphacteria. Cleon claimed the credit for this great victory, glorious not for the importance of the place but because of the unheard-of exploit of taking Spartans alive. Such was their reputation that they were expected to fight to the death in any encounter, and

(obscured) errᴀnt, ardᴇnt, actọr; ch, chip; g, go; th, thin; ŦH, then; y, you; (variable) ḍ as d or j, ş as s or sh, ṭ as t or ch, ᶎ as z or zh.

"come home either with their shields or on them." Demosthenes had made the disposition by which the surrender of the Spartans was accomplished. Later he commanded under Nicias in the unsuccessful expedition against Syracuse in 413 B.C. Having been captured in the retreat, he was put to death by order of the Syracusan assembly.

Demosthenes. Greatest of Greek orators. He was born at Paeania, in Attica, 384 B.C., and died on the island of Calauria, in the Saronic Gulf, 322 B.C. When he was seven years old, his father died and the guardians entrusted with his property made off with it. When Demosthenes, a weakly child reared by his mother, grew up, he brought an action against the guardians and, though they were prominent and attempted to frighten him, he won the case. Although most of his father's property had been lost, with the damages he won he fitted out a trireme and presented it to the Athenian fleet. He is said to have been the pupil of the orator Isaeus, and entered public life as a speaker in the popular assembly in 355 B.C. In that same year he delivered his speech *Against Leptines,* in which he favored the continuance of public grants of immunity from taxation which were awarded from time to time to those who had rendered outstanding service to the state. In 351 B.C. he delivered the first of a splendid series of orations directed against the encroachment of Philip II of Macedon, three of which are specifically denominated *Philippics.* In 346 B.C. he served as a member of the embassy which concluded with Philip the so-called peace of Philocrates. In the ten-member peace commission Demosthenes alone was not satisfied with the peace because of certain ambiguous clauses, and in the end refused the rich presents Philip offered the negotiators as was the custom, refused to be associated with them in the peace, and when he reached Athens proposed that the crown usually awarded to ambassadors be withheld from them all, including himself. As Philip immediately after broke this treaty, Demosthenes came forward as the leader of the patriotic party, in opposition to the Macedonian party which was headed by Aeschines. In the years immediately following, the ambassadors who had arranged the peace were violently attacked and some left Athens. Demosthenes came out against Aeschines in a speech *On the Embassy* (344 B.C.), but failed to convict him. In 340 B.C. he caused a fleet to be sent to the

fat, fāte, fär, fâll, àsk, fãre; net, mē, hèr; pin, pīne; not, nōte, möve, nôr; up, lūte, pùll; oi, oil; ou out; (lightened) ēlect, agǫny, ūnite;

relief of Byzantium, which was besieged by Philip. On the outbreak of the Amphictyonic War, he persuaded the Athenians to form an alliance with Thebes against Philip, who defeated the allies at Chaeronea in 338 B.C., and usurped the hegemony of Greece. The Macedonian party in Athens attacked Demosthenes, who called unceasingly for the overthrow of Philip, but the people were loyal to Demosthenes, his accusers failed to convict him, and he was chosen to pronounce the funeral oration for the fallen of Chaeronea. Athens was powerless to free herself from the alliance Philip had imposed on her. Following the murder of Philip (336 B.C.), Demosthenes was one of the leaders of the unsuccessful rising against Macedon. Alexander the Great razed Thebes to the ground and demanded that the leaders who had encouraged the Theban revolt, among them Demosthenes, be handed over to him. But on the representation of a trusted mediator, they were spared. In 324 B.C. Harpalus, treasurer of Alexander, fled with considerable treasure and some forces, his peculations and extravagance having been discovered, and came to Greece. The Athenians would not receive him as long as he was accompanied by an armed force. But when he came alone to Athens they received him and took from him, Demosthenes being the authority in charge, 700 talents which they placed in the Parthenon until such time as the stolen money could be returned to Alexander. This was a matter of honor with the Athenians. Before the money could be restored Harpalus escaped. The money that had been deposited in the Parthenon was counted and was found to amount to only about half the sum originally deposited. The Macedonian party raised a great hue and cry against Demosthenes, claiming he had taken it as a bribe. The amount he received, if any, could not be proved, but the case went against him and he was fined such a large sum he could not pay it and went into exile on the island of Calauria, off Troezen. On the outbreak of a fresh rising at the death of Alexander in 323 B.C. he was recalled by the patriotic party, and on the capture of Athens by Antipater and Craterus in 322 B.C. fled to Calauria again, where he took poison in the temple of Poseidon to avoid capture. His tomb was at Calauria, where he was especially honored. The chief of the orations of Demosthenes are three *Philippics* (351, 344, 341 B.C.), three *Olynthiacs* (349,

(obscured) err*a*nt, ard*e*nt, act*o*r; ch, chip; g, go; th, thin; ŦH, then; y, you;
(variable) ḍ as d or j, ṣ as s or sh, ṭ as t or ch, ẓ as z or zh.

349, 348 B.C.), *On the Peace* (346 B.C.), *On the Embassy* (344 B.C.), *On the Affairs of the Chersonese* (341 B.C.), *On the Crown* (330 B.C.). This last-named speech, the most famous of Demosthenes' orations, was in answer to Aeschines, who prosecuted Ctesiphon for moving that a crown be given to Demosthenes for his services to the state. Demosthenes was the great opponent of the Macedonian conquest of Greece, holding that Athens, traditionally and actually, was the heart of any Greek nation, and that it was necessary that the spark be rekindled that had died during the Peloponnesian War. Many legendary stories are told of how he obtained his oratorical power: a stammerer, he taught himself to speak slowly by putting pebbles in his mouth; he went to the seashore and declaimed to the waves so that the noise of an audience would not disturb him; he would run uphill while orating in order to strengthen his weak voice; he shut himself in a cave and copied Thucydides' history eight times in order to attain to a fine style. He seems actually to have had a speech defect; his style in oratory was not complex, but simple and pithy and effective.

Dentatus (den-tā′tus), *Manius Curius.* Roman tribune, consul, praetor, and censor; fl. in the first part of the 3rd century B.C. He is celebrated as a model of the early Roman virtues of simplicity, frugality, and patriotism. He defeated Pyrrhus in 275 B.C., and the Samnites (290) and the Lucanians (274 B.C.).

Diadochi (dī″ad′ō̧-kī). The Macedonian generals of Alexander the Great who, after his death in 323 B.C., divided his empire. Literally, the name means "Successors." The several empires that were established were the Seleucid in Syria and Asia Minor, the Ptolemid in Egypt, the Attalid in Pergamum, and the Antigonid in Macedonia.

Dieneces (dī-ȩ̄-nē′sēz). A Spartan in the company of Leonidas at the defence of the pass of Thermopylae (480 B.C.). According to Herodotus, he was warned by a Trachinian that the number of barbarians attacking was so vast that when they shot their arrows the face of the sun was darkened. Fearless, Dieneces replied that this was good news, for if the barbarians darkened the sun then the Greeks would be able to fight in the shade.

Diocles (dī′ō̧-klēz). Syracusan popular leader; fl. 5th century B.C. He was the reputed chief author of a code of laws named for him.

fat, fāte, fär, fåll, ȧsk, fāre; net, mē, hėr; pin, pīne; not, nōte, möve, nôr; up, lūte, půll; oi, oil; ou out; (lightened) ȩlect, agǫny, ụnite;

Dion (dī′on). Syracusan philosopher and statesman; born at Syracuse, c408 B.C.; assassinated there, 354 B.C. His sister Aristomache was one of two wives whom Dionysius the Elder, tyrant of Syracuse, married at the same time. Ultimately, Dion married Arete, the daughter of Dionysius and Aristomache. From his connection with Dionysius and because of his own wisdom and capacity, he gained an influential role in Syracusan affairs, and was one of very few who dared speak freely to Dionysius. Dionysius the Younger succeeded his father, and Dion became one of his counselors. Dion, a gifted and ardent disciple of Plato, earnestly wished Dionysius the Younger to put into practice some of Plato's theories of government. The young tyrant had had no education, because his father feared that if he mingled with intelligent and capable men, he might seek to overthrow him and seize the tyranny. Dion now encouraged him to seek the company of philosophers; he pointed out the magnificence in which the young ruler lived and advised him to furnish "the royal palace of his soul" as richly as he had furnished the palace of his body. He tried to instill in him the idea that with a just government his people would obey him out of respect and admiration rather than give him the sullen obedience they now rendered through fear. Dionysius was all enthusiasm for learning, and Plato was sent for. He arrived in Syracuse in 367 B.C. and was warmly welcomed, and a wave of enthusiasm for philosophy and letters swept Syracuse. It did not last long. Dion's influence was resented and feared by those who profited from the tyranny. They set all manner of criticisms of Dion afloat and declared that his aim was to depose Dionysius, seize power himself, and secure the succession for his sister's children. Dionysius, a weak and profligate man, believed the enemies of Dion, and when a letter Dion had written to the Carthaginians fell into his hands his suspicions against Dion seemed to be confirmed. By a trick he led Dion to the shore, accused him of treachery, commanded him to board a small boat waiting there, and ordered the crew to set Dion ashore in Italy. However, the Syracusans were so aroused by the departure of Dion that Dionysius was frightened and denied he had exiled him. He loaded two ships with the goods and treasure of Dion and sent them to him. After a time, Plato left Syracuse also, with a promise from Dionysius that he would recall Dion. Dion went to Athens and joined Plato. He visited cities through-

(obscured) errạnt, ardẹnt, actọr; ch, chip; g, go; th, thin; ᵮн, then; y, you; (variable) ḑ as d or j, ṣ as s or sh, ṭ as t or ch, ẓ as z or zh.

out Greece and was widely welcomed, the Spartans even going so far as to make him a citizen. Dionysius made no attempt to recall him. On the contrary, he discontinued sending him the revenues from his estates and forced Dion's wife to marry one of his friends. News came to Dion from Syracuse that the people were so discontented that they would overthrow Dionysius if Dion returned. He decided to do so. He collected a small force of Greek mercenaries on the island of Zacynthus, made a splendid sacrifice to Apollo, gave a feast, and was ready to depart. On the eve of departure there was an eclipse of the moon which frightened his soldiers, but seers said it betokened the eclipse of Dionysius. Another omen, swarms of bees that settled on the prows of the ships, was not publicly interpreted for the soothsayers feared it meant Dion's efforts would first prosper and then fail. Yet there were other definitely favorable signs: an eagle seized a spear, flew up with it, and then dropped it into the sea; sea water became sweet and drinkable for a whole day. The forces of Dion landed at Minoa in Sicily and marched toward Syracuse. Dionysius was away from the city, and letters warning him of the approach of Dion with an army failed to reach him. Dion, whose forces were increased by volunteers along the way, entered Syracuse without a struggle (357 B.C.), and was welcomed with joy. A week later, Dionysius sailed into the harbor, and though envoys were treating with Dion, he treacherously attacked the city. Dion rallied the defenders and won a victory, but not before Dionysius had gained the citadel where he took refuge. Dion was master of the city, but his aloof manner and determination to teach the Syracusans how to govern themselves under his direction offended them. The fickle people now appointed Heraclides as admiral of the fleet, but when Dion rebuked them for infringing the supreme power they had already give him, they withdrew the appointment. Dion himself then appointed Heraclides admiral, though his friends warned that Heraclides was not a friend to him. Philistus, a Syracusan exile, returned with a fleet to help Dionysius, who was under siege in the citadel, but Philistus was defeated and slain. Dionysius escaped through Heraclides' fleet and the people rose up in anger against Heraclides, but he diverted them by criticizing Dion, claiming that Dion's mercenaries got the best rewards and rousing the people against the

fat, fāte, fär, fåll, ȧsk, fãre; net, mē, hėr; pin, pīne; not, nōte, möve, nôr; up, lūte, pu̇ll; oi, oil; ou out; (lightened) ēlect, agǫny, ūnite;

foreign soldiers. He also suggested a land reform and proposed that the Syracusans choose new generals. The foolish
Syracusans swung over to his side and turned against Dion.
All sorts of unfavorable omens occurred the day the new
generals were to be chosen, but they were ignored. Twenty-
five new generals were selected, among them Heraclides,
and a threatening crowd sought to drive Dion and his
mercenaries out of the city. The Greek mercenaries would
have attacked the crowd but Dion would not turn against his
own city. Instead, his loyal mercenaries repelled the hostile
Syracusans with scowls and conducted him safely to Leontini, where they and he were welcomed (356 B.C.). In a short
time, Dionysius sent forces to Syracuse that took the city
with great slaughter. Envoys were hurriedly sent to Dion in
Leontini, begging him to come and save the city. Dion,
according to Plutarch, made a moving speech to his mercenaries, telling them he meant to return to Syracuse himself,
but would understand if they did not wish to accompany
him. "If, however, in your displeasure at the Syracusans, you
shall leave them to their fate, at least for your former bravery
and zeal in my behalf may you obtain a worthy reward from
the gods, and may you think of Dion as one who abandoned
neither you when you were wronged, nor, afterwards, his
fellow citizens when they were in distress." The mercenaries
leaped to their feet and shouted for him to lead them back.
When the enemy captain learned that Dion was coming to
the relief of the city, he sacked it and put it to the torch. Dion
found it in flames. With his mercenaries he overcame the
forces of Dionysius, who again took refuge in the citadel,
and put out the fires in the city. The son of Dionysius in the
citadel was compelled to surrender, and was permitted to
sail away. Dion was reunited with his wife and his sister, who
had been held in the fortress even since he returned from
Greece. All the Syracusans, with wildest rejoicing, went
down to the harbor to witness the departure of the son of
Dionysius. Dion was now at the height of his power and
prestige. He rewarded his friends, allies, and mercenaries,
but continued to live simply and modestly himself. His
friend Plato wrote that the eyes of the world were on him.
But Dion did not propose to restore a democracy; he favored a limited monarchy. However, he was, in fact, a new
tyrant of Syracuse. He brought in Corinthians to advise him

and by so doing aroused resentment among the Syracusans. Once again Heraclides stirred up discontent and plotted against him. This time Dion, who had always forgiven him though he was a known enemy, permitted his friends, who had been urging it for a long time, to go to the house of Heraclides and slay him. Dion gave him a splendid funeral and followed his body to the grave, but the murder of Heraclides oppressed him; he knew it was a stain on his honor. After this, a heavier blow fell. His dear friend, the Athenian Callippus, who had come to Syracuse with him, plotted to seize control. Dion's friends warned him, but he no longer wanted to struggle for the people of Syracuse or himself. He was ready to die, he said, if it had become necessary for him to live on his guard not only against his enemies, but even against his friends. Omens of death had already come to him. As he was sitting in his house, he saw a woman of great height, dressed like and resembling one of the Furies, and sweeping his courtyard with a broom; a few days later, his son threw himself from the roof in a fit of anger and was killed. Nevertheless, his friends, and especially his wife Arete and his sister Aristomache, tried to protect him. Callippus was charged with a plot but swore a most sacred oath that he was innocent. He then committed the greatest impiety of all. As Dion was sitting among friends, during the festival of the Coreia, in honor of the goddess in whose name Callippus had sworn his oath, Callippus attacked him and killed him (354 B.C.).

Dionysius (dī-ọ̄-nish′i-us, -nish′us). [Surnamed *the Elder.*] Tyrant of Syracuse, born c430 B.C.; died at Syracuse, 367 B.C. He was of obscure birth and had served as a clerk in a government office. In the siege of Acragas (406 B.C.), he fought bravely with the Syracusans who went to the relief of the city, was wounded, and left for dead on the field. His experience convinced him that the democratic government of Syracuse was so weak that a strong man could easily take control. He resolved to be that strong man. In an assembly he rose and denounced the generals of Syracuse who had failed to relieve Acragas. His views coincided with those of the populace. The generals were removed and a new board of generals, of which he was a member, was named. He soon discredited his fellow generals on the new board; they were deposed and he was made sole general (405 B.C.). He caused

fat, fāte, fär, fâll, ȧsk, fãre; net, mē, hėr; pin, pīne; not, nōte, mŏve, nôr; up, lūte, pụll; oi, oil; ou out; (lightened) ẹlect, agọny, ụnite;

a rumor to be spread that an attempt had been made on his life, demanded and was permitted a personal bodyguard. Through the fear of the Syracusans of Carthage they had allowed Dionysius to make himself tyrant of Syracuse, although he kept the outward forms of democracy.

He led a force to the relief of Gela, besieged by the Carthaginians, but through what was probably treachery on his part, an attack on the Carthaginian camp ended in failure. Rather than attempt to raise the siege he decided to remove the people of Gela; they abandoned their city at night. At Camarina he made the same decision, although Camarina had not even been attacked. His Italian allies withdrew in disgust. Some Syracusan horsemen thought he was a traitor, rode to his house, plundered it, and attacked his wife. Dionysius hurried to Syracuse, entered the city at night by burning the gate, and overcame his opponents. It seems that his activities in the case of Gela and Camarina were deliberate—he did not want the annihilation of Carthage in Sicily, for as long as Carthage presented a danger there was justification of his dictatorial power. In 404 B.C. he made a treaty with Himilco, the Carthaginian general, by which each side was to keep, in general, what it held at the time, but the significant clause of the treaty, from the standpoint of Dionysius, was that Carthage guaranteed his power in Syracuse.

He now set to work to fortify Syracuse, a city on an island. But his rule was not popular or secure. In a war against Herbessus the army mutinied. Dionysius withdrew to his fortified island and suffered siege by his own people (403 B.C.), who were assisted by forces from Rhegium and Messina. He called a council of his followers in the fortress. Some advised him to flee, others to stay; one Heloris remarked that "Sovereign power is a fair winding-sheet." Dionysius, as he did so often, resorted to stratagem. He asked the besiegers to let him depart from Syracuse with his possessions. They agreed, and so implicitly trusted him that they sent away some of their forces and relaxed the siege. Meantime, Dionysius sent a secret call for assistance to the Campanian mercenaries of Carthage. They came, in accordance with the treaty of Himilco guaranteeing his power. When they arrived they completely routed the rebels and Dionysius reestablished his control. He sold the inhabitants of the Greek cities of Naxos and Catana as slaves, gave Catana to Campanian mercenaries, and razed Naxos. Next he won back Leontini, which had been made independent by his treaty with Himilco. This left Sicily divided between Greek cities under control of Dionysius, and Carthaginian cities, except for Messina which remained independent. He expanded the fortifications of Syracuse, reorganized his army, introduced the catapult as an engine of siege warfare, and strengthened his fleet by building ships with five banks of oars. Having made such preparations, he was ready to move against the Carthaginians in Sicily. Gela, Camarina, Acragas, and Eryx gave him their allegiance. He besieged (398 B.C.) the Carthaginian city of Motya, a fortified island city, and after a tremendous effort and despite heroic resistance, he reduced and took it. This was the first Phoenician town taken by the Greeks.

Himilco was sent from Carthage to protect the Punic cities. He took Eryx by treason and recaptured Motya. Dionysius did not oppose him. He withdrew to Syracuse and sent a fleet, under command of his brother Leptines, to attack the Carthaginian fleet at Catana (396 B.C.). He observed the defeat of the fleet from the shore and again retreated to Syracuse, although his men were eager to stand and fight. The Carthaginians sailed into the harbor, their army disembarked and encamped in the marsh nearby, and laid siege to Syracuse. During the 11-month siege, discontent in the city was great. Outside, the army of Himilco was attacked by pestilence and greatly weakened. Dionysius chose the moment to counterattack. He ordered his fleet against the Carthaginian ships and himself led a land force out of the city. His attack was a great success; the Carthaginian fleet was burned, the land forces of Dionysius were victorious. The Carthaginians were routed, but Dionysius, on receipt of 300 talents, treacherously allowed Himilco to escape with 40 triremes. Himilco's mercenaries, deserted by their commander, were enslaved or slaughtered. Again, Dionysius was unwilling, for the sake of his own power, to allow the annihilation of Carthage in Sicily.

Following the victory, he extended his power in Sicily. In 392 B.C. the Carthaginians, under the command of Mago, returned, and were again defeated. They sued for peace. By the terms of the peace Syracuse became the acknowledged

fat, fāte, fär, fâll, ȧsk, fāre; net, mē, hėr; pin, pīne; not, nōte, mōve, nôr; up, lūte, pull; oi, oil; ou out; (lightened) ẹlect, agǫny, ūnite;

master of all the Greek communities of Sicily. The city of Tauromenium, once unsuccessfully besieged by Dionysius, was awarded to him, and he now began to expand his power on the mainland of Italy. Rhegium was a personal as well as a political enemy, for when he asked for a maiden of Rhegium for a wife he was told that the only maiden of Rhegium he could have was the hangman's daughter; Rhegium had sent assistance to the rebels who besieged Dionysius in his own city; and Rhegium controlled the strait between Sicily and Italy. He defeated the Italians at El-leporus (388 B.C.), and instead of killing his captives or selling them as slaves or even demanding ransom, he let them all go free. Thus he won the gratitude and friendship of all the Italian towns from which they came, and also isolated Rhegium, which he now (386 B.C.) besieged and captured. He scourged the defeated commander through his army and then drowned him, with all his relatives. With the capture of Rhegium he controlled both sides of the strait (he had earlier restored Messina), and in 379 B.C. he captured Croton. Continuing his expansion, he founded commercial settlements along the Adriatic coast up to what is now Venice. The Carthaginians returned in 379 B.C., Dionysius was defeated and forced to accept a humiliating peace. In 368 B.C. he again marched against the Punic cities, but failed to take Lilybaeum and died before peace could be concluded.

The tyranny of Dionysius lasted 38 years. It was maintained by force against all attempts to depose him and restore the Republic. He was harsh and cruel to his political enemies, but on the whole did not indulge in vengeance and murder for personal reasons. He had great capacity and energy, and above all, his ability to protect Syracuse from its enemies abroad continually kept his enemies at home off balance. Vast sums were needed to carry on his wars. He raised them by levying heavy taxes and by plundering the temples of their treasures. He even planned a raid on the holiest of Greek sanctuaries, Delphi, but was unable to put his plan into execution. He sent aid to Sparta several times, and was in turn aided by the Spartans.

Dionysius' first wife, abused by the Syracusans who had attempted to seize his power, killed herself in shame at her dishonor. He then married, so it is said, two wives at the same time, to whom he was equally devoted. One was a Locrian and bore his eldest son, Dionysius the Younger. The other was Aristomache, sister of Dion, one of his most trusted advisers. Dionysius accused the mother of his Locrian wife of drugging Aristomache so that she would not bear children and had her killed. Aristomache later had children, one of whom, Arete, was given in marriage to her brother Dion. Busy as he was in securing his own power, protecting Syracuse from Carthage and enlarging its sphere of influence, Dionysius found time to encourage letters. In 388 B.C. Dion invited Plato to Syracuse and became one of his most ardent disciples. He was anxious to have Dionysius hear the philosopher, in the hope that the tyrant might be imbued with some of his theories of a government based on law and justice. He took Dionysius to hear Plato lecture. That day the philosopher discoursed on the nature of tyrants. He branded them as timid men, who ruled with iron hands out of fear. He might have been speaking of Dionysius personally, for the tyrant was frighteningly aware of the hatred he had roused against himself among his own people. He was so afraid of assassination he would not allow a barber to cut his hair, but had it singed with live coals. No one was permitted to come before him who had not first taken off his clothes in an ante-chamber and put on robes supplied by the tyrant in which it would be impossible to conceal a weapon. On one occasion, his brother Leptines was describing some plans to him. To clarify his explanation he seized a spear and drew the plans in the sand. Dionysius had the man from whom the spear was borrowed slain for having brought a weapon into his presence. Once he dreamed a certain man had attempted to kill him. The next day he had the man put to death for his dream convinced him that this man would make an attempt on his life. He dared not trust his own children, and had his eldest son and heir, Dionysius the Younger, brought up in relative ignorance and isolation from public affairs, lest if he associated with intelligent men he try to overthrow his father. Nevertheless, to hear Plato discourse on the timidity of tryants enraged him, and shortly thereafter Plato left Syracuse. Dionysius gave orders to the captain of the ship on which he sailed to kill Plato if it was possible to do so quietly; if not, to sell him into slavery, for, said Dionysius, Plato claimed a just man was blessed, and

fat, fāte, fär, fåll, àsk, fãre; net, mē, hèr; pin, pīne; not, nõte, möve, nôr; up, lūte, pùll; oi, oil; ou out; (lightened) ēlect, agǫny, ūnite;

since he himself was just he would be happy even in slavery. The incident did not disturb Dion's relationship with Dionysius, and the latter continued to encourage letters and to work as a dramatic poet himself. He had several times sent his tragedies to compete in the Dionysia at Athens, and had won third and second prizes. In a later time, his son Dionysius the Younger met Philip of Macedon at a banquet in Corinth. Philip mockingly asked him when his father had found time to write the tragedies and poems he left behind. Dionysius the Younger answered, "When thou and I and all those whom men call happy are busy at the bowl." But Dionysius was not satisfied with second and third prizes. In 367 B.C., after his failure to take Lilybaeum from the Carthaginians, he learned that his tragedy, *Ransom of Hector*, had won first prize at the Lenaea in Athens. The news more than consoled him for his military failure. In his delight he celebrated mightily. He drank too much wine and was taken with a fever. The soporific drink he was given to calm him put him to sleep forever. Under the tyranny of Dionysius Syracuse became the leading state in Europe; his own power and influence are said to have exceeded those of any other Greek before Alexander the Great. Nevertheless, the "adamantine bonds" with which he boasted he had secured his power were loosened within a generation.

Dionysius. [Surnamed *the Younger*.] Tyrant of Syracuse, born c395 B.C.; died, probably at Corinth, after 343 B.C. He was the eldest son of Dionysius the Elder and his Locrian wife, Doris. His father deliberately denied him an education through the fear that if Dionysius mingled with intelligent and capable men he would attempt to seize the tyranny. Instead, Dionysius the Younger was kept in virtual isolation from public affairs, and occupied himself by making little wooden wagons, chairs, and tables, and in revelry with his friends. On the death of his father (367 B.C.), Dionysius the Younger became tyrant of Syracuse with no preparation for governing, but with a highly developed taste for debauchery and extravagant living. Dion, the adviser and brother-in-law of his father, now became adviser to the son. Dion was an ardent follower of the philosopher Plato. He hoped that with an education in philosophy Dionysius the Younger would become a wise and just ruler, that the tyranny might be converted into a benevolent monarchy under a constitu-

(obscured) errạnt, ardẹnt, actọr; ch, chip; g, go; th, thin; ᴛʜ, then; y, you; (variable) ḍ as d or j, ş as s or sh, ţ as t or ch, ẕ as z or zh.

tion along the lines proposed by Plato in the *Republic.* Dior was not an advocate of democracy; rather he hoped for a state that would prosper under a philosopher-king. He urged on the young tyrant the pursuit of knowledge and prevailed on him to send for Plato. The philosopher was reluctant to come, for his experiences in Syracuse under Dionysius the Elder had been unfortunate, but he admitted that he must not refuse the chance to put his theories to the test and sailed to Syracuse. Dionysius welcomed him warmly, and flung himself into the task of becoming a philosopher. To prepare him to become a philosopher-king, Plato insisted on a solid foundation of scientific study and set Dionysius to studying geometry. Soon the whole court of Syracuse was feverishly engaged in drawing diagrams on the sand, which served as a blackboard. But the mastery of geometry was slow and difficult. Dionysius soon tired of it; he was weak, impressionable, and easily swayed by those about him. Those who resented and feared the influence of Dion and Plato now brought their influence to bear. They flattered Dionysius, pandered to his extravagant tastes, and at last openly accused Dion of plotting against him. A letter Dion had written to the Carthaginians concerning negotiations between them and Syracuse was intercepted. Dionysius seized on it as evidence of treachery, and sent Dion away from Syracuse (366 B.C.). Frightened by the anger this roused in the Syracusans and by the threat of revolt, he sent Dion's treasure after him, declared he had not exiled him, and sent him the revenues from his estates at regular intervals. Dion went to Greece, where he traveled widely. Dionysius kept Plato in Syracuse, and became passionately attached to him, and jealously demanded to be the most loved and admired of his disciples. However, his mental equipment was inadequate, his will to discipline himself with work flickered, and his appetite for pleasure never faltered. Plato realized that Dionysius would never become the instrument to bring the ideal state into being. Having secured a promise from Dionysius that he would recall Dion, he returned to Athens. Dionysius made no attempt to recall Dion. Instead, when he learned how popular his former adviser was with the Greeks in the homeland he became fearful of him, lest he return and seize power in Syracuse.

fat, fāte, fär, fåll, àsk, fāre; net, mē, hèr; pin, pīne; not, nōte, möve, nôr; up, lūte, púll; oi, oil; ou out; (lightened) ĕlect, agǫny, ūnite;

He stopped sending the revenues of his estates to him and compelled his wife, his own half-sister, to marry one of his friends. He sent for Plato again, promising that he would show mercy to Dion if Plato returned, otherwise he would not. Whether it was from friendship for Dion or a lingering hope that he might influence Dionysius, Plato returned to Syracuse (361 B.C.). When he arrived, Dionysius, under the pretext of giving him an honor guard, kept him under virtual arrest for a time, then allowed him to return to Athens.

Syracuse was in a state of great unrest under the harsh, extravagant, and unpredictable rule of Dionysius. Dion returned with an army of Peloponnesian mercenaries and led a revolt against him. Dionysius was out of Syracuse when Dion arrived, and the city was taken without a struggle. A week later Dionysius sailed into the harbor with a fleet and attacked. He was defeated, but not before he had won the citadel of Syracuse, which was a fortified island guarding the city. Here he took refuge with many soldiers, much material, and with the wife and sister of Dion as his captives. When he found he could not raise the siege, he left command of the citadel to his son and escaped through the Syracusan fleet. He went to his mother's home (356 B.C.), in Locri, ruled it with an iron hand, and indulged his taste for profligacy. The hatred of the Locrians was so intense that when Dionysius at last left their city, abandoning his wife and children to the care of a small garrison, the Locrians seized them, outraged them in the streets, and slew them. They chopped up the bones of their victims, as ghosts could not rise from pulverized bones to haunt them, and served their flesh to the people of Locri, compelling all to taste of it on pain of being put under a terrible curse. The ashes of their bones were cast into the sea, along with any remains of their diced flesh. This occurred when Dionysius, after ten years of exile, returned to Syracuse (346 B.C.) and reëstablished himself as tyrant. Shortly after his return Hicetas, tyrant of Leontini, who had made a treacherous agreement with the Carthaginians, besieged him in Syracuse. The city was in despair. Carthaginian ships were in the harbor, the forces of Hicetas were in the city, and Dionysius had shut himself up in the island citadel. Corinth, the mother city of Syracuse, sent a force under Timoleon to relieve Syracuse.

Dionysius sent him a message offering to surrender to him
Timoleon sent a small force into the city in secret and took
him off the citadel and passed him in safety through the
encircling enemies. All the material Dionysius had stored in
the citadel and 2000 soldiers fell to Timoleon. Dionysius
sailed off to Corinth (343 B.C.) with his personal treasure.
There he lived aimlessly, occasionally mingling with the
great. On one occasion he was asked what was the cause of
the quarrel between him and Plato. He answered that the
worst evil of a tyranny was that no one spoke the truth to a
tyrant, and this cost him the good will of Plato. When he had
exhausted his treasure, he passed the rest of his life as a
mendicant priest of Cybele.

Dives (dī′vēz), **Crassus.** See **Crassus, Marcus Licinius.**

Divitiacus (div-i-tī′a̧-kus). Aeduan noble, brother of Dumnorix
He was an ally of Rome and a warm personal friend of
Caesar. He was the guest of Cicero during a political visit to
Rome. He rendered services to Caesar against Ariovistus
and against the Belgae. Through his intercession Dumnorix'
treason in 58 B.C. was pardoned by Caesar.

Dolabella (dol-a̧-bel′a̧), **Publius Cornelius.** Roman patrician,
born c70 B.C.; died at Laodicea in Syria, 43 B.C. He is noted
chiefly as the son-in-law of Cicero. Ruined by his profligate
habits, he sought to restore his fortunes by joining the
standard of Caesar in the civil war. He commanded Caesar's
fleet in the Adriatic in 49 B.C., and in 48 B.C. participated in
the battle of Pharsalus. He obtained the consulship after the
death of Caesar in 44 B.C. At first he acted in support of the
Senate, but was subsequently influenced by bribery to join
the party of Antony. He received from Antony Syria as his
proconsular province, but was defeated at Laodicea by Cassius. He was, at his own request, killed by one of his soldiers
in order not to fall into the hands of the enemy.

Domitian (dō-mish′a̧n). [Full Latin name, **Titus Flavius Do-
mitianus Augustus.**] Roman emperor (81–96); born at Rome,
Oct. 25, 51 A.D.; died there, Sept. 18, 96 A.D. He was the
second son of Vespasian and Flavia Domitilla, and the
brother of Titus, whom he succeeded. He undertook a campaign against the Chatti in 83, in the course of which he
began the construction of a boundary wall between the
Danube and the Rhine. This wall was guarded by soldiers
settled upon public lands (*agri decumates*) along its course.

fat, fāte, fär, fåll, àsk, fāre; net, mē, hèr; pin, pīne; not, nōte, mŏve,
nôr; up, lūte, pùll; oi, oil; ou out; (lightened) ēlect, agŏny, ūnite;

He carried on (86–90) unsuccessful wars against the Dacians under Decebalus, finally purchasing peace by the promise of a yearly tribute. He recalled Agricola, whose victories (78–84) in Britain aroused his jealousy. Though the beginning of his reign had been marked by sincere attempts to govern well, to enforce laws, to build temples, and to supervise the government closely, the last years of his reign were sullied by cruelty and tyranny, induced by fear of revolt and assassination. He was murdered by the freedman Stephanus, at the instance of the empress and several officers of the court, who were in fear of their lives.

Dorieus (dôr′i-us). Son of Anaxandridas, king of Sparta, and the first of his two wives to whom he was married concurrently. According to Herodotus, the reason for this unusual marital state was that the first wife of Anaxandridas bore him no children. The Spartans urged him to take a second wife, since he would not give up the first one, and maintain the two in separate houses and with nearly equal honors. The second wife bore Anaxandridas a son, Cleomenes, who became the heir to the throne. Some time thereafter, the first wife, who up to this time had seemed to be incapable of bearing children, also produced a son, whom she named Dorieus. In rapid succession she also bore Leonidas, later to become the hero of Thermopylae, and Cleombrotus. Dorieus was the most promising of the sons and, since Cleomenes seemed to be mentally unbalanced at times, Dorieus fully expected to succeed his father as king. However, when Anaxandridas died, the Spartans followed the law and made Cleomenes, the first-born son, the king. Dorieus could not bear to be subject to Cleomenes, and in anger sailed away with a company of Spartans to found a colony. In his disappointment, he failed to consult the oracle al Delphi, and to observe the customs before setting out to found a colony. He went to Libya and established a city there, but after three years was driven out. He returned to Sparta to consider what he should do, and was told by a seer to go to Heraclea in Sicily, for as a descendant of Heracles, he was entitled to the land. The claims of the Heraclidae to this region rested on the following grounds: When Heracles was driving the cattle of Geryon back to Argos, a bull escaped at Rhegium and swam across to Sicily. Heracles swam across after him. He landed in the kingdom of Eryx, in whose herds the bull had found a welcome. Eryx challenged Heracles to a series of contests, staking his kingdom against the bull. In the contests Heracles slew Eryx and won his kingdom, but left it to the inhabitants to enjoy until one of his descendants could come to claim it. Now Dorieus decided to be that descendant who recovered the land formerly won by Heracles. This time he went to the oracle at Delphi before he set out, and was assured by the priestess that he would gain the land as he intended. Dorieus returned to Libya, gathered up his followers, and proceeded to Sicily. On the way, according to some accounts, he stopped to help the people of Croton in a war against the Sybarites, and dedicated a temple to Athena in Sybaris after he had helped to take the city. The Crotoniats disclaimed this story entirely; they said Dorieus only came to their aid when victims foreshadowed defeat of the Sybarites, at which point he deserted them and came over to the side of the Crotoniats. From Sybaris he proceeded to Heraclea Minoa, in Sicily, helped the Selinuntians to overthrow their tyrant, and made himself tyrant of Selinus. After a while the inhabitants revolted against him, and though he fled to the altar of Zeus, they seized him and put him to death. Ironically, if Dorieus had been patient he would have become king of Sparta, for Cleomenes reigned only a short time and died without male issue. Leonidas, brother of Dorieus and half-brother of Cleomenes, became king in his place.

Draco (drā′kō) or **Dracon** (drā′kon). Athenian legislator; fl. in the last half of the 7th century B.C. According to tradition, he was appointed (c621 B.C.) to reform existing laws and to formulate the first written code of laws for Athens. Among his reforms was the establishment of 51 Ephetae (judges), chosen from the Eupatrids (nobles), to try cases of bloodshed that did not come before the Areopagus. The court of the Ephetae sat in various places, depending on the nature of the offense, as at Delphi, in the temple of Apollo, or at Phalerum, the old part of Athens. Those who had committed the crime of manslaughter abroad were not permitted to set foot on Attic soil until they were cleared of the charge. Since they had to make their defense standing in a boat drawn up near the shore, the court went to Munychia, the hill above the Piraeus, to hear their cases. (Telamon, charged with the murder of his brother Phocus, was not

fat, fāte, fär, fåll, åsk, fāre; net, mē, hėr; pin, pīne; not, nōte, möve, nôr; up, lūte, půll; oi, oil; ou out; (lightened) ĕlect, agǫny, ūnite;

permitted to land at Aegina, his father's home, to defend himself; he secretly built a mole and shouted his defense from the end of it that reached out into the sea.) According to Draco's code, one who was unable to pay a debt could be claimed as a slave by his creditor. On the completion of the code, there having been no written code previously, the people were so overjoyed that they smothered Draco accidentally under a deluge of cloaks. On account of the number of offenses to which it affixed the penalty of death, his code was said to have been written in blood. His code was superseded for the most part by that of Solon (594 B.C.).

Drusilla, Livia (drö-sil′a̱ liv′i-a̱). See *Livia Drusilla.*

Drusus (drö′sus), **Marcus Livius.** Roman politician, who died probably 109 B.C. He was tribune of the plebs conjointly with Caius Gracchus in 122 B.C., his election having been procured by the Senate, whose members were alarmed at the democratic innovations of the latter. In collusion with the Senate he opposed his veto to the bills brought forward by his colleague, and introduced instead bills of similar import, but making more extravagant concessions, which were passed by the Senate. He was consul in 112 B.C., and while governor of Macedonia, which he obtained as his province, defeated the Thracians and reached the Danube.

Drusus, Marcus Livius. Roman politician; son of Marcus Livius Drusus (d. 109 B.C.). Marcus Livius the son was assassinated at Rome in 91 B.C. He became tribune of the plebs (91 B.C.), whose favor he won by largesses of grain, and by the introduction of a bill providing for a new division of the public lands. This bill, together with another which restored to the Senate the places on the juries of which it had been deprived by Caius Gracchus, was passed by the comitia, but declared null and void by the Senate. He was assassinated as he was about to bring forward a proposal to bestow Roman citizenship on the Italians (that is to say, on the people of Italy as a whole and not simply those who lived in the city of Rome). His death gave the signal for the outbreak of the Social War.

Drusus, Nero Claudius. [Called **Drusus Senior;** surnamed **Germanicus.**] Roman general, born 38 B.C.; died in Germany, 9 B.C. He was the son of Livia Drusilla by Tiberius Claudius

Nero, and was born shortly after the marriage of his mother
with the emperor Augustus. With his older brother
Tiberius, who later became emperor, he was adopted by
Augustus, and at an early age married Antonia, the daughter
of Mark Antony. He subdued a revolt in Gaul in 13 B.C., and
starting in 12 B.C. from the left bank of the Rhine, undertook
four campaigns in Germany proper with his brother
Tiberius. In the course of these campaigns, whence his
name Germanicus, he led the Roman armies to the Weser
and the Elbe. He died on the way back, in consequence of
a fall from his horse.

Drusus Caesar. [Called *Drusus Junior.*] Son of Tiberius and
Vipsania, born c13 B.C.; poisoned 23 A.D., He quelled a
mutiny of the legions in Pannonia in 14 A.D., was consul in
15 A.D., was appointed governor of Illyricum in 17, was
consul in 21, and in 22 was invested with the *tribunicia potes
tas,* whereby he was declared heir apparent to the throne.
He is said to have lived an extremely dissolute life and so
angered his father thereby, that when Drusus died, Tiberius
curtailed the period of official mourning. Moreover, the tale
is told that when an embassy from Troy arrived to offer
condolences to Tiberius a month or two after the death of
Drusus, Tiberius ironically offered condolences to the
embassy on the loss of their eminent citizen, Hector. Later,
Tiberius learned that Drusus had not died from his excesses,
but that his wife Livilla had brought about his death by
poison, in alliance with Sejanus, the commander of the Praetorian Guard, favorite of Tiberius, and Livilla's lover.
When he learned this, Tiberius energetically sought to in-
vestigate the crime and eventually ordered the death of Sejanus.

Duilius (dū-il′i-us), *Caius.* Roman general; fl. in the 3rd century
B.C. He was consul in 260 B.C., when he defeated
the Carthaginians near Mylae (modern Milazzo), on the N
coast of Sicily. This was the first naval success gained by
Rome. Duilius, a land officer placed in charge of the fleet
by necessity, decided to fight the naval engagement as a
land battle, and won by using his new device, the *corvus.*

———E———

Empedocles (em-ped′ō̧-klēz). Greek poet, philsopher, and statesman, born in Acragas in Sicily, c493 B.C. He died probably in the Peloponnesus, c433 B.C. Although born of a rich and noble family, he was an ardent champion of liberty, and resisted the tyrants Theron and Thrasydaeus. On the expulsion of the latter he helped to set up a democratic constitution. Under it he exerted great influence through his vast learning, his powerful oratory, and his wealth. In later life it is thought he left Sicily, perhaps because of political disturbances, and went to the Peloponnesus, where he died. He followed Pythagoras and Parmenides in his teachings, but he was a real poet, and expressed his doctrine in poetic form. His system was based on the belief that there are four original elements—Fire, Earth, Water, and Air—and that these elements do not change in themselves but are mixed and moved by the action upon them of such non-physical forces as Love and Strife. The earth and all life on it originated from the endless mixing and moving of these elements. He also expressed in poetry his belief that the sinner who stained his hands with innocent blood, or was false to his oath, must wander through untold eons, never attaining the peace of the dead, received and cast out by Air, Sea, Earth, and Sun, and endlessly being transformed from one mortal shape to another. He professed magic powers, prophecy, and a miraculous power of healing. In support of such professions he is said to have stopped the etesian winds, drained a vast swamp, and restored a dead woman to life. He also prophesied the hour when the gods would summon him and, according to some accounts, he disappeared without trace and was believed to have passed away without dying. Others said he threw himself into the crater of Aetna in order that, from his sudden disappearance, the people might believe he correctly prophesied his own passing and was a god. It is claimed by these latter that they knew he hurled himself into the crater because one of his brass boots was cast up by the volcano. The general tradition i: that he died in the Peloponnesus. His influence on Greel and Arabian thought was great; books in his name appearec in both languages. Fragments of his hexameter poem, *O: Nature,* survive. It was very highly regarded in antiquity fo its content and its style. Some verses of his poem, *Purifica tions,* also survive.

Epaminondas (ē″pam-i-non′dạs). Theban general and states man, born c418 B.C.; died at Mantinea, Arcadia, Greece, 36: B.C. He was of a noble but impoverished family. Modest anc not personally ambitious, he determined to lighten his pov erty by the study of Pythagorean philosophy, to which h« had been introduced by Lysis, an exile from Tarentum. H« was as interested in music as he was in physical prowess, anc became an accomplished player on the lyre and the flute Further to lighten his poverty, he denied himself the luxur of taking a wife. He was the good friend of Pelopidas, a ma of wealth, and so high were his principles that he alone o the friends of Pelopidas refused to accept any financial hel from him. Pelopidas, since he could not share his wealt with Epaminondas, decided to share the poverty of hi friend—to some extent. Both were animated by ardent pa triotism, both were noted for their integrity. They were col leagues in government and in command. At the battle o Mantinea (385 B.C.), Thebes was an ally of Sparta. Pelopida fell, pierced by seven wounds. Epaminondas rescued hin from the enemy and saved his life. The Theban alliance witl Sparta was an unequal one. In 382 B.C. the Spartans seizec the citadel of Thebes and set a Spartan governor, with garrison of 1500 Spartan hoplites, over the Thebans Pelopidas flew to Athens rather than live under Spartan rule Epaminondas remained in Thebes, hoping for the day whe Spartan control would be thrown off. By a daring coup Pelopidas secretly returned to Thebes with six companion: and killed the Spartan rulers. Epaminondas, in the turmoi that then broke out in the city, came to his aid with an armec band, and urged the Thebans to expel the Spartan garrisor that had taken refuge in the citadel. But force was unneces sary, for the Spartans decided to withdraw under a truce Thebes was thus freed of the Spartan yoke (378 B.C.) and democratic constitution was proclaimed. An elite corps called the Sacred Band, was created. It consisted of 30(

young men of noble Theban families; 150 pairs of devoted friends determined to fight to victory or die together. The Sacred Band, maintained at the expense of the city, was the spearhead and rallying point of every attack. Epaminondas used it to revolutionize military tactics. In the years following the expulsion of the Spartans, Thebes repelled several Spartan attacks, and brought most of the Boeotian cities under her control. At a general peace conference between the various warring Greek states and their allies (371 B.C.), Agesilaus, the Spartan general, demanded that Epaminondas, the Theban envoy, allow every Boeotian city to sign the treaty separately. Epaminondas replied that he would if the Spartans would allow each of their vassal states to sign separately also. He knew that Sparta would not yield such control to her vassal states, and the result was that Thebes was not a party to the peace treaty. In the same year the Spartans, in violation of their treaty with their allies, decided to march against Thebes and free the Boeotian cities from Theban domination. At Leuctra they were met by Epaminondas and his army. The Thebans and their allies were appalled at the numbers and reputation of the forces marshaled against them and wished to withdraw. Epaminondas insisted that here was the place to make a stand, and his view prevailed. In accordance with a dream of Pelopidas, a roan colt was sacrificed to the daughters of the Theban Scedasus, Epaminondas permitted the Thespian allies, who had joined the Thebans against their will, to depart, and the next day, using the Sacred Band as a flying wedge, the Thebans defeated the Spartans at Leuctra (July, 371 B.C.). Cleombrotus, the Spartan king, was slain in the battle, 1000 Spartans fell, and 47 Thebans or their allies lost their lives. The Spartans admitted defeat by asking for a truce and were permitted to withdraw. By defeating them at Leuctra, Epaminondas destroyed the Spartan superiority in Greece that they had obtained 30 years before in the Peloponnesian War. The destruction of Spartan influence in Greek affairs was the most important and lasting of the accomplishments of Epaminondas. The Thespians, fearing the anger of Epaminondas because they had left him on the eve of Leuctra, withdrew to one of their strongholds, that at Ceressus, which had never been captured in its history. However, there was an oracle of Delphi saying Ceressus would fall

when "the Dorians have lost their glorious youth." Epami
nondas marched to Ceressus and took it. He then (370 B.C.
carried the war to the Peloponnesus in support of the Ar
cadians against Sparta. He restored the Mantineans of Ar
cadia to their city and persuaded the Arcadians to join i
building a great new city, Megalopolis, which would serve a
a bastion against Sparta. He marched to the very borders o
Sparta and ravaged southern Laconia. This created despai
in Sparta, which, for generations, had not known war so nea
its own lands. Next he went to Messenia, for he was advise
in a dream, some say, to restore the Messenians to thei
homeland from which they had been driven by the Spartans
Sparta now knew the humiliation of losing some of her terri
tory. Messenia was detached from her control. Using th
ancient citadel of Ithome as one wall, Epaminondas ordere
the boundaries of the new city of Messene to be marked ou
to the piping of flutes. To the city he recalled the Messenia
exiles. While he was in Messenia his one-year term a
boeotarch (commander) expired. Although it was against th
law, he retained his command, and when he returned t
Thebes he was brought to trial for ignoring the law. The jur
that heard the case did not even record their votes. Dul
elected boeotarch again, Epaminondas again defeated th
Spartans in the Peloponnesus. He marched into Sicyon (36
B.C.) and took many captives, including many Boeotians o
cities now under Theban control who had fled into Sicyon
It was the practice for the Thebans to allow prisoners of wa
to be ransomed, but for any Boetians captured in any en
gagement to be killed as traitors. As an example of his dis
like for unnecessary harshness, in this case Epaminonda
gave all the Boeotian captives a new nationality so that thei
lives might be spared. In 368 B.C. Pelopidas, who had gon
to visit Alexander of Pherae after a campaign in Thessaly
was treacherously thrown into prison by Alexander. Epami
nondas, no longer boeotarch, marched in the ranks of a
army sent to rescue him. The Thebans were surprised by th
army of Alexander in Thessaly and were thrown into confu
sion. The two legal boeotarchs voluntarily resigned thei
posts and handed over the command to Epaminondas. H
skillfully extricated the Thebans from a dangerous position
and the following year secured the release of Pelopidas with
out striking a blow.

On the advice of Epaminondas, the Thebans created a navy, of which he became the first admiral. Events in the Peloponnesus then caused him to lead an army into that region for a fourth time, to bring the disaffected cities there under Theban control again. He attacked the enemy—Spartans, Athenians, Mantineans, and others who had united against Thebes—at Mantinea (362 B.C.) and overwhelmed them. As he pursued the fleeing enemy he was mortally wounded by a spear thrust. Dying, he sent for the two men whom he wanted to appoint to succeed him in command. On learning that they had been slain he advised that peace be made with the enemy. By his death, a crushing victory was transformed into a stalemate, for when he pulled the spear from his body and died there was no one to take his place. Epaminondas was a brilliant military innovator, whose tactics were successfully imitated by Alexander the Great. He was noted for his patriotism, his learning and his eloquence (which was seldom employed, but then to great effect), and for the nobility and purity of his character. Notably successful as a general, he was unable, as a statesman, to secure the dominant place in Greek affairs which he had won for Thebes, and after his death Theban influence declined.

Ephialtes (ef-i-al′tēz). A Greek of Malis who betrayed the Spartans and other Greeks under the command of Leonidas at the pass of Thermopylae (480 B.C.). In the hope of reward, he went to Xerxes, whose forces had three times been thrown back by the Greeks, and offered to lead the Persians by a path over the mountains so that they could attack from the rear the Greeks defending the pass. Xerxes accepted his offer; Ephialtes led them over the mountain, and the Greeks, fighting with enormous valor, were wiped out. Ephialtes afterward fled and a price was put on his head by the Greeks. Some time later he returned from his exile to Anticyra, and there was slain, his slayer being greatly honored by the Spartans.

Ephialtes. Athenian statesman and general; died 461 B.C. He was the friend and partisan of Pericles, and was the principal author of a law which abridged the power of the Areopagus and changed the government of Athens into a pure democracy (i.e., for citizens). Ephialtes opposed Cimon, the leader of the oligarchic and aristocratic party. With Pericles he brought charges against Cimon of having accepted bribes

from the king of Macedon, but the charges were not presse◄
and Cimon was acquitted. Again, Ephialtes opposed Ci
mon's policy of aiding Sparta to put down a revolt of th◄
Helots (462 B.C.). It was while he was off at the head of a◄
expedition to aid Sparta in this affair that Ephialtes an◄
Pericles put through the reforms that made Athens a democ
racy. When Cimon returned he was banished, and short◄
afterward Ephialtes was mysteriously murdered. He wa◄
according to Aristotle, assassinated by Aristodicus of Tana
gra, at the instance of the oligarchs.

Eubulus (ū-bū'lus). Athenian statesman; fl. middle of the 4t◄
century B.C. He was in charge of the Theoric Fund from 35◄
to perhaps 346 B.C. This fund consisted originally of surplu◄
revenues of the state that were devoted to religious pur
poses, such as paying for the seats of the poor at the dra◄
matic festivals. By the time of Eubulus the manager of th◄
Theoric Fund was in effect the financial minister of Athens
Eubulus filled the office extremely ably. At a time whe◄
Athens was weak and the power of Macedon was growin◄
Eubulus favored a policy of peace with Philip II of Macedon
Nevertheless, he sent a force to rescue the Phocians whe◄
Philip defeated them (351 B.C.) and prepared to marc◄
through the Pass of Thermopylae. Philip withdrew. Eubulu◄
was an opponent of Demosthenes, who continually urge◄
the Athenians to destroy Philip before his power became to◄
great. After the fall of Olynthus (348 B.C.) which the Atheni
ans had not arrived in time to save, Eubulus was compelle◄
by the pressure of public opinion to send envoys to the citie◄
of the Peloponnesus for the purpose of organizing unite◄
resistance to Philip. In this case Eubulus acted against hi◄
own policy, which continued to be one of peace with Philip
the effort to organize resistance failed, and he bluntly tol◄
the Athenians they must accept Philip's terms for peace (34◄
B.C.). A peace was made, but because of the inflammator◄
speeches of Demosthenes against the envoys who ha◄
agreed to it Eubulus lost some of his influence.

Euchidas (ū'ki-dạs). According to Plutarch, a Plataean runner
After the battle of Plataea (479 B.C.), the oracle at Delph◄
commanded that all the fires of Greece, which had bee◄
polluted by the barbarians (Persians), must be extinguishe◄
and new fires kindled from the sacred fire at Delphi. Th◄
Plataeans extinguished their fires and sent Euchidas to Del◄

phi to fetch new fire. He ran to Delphi, purified himself, put a laurel crown on his head, took fire from the sacred altar and returned with it to Plataea on the same day. Arrived at Plataea, having covered a journey of 1000 furlongs (125 miles) in one day, he saluted his companions, delivered the fire, and fell dead. The Plataeans buried him in the temple of Artemis Eucleia.

Eumenes (ū'mȩ̄-nēz). Secretary to Philip of Macedon and to Alexander the Great and one of the successors of Alexander the Great. He was born at Cardia, Thrace, c361 B.C.; and was put to death in Gabiene, Elymaïs (Elam), 316 B.C. He controlled Cappadocia, Pontus, and Paphlagonia and in the struggle for power among the Diadochi, or successors, he sided with Perdiccas against Antipater, Antigonus I, Ptolemy I, and Craterus. He defeated Craterus in 321 B.C., was defeated by Antigonus, and was betrayed by his soldiers to Antigonus. He kept the diary, the *Royal Journal,* of Alexander the Great which he perhaps published after Alexander's death.

Eumenes II. King of Pergamum 197–c159 B.C.; died c159 B.C. He was the eldest son of Attalus I, whom he succeeded. He cultivated the friendship of the Romans, whom he assisted in the war against Antiochus the Great. He was present in person at the decisive battle of Magnesia (189 B.C.), and, on the restoration of peace, was rewarded by the addition of the Thracian Chersonese, Mysia, Lydia, and Phrygia to his kingdom. He was a patron of learning, and founded at Pergamum one of the famous libraries of antiquity.

Eurybiades (ū-ri-bī'ạ-dēz). Leader of the Spartan naval contingent during the Persian War; fl. 5th century B.C. Although the Athenians furnished the most ships in the war against the Persian invaders, the Spartans and the other Greek forces refused to serve under an Athenian commander. Eurybiades was appointed commander of the united fleet of the allied Greek states, with the consent of the Athenians. Aided by furious storms, he defeated the Persians in the naval battle of Artemisium, off the N end of Euboea, 480 B.C. The Persian army swept on down through Thessaly and occupied Attica. The Greek allies of Athens wished to withdraw to the Isthmus of Corinth and there make their defense against the oncoming Persians. Themistocles persuaded Eurybiades not to withdraw to the Isthmus, but to meet the

Persians in the narrow waters between the island of Salami
and the mainland, where the Greek ships would have th(
advantage of maneuver over the heavier Persian ships. Eury
biades was obliged to accept the strategy of Themistocle
when he learned that the Greek fleet in the waters of Salami
had been blockaded by the Persians. The victory the Greek
under Eurybiades won at Salamis (480 B.C.) was decisive.

Eurymedon (ū-rim′ẹ-don). Athenian general in the Peloponne
sian War; killed near Syracuse, 413 B.C. As commander o
an Athenian fleet, he was at Corcyra, 427 B.C., during th
revolution in which the democrats there overthrew the oli
garchs. He took no steps to prevent the excesses on tha
occasion and the oligarchs were massacred, except for abou
200 who escaped to the fortress of Istone. Two years late
he commanded a fleet that helped the Corcyraean demo
crats besiege the fortress of Istone. The besieged oligarch
at last surrendered, on condition that the Athenians be al
lowed to decide their fate. This condition being granted, th(
oligarchs marched out from the fortress, whereupon th(
Corcyraeans brutally murdered them in the courtyard wher(
they were assembled. Eurymedon made no effort to sav(
them. In 413 B.C. he sailed to Sicily as co-commander of .
force to rescue the expeditionary force sent out under Nicia
to take Syracuse. He was slain in the fighting at Syracus
(413 B.C.), in which the Athenians were annihilated.

Evagoras (ẹ̄-vag′ọ̄-rạs). King of Salamis, in Cyprus (c435–37
B.C.). He claimed descent from Teucer, the half-brother o
Telamonian Ajax who came to Cyprus and founded Salami
after the Trojan War. The descendants of Teucer rule(
Salamis for centuries and then lost the throne to the Phoeni
cians. Evagoras won it back by his own courage and enter
prise. He was said to be a wise and moderate ruler, wh(
encouraged and revived Greek culture in his kingdom. Afte
the defeat of the Athenians at Aegospotami (405 B.C.), Co
non, one of the Athenian admirals who escaped, found hos
pitality and protection at his court, and he took part in th(
battle of Cnidus (394 B.C.) in which the Spartans were de
feated by a Phoenician and Persian fleet under the comman(
of Conon. Because of his friendship for Athens he was mad(
a citizen and his statue was erected in Athens beside that o
Conon. He had been a tributary of the Great King of Persia
but as his own power grew in Cyprus, and was extended t(

fat, fāte, fär, fȧll, ȧsk, fãre; net, mē, hėr; pin, pīne; not, nōte, möv(
nôr; up, lūte, pu̇ll; oi, oil; ou out; (lightened) ẹlect, agọ̄ny, ūnit(

the coast of Asia Minor the Persians waged war on him as on a rebellious subject (c389 B.C.). For the next ten years he resisted the Persians. After a serious defeat at sea he withdrew to Salamis and endured siege, which he resisted so stubbornly that the Persians offered to raise it if he would pay tribute to Persia, "as a slave to his master." Evagoras refused the terms but finally agreed to pay tribute, only, however, as one king to another, and the siege was raised. The Athenians had at first helped him by sending ten ships, but with the signing of the King's Peace (386 B.C.), by which Cyprus was acknowledged as a Persian tributary, the Athenians ceased to support him, and he had carried on his war alone. He was slain (374 B.C.) by the eunuch of a man who had been forced to flee for plotting against him. The story is that the eunuch, left in charge of the beautiful daughter of the exile, told both Evagoras and his son of the loveliness of the girl and arranged appointments for each of them separately. Neither the father nor the son knew of the other's appointment. Each arrived at the stated times and each was slain by the eunuch who thus avenged his master.

F

Fabius Maximus (fā'bi-us mak'si-mus), *Quintus.* [Surnamed *Rullianus.*] Roman general; died c290 B.C. While he was master of the horse he defeated the Samnites (325 B.C.). In spite of the victory he was degraded because in waging the battle he had disobeyed orders, and he was compelled to leave Rome for a time. He afterward became consul a number of times, the first time in 322 B.C. He was named dictator (315) and suffered defeat at the hands of the Samnites. In 310 he defeated the Etruscans. As consul in 295 B.C. he distinguished himself in the third war against the Samnites, over whom and their allies he gained the decisive victory of Sentinum (295 B.C.)

Fabius Maximus, Quintus. [Surnamed *Cunctator,* meaning "the Delayer."] Roman general; died 203 B.C. He traced his descent from Hercules and a nymph, the parents of Fabius, founder of the Fabian family. Besides the well-known epithet, Cunctator, he was also surnamed *Verrucosus*, from a wart growing on his lip, and Ovicula *(Lambkin)*, because he was so gentle as a child. Because he was deliberate and cautious as a youth some thought he was rather stupid. He trained himself for war, recognizing the menace of Carthage, and for oratory so that he could persuade the Romans to follow him in their own interest. He became consul for the first time in 233 B.C., when by a victory over the Ligurians he obtained the honor of a triumph. In 230 B.C. he was censor, and in 228 he held the office of consul for the second time. In 218 B.C. he was at the head of the legation sent by the Roman Senate to Carthage to demand reparation for the attack on Saguntum. According to the story, he held up a fold of his toga and asked the Carthaginians whether they chose peace or war. The Carthaginians indicated that it was a matter of indifference to them. Fabius then dropped his toga and said, "Then take war." In the same year Hannibal came into Italy and was victorious at the Trebia. Reports of ominous portents added to the fears of the Romans: shields sweated blood, grain cut at Antium was found to have blood on it, fiery stones fell from the heavens. Fabius, in opposition to the consul Caius Flaminius, advised the Romans to let Hannibal exhaust himself, far from his base and with no allies in Italy. Flaminius was undaunted by the portents, ordered the tribunes to call out the armies, and was disastrously defeated at Lake Trasimenus (217 B.C.). News of the defeat threw Rome into a turmoil, and Fabius was chosen dictator a second time by the people. He surrounded the office with all the pomp and ceremony of which it was capable in order to impress the Romans with his power and make them submissive. He called on the people to honor and propitiate the gods, whose anger, he said, at the neglect and scorn of religious rites had caused the defeat; he consulted the Sibylline Books, and vowed sacrifices and festivals to the gods. All this was intended to encourage a belief in the Romans that the gods would bring them victory. But he, according to Plutarch, "put all his hopes of victory in himself, believing that heaven bestowed success by reason of wisdom and valor, and turned his attention to Hannibal." His strategy was to weaken the Carthaginians by numerous skirmishes which hit at stragglers and scouts, while at the same time keeping clear of the main body of Hannibal's troops, and at all events to avoid pitched battles (whence his name Cunctator, "Delayer"). His strategy was criticized by his soldiers, by the Romans, and by the enemy as well, who scorned him for a coward. Only Hannibal realized how wise he was, and determined to force him into an engagement. Among Fabius' own commanders was Minucius, his master of horse, who was seditious in his criticism of Fabius. When, having been trapped at Casilinum, on the Volturnus river, the Carthaginian not only escaped but spared the acres of Fabius when he burned the surrounding fields (to make it appear that Fabius was in collusion with him), the abuse of Fabius became violent. Fabius was summoned to Rome to assist in sacrifices and put his army in charge of Minucius, with orders not to give battle or engage the enemy. Minucius disobeyed and won a minor victory which was greatly exaggerated in Rome, whereupon he was, in a most unusual step, made co-dictator with Fabius. Rather than rotate the command, Fabius divided his forces with Minucius. Hannibal lured Minucius into battle. Fabius saw that his colleague was being destroyed. He exclaimed, "Hercules! How much sooner than I expected, but later than his own rash eagerness demanded, has Minucius destroyed himself!" Then he took the field and rescued Minucius, who publicly proclaimed his mistake, thanked Fabius, and put himself once more under his command. At the end of six months Fabius put down his office of dictator, as prescribed by law, and the war was again conducted by consuls—Paulus Aemilius and Terentius Varro succeeding him in command. At the outset they followed the policy of Fabius. But Varro boasted that he would conquer the enemy in a day, collected a force of 80,000 men, engaged Hannibal at Cannae (216 B.C.), and was defeated with frightful losses. Rome was almost defenseless, but Hannibal did not follow up his victory by marching on the city. In their terror and confusion the Romans again looked to Fabius, and he became consul for the third time (215 B.C., and again in 214). He limited the period of mourning and the offering of sacrifices in order to conceal to some degree the extent of the Roman losses, sent envoys to the oracle of Delphi, and when Varro returned saw that he was welcomed at Rome without recrimination. Two armies were sent out: one under Fabius, who now came to

be called the "Shield of Rome," and the other under the
daring and swift-moving Claudius Marcellus, Rome's sword.
In spite of his victories and the Italian cities that had gone
over to him after the victory of Cannae, Hannibal's army was
exhausting itself on foreign soil. He almost lured Fabius into
battle, but unfavorable auspices prevented Fabius from beginning operations, and he was saved. In 209 B.C. Fabius
became consul for the fifth time and won Tarentum, thanks
to the treachery of some Bruttians in the city. Rather than
acknowledge that his voctory was won by betrayal instead of
arms, he put the Bruttians who had made it possible to the
sword, killed many Tarentines, sold others into slavery, and
plundered the city. Among the spoils was a statue of Hercules, which he sent to Rome and had set up near a statue
of himself. The loss of Tarentum, which he had held for
three years, was a great blow to Hannibal and won a great
triumph for Fabius. Nevertheless, the Carthaginians were
still in Italy. In 205 B.C. Scipio became consul and proposed
to carry the war to Carthage. Whether from jealousy or from
some other reason, Fabius did all he could to hinder and
oppose him, but Scipio's view prevailed. The threat to Carthage forced Hannibal's recall from Italy and Fabius died
(203 B.C.) before Hannibal's defeat in Africa by Scipio.

Fabricius Luscinus (fa̱-brish′us lu-sī′nus), **Caius.** Roman consul
(282 B.C. and 278 B.C.), general, diplomat, and censor (275
B.C.); died c250 B.C. He was an envoy to King Pyrrhus in 280
B.C. to arrange for the ransom of Roman prisoners. Pyrrhus
is said to have attempted to bribe him but Fabricius, poor
as he was, refused the offers, much to the admiration of the
king. He was noted for his incorruptibility, austerity and
poverty.

Felix (fē′liks). Surname of **Sulla, Lucius Cornelius.**

Felix, Antonius. Roman procurator of Judea, 1st century A.D.
He was a freedman of Antonia, mother of the emperor
Claudius I, and was the brother of the latter's favorite, the
freedman Pallas. He was appointed procurator of Judea c55
A.D., and governed his province from Caesarea, whither
Saint Paul was sent to him for trial after his arrest at Jerusa-
lem (Acts, xxiii. 23,24). He married Drusilla, daughter of
Agrippa I and wife of Azizus, king of Emesa, whom he in-
duced her to desert, and procured the assassination of the
high priest Jonathan, who had offended him by unpalatable

advice. He was recalled c60 A.D., and was saved from the consequences of his tyranny and extortion by the intercession of his brother with the emperor Nero.

Flaccus (fla'kus), *Quintus Fulvius.* Roman soldier and statesman; fl. 3rd century B.C. He was consul in 237, 224, 212, and 209 B.C., censor in 231, pontifex maximus in 216, and urban praetor in 215 B.C. During his third consulship he won an important victory at Beneventum over the Carthaginians under Hanno. He laid siege to Capua, occupied by the Carthaginians, and though compelled to go to Rome, where Hannibal had caused a diversion, he returned and freed Capua from the invaders.

Flaccus, Marcus Fulvius. Roman politician, grandnephew of Quintus Fulvius Flaccus; fl. 2nd century B.C. After the death of Tiberius Gracchus (133 B.C.), of whom he had been a strong supporter, Flaccus took his place in the commission appointed for the redistribution of the land. He was consul, 125 B.C., and proposed that the allies of Rome be granted the citizenship. His proposal was rejected by the Senate, by whom he was considered a dangerous "democrat." He was sent out of Rome on the excuse of protecting the Massilians, allies of Rome, against the Ligurians. Successful in this, he returned to Rome in triumph, but left again (122 B.C.) to go to Carthage with Caius Gracchus to found a colony. He was killed in Rome in 121 B.C., at the same time as Caius Gracchus was killed.

Flamininus (flam-i-nī'nus), *Titus Quintius* (or *Quinctius*). Roman general and statesman; born c230 B.C.; died c174 B.C. He was consul in 198 B.C., defeated Philip V of Macedon at Cynoscephalae in 197, and proclaimed, at the Isthmian Games at Corinth, the freedom of Greece from Macedonian rule in 196 B.C. In 195 B.C. he defeated Nabis, tyrant of Sparta, and returned (194) to Rome in triumph. He was sent (192 B.C.) on a diplomatic mission to Greece and succeeded in rallying the wavering Greek states to the Roman side against Antiochus III of Syria. He negotiated with Bithynia for the surrender of Hannibal who had sought asylum there, but Hannibal committed suicide (183 B.C.) before any conclusion was reached.

Flaminius (flạ-min'i-us), *Caius.* Roman general and politician; killed in battle 217 B.C. He was tribune of the people in 232 B.C., in which year he procured the passage of a law distributing the *Ager Gallicus Picenus* (an area along the Adriatic coast) among the plebeians, for which he won great popularity. He defeated the Insubres (near modern Milan) while consul in 223 B.C., and while censor in 220 B.C. constructed two celebrated public works which bore his name: the Circus Flaminius for the plebeians, and the Flaminian Way. He was made consul for the second time in 217 B.C., after Hannibal had invaded Italy. He disapproved of the policy advocated by Fabius Maximus, which was to wear Hannibal out by harrassment rather than by engaging him in pitched battles. Numerous unfavorable portents frightened the Romans on the advent of Hannibal, but Flaminius scorned them. He ordered the tribunes to call out the army for the purpose of attacking Hannibal. When he sprang to his horse the animal trembled with fear and threw him. But even that ominous portent did not deter Flaminius. He met Hannibal at Lake Trasimenus (217 B.C.) in Tuscany. The opposing forces engaged in such a furious struggle that the occurrence of an earthquake in the midst of the battle is said to have gone unnoticed. The forces of Flaminius were nearly annihilated: 15,000 were slain and another 15,000 were taken prisoner. Flaminius, responsible for the disaster, fell in the battle. Hannibal sought his body, to give honorable burial to a valiant opponent, but it had disappeared.

Flaminius, Caius. Roman general; fl. 2nd century B.C.; son of Caius Flaminius (d. 217 B.C.). He served as quaestor under Scipio Africanus the Elder in Spain. He was elected praetor in 193 B.C., and obtained Hispania Citerior as his province. In 187 he became consul with M. Aemilius Lepidus, and in 181 B.C. he founded the colony of Aquileia near the head of the Adriatic Sea.

G

Galba (gal'bạ), ***Servius Sulpicius.*** Roman emperor (68–69). He was born c3 B.C. near Tarracina; died at Rome, Jan. 15, 69 A.D. The son of an aristocratic and ancient Roman house, he claimed descent from Jupiter on the one hand, and from

Pasiphaë, wife of King Minos of Crete, on the other. Various omens foretold his future role as emperor. During the reign of Tiberius it was predicted that he would become emperor when he was an old man. Tiberius, who expected to be safely dead by that time, was unmoved by the prediction and did not interfere with Galba's career. He took part in public affairs and, though still under the legal age, was made praetor (20 A.D.). While holding that office he had charge of the Games, at which, it is said, he introduced the spectacle of tight-rope-walking elephants. He was next appointed governor of the province of Aquitania for a year, and in 33 served as consul for six months. Under Caligula he became governor of Greater Germany and acquitted himself well, raising the standard of discipline and repelling a barbarian raid into Gaul (39). When Caligula was murdered (41) Galba was urged to make himself emperor. He won the favor of Claudius by refusing, and served the emperor well. In 45 he was named proconsul of Africa for two years. He restored order there and won a great reputation for his justice. On his return to Rome he received great honors. Nevertheless, he went into virtual retirement, apparently in fear of his life for, according to Suetonius, he never went anywhere during this period without a second conveyance that carried 10,000 gold pieces—to tide him over in case sudden flight became necessary. In his retirement at Fundi he was offered the governorship of Hispania Tarraconensis (Tarragonian Spain) by the emperor Nero and accepted it (60). He at first set about administering his office with vigor. Then, lest he win the disfavor of Nero by winning too great renown as an administrator and thus appearing as a possible rival, he became less active and careless in his duties. Even so, Nero feared him and gave a secret order for his assassination. By chance Galba discovered it. Shortly afterward, revolt broke out in Gaul, and he joined the insurrection of Caius Julius Vindex (68), and declared himself governor of all Spain, in the name of the Roman Senate and the Roman people. He accepted the title of commander-in-chief, began to raise an army, and announced his rebellion against Nero. His acts, according to Suetonius, were supported by propitious omens: a ring with a stone, engraved with an image of Victory raising a trophy, was found in the city where he made his headquarters; a ship carrying arms, but with no living person aboard, drifted ashore at Tortosa. Just as it appeared that his rebellion might fail through defections and the death of Vindex, news came from Rome that Nero was dead and that the praetorians had revolted and come out in his favor. Galba at once assumed the title of Caesar, and cruelly punished those who had resisted his rebellion. Arrived at Rome he soon lost the support of the Senate and the moderates. He removed many traditional privileges and immunities, savagely punished innocent men and protected his infamous friends. His unpopularity at once became apparent; the army violently opposed him because he refused to carry out a promise of gifts to the soldiers. The people opposed him for his miserliness. The soldiers in Germany refused to swear allegiance to him. Thinking it was because he had no son (his wife and two sons had died and he had long refused to consider remarriage) he adopted Calpurnius Piso Frugi Licinianus as his successor. But Marcus Salvius Otho, an early supporter, had hoped to succeed him, and now organized a revolt among the praetorians and marched against Galba. On false news that the rebels had surrendered, Galba went out to meet them, and was attacked in the Forum. Some say he realized his attackers meant to kill him, and bared his throat to their swords. No one came forward to defend him. His body was left where he was slain. The remains of his mutilated body were eventually buried in his own garden.

Gallus (gal'us), **Caius Asinius.** Roman politician and writer, consul with C. Marcius Censorianus in 8 B.C. He married Vipsania, formerly wife of Tiberius. He was condemned to death by the Senate (30 A.D.), at the instigation of Tiberius, and died of starvation after an imprisonment of three years. He was a son of C. Asinius Pollio. His works, all of which are lost, included *De Comparatione Patris et Ciceronis*, to which the emperor Claudius replied in his defense of Cicero.

Gallus, Caius Cornelius. Roman poet, orator, general, and politician. He was born at Forum Julii (modern Fréjus), in Gaul, 69 or 66 B.C. He committed suicide in 26 B.C. He supported Octavian, commanded a part of his army at the battle of Actium in 31 B.C., pursued Antony to Egypt, and was made first prefect of Egypt in 30 B.C. He incurred the enmity of Augustus, was deprived of his post, and was exiled by the Senate. Virtually nothing of Gallus' poetry survives,

fat, fāte, fär, fåll, åsk, fãre; net, mē, hėr; pin, pīne; not, nōte, möve, nôr; up, lūte, pull; oi, oil; ou out; (lightened) ĕlect, agŏny, ūnite;

but he was outstanding among the poets of his age for the development of the love elegy. Among others he is said to have influenced Vergil.

Gaumata (gô-mä′tạ) or *Gaumates* (-tēz). Median magus. See *Smerdis, False.*

Gelon (je′lon) or *Gelo* (je′lō). Tyrant of Gela (491 B.C.) and later of Syracuse (485 B.C.), in Sicily; died 478 B.C. He was the son of Deinomenes, a descendant of a noble and priestly family. In the wars against Naxos, Zancle, Leontini, and Syracuse carried on by Hippocrates, tyrant of Gela, Gelon distinguished himself as a general of cavalry. On the death of Hippocrates (491 B.C.), Gelon offered his support to the sons of Hippocrates, but on gaining power from an unwilling people, he swept aside the sons of Hippocrates and made himself tyrant. In 485 B.C. the nobles of Syracuse, who had been driven out by the people, appealed to Gelon for aid. He used their appeal as a pretext for marching against Syracuse, won control of it and made himself master, not only of the common people but of the nobles who had appealed for his aid as well. Gelon moved his court and half the inhabitants of Gela to Syracuse, which possessed great natural advantages for defense and for shipping. He enlarged Syracuse to include a high promontory on the mainland as well as the island of Ortygia, which was the site of the original city, and enclosed both within one great wall from the sea on one side to the inner harbor on the other. A new agora was laid out close to the harbor near the wall and installations for shipping were constructed to utilize the geographical advantages of the enlarged city. To secure inhabitants for his enlarged city he razed the city of Camarina to the ground and moved its inhabitants to Syracuse. New citizens were also drawn from the cities of Megara, a northern neighbor of Syracuse, and Euboea, farther up the coast. The nobles from these places became citizens of Syracuse. The common people were sold into slavery. Gelon was himself of the noble class and, though tolerant of the whims of the populace, he preferred his own class and looked upon the commons as "a thankless neighbor." At his own court he was supported by his brothers Polyzalus and Hieron. Envoys from Athens and Sparta went to seek Gelon's aid in the war that Xerxes was preparing to wage on Greece. According to Herodotus, Gelon offered his

(obscured) errạnt, ardẹnt, actọr; ch, chip; g, go; th, thin; ᵼн, then; y, you; (variable) ḍ as d or j, ṣ as s or sh, ṭ as t or ch, ẓ as z or zh.

assistance on condition that he be made commander of all the Greek forces, or, failing that, if he were made commander either of the land forces or of the fleet. Otherwise he would neither go himself nor send aid. He made this offer, he said, in spite of the fact that the Greeks had refused to help him against the Carthaginians. The Greeks could not accept his conditions and sailed home. As it happened, Gelon was fully engaged in Sicily. He was closely linked by ties of marriage to Theron, tyrant of Acragas. Theron quarreled with Terillus, tyrant of Himera, and drove him out. Terillus sought aid from the Carthaginians, who brought a vast army into Sicily under the command of Hamilcar, to recover Himera for Terillus. Theron besieged in Himera by the Carthaginians, appealed to Gelon for aid. Gelon immediately hastened to his rescue with a large force. By a stratagem he got some of his horsemen into the city. There they found Hamilcar sacrificing at the great altar of Poseidon. They captured and killed him, and set fire to his ships. When Gelon received the signal that they had been successful Gelon marched his army against the land forces of Hamilcar and, after a long and desperate struggle, won a complete victory (480 B.C.). The forces of the Carthaginians were annihilated. Some say this great victory of Gelon's over the Carthaginians fell on the same day as the victory of the Greeks over the Persians at Salamis. By the victory Gelon repulsed for some time to come the encroachments of the Carthaginians in Sicily. He died 478 B.C., leaving instructions to his brother Polyzalus to marry his widow, Damareta, daughter of Theron, and to share the rule of Syracuse with another brother Hieron.

Germanicus (jĕr-man'i-kus). See *Claudius I.*

Germanicus. See *Drusus, Nero Claudius.*

Germanicus, Claudius Tiberius. Original name of *Britannicus.*

Germanicus Julius Caesar (sē'zạr). Roman general, born 15 B.C.; died near Antioch, Oct. 9, 19 A.D. He was the son of Nero Claudius Drusus and Antonia the Younger, and was the nephew of the emperor Tiberius, by whom he was adopted. Germanicus was a noble example of the finest Roman traits: he was handsome, brave, kind, and possessed of a gift for winning the respect and devotion of his troops, his relatives, and the Roman people. He was skilled in Greek and Roman oratory and letters and translated Greek works into Latin.

His modest manner of living endeared him to the common people. His care to make sacrifices at the tombs of famous men emphasized his own humility and piety. His personal qualities so endeared him to Augustus that the latter had considered, some say, making Germanicus his heir, but decided instead on Tiberius and ordered him to adopt Germanicus. Added to his other qualities was great military ability. While still under the legal age for such offices he served as quaestor and as consul. He was in Germany with his troops when news of the death of Augustus arrived (14 A.D.). His devoted troops would have proclaimed him emperor in place of Tiberius, but he was loyal and forbade them to do so. The Senate appointed him commander of the forces in Germany. He conducted three campaigns against the Germans (14–16 A.D.), and in the latter year defeated Arminius in a great battle on the Campus Idistavisus between what are now Minden and Hameln, Germany. His successes and his popularity roused the jealousy of Tiberius and he was recalled, but the wild acclamation of the crowd at the triumph he was awarded at Rome (17 A.D.) did nothing to dispel the fears and jealousy of Tiberius. In 18 A.D. he was placed in command of the forces in the East and went there to restore order. He defeated the king of Armenia and reduced Cappadocia to the status of a province. He was taken ill at Antioch and died there, 19 A.D. His body was found to be covered with dark splotches and poison was suspected. It was said that Cnaeus Piso, the governor of Syria, poisoned him at the request of Tiberius. When his body was cremated, some say, his heart was not consumed. This was considered confirmation that he had been poisoned, for a heart steeped in poison was thought to be proof against fire. When news of his death reached Rome the people were wild with grief: temples were stoned, altars were overturned, and heads of families threw the household gods into the streets. Even the barbarians, both those fighting among themselves and those fighting against Rome, ceased fighting to mourn him. Cnaeus Piso was condemned to death by the Senate when he returned to Rome. Germanicus was married to Agrippina, the daughter of Marcus Vipsanius Agrippa and Julia, the daughter of Augustus. She bore him nine children, two of whom died in infancy and a third in early childhood. Of the remaining children who survived him, Agrippina the

Younger became the mother of the emperor Nero; two other daughters, Drusilla and Livilla, led notoriously immoral lives; his two sons, Nero and Drusus, were executed as public enemies during the reign of Tiberius, and his third son, Caius became the emperor Caligula.

Gordius (gôr'di-us). According to tradition, a Phrygian peasant who became king. One day as he was driving his ox-cart a royal eagle settled on the pole and remained there as he drove along. He made for the city of Telmessus where there was a famous oracle, but as he came to the gate of the city he was met by a prophetic maiden who noted the eagle on the pole of the cart and told him to make sacrifices to Zeus at once. He consented to do so if she would marry him. She agreed to do this as soon as the sacrifices were made. In the meantime the king of Phrygia died, and the oracle told the Phrygians that their new king was approaching with his bride in an ox-cart. As the Phrygians debated in the marketplace Gordius arrived in his ox-cart. The Phrygians, noting the eagle and the maiden, at once proclaimed him king. Gordius dedicated his cart, together with the yoke which was fixed to it with an intricate knot, to Zeus. It was afterward deposited in the temple at Gordium, a city founded by Gordius, and the oracle pronounced that he who could untie the knot joining the yoke and the ox-cart would become lord of all Asia. The cart and yoke were guarded in the temple for centuries. To this place came Alexander the Great. He looked at the knot, heard the oracular pronouncement concerning it, and with one stroke of his sword cut right through the knot.

Gracchus (grak'us). The distinctive *cognomen* of a branch of the Roman gens Sempronia: especially, the sons of Cornelia, the daughter of Scipio Africanus, and Tiberius Sempronius Gracchus (died 154 B.C.). They were: 1) Tiberius Sempronius Gracchus, born 168 or 163 B.C. He married Claudia, daughter of Appius Claudius, and was the brother-in-law of Scipio Africanus Minor whom he accompanied in his expedition against Carthage (146 B.C.). He was appointed quaestor in 137 B.C., and as such served under the consul Caius Hostilius Mancinus in the Numantine war in Spain. He was elected tribune of the people for 133 B.C. At this period the class of independent farmers of small holdings was rapidly disappearing from Italy. The land was being absorbed by the great estates of the rich and cultivated by slave labor; and the peasantry were forced to seek refuge in the cities, especially Rome, where they swelled the ranks of the unemployed. Gracchus sought to bring about a greater subdivision of the land and to restore the class of independent farmers by reviving, with some modification, the Licinian law, passed in 367 B.C. but allowed to fall into abeyance, which limited the amount of public land that each citizen might occupy. His proposals were carried in the *comitia tributa* in spite of the opposition of his colleague, who was deposed. At the end of his term he tried, contrary to precedent, to secure re-election, and a disturbance arose in consequence, in which he and 300 of his followers were killed. 2) Caius Sempronius Gracchus, younger brother of Tiberius. He served under his brother-in-law Scipio Africanus Minor in Spain, and was quaestor in Sardinia from 126 to 123 B.C., when he was elected tribune of the people. He renewed the agrarian law passed by his brother Tiberius, and brought forward a series of resolutions seeking to undermine the existing aristocratic republican form of government, securing the support of the poorer plebeians of the capital by the regular distribution of grain at the expense of the state. He was reëlected to the tribuneship in 122 B.C., but failed of election in 121 B.C., in consequence of the opposition among all classes to his project of extending the rights of citizenship to the Latins and Italians, and as the result of a campaign by the aristocratic party to discredit him by having one of their henchmen offer even more to the people than Gracchus did. He was killed in a disturbance which ensued in the city in 121 B.C. These two sons of Cornelia—the accomplished Roman woman who answered the boasts of a Roman matron about her jewels by pointing to her sons and saying, "These are my jewels"—were pointed out to Aeneas by Anchises when he visited the latter in the Underworld. Their spirits were awaiting to be born then and their illustrious future had already been decided, according to the *Aeneid*—which was, of course, written long after they had died.

Gyges (gī′jēz, jī′-). A king of Lydia (c685–c653 B.C.), and the founder of a new dynasty. Pressed by the Cimmerians, he invoked the help of Assurbanipal, and submitted to his supremacy. Afterward he allied himself with Psammetichus,

---

(obscured) errạnt, ardẹnt, actọr; ch, chip; g, go; th, thin; ŦH, then; y, you; (variable) ḍ as d or j, ṣ as s or sh, ṭ as t or ch, ẓ as z or zh.

king of Egypt, against Assyria, and seems to have fallen (c653 B.C.) in one of the repeated attacks of the Cimmerians, who were no longer checked by the Assyrian power. Plato's story is that Gyges, a shepherd of the king of Lydia, after a storm came upon a hollow, bronze horse in a chasm. Within the horse lay a corpse from which he took a magic ring which had the property of making the wearer invisible. Wearing the ring, Gyges killed the king, and thus became king himself. Herodotus tells still another story: Gyges was the trusted aide of Candaules who was king of Lydia and a descendant of Heracles. Candaules was madly in love with his wife and thought she was the most beautiful woman in the world. So carried away was he with the wonder of her beauty that he wished Gyges to see her naked, which was unlawful to do, so that his words might be confirmed by Gyges' eyes. He commanded Gyges to hide in the chamber where he and the queen slept and to behold her naked loveliness. Gyges was shocked at the idea but in the end obeyed his master as he valued his life above his honor. Candaules' wife entered the chamber, as Candaules had assured Gyges she would do, put off her clothes and went to bed, but out of the corner of her eye she saw Gyges hiding behind the door. She did not cry out or make any mention that she had seen him and Gyges slipped out of the room, as he thought, unobserved. The next day the queen sent for him. She informed him that she knew he had spied on her with her husband's aid, and had seen her naked which was unlawful. She now gave Gyges the choice of two alternatives; either he must kill Candaules and take her as his wife, that thus he would have looked on what was his own, or he must die himself, that only Candaules should have looked on what was his own. Gyges, who was truly loyal to his master, tried to appease her but the queen was immovable, and Gyges chose his own life rather than loyalty to the king. The queen gave him instructions for killing Candaules, in the very chamber where Gyges had spied on her. She gathered trusted friends to her support and Gyges slipped into Candaules' chamber at night and killed him as he slept. He then took the queen as his wife and declared himself king of Lydia. The Lydians were aroused to great wrath by the murder of their king and attacked Gyges, but as the attack was indecisive they agreed to consult the oracle at Delphi to learn whether Gyges should be allowed to reign. The priestess gave an answer favorable to Gyges and the Lydians accepted him as their king. Gyges sent rich offerings to Delphi, one of the earliest of the barbarians to do so, among them large amounts of silver and six golden goblets. In addition to confirming him as king, the priestess foretold that in the fifth generation the descendants of Gyges would suffer revenge at the hands of the descendants of Heracles. The king in the fifth generation was his descendant Croesus.

Gylippus (ji-lip′us). Spartan general; fl. 5th century B.C. He was a son of Cleandrides, who was expelled in 446 B.C. from Sparta after having been found guilty of taking bribes from the Athenians, exhibiting a weakness of character that his son apparently inherited. During the Peloponnesian War he was sent in 415 B.C. to help Syracuse against Athens. He defeated the Athenian forces in several engagements, compelling them to surrender (414–413 B.C.) with their generals, Nicias and Demosthenes. Later (404 B.C.), after the capture of Athens by Lysander, he was sent by the general to Sparta with the treasure taken in Athens, but he was unable to resist the temptation of unsewing the bags which contained large amounts of silver and of extracting from each bag a "considerable amount." He then sewed up the bags again and delivered them to the Spartan magistrates as he was ordered to do. Unfortunately, he did not know that each bag had in it a statement of its contents. When the bags were opened, his theft was discovered, and he was found guilty of having embezzled public funds and was sentenced to death. He managed to escape, fled the country, and died, like his father, in exile.

Hadrian (hā′dri-an). [Also: *Adrian;* full Latin name, *Publius Aelius Hadrianus.*] Roman emperor (117–138 A.D.); nephew and ward of Trajan, whom he succeeded. He was born probably at Italica, in Hispania Baetica (near modern Seville, Spain), Jan. 24, 76 A.D.; died at Baiae, Italy, July 10, 138. He

(obscured) errạnt, ardẹnt, actọr; ch, chip; g, go; th, thin; ᵵн, then; y, you;
(variable) ḍ as d or j, ş as s or sh, ţ as t or ch, ʐ as z or zh.

held several positions in various parts of the empire under Trajan, accompanying him in his campaigns. On the death of Trajan, it is said, he succeeded to the emperor's place through the slyness of Plotina, Trajan's wife, who announced Trajan's adoption of his nephew, then withheld news of Trajan's death until Hadrian could consolidate his position. Renouncing the policy of conquest, he abandoned the new provinces of Armenia, Mesopotamia, and Assyria, and established the Euphrates as the eastern boundary of the empire. In 119 he began a progress through the provinces, in the course of which he began the construction of the wall that bears his name, designed to keep the Picts and the Scots out of Britain. He returned finally about 131, having visited Gaul, Germany, Britain, Spain, Mauretania, Parthia, Asia Minor, Athens, Sicily, Rome (for a year), Syria, Palestine, Arabia, and Egypt. He promulgated the *Edictum perpetuum* (c130), a collection of the edits of the praetors by Salvius Julianus. This formed the groundwork for the *Corpus juris* of Justinian. In 132 a revolt was occasioned among the Jews by the planting of the Roman colony of Aelia Capitolina on the site of Jerusalem, and the building of a temple to Jupiter Capitolinus on the site of the Temple; the revolt, led by Bar Kochba, was suppressed in 135. Hadrian devoted himself to building and strengthening the position of the emperor. Through the *Edictum,* lawmaking by the praetors was ended; thereafter laws became a matter of senatorial confirmation of the suggestions of the emperor. He reduced taxes, provided for less arbitrary treatment of slaves, and fostered regulations to reduce immorality. His public works include the wall in Britain, similar structures in Germany, the Pantheons of Rome and Athens, and the temple of Olympian Zeus at Athens, as well as many other buildings in Rome and in the provinces. He was a patron of the arts and himself a poet; perhaps his most famous composition is the address to his soul, supposed to have been said on his deathbed, beginning: *"Animula, vagula, blandula,"* (Little soul, evanescent, pleasant . . .). Hadrian's first choice as his successor, Lucius Ceionius Commodus, died Jan. 1, 138, and Hadrian then chose Antoninus (Antoninus Pius).

Hamilcar (ham'il-kär, hạ-mil'kär). Carthaginian general of the 5th century B.C. During the Persian War envoys of Xerxes went to Hamilcar and arranged with him an attack on the

Greek settlements of Sicily, so that the latter could not, as requested by the homeland, send aid against the Persians. The occasion for the Carthaginian attack against Sicily was a quarrel between two Greek states there, in which the Greek tyrant of Himera was driven out of his city by the tyrant of Acragas and appealed to Hamilcar for aid. Hamilcar seized the opportunity to reduce Greek power in Sicily. He sailed with a huge armament to recover Himera and besieged the city (480 B.C.). He proposed to enlist the aid of the Greek gods to help defeat the Greeks in Sicily, but as he was unfamiliar with the forms and ceremonies, he sent to Selinus, a Greek city under Carthaginian dominion, requesting the people to send priests who could properly perform the ceremonies for a great sacrifice to Poseidon. Hamilcar's messenger to Selinus was intercepted by the forces of the tyrant of Acragas. They rode to the camp of Hamilcar on the appointed day and asked admittance as the men Hamilcar had sent for. The Carthaginians, unaware of the deception since all Greeks looked alike to them, admitted them to the camp by the sea. As Hamilcar stood waiting by the great altar of Poseidon he was overpowered and slain, and his ships were fired. The waiting Greek army, under the command of Gelon, tyrant of Syracuse, who had come to aid the tyrant of Acragas, received the signal that the trick had been successful and marched around the other side of the city where Hamilcar's land army was encamped and attacked it. After a desperate battle Gelon's forces were successful; Hamilcar's great force was utterly destroyed. The Carthaginians, unwilling to admit that Hamilcar was slain by a trick at the altar of the Greek god Poseidon, said that he stood throughout the hard-fought battle beside an altar of the Phoenician god, Baal, and that all day victims were hurled into the fire that blazed mightily. But when he saw his army in full retreat he offered himself as the greatest victim to his god; he leaped into the fire on the altar and was consumed in the flames.

Hamilcar Barca (or *Barcas*) (bär′kạ, bär′kạs). Carthaginian general, drowned in Spain, c229 B.C. He was the father of Hannibal; his surname Barca means "lightning." He held (247–244 B.C.) Mount Ercte (Monte Pellegrino), Sicily, against the Romans, transferred his troops and held (244–241 B.C.) Mount Eryx (Monte San Giuliano), and raided

Roman positions as far as the mainland. At the end of th
First Punic War in 241 B.C., he retired to Africa undefeate
There, his troops, their promised rewards being withheld b
the Carthaginian government, revolted and Hamilcar wa
called to defeat them. He suppressed the rising of th
mercenaries (241–238 B.C.), and became dictator of Ca
thage. He began (236 B.C.) the reduction of Spain to a Ca
thaginian province in order to have a base from which t
strike at Rome, but was drowned while withdrawing from
siege.

Hannibal (han'i-bạl). Carthaginian general, 5th century B.C
grandson of Hamilcar. His life was dominated by a desire t
avenge the death (480 B.C.) of his grandfather at Himera, i
Sicily. At an advanced age he persuaded Carthage to sen
a force to Sicily in reply to a request for aid from Segest;
a Greek city at war with Selinus. A great force was prepare
and sailed to Sicily under command of Hannibal. The flee
reached Sicily, and the armed force marched to Selinu
Selinus had never been attacked in the 250 years since i
founding and was completely unprepared to withstand th
Carthaginians. Its inhabitants resisted valiantly but afte
nine days the city fell to Hannibal (410 B.C.), and it becam
the first Greek city in Sicily to be taken by the Carthaginian
Such military installations as existed were destroyed, it
people were slaughtered or carried off into slavery, but th
city itself was allowed to stand. Hannibal now set out t
fulfill his real purpose in the expedition to Sicily, which wa
the destruction of Himera, the scene of his grandfather
defeat and death. He besieged Himera and breached it
walls by means of mines. The defenders drove his soldier
out. Just at that time appeared a fleet of 25 ships, sent fror
Syracuse to relieve Himera. Hannibal spread abroad a ru
mor that he was going to attack Syracuse, and the com
mander of the Greek fleet, having heard the rumor an
believing it to be true, immediately decided to withdraw. H
offered to take the inhabitants of Himera to safety in hi
ships. About half of the inhabitants, all he had room fo
boarded the ships and the fleet sailed. The remaining in
habitants continued desperate resistance to the Carthagin
ans. They maintained their resistance until the Syracusa
fleet returned to rescue them, but just as it appeared th
forces of Hannibal again breached the walls, poured into th

fat, fāte, fär, fåll, åsk, fâre; net, mē, hèr; pin, pīne; not, nōte, mōv
nôr; up, lūte, pùll; oi, oil; ou out; (lightened) ḛlect, agǫny, ŭnit

town, and by the time the Greek ships reached the harbor, Himera was already in Hannibal's hands. It is said that on the very spot where his grandfather had been slain Hannibal sacrificed 3000 human victims to appease his shade and avenge him. Afterward he completely destroyed the city and left the spot barren. Hannibal then returned in triumph to Carthage. In 406 B.C. he again invaded Sicily at the head of a great force and laid siege to Acragas. Because the ground about the city was low and made the siege difficult, he decided to build a great causeway, from which height his forces could attack the fortifications more effectively. He plundered the neighboring cemeteries of their grave stones and tombs to get material for the causeway. It is said that when the tomb of Theron, former tyrant of Acragas, was being broken into it was struck by a thunderbolt and seers advised that it be spared. Before the causeway was finished plague broke out in Hannibal's camp; he fell victim to it and died. The Carthaginians decided that the gods were angry because of the desecration of the cemeteries. They sacrificed a boy to their god Moloch and then completed the causeway, without further disturbing the tombs.

annibal. The great Carthaginian general, eldest son of Hamilcar Barca; born 247 B.C.; committed suicide at Libyssa, Bithynia, probably 183 B.C. He was with his father in Spain after c238 and, at his father's request swore, at the age of nine, his enmity to Rome, which had defeated Carthage in the First Punic War (261–241 B.C.). Following Hamilcar Barca's death in 228 B.C. Hannibal's brother-in-law Hasdrubal succeeded to the command of the Carthaginian forces in Spain; Hasdrubal was assassinated in 221 B.C. and Hannibal was chosen leader of the army. He set about extending the Carthaginian domain in Spain and by 219 B.C. had reached the Ebro, controlling all of Spain south of that river except the city of Saguntum (modern Sagunto, near Valencia), an ally of Rome. Hannibal laid siege to the city, despite specific warnings from Rome that such action would lead to war, and in eight months took it. When the Carthaginian government would not repudiate his action by surrendering Hannibal to the Roman envoys, the Romans declared for war. Hannibal now conceived a daring plan and in the spring of 218 B.C. marched northward, crossed the Pyrenees, evaded a Roman force sent to intercept him, reached the Rhône, and in October, with snow already in th high passes, crossed the Alps into Italy. Only some 26,00 men survived the crossing (which was probably by way of th Little St. Bernard Pass) of about 35,000–40,000 that ha started, yet this crossing of the Alps in late autumn, wit supplies and with the Carthaginian war-elephants, is sti considered among the greatest military achievements in hi tory. At the Ticinus River and again at the Trebia in Decen ber, Hannibal scored victories over the Romans and secure control of the Padus (Po) Valley. Reinforced by Gaulis tribesmen, he marched south in the spring of 217 B.C crossed the Apennines, and at Lake Trasimenus cut t pieces a Roman army under the command of the consu Caius Flaminius, who was killed in the battle. Rome now ha no army capable of risking another defeat in the field an Fabius Maximus, who was appointed military dictator, dare not risk a general engagement. Hannibal decided agains storming Rome itself and instead marched through Ital into Apulia, destroying as he went, but suffering the harry ing attacks of Fabius, whose tactics won him the surnam Cunctator ("Delayer"). Hannibal wintered on the Apulia plains and early the next summer (216 B.C.) faced the larges army Rome had ever put into the field, about 54,000 me at Cannae. Skillfully he encircled them, pushed one grou in on another until the Roman position was confused, an then cut them to pieces with his cavalry; more than half th Roman force was killed. As a result of the victory, sever Italian tribes came over to the Carthaginians, as did Capu where Hannibal wintered in 216–215 B.C. Syracuse deserte the Roman cause and allied itself with Carthage; Philip V o Macedon became an ally, although he never did sen material aid. Hannibal had now reached the peak of h power; Rome, in his eyes, was impregnable, and her neare allies were not deserting her; his failure to attack Rome afte Cannae, when she was probably helpless, has been criticize as his fatal mistake. He compaigned in southern Italy fo several years, captured Tarentum in 213 B.C., and in 21 won a victory at Herdoniae, but the strain on his manpowe was great. In 212 B.C. Syracuse, under siege for three year fell to the Romans, and in 211 B.C. Capua, too, was capture and sacked, despite Hannibal's attacks on the surroundin Roman armies and a feint on Rome itself. Help was require from Carthage's armies elsewhere, and Hannibal's brother Hasdrubal, who had been fighting the Romans in Spain, crossed the Alps with a large force. But before Hannibal could reach him from the south Hasdrubal was defeated and killed at the Metaurus in 207 B.C. Hannibal took refuge in the mountains of Bruttii, where he maintained an unassailable position for some years. At last, with help not forthcoming, with Mago defeated in Liguria, and with Scipio advancing victoriously in Africa against Carthage itself, he was recalled to Carthage in 203 B.C. There he hastily put together an army of his veterans from Italy and a levy from the African tribes and met the Romans at Zama in 202 B.C.; the Carthaginian force was practically annihilated and Carthage had to make peace. To pay the resulting indemnity (Carthage also gave up all claims to the Mediterranean islands), Hannibal, appointed chief magistrate, reformed the financial structure of the Carthaginian state and thereby came into conflict with the oligarchy. But his methods succeeded and within a few years Carthage was not only paying the indemnity but was reëstablishing itself as a Mediterranean power. Alarmed, Rome thereupon demanded that Carthage surrender Hannibal and he was forced to flee (c195 B.C.). He stayed in Syria for some time as a general with Antiochus III, but when Syria was defeated by the Romans he once again fled, to the court of Prusias, king of Bithynia. There the Romans again sought him and demanded his surrender by Prusias. Rather than give up to his sworn enemies, Hannibal committed suicide; the year 183 B.C. is given as the date of his death by Livy, the same year that Scipio Africanus and Philopoemon, general of the Achaean League in Greece, died, but the specific date is conjectural.

Hanno (han'ō). [Called *Hanno the Great.*] Carthaginian leader; fl. in the 3rd century B.C. He was the leader of the aristocratic party at Carthage and an opponent of Hamilcar Barca and Hannibal. He opposed the war with Rome and all other trans-Mediterranean adventures. His opposition to paying Hamilcar's troops led to their revolt, and his refusal to support Hannibal with sufficient aid was a principal contributory cause of Hannibal's failure.

Harmodius (här-mō'di-us) and *Aristogiton* (a̧-ris-tō̧-jī'to̧n, ar″-is-tō-). Killed 514 B.C. Two Athenian youths who killed Hip-

parchus, tyrant of Athens, in 514 B.C. They are represente
as entertaining a strong affection for each other, which r
mained unaltered despite the endeavors of Hipparchus
draw that of the young and beautiful Harmodius towa
himself. Enraged at the indifference of Harmodius, Hippa
chus put a public insult upon him by declaring his sist
unworthy of carrying the sacred baskets at the religio
procession of the Panathenaea, in revenge for which t
youths organized a conspiracy to overthrow both Hippa
chus and his brother Hippias. They chose the feast day
the Panathenaea for the execution of their plot because
was the only day when the citizens could meet togethe
armed, without arousing suspicion. They had only a fe
accomplices, but they hoped that the stir made by the dea
of Hipparchus would rouse the citizens to throw off the yo
of tyranny. However, revolution was incidental, and wa
hoped for only as a means of saving themselves. As the tim
for the festival arrived the conspirators saw Hippias stan
ing in the Ceramicus talking with one of their accomplice
They immediately concluded, falsely, that their plot w
exposed and resolved to act at once. They found Hippa
chus by the Leocorium and struck him down. Harmodiu
was captured by the guards and slain on the spot. It is sai
that Hippias, to whom the news was brought as he still stoo
in the Ceramicus, kept his features composed as if nothin
had happened, pointed to the armed men in the processic
whom he thought were implicated in the plot, ordered the
to withdraw and had them disarmed. Aristogiton escape
temporarily through the excited crowd, but was shortly ca
tured. When put to torture to reveal his accomplices, h
named the principal friends of Hippias, who were execute
When pressed for further revelations, he answered th
there remained no one whose death he desired, except t
tyrant. Aristogiton then died under torture. Following t
death of Hipparchus, Hippias, who hitherto, according
Thucydides, had maintained the laws, beautified the cit
and carried out the wars of the Athenians and the sacrific
as prescribed, now became fearful of further plots. Fro
this time on his rule became more oppressive, so that, a
cording to Thucydides, and Herodotus also, the death
Hipparchus deepened, rather than lessened, the tyranny
the Pisistratidae. At the time of the murder of Hipparchu

not much attention was paid to Harmodius and Aristogiton by the citizens. But as the rule of Hippias became more oppressive the conspirators came to be regarded as heroes, and after the expulsion of Hippias (510 B.C.), they were honored as such. A statue of them was placed in the market-place, on the way to the Acropolis opposite the Metroum; a copy of this is in the Museo Nazionale at Naples. They were the first men to have their statues set up in the market-place at Athens. The subject of Harmodius and Aristogiton became a favorite with painters and sculptors when popular fancy transformed them from murderers to tyrannicides.

Harpagus (här'pạ-gus). General of Cyrus; fl. 6th century B.C. According to Herodotus, he was descended from a noble Median house, and was the attendant of Astyages, who charged him with the duty of exposing the infant Cyrus, grandson of Astyages. Instead of performing that duty in person, he delegated it to the herdsman Mitradates, who substituted a still-born child of which his wife had just been delivered. When the identity of Cyrus, who had been brought up by Mitradates and his wife as their own child, was discovered, Astyages punished Harpagus by serving up to him at a banquet the flesh of his own son. Harpagus waited until Cyrus had grown to manhood, then incited him to rebel against Astyages, and effected the downfall of the latter by deserting with the army to Cyrus. He was afterward one of the most trusted generals in the service of Cyrus, and played a prominent part in the conquest of Asia Minor.

Hasdrubal (haz'drü-bạl, haz-drö'bạl). [Also: *Asdrubal.*] Carthaginian general and politician, who died in Spain, 221 B.C. He rose to prominence as a leader of the democratic party in Carthage in the interval between the First and Second Punic wars, and married a daughter of Hamilcar Barca, whom he accompanied to Spain in 238 B.C. He subsequently returned to Africa to assume command in a war against the Numidians, and reduced them to submission. In 229 B.C. he succeeded his father-in-law as commander in Spain, where he founded the city of Carthago Nova (New Carthage, modern Cartagena), and largely extended the Carthaginian power, fixing by treaty the boundary between the Carthaginian and Roman possessions in Spain at the Iberus (Ebro). He was assassinated by a Celtic slave whose master he had put to death.

Hasdrubal. [Also: *Asdrubal.*] Carthaginian general; son o
Hamilcar Barca and younger brother of Hannibal (c247-
c183 B.C.); died 207 B.C. He was left in charge of the Car
thaginian forces in Spain when Hannibal set out on hi
expedition to Italy in 218 B.C. He maintained the war agains
the Romans under the brothers Cnaeus and Publius Scipic
with varied success until 212 B.C. Then, having been rein
forced by two armies under Mago and Hasdrubal (d. 20(
B.C.), son of Gisco, he was enabled to inflict a decisive defea
upon Cnaeus, who fell in the battle, Publius having beer
killed a short time previously in a cavalry engagement. He
was defeated by Scipio Africanus at Baecula (Bailén) in 20(
B.C., and probably in the same year crossed the Pyrenees or
his way to join his brother in Italy. He crossed the Alps in
207 B.C., but was attacked and defeated by the Roman
under Caius Claudius Nero and Marcus Livius on the Metau
rus (Metauro) River in the same year before he could effec
a junction with Hannibal. He fell in the engagement, and
according to Livy, his severed head was thrown into the
camp of Hannibal by the victorious Romans.

Hasdrubal. [Also: *Asdrubal.*] Carthaginian general, son o
Gisco; died c200 B.C. He was sent to Spain with an army ir
214 B.C., and on the departure (c209 B.C.) of Hasdrubal, so
of Hamilcar, on his expedition to join Hannibal in Italy, wa
left with Mago in command of the Carthaginian forces ir
Spain. He was defeated with his colleague at Silpia by Scipic
Africanus in 206 B.C., was in command of an army opposec
to Scipio in Africa in 204 B.C., when his camp near Utica wa
fired by the Romans and nearly the whole of his army de
stroyed, and is said by some authorities to have taken poisor
to escape the fury of the Carthaginian populace.

Hasdrubal. [Also: *Asdrubal.*] Carthaginian general. He wa
commander-in-chief in the war against Masinissa in 150 B.c
Having sustained a decisive defeat, he was punished with
exile. He was, however, recalled on the outbreak of the
Third Punic War in 149 B.C., and was placed in command
of the forces outside the walls of Carthage. He defeated the
consul Manilius in two engagements (c148 B.C.). He subsequently became commander of the forces within the city
which he defended with great obstinacy against Scipio
Aemilianus in 146 B.C. He finally surrendered, and, after
gracing the triumph of Scipio, was allowed to spend the res

of his life in honorable captivity. It is said that at the time
of his surrender his wife upbraided him for cowardice, and
threw herself and her children into the flames of the temple
in which she had taken refuge.

Hephaestion (hē-fes'ti-ǫn). Macedonian of Pella; died at Ecbatana (now Hamadan, Iran), 324 B.C. He was the intimate
friend and companion of Alexander the Great, whom he
accompanied on the campaigns in Asia. Alexander called
him "the friend of Alexander," whereas his other close companion he named "the friend of the king." When Alexander
crossed the Hellespont (334 B.C.) and laid a garland on the
tomb of his hero and supposed ancestor, Achilles, Hephaestion did homage at the grave of Patroclus, for he was linked
to Alexander as Patroclus was to Achilles. When Alexander
increasingly adopted barbarian (Oriental) customs as he
continued his conquest of Asia, Hephaestion did the same,
although other of Alexander's closest companions resented
the influence the barbarians seemed to be wielding on their
king. On the march into India, Hephaestion, with three regi-
ments, went by the Khyber Pass to the Indus River, where
he was to arrange transport for the crossing of the army. On
the return from India Alexander rested at Ecbatana, the
Median capital. Thousands of poets and actors came from
Greece to entertain the king; great feasts and celebrations
were held. Hephaestion fell ill of a fever. He disregarded his
physician's orders to rest and abstain from feasting, and
joined Alexander at a banquet. He suffered a relapse and
died. Alexander was wild with grief. He ordered the manes
and tails of the horses and mules to be cut, razed the fortifications of neighboring cities as a sign of mourning, crucified
the physician who attended Hephaestion, and forbade the
playing of music until an oracle of Ammon arrived instructing him to sacrifice to Hephaestion and worship him as a
hero. He fell on the tribe of the Cossaeans and destroyed
them, some say as a sacrifice to Hephaestion. When he arrived in Babylon, 323 B.C., he caused a funeral pyre 200 feet
high to be raised, on which his friend's body was burned.
For the funeral, of unsurpassed magnificence, he had set
aside 10,000 talents. The last honor he paid his friend was
the erection of shrines, in which Hephaestion would be worshiped as a hero, at Alexandria in Egypt and in other cities.

Hermann (her'män). See **Arminius.**

Hermocrates (hėr-mok'rᴀ-tēz). Syracusan general and politi
cian; killed at Syracuse, c407 B.C. At a congress at Gelᴀ
attended by delegates from all the Greek cities of Sicily anᴅ
called (425 B.C.) for the purpose of considering whether thᴇ
cities should ally themselves with Athens against Syracuse
Hermocrates formulated a policy of Sicily for the Sicilians
He advised the representatives not to invite outsiders in tᴏ
settle the quarrels of the Greek cities with each other, anᴅ
to unite to repulse any interference in their affairs by outsiᴅ
ers. His policy was not adopted, nor in the end was he ablᴇ
to follow it himself, but for the time being the interventioɴ
of Athens in Sicilian affairs was postponed. Ten years latᴇ
an Athenian expedition arrived in Sicily at the request oᴏ
Segesta, which was engaged in a quarrel with Selinus, anᴅ
to restore Leontini, which had been taken by Syracuse. Herʜ
mocrates was appointed general to defend Syracuse. A fleeᴇ
was assembled and walls were built. With the aid of thᴇ
Spartan general Gylippus, who came in response to Syracu
san appeals for help, the Athenians were completely dᴇ
feated at sea (413 B.C.), and cut to pieces or enslaved as theʏ
attempted to retreat overland. After the defeat of thᴇ
Athenians Hermocrates was appointed commander of ᴀ
fleet that was sent to the aid of Sparta in the Aegean anᴅ
took part in the battle of Cynossema (411 B.C.). While he waᴏ
gone a resurgence of democratic feeling in Syracuse waᴏ
used by his political opponent, Diocles, to secure his banishʜ
ment and to deprive him of his command. He went to Persiᴀ
and served the Spartans under the satrap Pharnabazus. Iɴ
408 B.C. he returned to Sicily, but was not allowed to returɴ
to Syracuse. He built a small fleet, hired mercenaries, anᴅ
gathered a band of followers from Himera, the city jusᴛ
destroyed by the Carthaginians, and set about to drive bacᴋ
the Carthaginians. He had great success and hoped now tᴏ
win back his own city, but Diocles prevented his recall. Herʜ
mocrates thereupon went to the ruins of Himera and gathʜ
ered the bones of the soldiers of Diocles who had falleɴ
there and whose bones Diocles had neglected to inter. Herʜ
mocrates loaded the bones on wagons and sent them intᴏ
Syracuse, while he waited outside the city walls, hoping tᴏ
be recalled. Diocles was banished for having failed to burʏ
the dead, but Hermocrates was not recalled. All else failinɢ
he now resolved to take the city by force. With a few follow

ers he was secretly admitted to the city by his supporters inside it, but before the main body of his supporters could join him his presence in the city became known, and he was overpowered and slain (c407 B.C.).

Hiero I (hī′e̯-rō) or **Hieron I** (-ron). Tyrant of Syracuse, who died 467 B.C. He was the brother of Gelo, whom he succeeded as tyrant in 478 B.C. Cyme (Cumae), the northern outpost of the Greek settlements on the Italian coast, harried by its neighbors the Etruscans, appealed to Hiero for aid. He sailed at the head of a large Syracusan fleet and defeated the Etruscans at the Battle of Cyme (474 B.C.). Thenceforth Etruscan power in Italy declined. Hiero and Syracuse, like the other Greek settlements in Italy and Sicily, were strongly attached to their motherland, and honored and preserved Greek customs and Greek gods. From the spoils taken from the Etruscans at Cyme, Hiero dedicated a fine bronze helmet at Olympia. Hiero's court was wealthy and luxurious, and its ruler a generous patron of literature. The poet Pindar was an ardent admirer of Hiero and was a welcome guest at his court. He wrote the *First Pythian Ode* to celebrate the victory at Cyme. Hiero reverenced the sacred sanctuary at Delphi, to which the tyrants of Syracuse made rich gifts. He sent his horses and chariots to take part in the great games at Olympia. His entries won victories there in 476, 472, and 468 B.C., and at the Pythian Games, in which he also participated, in 482, 478, and 470 B.C. Pindar and Bacchylides, another poet who was welcomed at his court, commemorated his victories in their odes. To memorialize the founding of the city of Aetna, which Hiero accomplished by removing all the inhabitants of Catana and repeopling and renaming it, Aeschylus, visiting at Hiero's court, wrote a play, *Women of Aetna.* The play has been lost, and the city as Aetna did not long survive; it soon became Catana again. A quarrel between Hiero and Theron, tyrant of Acragas, was settled, so it is said, by the poet Simonides, who spent the last years of his life in Syracuse. Under his successor, the work of Hiero as a tyrant was undone. His defeat of the Etruscans at Cyme was a lasting benefit to the Greek settlements of Italy, and his generosity as a patron of literature bore fruit which survives to our own age.

Hiero II or **Hieron II.** King of Syracuse, born c307 B.C.; died 216 B.C. He became (275 B.C.) general of the Syracusans,

and as a result of his victory over the Mamertines, who were
spreading into Syracusan territory, was chosen king in 270
or in 265 B.C. The Carthaginians, looking for a chance to
gain possession of a base in Sicily, came to the Mamertines
aid, but they in turn had called on Rome for help. Hiero
therefore became an ally of Carthage in 264 B.C., but driven
back by the Romans, he became a permanent ally of Rome
in 263 B.C. and remained on their side during the First and
Second Punic wars.

Hieronymus of Cardia (hī-ę-ron′i-mus; kär′-di-ạ). Greek general
and historian; fl. end of the 4th century B.C.; died c250 B.C.
He was possibly one of Alexander the Great's generals.
After Alexander's death he joined Eumenes, was taken prisoner by Antigonus, who pardoned him, and was later made
military governor of Boeotia by Demetrius Poliorcetes. He
wrote a carefully documented history of the Diadochi
(successors of Alexander) from the death of Alexander to
the Pyrrhic War. His work was an important source for Arrian's history of Alexander the Great. Hieronymus lived to
an extremely advanced age and died at the court of Antigonus Gonatas.

Himilco (hi-mil′kō). Carthaginian general (fl. c400 B.C.). He
was a cousin of Hannibal (d. 406 B.C.), whom he accompanied at the siege of Acragas (406 B.C.). In order to attack
the walls, Hannibal ordered a causeway to be built and plundered the tombs of cemeteries outside Acragas for material.
Plague broke out and Hannibal was one of its first victims.
Himilco succeeded to the command. Feeling that the gods
were angry at the plundering of the tombs, Himilco sacrificed a boy to the Carthaginian god Moloch, and finished
building the causeway, but without taking any more material
from the tombs. He besieged the city and at the end of eight
months the defenders, in despair, decided to abandon their
homes and their gods. Practically the entire population
marched out at night, unhindered by the Carthaginians, and
left their city to be plundered and occupied (406 B.C.) by
Himilco's forces. The following year he marched against
Gela, besieged the city, and took it when its inhabitants also
fled. In 397 B.C. Himilco returned to Sicily to protect the
Carthaginian cities from the attacks of Dionysius the Elder,
tyrant of Syracuse. He retook the city of Motya, captured
and almost completely destroyed by Dionysius the year

fat, fāte, fär, fâll, ȧsk, fāre; net, mē, hėr; pin, pīne; not, nōte, möve;
nôr; up, lūte, pu̇ll; oi, oil; ou out; (lightened) ę̄lect, agǫny, ūnite

before, and founded a new city, Lilybaeum, nearby, and the city of Tauromenium on the heights above the Sicilian city of Naxos. He defeated the Syracusan fleet at Catana and marched to besiege Syracuse. His army encamped in a marsh, but Himilco pitched his tent on higher ground, in a precinct of Olympian Zeus. This insult to Greek gods, and a more horrendous sacrilege—the plundering of a temple of Demeter—were thought by the Syracusans to have caused the plague that now broke out in the Carthaginian camp. The pestilence so weakened the besiegers that a well-planned assault by the besieged on the plague-stricken camp succeeded, and the forces of Himilco were defeated. But Himilco himself came to a secret arrangement with Dionysius, treacherous on both sides, whereby, in return for the payment of 300 talents, Dionysius allowed Himilco to escape with 40 triremes and his Carthaginian soldiers, leaving his allies and mercenaries to their fate at the hand of Dionysius. Upon returning home Himilco committed suicide.

Hipparchus (hi-pär′kus). Younger son of Pisistratus and brother of Hippias. The brothers succeeded their father (527 B.C.) and reigned as tyrants of Athens conjointly. The night before the Panathenaic Festival, according to Herodotus, Hipparchus dreamed that a tall and handsome man stood over him and made the following statement: "Bear thou unbearable woes with the all-bearing heart of a lion,/ Never, be sure, shall wrong-doer escape the reward of wrong-doing." The next day Hipparchus offered sacrifices to ward off the evil portended by the dream and then led the Panathenaic procession. While leading it he was murdered (514 B.C.) by Harmodius and Aristogiton, Gephyraeans whose ancestors were said to have come to Boeotia from Phoenicia with Cadmus and who, being driven from Boeotia, fled to Athens for refuge. The murder of Hipparchus did not end the tyranny of the Pisistratidae but, according to Herodotus, merely exasperated them. Hipparchus was a great patron of the arts. It was his invitation which brought the poets Anacreon and Simonides to Athens. The great advances in vase-painting, sculpture and architecture of Pisistratid Athens are due in great part to this cultured ruler.

Hippias (hip′i-as). Tyrant of Athens, 527–510 B.C. He was the eldest son of Pisistratus and with his brother Hipparchus succeeded him as ruler of Athens, 527 B.C. After the murde of Hipparchus (514 B.C.), he became sole ruler and tyrant Athens. As a result of the extremely harsh rule to which h subjected the Athenians the Alcmaeonidae, who had bee banished by the Pisistratidae, joined other exiles and soug to free Athens. With the assistance of the Spartans und Cleomenes, the Athenians compelled Hippias to leave th country (510 B.C.). He went to Sigeum on the Scamand River in Asia Minor. Later the Spartans, fearing lest a fr Athens become as strong as Sparta, sent to Hippias in S geum, invited him to Sparta, and proposed to restore hi to power in Athens. However, the allies of Sparta, especial the Corinthian representative, rebuked the Spartans f seeking to restore a tyrant, and since they refused to partic pate in the undertaking it was abandoned. Hippias wer again to Sigeum where he embarked on an intense progra of interesting Artaphernes, nephew of the Persian kin Darius, in making war against Athens. The Athenian learned of his activities and sent messengers to Artapherne to whom he replied that if they valued their safety they mu take back Hippias. As the Athenians refused to do th henceforth they were open enemies of the Persians. Hippi accompanied Artaphernes when he invaded and too Eretria. A dream convinced him that he would be restore to Athens with all his former power and that he would li to old age in his native land. He now assumed the role guide to the Persians and led them to the plain of Maratho as he considered it a favorable ground for the Persian ca alry. When he had arrived at Marathon it happened that h sneezed violently and as he was then of advanced year probably well over 60 at the time, one of his teeth was force out by the violence of his sneeze and fell in the sand. Hippi searched for it but could not find it. To him this was th fulfillment of his dream and it now seemed to him that aft all the land would never fall to the Persians, and that all h share of it would be the part occupied by his lost tooth. I the ensuing battle of Marathon (490 B.C.) the Persians wer completely defeated, and Hippias died shortly thereafte c490 B.C.

Hippocrates (hi-pok′ra̤-tēz). Tyrant of Gela, in Sicily; died 49 B.C. He extended the power of Gela over Naxos, Zancle, an other Greek cities of Sicily. He waged war on Syracuse an

---

fat, fāte, fär, fåll, a̤sk, fāre; net, mē, hėr; pin, pīne; not, nōte, mö nôr; up, lūte, půll; oi, oil; ou out; (lightened) e̤lect, agǫny, ūnit

defeated the Syracusans at the Helorus River, but was prevented from taking Syracuse when aid arrived for that city from Corinth and Corcyra. He was killed while attacking the city of Hybla (491 B.C.).

Iirtius (hėr'shi-us), **Aulus.** Roman politician; killed near Mutina (Modena), Italy, 43 B.C. He was a friend of Caesar and the reputed author of the eighth book of Caesar's *Commentaries on the Gallic War,* and of the history of the Alexandrian war. As consul with Pansa (43 B.C.) he defeated Antony at Mutina, but less than two weeks later was killed in another battle there.

Iistiaeus (his-ti-ē'us). Tyrant of Miletus, through the friendship of Darius the Persian, at the end of the 6th century B.C. He was executed at Sardis, Asia Minor, 494 B.C. When Darius attacked Scythia (c512 B.C.), the Ionian leaders who were allied to Darius and who had been left to guard the bridge by which Darius crossed the Ister (Danube), considered whether they would revolt against Darius and regain their freedom. Histiaeus urged them not to revolt and suggested a means by which they could preserve the bridge from the attacks of the Scythians. To reward him for this service Darius promised him whatever boon he asked. Histiaeus asked for Myrcinus on the Strymon River in Thrace, that he might build a city there. His request was granted. Histiaeus took the town and began to raise a wall about it. Darius now feared that he meant to make himself master of the area. He sent for Histiaeus, on the pretext that he needed his advice, compelled him to relinquish the throne of Miletus, and kept him in honorable confinement at the court of Susa, Miletus being left under the regency of Aristogoras, nephew and son-in-law of Histiaeus. Histiaeus longed to return to Miletus but could not go as Darius pretended he needed him, nor could he send out any messages to Aristogoras as he was closely watched. He finally hit on the following scheme: He chose his most trusted slave, shaved his head, and pricked a message on his scalp. When the hair had grown back he sent the slave to Aristagoras in Miletus with instructions to Aristagoras to shave the head of the messenger and look at it. Aristagoras did as commanded and found orders to revolt against Darius. Histiaeus incited the revolt because he thought if Miletus rebelled Darius would send him to quell the revolt. All Ionia revolted and, as he had planned, Histiaeus was sent to put it down. Being now freed of Darius' restraint, he warred against Persia. He was finally captured in Mysia and handed over to the Persian satrap Artaphernes. The latter, fearing that Darius might even now forgive Histiaeus because of his former services, impaled his body, cut off his head and sent it back to Darius at Susa.

Hortensius Hortalus (hôr-ten′shi-us, -shus; hôr′ta-lus), *Quintus.* Roman orator, born 114 B.C.; died 50 B.C. He was a leader of the aristocratic party, a minor historian, collector of art and a composer of love poems. Catullus twice addresses him. As a pleader he defended the notorious Verres (70 B.C.), whose conviction by Cicero was a notable defeat for Hortensius. Many stories circulated concerning his luxurious habits. (JJ)

Hyksos (hik′sōs, -sos). ["Princes of the Desert"; wrongly called (from an incorrect etymology) the "Shepherd Kings."] Name given to the kings of Egypt, of a foreign (probably Semitic) race, whose rule (c1800–c1575 B.C.) fell between the XIIIth and the XVIIIth Dynasties. They introduced into Egypt the horse and chariot.

Hyperbolus (hī-pèr′bō-lus). Athenian politician and demagogue; killed at Samos, c411 B.C. He was a lamp-maker who rose in politics during the Peloponnesian War. His pretensions made him the butt of the comic poets and he endured all manner of abuse, but cared not at all what men said of him and continued to pursue his ambitions. Thucydides called him "a rascal and a disgrace to the city." He was allied with Alcibiades, leader of the radical party, against Nicias, leader of the aristocratic party. In 417 B.C. he engineered a vote of ostracism in an attempt to get rid of Nicias. He thought the radicals would vote against Nicias and that he would be ostracized; if not, the supporters of Nicias would surely vote against the radical Alcibiades. In either case one of them, so he reasoned, would be removed and he could compete on more equal terms against the one who remained. But Alcibiades deserted him and joined forces with Nicias. In the resulting vote Hyperbolus was himself ostracized and sent into exile. Candidates for ostracism had been the leaders of the state, prominent men whose very prominence and influence were considered to be a possible danger to the democracy. Ostracism was thus a backhanded honor. When the vote fell on Hyperbolus it was felt that the process of ostracism had been degraded. He was the last Athenian ever to be ostracized; afterward, the practice fell into disuse. He went to Samos and was murdered there (c411 B.C.) by the oligarchic party that supported the government of the Four Hundred at Athens.

Hyperides (hī-pẹ-rī′dēz or hī-per′i-dēz). One of the Ten Attic Orators, born c390 B.C.; died 322 B.C. He studied with Plato and Isocrates and achieved an important position in Athenian forensic circles. His gay private life and natural wit made him a favorite topic of comedy. In politics he was allied with Demosthenes against the Macedonian Party which favored peace with Philip of Macedon. After the destruction of Thebes (335 B.C.) by Alexander, he and Demosthenes, only with the greatest difficulty, escaped being handed over to the Macedonians. In 324 B.C. he was one of the prosecutors of Demosthenes, on charges of bribery. However, in seeming to prosecute Demosthenes, Hyperides actually defended him, and his action in this case led to no breach in their friendly relations. After the death of Alexander, Hyperides and Demosthenes joined forces to rouse the Peloponnesus to war. The Lamian War broke out and was pursued to disaster for Greece. The Macedonian general demanded the surrender of Hyperides and Demosthenes. His death sentence was signed but he fled to a temple in Aegina for refuge. He was seized there, and by order of the Macedonian commander Antipater was put to death in 322 B.C. Some consider the work of Hyperides to rank next to that of Demosthenes in forcefulness, and superior to it in charm. Large fragments of five speeches, found in Egyptian papyri in the 19th century, show that his work was marked by forthrightness, humor, and grace.

Hystaspes (his-tas′pēz). Persian general; fl. c517 B.C. He was an Achaemenid, related to and a contemporary of Cyrus the Great. Ordinarily, it would have been he who succeeded to the vacant throne when Cambyses III died without issue, but instead Hystaspes saw his son Darius I become king and served under him. He was satrap of Parthia and Hyrcania, and is thought by some to have been the patron of Zoroaster. Among his other sons were Artabanus, Artaphernes, and Artanes.

(obscured) errạnt, ardẹnt, actọr; ch, chip; g, go; th, thin; ŦH, then; y, you; (variable) ḍ as d or j, ṣ as s or sh, ṭ as t or ch, ẓ as z or zh.

I

Intaphernes (in-tạ-fêr′nēz). A Persian noble who, with Darius, was one of seven conspirators who overthrew the False Smerdis and made Darius ruler of the Persians. Among the privileges which the six were to enjoy when Darius was made king was that they were free to enter the palace unannounced whenever they chose, except when the king was with a woman. This privilege led to the death of Intaphernes. Acting on it, he wished to enter the palace on a matter of business with the king. Guards sought to bar his way on the grounds that the king was with a woman. Intaphernes thought they were lying, and drawing his scimitar, he cut off their ears and noses and strung them on his bridle. The guards went to Darius and told him what had happened. Darius, fearing that this was part of a plot against him, secretly consulted the other conspirators. He learned from their answers that they knew nothing at all of Intaphernes' insolence. Relieved on this score, Darius seized Intaphernes, his children and his close relatives, put them in fetters and condemned them to death. Each day the wife of Intaphernes stood before the palace gate weeping. Darius took pity on her and offered to grant her as a boon the life of one of the condemned family. She answered that if she could save the life of one only she chose that of her brother. Darius was surprised at this choice and asked why she had not chosen her husband or one of her children. Her answer was that the gods might grant her another husband and more children, but as her father and mother were dead she would never have another brother. Darius saw the worth of such reasoning. He not only spared her brother's life but that of her oldest son as well. Intaphernes, with the rest of his children and relatives, was put to death.

Iphicrates (ī-fik′rạ-tēz). Athenian general, from Rhamnus; fl. first half of the 4th century B.C.; died c353 B.C. He was noted for his military reforms. He equipped his soldiers, called *peltasts*, with light shields and javelins, which gave them

fat, fāte, fär, fảll, ȧsk, fāre; net, mē, hėr; pin, pīne; not, nōte, mȯve, nôr; up, lūte, pu̇ll; oi, oil; ou out; (lightened) ẹlect, agǫny, ụnite;

much greater mobility for the raiding tactics he increasingly employed than the heavy armor worn by the hoplites. He emphasized drill and discipline; he lengthened the swords and javelins the soldiers carried, and introduced the wearing of leggings, called "Iphicratid boots." In the Corinthian War (c391 B.C.) he attacked a band of 600 Spartan hoplites and destroyed them. In 388 B.C. he was sent to the Hellespont with 1200 peltasts and defeated a Spartan force near Cremaste, and assured Athenian command of the Hellespont and the Bosporus, for the time being at least. With his band of mercenaries he served various princes of Thrace. About 378 B.C. he married a daughter of the Thracian king Cotys. He later served the king of Persia, and then returned to Athens. From there he was sent to the relief of Corcyra, besieged by the Spartans. On his way he encountered a fleet of ten Syracusan ships, sent to help Sparta. He attacked and captured all but one of them (372 B.C.). As a captain of mercenaries he served sometimes against his own country. He was adopted by Amyntas, king of Macedonia, and with the fleet he was operating off the Macedonian coast he helped to secure the throne for Perdiccas, son of Amyntas, on the latter's death (368 B.C.). He sided with the Thracian king Cotys against Athens in a war over the Chersonese, but the Athenians later pardoned him, and made him commander, with Timotheus and Chares, of a fleet to put down a revolt of Chios. Timotheus and Iphicrates, experienced soldiers, disagreed with Chares' plan to attack Chios and refused to take part in it. Chares was driven off with losses. He accused Iphicrates and Timotheus of treachery. They were tried, but Iphicrates was able to secure his acquittal.

Isocrates (ī-sok′ra̤-tēz). One of the Ten Attic Orators, a professional speech-writer and teacher of rhetoric. He was born (436 B.C.) at Athens, the son of a wealthy flute manufacturer, and received a good education. When his father lost his money in the Peloponnesian Wars Isocrates was compelled to earn his living. He studied with Gorgias, and then went to Chios, where he taught rhetoric. On his return to Athens he opened a school (c392 B.C.) of rhetoric and philosophy. This school, intended to further the study of history, dialectics, mathematics, literature, and the use of language, was highly successful. He numbered among his pupils states-

(obscured) errạnt, ardẹnt, actọr; ch, chip; g, go; th, thin; ᴛʜ, then; y, you;
(variable) ḍ as d or j, ş as s or sh, ṭ as t or ch, z̧ as z or zh.

men, poets, historians, and the orators Isaeus, Hyperides, and Lycurgus. Isocrates' view of life, expounded in his *Speech on the Exchange of Property*, was to steer a middle course between the purely practical and the purely philosophic. He defended his course on the ground that the practical man lacks culture and imagination, while the philosopher becomes too detached from life. He found that his course was much criticized from both directions, but his school and the culture he imparted in it were extremely popular. It is said that through shyness and because of a weak voice he kept aloof from an active public life. He attempted to exercise political influence through his writings. His *Panegyricus*, written (380 B.C.) for the Hundredth Olympiad, extolled the contributions of Athens to Greece, urged the Spartans to share supremacy of Greece with Athens, and exhorted all the Greek states to abandon their rivalries and unite against the barbarians. He was a friend and admirer of Evagoras of Salamis who alone fought against the Persians for eight years. When Evagoras was assassinated Isocrates transferred his admiration to his son. In 356 B.C. Isocrates addressed himself to Archidamus, king of Sparta, urging him to unite the Greeks on the mainland and free the Greeks in Asia. Archidamus failed him. Isocrates recognized that Philip of Macedon was the rising power. With unimpaired patriotism after the first peace with Philip (346 B.C.), he addressed him and urged him to seize the magnificent opportunity he now had to unite Greece, make himself the champion of liberty, and become the benefactor of the world. His views on Philip and the Macedonians made him extremely unpopular. He lived, in full vigor of mind and body, nearly 100 years, and saw all his hopes for Greek unity and democracy completely crushed. In 338 B.C., a few days after the Battle of Chaeronea in which Philip defeated the Athenians and the Boeotians, Isocrates died. Some say he starved himself to death in despair over the loss of Greek liberty. Isocrates was a master of style, whose influence extended to all subsequent Greek prose. According to Gilbert Murray, the essay-writing of Isocrates' school "forms in one sense the final perfection of ancient prose, in another the ruin of what was most characteristically Attic or indeed Hellenic. It is smooth, self-restrained, correct, euphonious, im-

fat, fãte, fär, fâll, àsk, fãre; net, mē, hèr; pin, pīne; not, nōte, mõve, nôr; up, lūte, pùll; oi, oil; ou out; (lightened) ēlect, agǭny, ūnite;

personal. . . . It has lasted on from that day to this, and is the basis of prose style in Latin and in modern languages." Of the *Orations of Isocrates,* which he did not speak himself but wrote for others, 21 are extant.

Josephus (jō-sē'fus), *Flavius.* [Usually shortened to *Josephus.*] Jewish priest, soldier, statesman, and historian; born at Jerusalem, 37 A.D.; died at Rome, sometime between 95 and 100 A.D. The son of a priest and descendant of royalty, he studied Hebrew law and Greek and Hebrew literature. After spending three years in the desert with Banus, a hermit, he was chosen to serve as a delegate to Nero in 64. Upon his return from Rome, he was appointed governor of Galilee by the Sanhedrin, the great council of the Jews at Jerusalem. In 66 he was active in the Jewish revolt against Rome, and led in the defense of Jotapata for 47 days before he surrendered to Vespasian. He won the favor of the latter (as he had previously won that of Nero's mistress Poppaea Sabina) by making predictions calculated to please his hearers (he told Vespasian that he would become emperor). He went with Vespasian to Alexandria, was later freed, adopted the family name of Vespasian (Flavius), became a Roman citizen, and was given a pension and a considerable estate in Judea. He continued to enjoy the protection of Vespasian, and later of Titus and Domitian (he was with Titus at the fall of Jerusalem in 70 A.D.). His works are a *History of the Jewish War,* in seven books, first written in Aramaic and then translated into Greek; *Antiquities of the Jews,* in 20 books, dealing with the history of the Jewish people from the beginning of time to the year 66; *Vita* (his autobiography), in which he denies the charges made by his enemy, Justus of Tiberias, that he was responsible for the Jewish rebellion; and *Contra Apionem,* two essays in which he defends the Jews against the attacks of Apion, an anti-Semitic Alexandrian.

Juba I (jö'ba). [Also: *Iuba.*] Committed suicide, 46 B.C. King of Numidia, an ally of Pompey. He defeated the Caesareans under Curio in 49 B.C., and in 47–46 B.C. supported Metellus Scipio, whose forces were defeated at Thapsus. Following this, Juba died by his own hand at Zama.

Juba II. [Also: *Iuba.*] King of Mauretania, son of Juba I of Numidia; died c19 A.D. He was taken to Rome (46 B.C.) as a young child to form part of Caesar's triumphal procession and eventually became a protégé of Octavian. He was made king of Numidia c30 B.C., married Cleopatra Selene, daughter of Antony and Cleopatra, in 29 B.C., and was transferred by Augustus to Mauretania in 25 B.C. He established his capital at an old Carthaginian depot, Iol, which he renamed Caesarea (modern Cherchel). He was noted as a man of broad culture, as an art collector and author, in Greek, of many works on history and natural history, now all lost. (JJ)

Jugurtha (jö-gėr′thạ). [Also: *Iugurtha.*] Executed at Rome, 104 B.C. King of Numidia; son of Mastanabal and grandson of Masinissa. On the death of his uncle Micipsa in 118 B.C., he and Micipsa's two sons inherited the kingdom. He usurped western Numidia in 117 B.C. and eastern Numidia in 112. A war with Rome commenced as a result in 111, and he contended against Metellus in 109 and 108 and against Marius in 107 B.C. He was captured by Sulla, was exhibited by Marius in a triumphal procession at Rome in 104 B.C., and was then put to death by strangling.

Julia (jöl′yạ). Daughter of Julius Caesar and his first wife Cornelia. She was born c83 B.C.; died 54 B.C. She was betrothed to Servilius Caepio, but instead became the wife of Pompey the Great in 59 B.C. At this point in his career Caesar needed Pompey's armies and his influence, and he used his daughter as a means of gaining Pompey's support. When she died in childbirth, Caesar gave a gladitorial show and a public banquet in her honor.

Julia. Daughter of Augustus Caesar and Scribonia, born 39 B.C.; died at Rhegium, 14 A.D. She was married in 25 B.C. to Marcus Claudius Marcellus, on whose death in 23 B.C. she became the wife of Marcus Vipsanius Agrippa, by whom she became the mother of Caius and Lucius Caesar, Agrippa Postumus, Julia, and Agrippina. After Agrippa's death in 12 B.C., she married Tiberius for reasons of state. Her private life was the scandal of Rome, and it was particularly galling to Augustus when he learned of it, as he regarded himself as the upholder of public morals. Tiberius divorced her, and Augustus banished her, first to the island of Pandataria, and afterward to Rhegium.

Julian Emperors. Collective name for the Roman emperors Augustus, Tiberius, Caligula, Claudius, and Nero, as members by birth or adoption of the family of Julius Caesar.

L

Labienus (lab-i-ē′nus), *Quintus.* Roman general; son of Titus Labienus. As a republican opposed to Antony and Octavian, and commander of Parthian mercenaries, he invaded (41–40 B.C.) Syria and Asia Minor where after some successes, he was defeated and killed in 39 B.C.

Labienus, Titus. Roman general; killed in battle, 45 B.C. He was early a partisan of Caesar and helped him to secure the office of Pontifex Maximus (63 B.C.). He was distinguished as Caesar's legate in the Gallic War, and acted as his chief subordinate in Gaul. As a general in Gaul, he defeated the Treviri (54 B.C.), made an expedition against Lutetia (Paris, 52), and defeated the Aedui (52 B.C.). When civil war broke out, he joined Pompey (49 B.C.). After the defeat at Pharsalus he fled to Africa. From there he went to Spain and joined the forces of the younger Pompey, and was killed at the battle of Munda, 45 B.C.

Laelius (lē′li-us), *Caius.* Roman general and consul; fl. c200 B.C. He was a friend of the elder Scipio Africanus, whom he accompanied on his campaign in Spain (210–206 B.C.). In 205 B.C. he led an expedition to Africa, and in the battle of Zama (202 B.C.) distinguished himself as commander of the cavalry. He served as aedile (197), praetor (196), and consul (190 B.C.).

Laelius, Caius. [Surnamed *Sapiens,* meaning "the Wise."] Roman statesman and philosopher, praetor in 145 B.C., consul in 140 B.C., and closely associated with the younger Scipio Africanus. He is the chief character in the *De Amicitia* of Cicero, which is therefore often called *Laelius,* and appears as a speaker in Cicero's *De Senectute* and *De Republica.* He was

(obscured) errạnt, ardẹnt, actọr; ch, chip; g, go; th, thin; ŦH, then; y, you; (variable) ḍ as d or j, ṣ as s or sh, ṭ as t or ch, ẓ as z or zh.

one of the aristocratic party in opposition to the reforms of the Gracchi.

Laevinus (lē-vī′nus), **Publius Valerius.** Roman consul, 280 B.C. He advanced with an army to meet Pyrrhus at Heraclea, and when Pyrrhus sent word to him that he would act as mediator between the Romans and the Greeks in Italy, Laevinus replied that he "neither accepted Pyrrhus as a mediator nor feared him as an enemy." At the battle which took place, 280 B.C., he was defeated by Pyrrhus with heavy losses on both sides.

Lamachus (lam′a-kus). Athenian general, killed in Sicily, 414 B.C. With Alcibiades and Nicias he was one of the three commanders in charge of the Athenian expedition to Sicily, 415 B.C. He was not a rich man and had to be reimbursed for all expenditures he made for himself on his campaigns. Perhaps for this reason he was mocked by the comic poets. However, he was a brave and able soldier. When the Athenian expedition arrived in Sicily to aid the Egestaeans against the Selinuntines, allies of Syracuse, the commanders learned to their dismay that the Egestaeans were unable to advance the gold they had promised. Lamachus, with a purely military view, advised the Athenians to attack Syracuse at once, although this had not been the announced target of the expedition. He argued that Syracuse was the real enemy, and that the Athenians should take advantage of the unprepared state of the Syracusans and the panic into which the sight of the Athenian flotilla would throw them; for after a time, he warned, the Syracusans would recover their composure and prepare themselves for battle, and the advantages of surprise would be lost. The advice of Lamachus was ignored. In a skirmish before the city of Syracuse Lamachus was killed, 414 B.C.

Lentulus (len′tū-lus), **Publius Cornèlius.** [Surnamed **Sura.**] Roman politician; executed at Rome, Dec. 5, 63 B.C. He was praetor (75 B.C.), and a conspirator with Catiline in 63 B.C. He planned to kill Cicero and burn Rome. He divulged the plot to the Allobroges in the hope of securing their assistance and they betrayed the plot. The conspirators in Rome were seized; they confessed and were executed. He received his surname, Sura, because when Sulla accused him of carelessness with public funds (81 B.C.), instead of defending himself he held out the calf of his leg *(sura).* This was in

fat, fāte, fär, fåll, àsk, fāre; net, mē, hèr; pin, pīne; not, nōte, möve, nôr; up, lūte, pùll; oi, oil; ou out; (lightened) ēlect, agǫny, ūnite;

imitation of boys who did this to receive punishment when they committed a fault in their games.

Leonidas (lē-on'i-dạs). King of Sparta, early in the 5th century B.C. He was reputed to be the 20th generation in direct descent from Heracles, and became king of Sparta, c490 B.C., on the death of his two elder brothers, who died childless. When Xerxes marched with his host against Greece and invaded the mainland as far as the borders of Locris, Leonidas went to defend the narrow pass at Thermopylae (480 B.C.), through the mountains south of the Sinus Maliacus. Through it ran the main road into Greece by which the Persian land forces meant to enter Locris and press on to the Peloponnesus. Under his command Leonidas had a force of 4000 soldiers, including 300 Spartans, 700 Thespians, and groups of varying numbers from Arcadia, Corinth, Mycenae, Thebes, and other cities. The plan was to send him more soldiers as soon as the Olympic Festival, which fell at this time, was over. However, before reinforcements arrived, Xerxes learned from his spies the small size of the force which opposed him. He questioned Demaratus, a former Spartan king who had fled to Xerxes before the Persian invasion and who now accompanied him. Did Demaratus think these Spartans, whom his spies had observed combing their hair and going through gymnastic exercises, would dare fight the host of the Persians? Demaratus assured him that the Spartans were the bravest of the Greeks, that it was their custom to dress their hair when they were about to risk their lives in battle, and that they were trained to give up their lives in glorious combat rather than retreat or surrender. Xerxes was incredulous. He thought it was ridiculous that such a small force would attempt to resist his vast army. He waited four days, thinking the Greeks would surely retire. Finding that they did not do so, he sent the Medes and Cissians against them. The Greeks fought like gods in the narrow pass, caused immense slaughter among the barbarians, and compelled them to withdraw. Xerxes next sent his Persian Immortals against them. This was a band of 10,000, called Immortals because when one of their number fell he was replaced immediately, that the number might remain always at exactly 10,000. They too suffered enormous casualties and fell back. The next day the Persians attacked again, and were again driven back. Now as Xerxes pondered what should be done, a Malian, one Ephialtes, out of desire for gain betrayed the Greeks. He went to Xerxes and offered to lead the Persians across the mountains by a path he knew so that they could attack the Greeks from the rear. Xerxes gladly accepted his services. At nightfall he sent a band of Persians off under the guidance of Ephialtes. Leonidas was first warned of the destruction that was coming by the seer Megistias, who learned of it from his sacrificial victims. The seer's warning was confirmed by scouts. On learning of the destruction that was imminent, Leonidas decided that he and his Spartans could not honorably withdraw, but he allowed the soldiers from all the other cities to retire, except the Thebans, who had come unwillingly in the first place, and whom he kept as hostages. The Thespians remained of their own accord, refusing to desert Leonidas. According to Herodotus, who gives us a description of the heroic defense of the pass, Leonidas had earlier been told by an oracle that either Sparta or its king must fall before the barbarians. He chose to remain and perish at their hands, thus fulfilling the oracle, that Sparta might be spared. The next day, the Persians fell upon them again. Leonidas and his forces met the attack with unparalleled courage, knowing they were doomed to die. They boldly sallied out from the narrow pass and in a furious onslaught slew many of the barbarians before them and flung others into the sea. On this wild day the brave Leonidas perished in furious battle. Many valiant Spartans and brave Persians, among them kin of Xerxes, also died. After inflicting immense casualties and losing many of their own number, the Greeks, except the Thebans who surrendered, again withdrew to the pass. Here they were attacked on their other side by the Persians who had crossed the mountain. A smaller band now, they formed a tight group on a hillock near the entrance to the pass and continued to defend themselves. They fought with immortal valor until not one Greek survived. A stone lion in honor of Leonidas was set up to mark the spot where the Spartans perished, and the names of the 300 Spartans were engraved on a pillar, set up in Sparta, which existed at least until the 2nd century A.D. In honor of the 4000 of the original group, before Leonidas sent the allies away, an inscription marked the spot, which read:

fat, fāte, fär, fȧll, ȧsk, fãre; net, mē, hėr; pin, pīne; not, nōte, mȯve, nôr; up, lūte, pu̇ll; oi, oil; ou out; (lightened) ĕlect, agǫny, ūnite;

Here did four thousand men from Pelops' land
Against three hundred myriads bravely stand.

The Spartans alone were immortalized in another inscription:

Go, stranger, and to Lacedaemon tell
That here, obeying her behests, we fell.

It is said that Xerxes, examining the field after the battle, came upon the body of Leonidas and knew him to be the Spartan king and commander. He ordered the head cut off and the body hung on a cross. This was a measure of his wrath against Leonidas, for ordinarily fallen enemies were honorably treated. It is also said that Xerxes tried to conceal the number of men he had lost, 20,000, in this engagement with first 4000 and then 1000 Greeks. He buried 19,000 of his dead in trenches which he camouflaged with branches. The bodies of 1000 he left scattered about the field. But this attempt at deception fooled no one. Many years after his death the bones of Leonidas were removed to Sparta by Pausanias, the victor at Plataea. In after times, speeches were annually delivered over the tombs of Leonidas and Pausanias, and contests were held in which none save Spartans could compete.

Leonnatus (lē-ō-nā′tus). General of Alexander the Great; died 322 B.C. He was one of the ablest of Alexander's generals. On the return from India Alexander pursued the Malli and attacked them in their city, the modern Multan, 325 B.C. He recklessly mounted the wall of the city and leaped down among his enemies before his men had gained entrance into the city. Leonnatus was one of three who succeeded in scaling the wall to go to his aid. He guarded the king, who had been wounded as he faced his enemies, until rescue arrived. On Alexander's death (323 B.C.), Leonnatus received the satrapy of Hellespontine Phrygia. He fell in battle against the Athenians and their allies while seeking to relieve Antipater who was blockaded in Lamia.

Leosthenes (lē-os′the-nēz). Athenian general; died 322 B.C. He was commander of the combined Greeks armies in the Lamian War, 323 B.C., defeating Antipater and forcing him to take refuge in Lamia, the siege of which city gave the war its name. Leosthenes was killed in the course of the siege.

Leotychides (lē-ō-tik′i-dēz). King of Sparta, c491–c476 B.C. He was the son of Menares and was reputed to be a direct descendant of Heracles. All his ancestors except the seven immediately preceding him had been kings of Sparta. Cleomenes, co-king of Sparta with Demaratus, sought to depose Demaratus, and agreed to make Leotychides king in his place if the latter would help him against the Aeginetans. Leotychides was the more willing to destroy Demaratus because Demaratus had stolen the bride to whom he was betrothed and married her himself. Leotychides brought charges against Demaratus, claiming he was not the true son of Ariston. The priestess of Delphi, bribed by Cleomenes, confirmed his charges, and Leotychides became king in his place. In fulfillment of his agreement he then assisted Cleomenes in a successful attack on the Aeginetans. Leotychides commanded the Spartan fleet that sailed against the Persians at Mycale in Asia Minor, and defeated them there in 479 B.C., traditionally on the same day as the Greeks at Plataea defeated the Persian forces under Mardonius. Later he commanded the Spartans in a war against Thessaly and might have conquered the whole region but for his probable acceptance of a bribe. Discovered in his tent with a large sum of silver, he was brought to trial and fled, or was banished, from Sparta. His house was destroyed and he took refuge at Tegea where he subsequently died, c469 B.C.

Lepidus (lep'i-dus), **Marcus Aemilius**. [Surnamed **Porcina**.] Roman consul (137 B.C.) and orator. He was sent into Spain during his consulship, and conducted an unsuccessful war against the Vaccaei.

Lepidus, Marcus Aemilius. Roman politician; died c77 B.C. He was the father of Lepidus the triumvir (died 13 B.C.). He was praetor of Sicily, 81 B.C., took the side of Sulla in the civil war, but then abandoned him and with Pompey's help became consul, 78 B.C. He unsuccessfully attempted to alter Sulla's constitution and was then ordered to a provincial post by the Senate to remove him from Rome. On his way to his post, Transalpine Gaul, he began to raise an army in defiance of the Senate, which thereupon declared him an enemy of Rome. Pompey and Catulus led the resistance when he marched on Rome, 77 B.C., and defeated him in the Campus Martius. He went to Sardinia and died shortly thereafter.

Lepidus, Marcus Aemilius. Roman politician; died 13 B.C. He was consul, 46 B.C., and took the side of Caesar in the civil

fat, fāte, fär, fåll, åsk, fāre; net, mē, hèr; pin, pīne; not, nōte, möve, nôr; up, lūte, pùll; oi, oil; ou out; (lightened) ēlect, agǫny, ūnite;

war. When Caesar was assassinated (44 B.C.), Lepidus was at the head of an army preparing to go to Gaul. In the disturbances that followed Caesar's death he allied himself with Mark Antony, and became a member of the Second Triumvirate with Octavian and Antony in 43 B.C. Octavian and Antony took away his provinces of Spain and Gaul and relegated him to a minor role in the affairs of government. He was later given command of 20 legions in Africa and became so convinced of his strength that he demanded an equal role in the Triumvirate, but without success. In 36 B.C. he sailed to Sicily to raise rebellion against Octavian but was betrayed by the soldiers, who went over to the latter. Lepidus was sent into permanent exile, which he passed at Circeii.

Licinius (lī-sin'i-us). [Full name, *Caius Licinius Calvus Stolo.*] Roman tribune (377 B.C.) who proposed the Licinian Laws, which provided that one of the consuls must be a plebeian; that no person could occupy more than 500 *jugera* (somewhat more than 300 acres) of the public land; that interest on debts should be deducted from principal and the balance paid in three years; and that plebeians should be admitted to the College of the Sibylline Books. The laws brought a peaceful end to the struggle between patricians and plebeians. Licinius, who was active 377–361 B.C., was consul in 364 and 361 B.C. He was afterward fined for possessing more of the public land than was allowed by his own laws.

Livia Drusilla (liv'i-a̤ drö-sil'a̤). First Roman empress, born 56 B.C.; died 29 A.D. She was the daughter of Livius Drusus Claudianus and was married first to Tiberius Claudius Nero (the father of her sons Tiberius and Drusus), who was compelled to divorce her (38 B.C.) in order that she might become the wife of Octavian, the future emperor Augustus. She was accused of committing various crimes, even of hastening the death of her husband, in her endeavor to secure the succession to her son Tiberius. For a time after the accession of Tiberius she was all-powerful in the state, but was soon forced to retire from public affairs by her son.

Livius Drusus (liv'i-us, drö'sus), *Marcus.* See *Drusus, Marcus Livius.*

Longinus (lon-jī'nus), *Caius Cassius.* See *Cassius Longinus, Caius.*

Lucullus (lö-kul'us), *Lucius Licinius.* [Surnamed *Ponticus.*] Roman general, born c117 B.C.; died 56 B.C. He served under

Sulla in the East, and was curule aedile in 79 and consul in 74 B.C. He defeated Mithridates VI of Pontus in Asia Minor, 74–71 B.C., defeated Tigranes near Tigranocerta in 69, and was recalled to Rome in 66 B.C. He was afterward famous for his wealth and his luxury. His villas at Tusculum and near Neapolis (Naples) were famous for their splendor, and he is said to have spent fabulous sums on his table (a rich banquet is still called a Lucullan feast). One anecdote tells that his dining-rooms were coded, so that a message to his chef naming only the room in which dinner was to be served indicated the degree of extravagance and ostentation with which he wished to celebrate the occasion. He is said to have been the first to introduce cherries into Italy. He was also a collector of books and a patron of learning.

Luscinus (lu-sī'nus), *Caius Fabricius*. See *Fabricius Luscinus, Caius.*

Lycurgus (lī-kėr'gus). Spartan legislator, the traditional author of the laws and institutions of Sparta. Some say he lived in the 9th century B.C. Others say he lived in the 7th century B.C.; and still others say he was not a historical person at all, but a legendary figure to whom was ascribed the authorship of the Spartan way of life which was so consistent that it was thought to have been developed by one person. According to Plutarch, Lycurgus was descended from the Heraclid Aristodemus, and was a descendant of Soüs and of the Eurypontid line of Spartan kings. He lived at a time when Sparta was in a state of anarchy. King Polydectes, his half-brother, died and left a wife who was about to bear a child. Lycurgus declared that if the child was a boy, he would be the king. Polydectes' widow proposed to Lycurgus that she should destroy her unborn child and marry him, and that he should claim the throne. He was shocked, but pretended he would be delighted to marry her at some later time, and persuaded her not to interfere with the natural course of her pregnancy. In due course she bore a son. Lycurgus proclaimed him king, named him Charilaus, and acted as his regent. The widow of Polydectes made accusations against him, and for the sake of peace in Sparta he went into voluntary exile. He went to Crete where, impressed by the sober and temperate character of the Cretans, he studied their laws with the view to applying them to Sparta. Some say he went from Crete to Asia Minor, where he first came in contact with the poems of Homer and transcribed them for his own people. And some say he also visited Egypt and that it was there that he got the idea, later introduced into Sparta, of separating the military class from the rest of the people. At last he returned to Sparta, resolved to make certain reforms and to restore order to his country. He went to consult the oracle at Delphi, to learn whether his plans were wise. As he entered the shrine the priestess exclaimed,

"O thou great Lycurgus . . .
Whether to hail thee a god I know not, or only a mortal,
But my hope is strong that a god thou wilt prove, Lycurgus."

Because of this oracle some afterwards claimed that Lycurgus was indeed a god, and there was a temple of Lycurgus erected in Sparta. But at the time, the response of the priestess encouraged him and he introduced his reforms. Some say it was he who established a body of 30 overseers or administrators, which included the two kings. These *ephors,* as they were called, proposed measures to the citizens who assembled before them. The citizens could vote to adopt or reject their proposals, but could not modify them nor propose measures of their own, and the ephors might withdraw their own proposals if they wished. The effect of having 28 ephors to act with the kings was to weaken the absolute power of the kings, but Sparta did not become a democracy through this because the voice of the citizens was so limited in state affairs. Another change attributed to Lycurgus was of great importance to the future development of Sparta. He is said to have called in all the gold and silver and to have established a system of iron money. The purpose was to reduce all the citizens to the same level and to eradicate the evils of greed and robbery which gold and silver brought in their train. The iron from which money was made was first quenched in vinegar so that it could not be worked and therefore had no practical use; it was so cumbersome that large amounts could not be transported or hidden; it was worthless in trade with other Greek states and therefore weakening luxuries were not imported into Sparta from other areas. Conditioned to valueless iron money, the Spartans became impervious to bribery. It was not until the time of Agis (died 399 B.C.) that gold and silver again came into use in Sparta. The entire education and training of Spartan

---

(obscured) errȧnt, ardȩnt, actǫr; ch, chip; g, go; th, thin; ᴛʜ, then; y, you;
(variable) ḑ as d or j, ş as s or sh, ţ as t or ch, ẓ as z or zh.

youth was designed to create a military state, not for the purposes of conquest, but to protect Sparta in the midst of her enemies. Children were considered to belong to the state. Those that were puny at birth were exposed on Mount Taÿgetus. Lycurgus established rules for the training and physical development of young women so that they would bear strongs sons, and of young men so that they would become excellent and obedient soldiers. The males were brought up together according to prescribed rules from the age of seven. Even as men they ate together in a common mess. Not all the citizens favored the changes brought about by Lycurgus. The wealthy especially opposed them. Lycurgus was attacked and chased into the market place, where his attacker put out one of his eyes with his spear. The Spartans were ashamed that their leading citizen had been injured, and turned his attacker over to him. Lycurgus punished him mildly by compelling him to serve him at table, and ultimately converted him into one of his greatest admirers. Lycurgus raised a temple to Athena Ophthalmitis in gratitude that he still had one eye, and the Spartans made a law that no one should carry as much as a staff in the public assemblies. To provide a livelihood for the citizens whose lives were entirely devoted to military training, the land was redistributed in lots which would produce certain amounts of grain, oil, and wine. It is said that once when he returned to Sparta from a journey at harvest time and saw all the stacks of grain standing, equal and alike, Lycurgus remarked with pleasure that "all Laconia looks like one family estate just divided among a number of brothers." The land was worked by *helots*, a slave class that was continually threatening to revolt. As part of the training of a Spartan youth, he was permitted to seek out and slay any helot who he thought might become a leader of rebellion.

When Lycurgus had brought about these changes and thought that they were good, he won a promise from the Spartans that they would observe his laws until he returned. He went to Delphi to learn from the priestess whether his laws were good. The priestess of Apollo assured him that they were, and that Sparta would thrive as long as they were followed. Lycurgus sent on the words of the priestess to Sparta. He sacrificed again to Apollo and said farewell to his relatives and friends. Determined to compel the Spartans to

fat, fāte, fär, fȧll, ȧsk, fãre; net, mē, hėr; pin, pīne; not, nōte, möve, nôr; up, lūte, pu̇ll; oi, oil; ou out; (lightened) ēlect, agǫny, ṳnite;

observe his laws until he returned, he resolved not to return at all and, some say, starved himself to death. But others say he went to Crete, the place of origin of many of his laws, and died there. His ashes were scattered on the sea, they say, so that his bones could never be collected and returned to Sparta and release the Spartans from their oath. And, of course, some say that there never was any such person as Lycurgus at all, but all admit that he, or his legend, had great effect on the development of the Spartan character.

Lycurgus (lī-kėr′gus). One of the Ten Attic Orators, born at Athens, c396 B.C.; died 324 B.C. He was the son of Lycophron of the aristocratic family of the Eteobutadae. With Demosthenes and Hyperides he was a leader of the anti-Macedonian party. He was thrice appointed manager of the Athenian finances for terms of five years each. During his tenure he improved the revenues of the city and beautified Athens with magnificent buildings. He was also responsible for causing copies of the plays of Aeschylus, Sophocles, and Euripides to be deposited in the public archives. Only one of his speeches, *Against Leocrates*, is extant. A man of unblemished patriotism and integrity himself, he accused Leocrates of cowardice for leaving the city after the battle of Chaeronea, and demanded the death sentence as punishment; Leocrates, however, was spared.

Lysander (lī-san′dėr). Spartan commander, killed near Haliartus in Boeotia, 395 B.C. He was the son of Aristoclitus of the line of the Heraclidae. Reared in poverty and in the strict Spartan discipline, he showed himself unusually subservient, according to Plutarch, to men of influence and power with the object of furthering his own ambitions. He was appointed *navarch* (admiral) of the Peloponnesian fleet in 408 B.C. He sailed to Ephesus where the Spartans were cordially received, and set up a base there. At this time he became friendly with Cyrus the Younger, the son of the Persian king, Darius II, and the satrap at Sardis with jurisdiction over Cappadocia, Phrygia, and Lydia. Lysander won his complete confidence and promises of help for the Spartan cause by his refusal to accept any gift from Cyrus for himself. In 407 B.C. he defeated an Athenian fleet at Notium. According to Spartan law, he now had to give up his post as navarch, having served the legal term of one year. Callicratidas was appointed the new navarch but (again according to Plutarch) Lysander wished to hamper Callicratidas and sowed disaffection among his men before turning over his command. In 406 B.C. Callicratidas was defeated at Arginusae by the Athenians and fell in the battle. The Spartan allies and Cyrus the Younger wanted Lysander reappointed as admiral, but because of the Spartan rule that no man could twice be navarch, it was impossible to give him the title. He was, however, given the power. He went to Sardis and obtained funds from Cyrus the Younger, over whom he continued to exercise his influence. Cyrus entrusted him with the administration of his satrapy and the collection of the tribute therein while he went off to see his dying father, Darius II. Thus restored in funds and power, Lysander sailed forth. The Athenians sought to engage him at Ephesus, but he refused to meet them in battle there. Instead, after sailing to Attica where he conferred with Agis II, the Spartan king, he recrossed the Aegean, laid siege to Lampsacus on the east shore of the Hellespont, took it, and gave it over to his men to plunder. The Athenians determined to engage him and met him at Aegospotami. In the battle that finally took place there (405 B.C.) it was said that twin stars appeared on each side of Lysander's ship as he sailed into battle. These stars represented the Dioscuri, ever-protecting deities of Sparta. Lysander was completely victorious in the battle at small cost to Sparta. Three or four thousand Athenians were taken prisoner and put to the sword; only 20 Athenian ships escaped. Lysander was prevented from pursuing those by the quick action of the Athenian admiral Conon. It was the custom of the Greeks to unship their sails in preparation for a naval battle, and the Peloponnesians had deposited theirs at Cape Abarnis near Lampsacus before the battle of Aegospotami. Conon swooped down on the Cape and seized the sails. However, the complete defeat of the Athenians at Aegospotami was the effective end of the Peloponnesian War. Lysander sailed to blockade Athens. He set up Spartan *harmosts* (governors) over the Athenian cities of Greece and Asia, established Spartan supremacy, and restored Melos which had been taken and depopulated by the Athenians (416–415 B.C.), and also restored Scione, which had suffered the same fate (421 B.C.). At this moment the power of Lysander was supreme. Athens, on the verge of starvation because of the blockade, was compelled to ask for peace. According

fat, fāte, fär, fâll, ȧsk, fãre; net, mē, hėr; pin, pīne; not, nōte, mȯve, nôr; up, lūte, půll; oi, oil; ou out; (lightened) ẹlect, agọny, ụnite;

to the terms of it the Long Walls and the fortifications of the Piraeus were demolished to the piping of flutes; Athens surrendered all but 12 of her ships; her possessions were taken away from her; she was compelled to readmit those who had gone into exile, and to become a subordinate ally of Sparta. To memorialize his victory, Lysander set up twin golden stars of the Dioscuri as a trophy at Delphi. (These were the stars which were said to have disappeared in 371 B.C., just before the Battle of Leuctra in which the Spartan supremacy won in the time of Lysander was destroyed by the Thebans under Epaminondas.) Lysander sailed off to reduce Samos, but intervened in Athenian politics to establish the Tyranny of the Thirty (404 B.C.) and to write a new constitution. He placed Spartan harmosts over the cities which had been freed from Athens, choosing for these posts friends whom he wished to reward, regardless of their capacity or honesty. His arrogance increased as he was successful in his ambitions. At Samos he was awarded, and graciously received, divine honors, the first living man to be so honored. The Samians changed the name of their festival of Hera to *Lysandria* in a slavish desire to win his favor. To please his friends, he wantonly ordered the death of their enemies. To exiles whom he distrusted, he promised amnesty if they returned; once they did so, he had them executed. He pillaged the coasts of Asia to reward his friends and to send rich treasure back to Sparta, but took nothing for himself. Such actions roused strong resentment in the Persian satrap and he complained to Sparta. Lysander was recalled. With him he carried a letter from the Persian satrap Pharnabazus who had been a faithful ally of the Spartans in their war against Athens. Lysander thought the letter justified his actions, but at the last moment Pharnabazus had substituted a highly critical account, denouncing Lysander, and it was this letter that he handed to the Spartan ephors with his own hand. The accusations of the letter and the fact that he had been duped by Pharnabazus into delivering it himself made Lysander's position in Sparta equivocal. With some difficulty, he secured permission to depart on a visit to the temple of Zeus Ammon in Libya. He subsequently returned, and such was his fame for his victory over the Athenians that he was influential in securing the throne for Agesilaus II on the death of Agis II. He encouraged Agesilaus to wage war on the Persian king, and accompanied him on an expedition to Asia, fully expecting that he would be the actual commander of the expedition because of his supposed influence with Agesilaus and his experience in the area. Agesilaus soon disabused him of that notion. He refused to aid those who came to him recommended by Lysander; on the other hand, he ostentatiously helped those known to be unfriendly to Lysander; finally, while he gave others of his train positions of command, he appointed Lysander as his official Carver-of-Meats. Lysander understood the insult, asked leave to depart and was granted permission. Unhonored, he sailed back to Sparta plotting revolution. He planned to unseat Agesilaus by changing the Spartan rule from hereditary kingship to elective kingship. To justify his proposals he sought favoring oracles from Delphi. The priestess there, as at Dodona, was impervious to both persuasion and bribery. The priests of Ammon were so incensed by his attempts to corrupt them that they sent word to Sparta denouncing him, but the Spartans acquitted him. In lieu of valid responses he gathered a number of spurious oracles to place before the Spartans. His intrigue failed and was not discovered until after his death. Sparta became involved in a war against Thebes in support of Phocis, the Spartan ally. Lysander marched out from the revived Spartan colony of Heraclea near Themopylae, against Thebes. The Spartan king Pausanias, coming with a second force from the south, was to join him at Haliartus, in Boeotia. Lysander arrived first and attacked the town. The soldiers within it rushed out in a surprise raid, repulsed the Peloponnesians, and killed Lysander (395 B.C.).

A skillful diplomat and an able general, Lysander was for a time supreme in Greece. His great capacity was betrayed by his personal ambition, his harshness when he had won supreme power, and his irresponsible choices of subordinates. Personally incorruptible and scornful of wealth, he undermined the ancient Spartan discipline, which depended on iron money that had no real value and hence presented no temptation, by sending into the state great treasure taken by plunder. He thus opened up Sparta to the corruption brought by wealth and completely changed the Spartan character. Honest men considered him unscrupulous and deceitful, treacherous to his friends as well as to his foes. He

fat, fāte, fär, fåll, àsk, fãre; net, mē, hėr; pin, pīne; not, nōte, möve, nôr; up, lūte, půll; oi, oil; ou out; (lightened) ĕlect, agŏny, ūnite;

justified his deceit in war by saying, "Where the lion's skin will not reach, it must be patched out with the fox's." Some say the image of a long-haired, bearded man that was set up in the treasury of the Acanthians at Delphi was that of Lysander to honor him for his part in winning Acanthus from Athens (424 B.C.).

Lysias (lis′i-as, lī′si-as). One of the Ten Attic Orators. He was born in the Greek colony of Syracuse, c450 B.C., and died in 380 B.C. His father Cephalus, whose portrait appears in Plato's *Republic,* was invited by Pericles to come to Athens. There, at the Piraeus, he had a shield factory, and was the owner of some property. When he was 15 years old, Lysias went to Thurii, in Italy, and studied rhetoric. In 413 B.C. he took part in the defeat of the Athenians in Sicily, after which he returned to Athens and went into his father's business with his brother Polemarchus. When the Thirty Tyrants took control of Athens (404 B.C.), they attacked the wealthy aliens. Polemarchus was killed, much of his property was confiscated, and Lysias escaped to Megara. Henceforth Lysias espoused the cause of democracy and gave money to support it. In 403 B.C. the Tyrants were expelled. Lysias was given Athenian citizenship, but it was withdrawn shortly thereafter. Unable to take a part in the politics of the city, he occupied himself with writing speeches for others to deliver. One of the speeches, still extant, which he himself made was *Against Eratosthenes.* Eratosthenes was one of the tyrants, who had been given amnesty on the restoration of the democracy. Lysias was noted for being able to make the speeches he wrote for others sound as if they had been prepared by the person who gave them. It was said of him that he was never more persuasive and convincing than when he had a shaky case. Of his more than 200 speeches, 34 which bear his name are extant, though of some the authenticity has been challenged. Titles or fragments of a hundred others remain. They show him to have been somewhat cynical, able, and possessed of tact and agility. In style he avoided bombast, used simple and lucid language, and achieved his effects by vivid narrative description, concise points, and a faithful or skillful presentation of the character of the person who gave the speech.

Lysimachus (lī-sim′akus). Macedonian general under Alexander the Great. He was born probably at Pella, in Macedonia, c360 B.C.; and was killed at the battle on the plain of Corus, Asia Minor, 281 B.C. He was buried at Lysimachia, a town he founded in the Thracian Chersonese between Cardia and Pactye. He was a member of Alexander's bodyguard and served with distinction in the campaigns in Asia. According to one implausible account, Alexander, angered at Lysimachus, shut him up in a chamber with a lion. Lysimachus overpowered the beast and emerged unscathed. Ever after, Alexander treated him with great respect. Following Alexander's death Lysimachus received the kingdom of Thrace. He joined Cassander, Ptolemy, and Seleucus in the league against Antigonus in 315 B.C., assumed the title of king in 306 B.C., and was one of the victors at Ipsus in 301 B.C., when Antigonus was killed. In the division of Antigonus' realm, Lysimachus received a large part of Asia Minor. He destroyed Lebedos and Colophon and refounded Ephesus with inhabitants he removed from the former cities. Demetrius, son of Antigonus, took advantage of his absence in Greece (297 B.C.) to renew the war. By the peace which ended the war Demetrius became king of Macedonia, but in 288 B.C. Lysimachus, with Pyrrhus, invaded Macedonia, and drove Demetrius out. Pyrrhus, king of Epirus, held the throne for a time, but was soon driven out in his turn by Lysimachus, who thus obtained Macedonia for himself. Before the battle of Ipsus Lysimachus had married Amastris, the widowed queen of Heraclea in Pontus. She later divorced him and he married Arsinoë, daughter of Ptolemy, to strengthen himself against Seleucus, who now appeared to threaten him. Amastris was slain by her sons. Lysimachus had them put to death. Arsinoë asked him to give her Heraclea, and he did so. Then to secure the succession for her own children, Arsinoë plotted against Lysimachus' eldest son Agathocles. He was accused of conspiring to seize the throne. Lysimachus believed the accusations and had him put to death. The widow of Agathocles fled to Seleucus, who at once invaded the territory of Lysimachus in Asia. The towns the latter had taken in Asia Minor rose up in revolt. He crossed the Hellespont to engage Seleucus. A battle took place in the plain of Corus in Lydia, and Lysimachus was killed (281 B.C.). It is said that his body, left lying on the field of battle, was guarded for several days by his dog, until it was recovered and delivered to his son Alexander.

fat, fāte, fär, fåll, àsk, fãre; net, mē, hèr; pin, pīne; not, nōte, mŏve, nôr; up, lūte, pùll; oi, oil; ou out; (lightened) ēlect, agǒny, ūnite;

——M——

Maecenas (mē̠-sē′n̠as), **Caius Cilnius**. Roman statesman and patron of literature, died 8 B.C. He was descended from an ancient Etruscan family and belonged to the equestrian order. He appears in 40 B.C. as the agent of Octavian (afterward emperor under the title of Augustus) in negotiating a marriage with Scribonia, daughter of Libo, the father-in-law of Sextus Pompeius. He was entrusted with the administration of Rome during the absence of Octavian on an expedition against Pompey in 36 B.C., and after the battle of Actium in 31 B.C., when Octavian made himself master of the Roman world, urged him to establish an empire instead of restoring the Republic. He remained, with Agrippa, the chief adviser of Augustus down to 16 B.C., when he became estranged from his master and retired to private life. He was the friend and patron of Horace and Vergil, and wrote a number of works of which only fragments are extant. His name has become a synonym for the generous patron of the arts.

Mago (mā′gō). Carthaginian naval commander; fl. 4th century B.C. He commanded the Carthaginians in the wars against Syracuse (396–392 B.C.), and was compelled by Dionysius of Syracuse to make a peace which put all the Greek cities of Sicily under the dominion of Syracuse. By this peace the Carthaginians were forced to withdraw to the western corner of Sicily. In a later war with Dionysius, Mago was killed in Sicily, c378 B.C.

Mago. Carthaginian general; fl 4th century B.C. He was the commander of the Carthaginian forces in Sicily, 343 B.C., and allied himself with Hicetas, tyrant of Leontini, in his struggle with Timoleon who sought to overthrow the tyrants. Mago's conduct of the campaign was marked by inexplicable cowardice. On his return to Carthage he committed suicide, and his body was nailed to a cross by his countrymen.

Mago. Carthaginian general; died c203 B.C. He was a younger

(obscured) err̠ant, ard̠ent, act̠or; ch, chip; g, go; th, thin; ᴛʜ, then; y, you; (variable) d̠ as d or j, s̠ as s or sh, t̠ as t or ch, z̠ as z or zh.

brother of Hannibal, whom he accompanied to Italy in 218
B.C. and in whose victories he shared in the first years of the
war. He returned to Carthage and then was ordered to Spain
(215 B.C.) to support his brother Hasdrubal there. When
Hasdrubal went to Italy to support Hannibal, Mago remained in Spain. He was defeated by Scipio Africanus at
Silpia in 206 B.C. He later landed in Liguria and was defeated in Cisalpine Gaul by the Romans (203 B.C.). On his
journey back to Carthage he died of his wounds.

Manilius (ma̧-nī′li-us), *Caius*. Roman tribune (67 B.C.); fl. in the
first half of the 1st century B.C. He proposed the Manilian
Law in connection with the voting privileges of freedmen
and the law conferring on Pompey the command of the
Mithridatic War.

Manlius Capitolinus (man′li-us kap″i-tō̧-lī′nus), *Marcus*. Roman
patrician, consul 392 B.C.; died 384 B.C. When Brennus and
the Gauls attacked Rome, 390 B.C., most of the inhabitants
fled. Brennus found the gates open and unguarded. He
pillaged and burned the city and put to the sword those
whom he took captive. Manlius and some companions fled
to the citadel on the Capitoline Hill and successfully resisted
Brennus who laid siege to the Capitol. In the course of the
siege, Pontius Cominius, an envoy from the exiled dictator
Camillus, secretly penetrated the enemy ring about the
Capitol, and by a way he knew ascended the lower slopes of
the Capitol and was hauled to the top by the defenders. He
left by the same route, and returned safely to Camillus. A
few days later one of the Gallic soldiers noticed the broken
branches and gouged places in the hill which marked the
path taken by Cominius up the slope, and he pointed this
out to Brennus. The leader of the Gauls realized that there
was a way to the top, and sent a force of Gauls up to attack
the Capitol at night. According to tradition, the Gauls made
their way in safety to the top, but as they were about to attack
the Romans, some sacred geese in the temple of Juno heard
them, cackled, and woke the sleeping Romans, who leaped
up to defend themselves and the Captiol. The Gallic party
was slain, and next day their leader was hurled from the rock
into the enemy camp. Because he was the commander and
preserved the Captiol from the Gauls, Manlius was given the
surname Capitolinus (but some say his father before him
had that name, and it had nothing to do with the defense of

the Capitol). After the Gauls had been driven out of Rome, Manlius began (385 B.C.) to champion the cause of the plebeians against the patricians with a view to making himself ruler of Rome. In the following year he was arrested by Camillus, who had been appointed dictator by the Romans, and cast into prison. But Manlius had so won the people that when they learned of his imprisonment they went about the streets clad in mourning, and Camillus was forced to release him. Manlius continued his seditious activities against the Republic and was brought to trial. The Campus Martius, where the trial was held, was in full view of the Captiol. Marcus Manlius stretched out his hands toward it and recalled how he had gloriously defended it against the Gauls. This aroused so much sympathy that the judges dared not convict him. On the other hand, he could not be acquitted because proof of his crimes against the state was plain. Camillus settled it by transferring the place of the trial. Manlius was convicted of treason and hurled to his death from the Tarpeian Rock on the Capitol, so that this place was the scene of his greatest glory and his deepest shame. The house of Manlius on the Capitoline Hill was razed, a temple of Moneta was erected in its place, and henceforth it became the rule that no patrician should have a house on the Capitoline Hill.

Manlius Imperiosus Torquatus (im-pir-i-ō'sus tôr-kwā'tus), **Titus.** Roman hero of the 4th century B.C. He was elected military tribune in 362 B.C., and in 361 served under the dictator Titus Quintius Pennus against the Gauls. During this campaign he slew a gigantic Gaul in single combat in the presence of the two armies, and despoiled him of a *torques* (chain) which he placed around his own neck (whence the surname *Torquatus*). He was appointed dictator in 353 and again in 349 B.C., and was consul in 347, 344, and 340 B.C. During his third consulship, while engaged with his colleague Publius Decius Mus in a campaign against the Latins, he put to death his own son, who, contrary to orders, had fought and killed in single combat an enemy from the opposing army.

Manlius Torquatus, Titus. Roman general, died 202 B.C. He was consul in 235 and 224 B.C., and dictator in 208 B.C. During his first consulship he conquered the Sardinians, after whose subjugation the Romans enjoyed a brief period of universal peace, the temple of Janus being closed for the first time since the reign of Numa Pompilius at the very beginning of Roman history. He opposed the ransoming of the prisoners taken by Hannibal at Cannae in 216, and gained a decisive victory over the Carthaginians in Sardinia in 215 B.C.

Marcellus (mär-sel'us). The name of an illustrious Roman family. Among its members were: 1) **Marcus Claudius,** who was born before 268 B.C. In 222 B.C. he became consul for his first of five terms, and defeated the Gauls at Clastidium, slaying with his own hand their leader, Viridomarus or Britomartus. He defended Nola against Hannibal in 216 B.C. For his daring and swift action in the Second Punic War, he came to be known as the "Sword of Rome," as Fabius Cunctator, his great colleague, became the "Shield of Rome." He captured Syracuse in 212 and, taking command in Apulia, contended against Hannibal in southern Italy until his death (208 B.C.) in a skirmish near Venusia (Venosa). 2) **Marcus Claudius,** consul in 51 B.C., was an adherent of Pompey and an opponent of Caesar. He exiled himself to Mytilene after the battle of Pharsalus (48 B.C.). An appeal by the Senate in his favor caused Caesar to pardon him. He was killed on his way back to Rome, 45 B.C. 3) **Marcus Claudius,** the son of Octavia, born 42 B.C. He was the nephew of Augustus, and the adopted son and favorite of the emperor, whose daughter Julia he married. His early death (23 B.C.) was noted by Vergil *(Aeneid)* and other writers; Augustus read the funeral oration.

Mardonius (mär-dō'ni-us). Persian general, son-in-law and nephew of Darius, and cousin of Xerxes. After Darius had put down the Ionian revolt (494 B.C.), he sent Mardonius to resubdue Thrace and Macedonia, and to punish Athens and Eretria for the aid they had lent the Ionians. Mardonius succeeded in subduing Thrace, and Macedonia submitted, but on the way to punish the two Greek cities a violent storm shattered the Persian fleet off the promontory of Athos, and Mardonius returned to Susa, having carried out the more important part of his task. Darius died before he could punish the Greeks, who in the meantime had added to the Persian desire for vengeance by defeating Datis and Artaphernes at Marathon (490 B.C.). The desire to punish the Greeks burned fiercely in Mardonius, who besides hoped to win glory in an expedition against Athens. It was he, according to Herodotus, who continually urged Darius' successor Xerxes to make a punitive expedition against Greece. In the war that Xerxes undertook, after enormous preparation, the Persians captured and burned Athens, but suffered a humiliating defeat by the combined Greek fleet at Salamis (480 B.C.). Xerxes decided to return to Persia, and left Mardonius, at his earnest request, with a large land force to prosecute the war. The Persian forces under Mardonius withdrew to Thessaly and spent the winter. The Greek states that had so valiantly resisted at Salamis fell into violent disagreement on the best way to resist further Persian attacks. Mardonius, aware of this, tried to separate Athens from her Peloponnesian allies. He sent a distinguished ambassador to offer to repair the damage Athens had suffered from the Persians, and proposed an alliance with Athens, as with an equal and independent state. The terms were generous. According to Herodotus, the Athenians answered him in this manner, "We know, as well as you do, that the power of the Persians is many times greater than our own: we did not need to have that cast in our teeth. Nevertheless, we cling so to freedom that we shall offer what resistance we may. Seek not to persuade us into making terms with the barbarian—say what you will, you will never gain our assent. Return rather at once, and tell Mardonius that our answer to him is this, 'So long as the sun keeps his present course, we will never join alliance with Xerxes. Nay, we shall oppose him unceasingly, trusting in the aid of those gods and heroes whom he has lightly esteemed, whose houses and images he has burnt with fire.' And come not again to us with words like these; nor, thinking to do us a service, persuade us to unholy actions." On learning of the answer Mardonius broke camp and marched to Thebes and thence to Athens, which he found abandoned as the Athenians had again withdrawn to Salamis. Again he offered terms, and again his terms were rejected, as the Spartans rallied to the Athenians. A Spartan force was sent out under Pausanias. Mardonius, seeing his overtures were fruitless, burned Athens and resolved to withdraw from Attica, since the ground was not suitable for his cavalry, and was not advantageous for a retreat in case he should suffer defeat. He decided to return to the friendly neighborhood of Thebes, but first he

marched into the region of Megara, the farthest point in
Europe to which the Persians penetrated, ravaged it, and
afterward withdrew to Thebes. The Greeks under Pausanias
advanced to Plataea. Mardonius came out to meet them, but
on both sides the victims of sacrifices gave unfavorable
omens and the battle was delayed. At last Mardonius resolved to ignore the omens, to still the fears roused by
various oracles, and to begin the battle. In the struggle that
followed, after much maneuvering and many harassing attacks by the Persian horse, Mardonius fought like a lion, and
as long as he lived, his men defended themselves and killed
many Greeks. But Mardonius was slain (479 B.C.) by a Spartan, and after his death the Spartans drove the Persians
back, pursued them, and hacked them to pieces. When the
battle was over, it was proposed to Pausanias, the victorious
Spartan general, that he behead the corpse of Mardonius
and hang the body on a cross, as Xerxes had done to Leonidas after Thermopylae. Pausanias replied that such actions
were more fitted to barbarians than to Greeks, and even in
barbarians they were detestable. Moreover, the great victory
more than avenged Leonidas. The next day the body of
Mardonius disappeared, and none could say who had taken
it, although Herodotus says he knew of many who were paid
large sums by the son of Mardonius on this account.

Marius (măr'i-us), *Caius*. Roman general, born near Arpinum,
Italy, 157 B.C., died Jan. 13, 86 B.C. He was the son of poor
and obscure parents, which probably accounted for his lifelong opposition to the aristocratic conservative party at
Rome. He served with distinction under Scipio Africanus
the Younger in the Numantine War in Spain (134 B.C.), and
won the affection and respect of his commander. It is said
that one evening when Scipio was sitting around the
campfire talking with his men, one of them asked where
Rome would find another such general when Scipio was
gone. Scipio put his hand on Marius' shoulder and said
"Here, perhaps." This incident was supposed to have been
a great inspiration to Marius. He became tribune of the
people in 119 B.C. During his term of office he proposed a
law to improve the election procedure, but also opposed a
proposal for free distribution of grain to the people. When
his term as praetor (115 B.C.) expired he cleared Spain of
robbers; then he returned to Rome, where he won

popularity and married Julia, the aunt of Julius Caesar. He
was legate under the consul Caecilius Metellus, and fought
with him against Jugurtha in Africa (109–108 B.C.), winning
great distinction and the devotion of his soldiers, whom he
had organized into a well-disciplined force. Metellus became alarmed at his growing power and found excuses to
delay him from returning to Rome to seek the consulship.
But Marius returned in time and promised, if given command of the war in Africa, that he would either kill Jugurtha
or take him alive. He became consul, 107 B.C., and soon
alarmed the conservatives by his bold and insolent speeches.
His policy was one of attack on the patricians to win the
support of the delighted commons. He returned to Africa to
finish the war (107–105 B.C.), but did not have the honor of
capturing Jugurtha. This distinction fell to Sulla, a general
serving under Marius, and this event was the beginning of
the rivalry between them that ended in civil war. In 102 B.C.
Marius illegally became consul, while he was outside Rome,
and went to subdue the Cimbri and Teutones. He defeated
(102 B.C.) the Teutones at Aquae Sextiae (Aix), and the
Cimbri at the Raudian Fields near Vercellae (101 B.C.). For
these successes in protecting Rome from the invaders he
was named "Third Founder of Rome." He returned to
Rome and sought the consulship again with the most servile
flattery of the people. With the aid of two lawless mob leaders he had Metellus, whom he feared, expelled from Rome,
and won the consulship for the sixth time, 100 B.C. In his
efforts to get the office he had become even more objection-
able to the aristocrats. He lost the favor of the people when
he was unable to save one of the leaders who had helped him
to win it. In the Social War he defeated (90 B.C.) the Marsi,
but Sulla had also won great successes in the Social War, and
was more than ever a threat to Marius. When the war was
over, Rufus Sulpicius demanded that Marius be named commander of the war against Mithridates, and he invaded the
Senate with his personal armed guard to enforce his demand. Sulla escaped to the house of Marius, from which he
departed in secret to rejoin his army, and Marius was named
to command the Mithridatic War. However, when tribunes
went to take over Sulla's army, they were stoned. In Rome,
Marius attacked the friends of Sulla, put many of them to
death, and seized their property. Sulla now marched on

Rome at the head of his loyal army, and Marius fled (88 B.C.)
He took ship from Ostia and sailed along the coast, bu
when the provision for his party ran out, his companions
deserted him. He was put ashore and was found by a search
party hiding in the marshes of the Liris River. Marius did no
give up hope. An ancient oracle, which he quoted many
times, said he would serve as consul seven times. Up to thi
time he had held the office six times, in 107, 104, 103, 102
101, and 100 B.C. Until the oracle was fulfilled, he believed
he was safe. He was ordered executed, but the people o
Minturnae, where he was imprisoned, freed him and put him
aboard a boat for Carthage. There he was joined by his sor
Marius the Younger. He learned that Cinna had seized
power in Rome after Sulla's departure for the East, and wa
engaged in destroying the friends of Sulla to increase hi
own power. Marius decided to join Cinna, and soon afte
landed in Tuscany, where he gathered a force and joined
Cinna (87 B.C.). He seized the grain ships and the port o
Ostia, marched to Rome and bathed the city in blood as he
gave full rein to his desire for revenge on Sulla and the
aristocrats. In 86 B.C. he became consul for the seventh time
and the oracle was fulfilled. His thirst for blood was unas
suaged, and even Cinna was shocked by his crimes. He had
been consul for only a few days when news of Sulla's victor
over Mithridates and his approach to Rome came to him
Marius had no more heart to fight him. He retired to hi
home and soon after sickened and died. According to Plu
tarch, the Romans were delirious with joy when they learned
of his death.

Masinissa or *Massinissa* (mas-i-nis′ạ). King of Numidia, born
c240 B.C.; died 149 B.C. He fought as ally of the Carthagini
ans in Spain, but later went over to the Romans. As an all
of Rome he served (204–203 B.C.) with Scipio against Sy
phax. Syphax was defeated and his capital fell, one of the
prisoners being his queen Sophonisba, who had once been
betrothed to Masinissa. Scipio refused to sanction their mar
riage and, rather than see Sophonisba paraded in triumph
through Rome, Masinissa sent her a bowl of poison which
she drank. He later served (202 B.C.) at Zama, the decisiv
battle of the Second Punic War. He became (201 B.C.) rule
of all Numidia and ruled in peace for 50 years.

Massinissa (mas-i-nis′ạ). See *Masinissa.*

Mausolus (mô-sō'lus). King or *dynast* of Caria, who died 353 B.C. He first appears in history in the revolt of the satraps against Artaxerxes II (Artaxerxes Mnemon) in 362 B.C. He married his sister Artemisia, who after his death completed at Halicarnassus the celebrated monument named after him, the Mausoleum. A Greek statue of Mausolus from the Mausoleum (352 B.C.) is in the British Museum.

Maximus (mak'si-mus). A title, "greatest," given to Fabius, surnamed Rullianus, and to his descendants, the most illustrious of whom was Fabius Cunctator. Fabius Rullianus, who died about 290 B.C., was a consul and general, who distinguished himself in the Third War against the Samnites, over whom he gained the decisive victory of Sentinum in 295 B.C.

Maximus, Quintus Fabius. See *Fabius Maximus, Quintus.*

Megacles (meg'a-klēz). An Athenian noble of the Alcmaeonid family. He was archon at the time of the uprising of Cylon (c632 B.C.) and was responsible for the death of the followers of Cylon in violation of a pledge to spare their lives if they surrendered. For violating the oath and insulting the gods, Megacles and the Alcmaeonids were tried for sacrilege, their property was confiscated, and they were driven into perpetual exile. The bodies of those Alcmaeonids who had died between the time of the murders and the sentencing for sacrilege were dug up and reburied outside the city. Although the curse on the Alcmaeonids was not allowed to be forgotten for over 200 years, members of the family returned to Athens under an amnesty enacted by Solon.

Megacles. An Athenian noble, son of Alcmaeon. He lived in the 6th century B.C. He married Agariste, daughter of Clisthenes of Sicyon, who bore him Clisthenes, future ruler of Athens, and Hippocrates, later grandfather of Pericles. He was the leader of the party of the Coast in Athens, in opposition to Lycurgus, leader of the Plain. While they contended, Pisistratus at the head of a third party, the Hill, gained control. After a period of struggle in which Pisistratus was driven into exile, Megacles agreed to aid Pisistratus to return on condition that the latter marry his daughter. Pisistratus agreed and gained control of Athens a second time. However, as he already had two sons, and as the Alcmaeonids were under a curse for having slain the followers of Cylon, he refused to have children by the daughter of Megacles. Megacles was furious when he learned of this insult. He

allied himself to the enemies of Pisistratus and drove him
into exile a second time. But when Pisistratus was again
restored (c544 B.C.), the Alcmaeonids fled and their property was seized.

Megistias (mē-jis'ti-as). An Acarnanian seer, said to be a descendant of Melampus. He was in the train of Leonidas a
the defense of the pass of Thermopylae (480 B.C.). From
observing his sacrificial victims he foresaw the imminen
doom of the Greeks. Scouts soon confirmed his deductio
with news that the Persians were coming by a path over th
mountain to attack the Greeks in the rear. Leonidas gav
Megistias permission to retire with the allies when they lef
him alone with the Spartans and Thespians to resist th
Persians. Megistias scorned to desert Leonidas himself, bu
sent his only son back with the allies. He died along with th
Spartans and Thespians in their heroic defence of the pass
and was memorialized by the poet Simonides as follows:

> The great Megistias' tomb you here may view,
> Whom slew the Medes, fresh from Spercheus' fords.
> Well the wise seer the coming death foreknew,
> Yet scorned he to forsake his Spartan lords.

Melissus (me-lis'us). Greek philosopher and admiral, who wa
active in the middle of the 5th century B.C. As an admiral c
the Samian fleet he once defeated Pericles. He was a discipl
of Parmenides and a representative of the Eleatic schoo
Fragments of his writings have been preserved.

Menon (mē'non). Thessalian mercenary; killed c400 B.C. H
was one of the leading generals in the expedition of Cyru
the Younger against Artaxerxes. After the death of Cyrus a
Cunaxa (401 B.C.) the Greek mercenaries, who had bee
victorious in the battle against Artaxerxes in which Cyru
was killed, refused to surrender when Cyrus' oriental troop
fled, and forced the Persians to supply them with provision
and a guide back to Sardis. The satrap Tissaphernes becam
their guide. After crossing the Tigris and proceeding int
Media, hostility between the Greeks and their Persian esco
broke out. Tissaphernes invited all the Greek generals (fiv
of them), including Menon, as well as the leading Gree
captains to a conference in his tent. When they were gath
ered there, he treacherously caused the captains to be take
and slain. The generals were sent off to the Persian court i
chains. Menon was put to torture and finally killed.

fat, fāte, fär, fåll, àsk, fāre; net, mē, hèr; pin, pīne; not, nōte, möv
nôr; up, lūte, pùll; oi, oil; ou out; (lightened) ēlect, agǫny, ūnit

Messala (or *Messalla) Corvinus* (me-sä'lạ, me-sal'ạ, kôr-vī'-nus), *Marcus Valerius.* Roman general, official, orator, historian, and patron of literature (64 B.C.–8 A.D.) He fought for Antony at Philippi (42 B.C.) but later was on Octavian's side at Actium (31 B.C.). He was consul in 31 B.C.

Messalina or *Messallina* (mes-ạ-lī'nạ), *Valeria.* Roman empress. Before 41 A.D., she became the third wife of Claudius who afterward ascended the imperial throne. Their children were Octavia, later married to Nero, and Britannicus (Claudius Tiberius Caesar). She was a woman of infamous vices, and during a temporary absence of her husband publicly married her favorite, Caius Silius. Her partner in influence over Claudius, the freedman Narcissus, informed the emperor, and she was put to death (48 A.D.) by order of Claudius.

Metellus (mẹ-tel'us), *Lucius Caecilius.* Roman general; died c221 B.C. As proconsul he defeated the Carthaginians at Panormus in 250 B.C.

Metellus, Quintus Caecilius. [Surnamed *Macedonicus,* meaning "the Macedonian."] Roman general; died 115 B.C. As praetor he was distinguished for his victories in Macedonia and Greece (148–146 B.C.). He was consul in 143, and censor in 131 B.C.

Metellus, Quintus Caecilius. [Surnamed *Numidicus,* meaning "the Numidian."] Roman general; died c91 B.C. He was a nephew of Metellus Macedonicus. As consul and proconsul he defeated Jugurtha in Numidia in 109 and 108 B.C. He was exiled (c100 B.C.) by his political opponents.

Metellus, Quintus Caecilius. [Surnamed *Pius.*] Roman general; died c64 B.C. He was a son of Metellus Numidicus. He was commander under Sulla in the civil wars, was consul in 80 B.C., and commanded later in Spain against Sertorius.

Metellus, Quintus Caecilius. [Surnamed *Creticus,* meaning "the Cretan."] Roman general; died probably c56 B.C. He was consul in 69 B.C., and subdued Crete (68–66 B.C.).

Metellus Celer (sē'lẻr), *Quintus Caecilius.* Roman statesman; died 59 B.C. He was praetor in 63 B.C., opposed the conspiracy of Catiline, and was consul in 60 B.C.

Metellus Nepos (nē'pos), *Quintus Caecilius.* Roman statesman; died c55 B.C. He was a partisan of Pompey. He was tribune in 62 and consul in 57 B.C.

Metellus Pius Scipio (pī'us sip'i-ō), *Quintus Caecilius.* Roman statesman; committed suicide 46 B.C. He was the son of Scipio Nasica, and the adopted son of Metellus Pius. He was consul with Pompey in 52 B.C., and Pompeian commander in Syria and Egypt.

Milo (mī'lō), *Titus Annius Papianus.* Roman partisan leader, a rival of Clodius; killed in Lucania, Italy, 48 B.C. The gangs of toughs hired by the two rivals kept Rome in constant uproar during the struggle between Pompey and the conservative group on the one hand, and the democratic party on the other. Milo, an adherent of Pompey, was tribune of the plebs in 57 B.C. and had Cicero recalled from exile. The struggle came to a climax in 52 B.C., when Milo and Clodius met by chance at Bovillae; Milo's band, at his orders, set upon Clodius' and Clodius was killed. Feeling ran high and Milo, after a trial, was exiled to Massilia. Cicero's speech in his behalf was not delivered for fear of violence; the oration (*Pro Milone*) which we possess is an expanded version published after the trial. Milo joined with Marcus Caelius Rufus in a revolt (48 B.C.) against Caesar and was killed. He was married to Sulla's daughter Fausta.

Miltiades (mil-tī'a-dēz). Son of Cypselus, lived 6th century B.C. He governed the cities of the Chersonese (Gallipoli Peninsula), which came into his possession, according to Herodotus, in the following manner: The Dolonci, a Thracian tribe of the Chersonese, sent envoys to Delphi to inquire of the oracle how they could settle a war they were waging against their northern neighbors. The priestess told them to take back to the Chersonese with them the first man to offer them hospitality after they left the temple. The envoys journeyed all the way from Delphi to Athens without being offered hospitality, but when they passed the house of Miltiades, he noticed their strange dress and the lances they carried and called them into his house for refreshment and lodging. After they had eaten, the Dolonci told Miltiades of the oracle and urged him to accompany them to the Chersonese. This was during the reign of the tyrant Pisistratus in Athens, and Miltiades, his political enemy, chafed under his government. He agreed to accompany the Dolonci and took with him many Athenians as colonists. Arrived in the Chersonese, Miltiades became as autocratic a ruler, over the Dolonci and the Athenians who had come with him, as Pisistratus was over the Athenians in Athens. He built a wall across the narrow neck of the Chersonese to safeguard it from attacks. Next he crossed the Hellespont (Dardanelles) and attacked Lampsacus. In the engagement he was taken prisoner, but when Croesus, king of Lydia, an admirer of Miltiades, heard of this he threatened to cut down the Lampsacenes "like a fir" unless they released Miltiades. The Lampsacenes learned from one of their wise men that the particular reference to the "fir" was made because the fir of all trees is the only one that does not put forth new shoots when it is cut down, but dies completely. They immediately freed Miltiades. After his death the people of the Chersonese made sacrifices to Miltiades as the founder of their country, and established games in his honor, in which Lampsacenes were forbidden to take part.

Miltiades. Athenian general, c550–489 B.C. He was the son of Cimon and the nephew of Miltiades, son of Cypselus, whom he ultimately succeeded as ruler of the Chersonese (c524 B.C.). When he arrived in the Chersonese to take up the government, he confined himself in his house on the pretext of mourning his brother, his immediate predecessor. According to Herodotus, the leading men of the area came to his house to offer him comfort. Miltiades had them all cast into prison, although they had shown no enmity to him, and made himself tyrant. He married Hegesipyle, daughter of Olorus, king of Thrace. When Darius I, king of Persia, subdued Thrace and then marched into Scythia (c516–513 B.C.), Miltiades commanded the Chersonesites at the Ister (Danube) against the Scythians. Darius crossed into Scythia by means of a bridge he caused to be built over the Ister. He left Ionians to guard the bridge against his return. The Scythians circled around the forces of Darius and reached the bridge before him as he retreated from their country. The Scythians urged the Ionians to destroy the bridge and prevent Darius from using it on his return. According to Herodotus, Miltiades also advised the destruction of the bridge but was outvoted by Ionian tyrants loyal to Darius. Thus he became an enemy of the Persian king. That this story is of doubtful validity is shown by the fact that Miltiades was not disturbed subsequently by Darius. He went back to the Chersonese at the request of the Dolonci. During the Ionian revolt against Persia that broke out in 499 B.C., Miltiades seized the islands of Lemnos and Imbrus. As the forces of Darius drew nearer to the island of Tenedos, Miltiades fled to Athens (493 B.C.). On his arrival there he was accused of tyranny, but was acquitted by his fellow citizens because his conquest of Lemnos and Imbrus brought them under Athenian dominion. Darius resolved to punish Athens and Eretria for their part in the Ionian revolt and sent Artaphernes and Datis at the head of an expedition to attack them. The Persians took Eretria, enslaved the population, and burned the temples. They then pushed on toward Athens. Led by Hippias, exiled tyrant of Athens, they landed at Marathon. Before the threat of the Persian attack Miltiades was made one of the ten generals to direct the defense. He was a bitter enemy of Hippias; he was the best acquainted of all the Athenians with Persian methods of warfare, and he became the guiding spirit of the resistance at Marathon. According to the traditional account, the ten generals were equally divided on the question of resisting the Persians at Marathon. Miltiades, hot for the attack, persuaded the polemarch Callimachus who had the power (at this time in Athenian history) to supervise military matters and to cast a vote with the generals. According to Herodotus, Miltiades told Callimachus that by his vote he could make his country free or could enslave it. Callimachus voted to attack. The Persians, planning an amphibious invasion of Athens, embarked part of their army on ships and the remainder began to march on Athens. On the plain of Marathon they were met by the Greeks, led into a trap by the apparent collapse of the Greek center, and slaughtered by the more heavily-armed though outnumbered Greeks. Miltiades then turned quickly and marched back to Athens to face the threatened landing from the Persian ships, but the Persians, rather than land, drew off and gave up their expedition. After this great and decisive victory Miltiades was held in the highest esteem by the Athenians. He was given command of a fleet of 70 Athenian ships, with which he attacked, for reasons now uncertain, the island of Paros. The Parians withdrew into their city and submitted to siege. According to their account as given by Herodotus, Miltiades, unable to overcome them, received a Parian priestess, Timo, who suggested to him if he wished to take the city he must do certain things in the sacred precinct of Demeter which lay outside the walls of the city. He acted on her advice, went

fat, fāte, fär, fåll, åsk, fâre; net, mē, hèr; pin, pīne; not, nōte, möve, nôr; up, lūte, pull; oi, oil; ou out; (lightened) ĕlect, agǫny, ūnite;

to the precinct, leaped over the wall, and proceeded to the sanctuary. There, according to Herodotus, he was overcome with horror at what he was about to do (Herodotus does not know what it was), and turned back, but on leaping again from the wall he injured his leg. Because of his injury and the stubbornness with which the Parians resisted, he was forced to withdraw from Paros after a siege of 26 days without adding anything to the wealth or power of Athens. On his return to Athens he was charged with having deceived the Athenians concerning the use of the 70 ships they had granted him. His life was spared because of his former contributions to Athens, but he was fined 50 talents. His wound had turned gangrenous so that he could not defend himself, and he died of it before the fine could be paid, but this was ultimately done by his son Cimon. The Parians, when they learned of Timo's treachery, asked the oracle if she should not be put to death. They were told by the oracle to spare her, as it had been decreed that Miltiades would come to an unhappy end and Timo had been merely the instrument that lured him to his destruction.

Minucius Rufus (mi-nū′shus rō′fus), *Marcus.* Roman commander; fl. last half of the 3rd century B.C. He was named *magister equitum* (master of the horse, or cavalry commander) under the dictatorship of Fabius Maximus Cunctator (217 B.C.). As did the Roman soldiers, citizens, and the Carthaginian enemy, he scorned the harrying tactics of Fabius against Hannibal, and urged an attack on him. In the absence of Fabius he engaged in a skirmish with a part of Hannibal's forces in disobedience of an order from Fabius, and won a victory which was greatly exaggerated in Rome. Fabius threatened to punish him but such was the joy in Rome over the success of Minucius that, in an unusual step, Minucius was named co-dictator with Fabius. The Roman army was divided between the two commanders. Minucius moved the troops in his command to a separate camp beyond a hill that separated him from Fabius. Hannibal, occupying the hill, lured Minucius into a battle, surrounded him and would have destroyed him if Fabius had not rushed to his rescue and driven off the Carthaginians. According to the accounts, Fabius uttered no word of recrimination against Minucius, but the latter publicly acknowledged his mistake, presented himself in Fabius' camp to thank him, and put himself once more under the command of Fabius. Minucius fell at the battle of Cannae (216 B.C.).

Mithridates or *Mithradates VI* (mith-ri-dā'tēz or mith-rạ-dā'-tēz). [Also: *Mithridates VI Eupator;* called *Mithridates the Great.*] King of Pontus (120–63 B.C.), born 132 B.C.; died 63 B.C. He succeeded his father at about the age of 11, but his mother made so many attempts to have him slain that he fled to the mountains and lived as a hunter until he felt strong enough to overcome his enemies. He became noted in antiquity for his courage, his strength, his skill in military arts, and for his swiftness of foot. He was a daring rider, skilled hunter, and tremendous eater, and had an enormous capacity for drinking. With these physical qualities was united a keen intelligence. He surrounded himself with Greek men of letters and awarded prizes to the greatest poets, as he did also to the best eaters. But it was an uneasy state to be among his friends, for he distrusted everyone and was ruthless to any who threatened or seemed to threaten him. In 111 B.C. he returned to Sinope and regained his throne by casting his mother into prison and putting his younger brother to death. Ultimately, he murdered his mother, his own sons, and the sister Laodice whom he had married, and once killed all the concubines in his harem to prevent their falling into the hands of his enemies. Having secured his power, he at once undertook a program of conquest. He subjugated the peoples on the eastern shore of the Euxine Sea, and conquered what is now the Crimea and southern Russia. He next attacked Paphlagonia, Cappadocia, and Bithynia, client states of Rome, which caused the interference of that power. He had seized the thrones of Bithynia and Cappadocia. Sulla, as propraetor of Cilicia, restored Ariobarzanes to the throne of Cappadocia (92 B.C.) and Nicomedes III was restored to his throne in Bithynia. Mithridates prepared for war on Rome in consequence, and the First Mithridatic War broke out in 88 B.C. Mithridates rapidly made himself master of all the Roman possessions in Asia Minor, except Magnesia on the Maeander, and caused a general massacre of the Roman inhabitants, said to have numbered 80,000, or according to others, 150,000. He also instigated a rising of the European Greeks, to whose aid he sent a formidable land and naval force under his general Archelaus. Mithridates was now at the height of his power.

His general controlled the sea, his sons were in Thrace and on the Bosporus, he himself had won large areas of Roman interest in Asia, and he sat in Pergamum, handing out provinces and principalities to his friends. There an omen of evil came to him. As he sat in the theater a Victory, bearing a crown in her hands, was being lowered over him so that the crown would be deposited on his head. As it was about to touch his head, the mechanism failed; the Victory fell and was smashed to pieces. The portent was followed by the defeat of Archelaus by Sulla at Chaeronea in 86 and at Orchomenus in 85 B.C. Sulla crossed the Hellespont to Asia. Mithridates was forced to sue for peace. He met Sulla at Dardanus in the Troad in 84 and was compelled to accept the peace the Roman general dictated. Mithridates surrendered his fleet, paid a heavy war indemnity, and restored all his conquests, retaining Pontus only. He did not honor all the terms of the peace, failing to evacuate Cappadocia completely, and the Second Mithridatic War broke out in 83. The propraetor Murena invaded Pontus, but was defeated and forced to withdraw. Peace was restored in 81 on the basis of the treaty of Dardanus. In 74 the Third Mithridatic War broke out, occasioned by an attempt on the part of Mithridates to take possession of Bithynia, which had been bequeathed to the Romans by his son-in-law Nicomedes III, late king of Bithynia. Mithridates defeated Marcus Aurelius Cotta at Chalcedon in 74 but was expelled from his own kingdom by Lucullus, and took refuge with his son-in-law Tigranes, king of Armenia. Lucullus defeated the latter at Tigranocerta in 69, but was unable to prevent Mithridates from reconquering Pontus and ravaging Bithynia and Cappadocia because his troops mutinied. Lucullus was superseded by Cnaeus Pompeius Magnus (Pompey the Great), who defeated Mithridates in 66 B.C. and compelled the surrender of Tigranes at Artaxata. Mithridates fled to Panticapaeum (modern Kerch in the Crimea), and was planning a new campaign when his troops revolted. He tried to commit suicide by poison. He had taken small doses of poison for years, however, and his body was immune to its action. He was compelled to order a mercenary soldier to kill him. His body was sent to Pompey, who caused it to be buried in the royal tomb at Sinope.

Mummius (mum'i-us), *Lucius*. [Surnamed *Achaicus*.] Roman

consul, active in the middle of the 2nd century B.C. During
his consulship (146 B.C.) he defeated the Achaean League
and captured Corinth, completing the Roman conquest of
Greece. Mummius is noted for the barbarity with which he
treated Corinth; according to contemporary sources, all its
inhabitants were killed, its art treasures were sent to Rome,
and the city was burned to the ground. The material
brought to light in the extensive excavations by the American School of Classical Studies at Athens, however, indicates
that the city was not completely depopulated, that some
inhabitants survived or, having fled, returned to maintain
life in the ruins until the city was officially refounded in 44
B.C.

—N—

Nabis (nā'bis). A son of Demaratus and tyrant of Sparta from
207 to 192 B.C. when he was killed. He was conquered by the
Romans under Flamininus in 193 B.C.

Nabonidus (nab-ọ-nī'dus). [Babylonian, *Nabuna'id.*] Last king
of Babylonia (556-c538 B.C.). He was the father of Belshazzar. He seems to have belonged to the priestly class, and was
zealous in the repairing of sanctuaries, but neglected the
gods Merodach (or Marduk) and Nabu (or Nebo), on account of which he estranged himself from the priesthood;
this to some extent facilitated the easy conquest of the
Babylonian Empire by Cyrus of Persia in 538 B.C. According
to Eusebius, Nabonidus after the fall of Babylon fortified
himself in Borsippa, and when this was taken by Cyrus, the
conqueror generously gave him a region in Carmania as his
residence. But from a cylinder (cuneiform record) of Cyrus
it seems that Nabonidus was treacherously delivered into
the hands of Gobryas, the general of Cyrus, and died in a
mysterious manner. It appears, from inscriptions of his
which have been recovered, that he had a strong historical
interest, and several historical statements of great importance for the chronology of the Babylonian Empire are re-
corded by him.

fat, fāte, fär, fâll, àsk, fāre; net, mē, hèr; pin, pīne; not, nōte, möve,
nôr; up, lūte, pùll; oi, oil; ou out; (lightened) ẹlect, agọny, ụnite;

Nabopolassar (nab"ō-pō-las'ạr). [Babylonian, *Nabu-bal-uçar*.] Founder of the new Babylonian Empire, active c625–604 B.C. He ruled, it seems, first over Babylonia as viceroy of Assyria. He then entered into an alliance with the Median king Cyaxares, who gave his daughter in marriage to Nabopolassar's son Nebuchadnezzar, and by their united efforts the destruction of the Assyrian Empire was brought about in 606 B.C.

Nearchus (nē-är'kus). Macedonian officer, born in Crete, active in the second half of the 4th century B.C. He was an intimate friend and trusted officer of Alexander the Great, and was admiral of the fleet which Alexander sent out (325–324 B.C.), and voyaged from the mouth of the Indus to that of the Euphrates. An account of his voyage is given by Arrian in his *Indica.*

Neoptolemus (nē-op-tol'ẹ-mus). King of Epirus; fl. 4th century B.C. He was the father of Olympias and the grandfather of Alexander the Great.

Nepos (nē'pos, nep'os), *Quintus Caecilius Metellus.* See *Metellus Nepos, Quintus Caecilius.*

Nero (nē'rō, nir'ō). [Full name, *Nero Claudius Caesar Drusus Germanicus;* original name, *Lucius Domitius Ahenobarbus.*] Roman emperor (54–68 A.D.); born at Antium, Italy, Dec. 15, 37 A.D.; committed suicide near Rome, June 9, 68. He was the son of the consul Cn. Domitius Ahenobarbus and Agripina (daughter of Germanicus Caesar). His father died when he was three years old and, since his mother had been banished the year before by the emperor Caligula, Nero was taken into the house of his aunt Domitia Lepida. The emperor Claudius recalled Agrippina, who at once began an unrelenting campaign to have Nero succeed Claudius in place of his son Britannicus. Agrippina married Claudius in 49 and persuaded him to adopt Nero as his son the following year. Seneca was recalled from exile and became his tutor. In 55 Nero married Octavia, the daughter of Claudius by Messalina. In 54 Claudius was poisoned by Agrippina, probably with the knowledge of Nero. She caused Nero to be proclaimed emperor to the exclusion of Britannicus, the son of Claudius, who was Nero's ward. The partisans of Britannicus made no great resistance; Nero was well received by the public, and the opening of his reign was propitious. His former tutors, the philosopher Seneca and Burrus, commander of the praetorian guards, were placed at the head of the government. The early years of his reign were marked, on the whole, by clemency and justice. To be sure, he caused his rival, Britannicus, to be removed by poison (55) but such removals of threats to the imperial power had become so common as to be taken for granted, and did not particularly arouse resentment against him. The Senate recovered some of its power, taxes were lowered, many abuses were corrected, and the provinces were left in peace. In this time a great struggle for domination over the young emperor was being waged by Agrippina and Seneca. Agrippina's influence had been supreme, for she had made him emperor. But when Nero fell in love with Acte, a beautiful freedwoman, and was encouraged in the affair by Seneca, Agrippina rebuked, harried, and ultimately threatened her son. Nero deprived her of her Roman and German bodyguards, took away her power, and sent her away from his palace. Her continued threats and violent behavior so frightened him that he decided to put her out of his way. It is said he tried three times to poison her, but that each time she had taken an antidote in advance. He had a mechanical contrivance rigged up in her bedroom that would hurl the ceiling down and crush her as she slept, but someone revealed the presence of the device. Later, he pretended reconciliation and invited her to visit him at Baiae. He arranged to have the galley in which she arrived collide with another so that it was no longer seaworthy. After a seemingly affectionate reunion, he kissed her and put her aboard a vessel for her return home. This vessel was so constructed that it would collapse and fall apart on signal. On the way home the vessel collapsed as planned, but Agrippina saved herself by swimming to shore. In the end, Nero sent a group of soldiers to surround her house and murder her in her bedroom (59). Then at once he became fearful of the consequences of his crime, and claimed to be haunted by her ghost. He said the Furies hounded him with whips and flaming brands, and he asked magicians to intercede with her ghost and compel it to cease haunting him. The report was circulated that Agrippina had died as a result of her own plots against him, and congratulations came to him from all quarters that he had been spared. He was tumultuously welcomed when he returned to Rome. In 61 a savage revolt erupted in Britain. One Roman legion was destroyed before it was put down. Burrus died in 62, whereupon Seneca retired from public life. Freed from the restraint of his former advisers, Nero gave free rein to a naturally tyrannical and cruel disposition. He divorced Octavia in order to marry Poppaea, who had been his mistress for several years. He had several times tried to strangle Octavia, and when he divorced her, his act was so unpopular that he banished her to the island of Pandataria and shortly afterward had her put to death (62). Poppaea ultimately died (65) from the effects of a kick administered by her brutal husband. He also married Statilia Messalina, whose husband he murdered. In 63 the Romans lost the province of Armenia. Having been accused of kindling the fire which in 64 destroyed a large part of Rome, he sought to divert attention from himself by ordering a persecution of the Christians, whom he accused of having caused the conflagration. Traditionally, Peter and Paul both died in this persecution, but this is unlikely. Legend states that Nero, having set the fire, watched it spread while playing music on his lyre. The fire raged for six days, subsided, and then broke out anew. Nero made what provision was possible to shelter the many who were made homeless, brought in food from Ostia, and lowered the price of grain. In the rebuilding of the city an attempt was made to prevent future conflagrations by leaving open spaces about the new houses which were to be at least partly of stone, and by replacing the narrow winding alleys with broad streets. Nero took the opportunity offered by the fire to erect the "Golden House" between the Palatine and Esquiline Hills. It was built with no consideration for cost, decorated with gold and precious stones, and surrounded by magnificent grounds. The provinces were taxed heavily to pay for it. From the time of the fire Nero's popularity waned rapidly. The fire was thought to be a sign of the wrath of the gods, and was followed by a plague. In addition, his personal and public excesses, his wild extravagance, his cruelty and licentiousness, disgusted and terrified the people. A group of enemies conspired to murder him and put Caius Calpurnius Piso, a young noble who was one of his closest companions, in his place. The conspiracy was discovered (65) and ten leaders were put to death. Nero was terrified by the plot and the extent of the enmity against him it revealed. He seized many citizens and had them put to

(obscured) errạnt, ardẹnt, actọr; ch, chip; g, go; th, thin; ᵺн, then; y, you; (variable) ḍ as d or j, ṣ as s or sh, ṭ as t or ch, ẓ as z or zh.

death, among them Seneca. From this time on he killed Roman citizens more or less at will. From his youth Nero had been interested in the lyre and singing; he had studied and worked at this interest, and had arrived at a point where he considered himself a serious and accomplished musician. In 67 he went to Greece and entered as a contestant in the chariot races and musical competition. To accommodate him, all the great festivals were held in one year. He won the prizes in every contest, whether he actually competed or not, but he usually went through the motions of competing on the same terms as the other entrants. He was pleased with his reception in Greece and made lavish presents. While there he planned to cut a canal across the Isthmus at Corinth, and even went so far as to remove the first spadeful of earth himself. When he returned to Italy (68) he had great sections of the walls of the towns he visited torn down to permit his entry, as was fitting to a victor in the Greek games, and gave many musical entertainments, from which no one was permitted to depart while he was still performing. In his absence in Greece unrest at Rome had increased. More dangerous to him was the unrest and outright spirit of rebellion that had arisen in the provinces. Revolt broke out in Gaul. It was put down, and the troops who quelled it offered the throne to their commander. He refused it. This revolt was followed by one in Spain where Galba, the leader, proclaimed himself emperor. When Nero at last decided to take action to save his tottering power he found himself deserted even by his palace guards. He fled from Rome to the house of a freedman and there, with the aid of his secretary, stabbed himself and expired just as the troops who had been sent to take him alive arrived. Acte, the beautiful freedwoman he had earlier loved, had his body buried in the family tomb on the Pincian Hill. Many people refused to believe he was dead, and in ensuing years several appeared who pretended, with success in certain quarters, to be Nero. With the death of Nero the line of the Julian emperors came to an end. Suetonius tells that when Livia was returning to Rome after marrying Augustus, an eagle swooped down and deposited a white pullet in her lap. The pullet held a laurel twig in its beak. She kept the pullet and planted the twig. The pullet produced a great flock of poultry and the twig grew into a luxuriant tree. The Caesars henceforth were

fat, fāte, fär, fåll, åsk, fâre; net, mē, hėr; pin, pīne; not, nōte, möve, nôr; up, lūte, pully; oi, oil; ou out; (lightened) ẹlect, agǫny, ụnite;

crowned with laurel from this tree in their triumphs. The deaths of the Julian emperors were foretold by the tree, whose leaves unfailingly wilted just before one of them died. In the last year of Nero's reign the original laurel tree, and those that had been raised from it as slips, died at the root, and the whole flock of chickens, descended from the original pullet, also died, thus faithfully prophesying the death of Nero and the end of the Julian line.

Nero, Caesar Tiberius Claudius. See *Tiberius.*

Nero, Caius Claudius. Roman consul in 207 B.C. He marched against Hasdrubal, and (with Marcus Livius Salinator) defeated him in the decisive battle of the Metaurus in 207 B.C.

Nero Claudius Drusus (klod'i-us drö'sus). See *Drusus, Nero Claudius.*

Nerva (nėr'va̧), *Marcus Cocceius.* Roman emperor (96–98 A.D.); born c30 A.D.; died Jan. 27, 98. He was consul with Vespasian in 71 and with Domitian in 90, and was raised to the throne (96) after the latter was murdered. He was a mild and just ruler and accomplished reforms in laws, taxation, and expenditures. He was unable, however, to control the Praetorian Guard and therefore adopted (97) Trajan as his successor.

Nicator (nī-kā'tôr, -tọr). See *Seleucus I.*

Nicator, Demetrius. See *Demetrius II* (of *Syria*).

Nicias (nish'i-a̧s). Athenian general and politician; killed 413 B.C., in Sicily. He was the son of Niceratus and, although he was wealthy, he was the leader of a moderate party at Athens. He favored peace with Sparta and was continually opposed by Cleon and others who had lately won influence in the assembly and who pursued a policy of empire and war with Sparta. Nicias maintained his popularity with the people by his deserved reputation for incorruptibility, his undeserved reputation as a general, and his conspicuous piety. In the latter connection, he played a leading part in the "cleansing" of Delos. This was done (426 B.C.) to propitiate Apollo that he might never again send plague to Athens. The bodies of the dead were removed from their tombs on Delos and transferred to another island. It was ordered that henceforth those on the island who were near death, or women who were about to bear children, should be removed to neighboring Rhenia to keep Delos pure. Under his leadership the Athenians reëstablished the ancient games of Apollo and held them every four years at Delos. A few years later all the inhabitants were moved from the island to complete the purification. Such manifestations of piety were intensely gratifying to the Athenians. Nicias ever held their respect and support. He was *strategus* (general) when the Spartans were besieged in Sphacteria (425 B.C.), and replied to the taunts of Cleon, who claimed he would capture the Spartan garrison himself if he were commander, by resigning his command to Cleon in order to permit the latter to carry out his boast. To the surprise of all, Cleon did so. To counteract the growing influence of Cleon that ensued from this success, Nicias went to the Peloponnesus and established a garrison at Methone (425 B.C.), and captured the island of Cythera (424 B.C.) from which the Athenians could raid Sparta. In 423 B.C. he negotiated a one-year truce with Sparta. The truce was violated in Thrace, whither Nicias now sailed at the head of a fleet of 50 ships and recovered Mende which had revolted. In 421 B.C. he was the chief Athenian negotiator of a peace, with Plistoanax the Spartan king, that was to last for 50 years. In 420 B.C. Alcibiades was elected strategus and Nicias was not. An expedition was made against Epidaurus; Sparta came to her assistance; Athens claimed Sparta had broken the peace. Nicias was returned as strategus (418 B.C.), continued to advocate peace, but found himself, through the vagaries of political fortunes, now in alliance with the warlike and far from pious Alcibiades.

In 416 B.C. Segesta, a city of Sicily, asked Athens for aid in a war with her neighbor Selinus. Alcibiades was all eagerness for a war in Sicily. He painted a glowing picture of the aggrandizement of Athens as the result of such a war. The younger generation of Athens responded to his clamor for war as if in a hypnotic trance. Nicias opposed sending aid to Segesta. In the first place, he doubted—correctly as it turned out—that the Segestaeans had the money they promised for the war. He pointed out that the Athenians had enough enemies near at hand without going abroad for more. Even if an expedition to Sicily should succeed, it would be impossible to keep an enemy subdued at such a distance. It would be more to the purpose to concentrate on the enemies at hand. But the Athenians were so in love with the idea of conquering Sicily, about which they had only the

vaguest ideas, that they paid no attention at all to his good
advice, nor were they deterred in the least when he presented a formidable estimate of the cost of such an expedition. They voted all he asked for and made him, against his
wish and judgment, one of three commanders of the expedition with full power to help Segesta against Selinus, restore
the Leontini to their city that had been taken by Syracuse,
and promote Athenian interests in all matters. The other
two commanders were Alcibiades and Lamachus. The most
splendid and costly armament ever prepared by one city for
the longest passage away from home ever attempted, sailed
in a carnival atmosphere from the Piraeus (415 B.C.), libations having been poured and prayers uttered by a herald.
At Corcyra the fleet, 134 galleys, was divided into three
squadrons, each under one of the three commanders. Arrived at Rhegium, Nicias wanted to sail directly against Selinus to settle the affair of the Segestaeans. Alcibiades
prevailed on him to prepare for an attack on Syracuse, but
before it could be mounted, Alcibiades was recalled to
Athens to answer a charge of impiety. Nicias and Lamachus
divided the command between them. Lamachus now urged
immediate attack on Syracuse, while the Syracusans were
still unprepared and overawed by the size of the armament
the Athenians had brought against them. Nicias rejected his
advice. Instead the summer was spent sailing about, engaging in ineffectual skirmishes, while Nicias tried to make up
his mind. In the meantime, the Syracusans recovered from
their first shock and began energetic preparations to defend
themselves. The Athenians frittered away their time, their
money, and their striking power sailing up and down the
coast, and then returned to Syracuse. In the first engagements there they were successful, but in one of them Lamachus was slain (414 B.C.), leaving the sole command to
Nicias. He was not only incapable of making decisive moves
but was ill. The Syracusans sent to Sparta and Corinth for
aid and the Spartan general Gylippus arrived to aid them. A
furious contest of building walls about Syracuse took place
between the Athenians, to protect access to their ships and
cut off the city, and the Syracusans, to protect their city and
cut off the Athenians. As the strength of Syracuse under
Gylippus grew, Nicias sent to Athens for help. Demosthenes
and Eurymedon were sent out with a fleet. Demosthenes,

driven back in an attempt to take one of the heights of
Syracuse, advised Nicias to withdraw while he could still save
his fleet, as he was convinced that Syracuse, made strong by
her own preparations and by her allies, could not be taken
by siege, and as he realized the danger in which the
Athenian fleet was placed in the harbor. Nicias was fearful
of his reception in Athens if he should retreat from Syracuse, and would not leave unless he was ordered to do so
from Athens. To receive such an order would take a long
time. He would not even withdraw to Catana, from which his
army would have room to maneuver in open territory as
Demosthenes advised, for at Syracuse the Athenians were
cramped by the physical limitations of the location. When
Gylippus returned to Syracuse with reinforcements, Nicias
saw that his position was hopeless and decided to withdraw
under cover of darkness. All was in readiness and the
Syracusans were unaware of his intention. But that night
there was an eclipse of the moon. One might have said the
gods were aiding the Athenians with total darkness for their
withdrawal. But many regarded the eclipse as an evil omen.
Nicias consulted the soothsayers and decided to wait the 27
days they had prescribed. In that time the Syracusans
learned that he meant to retreat. Emboldened by this obvious sign of weakness, they resolved to prevent the withdrawal they would earlier have welcomed. They defeated
the Athenians in a sea fight and bottled their remaining
ships in the harbor. The crews refused to board the ships for
another attempt to get through the enemy fleet. Nicias was
now compelled to retreat overland. Even in this extremity he
let time help the Syracusans. They were celebrating their sea
victory and would have been in no condition to march out
and stop the Athenians, but Nicias delayed, duped by a
stratagem of the Syracusan Hermocrates. When he led his
forces overland in retreat, the Syracusans were ready and
attacked them as they fled. The forces were divided between
Demosthenes and Nicias, Eurymedon having been slain.
Those under Demosthenes fell behind and were forced to
surrender. Nicias, unaware of the surrender, pushed on to
the Asinarus River. His men were harried by Syracusan attacks and many were lost; they were exhausted by lack of
provisions and by thirst. When they came to the Asinarus
River, they tumbled into it like madmen to allay their thirst.

fat, fāte, fär, fåll, ȧsk, fãre; net, mē, hėr; pin, pīne; not, nōte, mȯve,
nôr; up, lūte, pu̇ll; oi, oil; ou out; (lightened) ĕlect, agǫny, ṵnite;

The Syracusans and their Peloponnesian allies, lined atop the steep opposite bank, butchered them with arrows and javelins as they drank. Nicias, who had now learned of the surrender of Demosthenes, offered to surrender. The Syracusans might do as they like to him if they would stop the slaughter of his men. Gylippus accepted his surrender. According to Thucydides, Gylippus would have preferred to lead Nicias back as a captive, but the exultant Syracusans butchered him, and Demosthenes as well. The men were enslaved and imprisoned in a quarry. A few escaped and brought back the terrible news to Athens—news that the entire armament was destroyed and that those who were not killed were enslaved. This was the greatest disaster Athens had ever suffered and she did not recover. According to Thucydides' account of it in his *History of the Peloponnesian Wars,* if any one man was responsible for it that man was Nicias, whose incapacity and indecision along with his obstinacy were not only incredible but tragic for Athens. In his defense it must be said that he was personally brave, scrupulously honest, pious to the point of blind superstition, and commander of the expedition by popular demand and against his own will.

Ochus (ō′kus). Original name of *Darius II* (of *Persia*).

Octavia (ok-tā′vi-ạ). Sister of Caius Octavius (Octavian; after 27 B.C. known as Augustus). She died 11 B.C. She was the wife first of Caius Marcellus, and afterward of Mark Antony. Her son by Caius Marcellus was the first husband of her brother Octavian's (Augustus) daughter Julia. Octavia was married to Mark Antony to cement the alliance between Augustus and Mark Antony. When Antony went to the East and carried on his affair with Cleopatra with flagrant disregard for Roman morality and the feelings of his wife, Augustus used this as one of his reasons for making war on Antony and eliminating him as a rival for power in Rome. Octavia was divorced from Antony in 32 B.C.

Octavia. Daughter of Claudius I and Messalina; born c40 A.D.; killed 62 A.D. She was the wife of Nero. He divorced her in order to marry Poppaea and soon afterward contrived to have her killed, after banishing her to the island of Pandataria.

Octavian (ok-tā′vi-an). Name by which Caius Octavius, who afterward became Augustus, was known after he became the heir of Julius Caesar and, under the terms of his will, took the name Caius Julius Caesar Octavianus. After 27 B.C. he is properly known as Augustus.

Octavius (ok-tā′vi-us), **Caius.** Original name of Augustus.

Olympias (ọ-lim′pi-as). Wife of Philip II of Macedon, and mother of Alexander the Great; put to death 316 B.C. The daughter of Neoptolemus, king of Epirus, she met Philip at Samothrace, where he had gone to be initiated into the mysteries, and married him in 357 B.C. According to tradition, before Alexander was born, she dreamed a thunderbolt fell on her body and that from it flames spread out in all directions and then were extinguished. This was taken as an omen that her son would have brilliant successes. Of a strongly mystical temperament, it is said that at the religious orgies she twined tame serpents about her body, a sight men could not bear to see. Once also, it is said, Philip found a serpent lying beside her as she slept. From that time on he found her distasteful and turned his attention to other women. Her proud and tumultuous spirit was roused to fury and desire for revenge by his flagrant infidelities. She found some satisfaction in turning her son against his father. In 337 B.C. Philip inflicted the supreme insult by casting her aside altogether and marrying Cleopatra, the niece of his general, Attalus. At the wedding feast Attalus asked the assembled company to pray for a legitimate heir, thus bringing into the open rumors that Olympias was, though more discreet, no less unfaithful than Philip, and that Alexander was not his son. Alexander hurled a cup into Attalus' face for his insult to his mother. Philip rose to run his son through with his sword but tripped over a couch as he lunged. After this Alexander took his mother to her old home in Epirus. She continued to intrigue against Philip for revenge and for power. At the marriage of Philip's daughter to her brother, the king of Epirus, Philip was murdered as he walked in the wedding procession. Olympias did not wield the dagger that killed him, but it has been said on the basis of evidence of doubtful validity that she was the architect of the plot. Still thirsting for revenge, she caused the infant son of Philip and Cleopatra to be slain in his mother's arms and compelled Cleopatra to hang herself. This not only avenged her honor but also cleared a possible rival from Alexander's path. After Alexander's accession (336 B.C.) she maintained her influence at court, especially during Alexander's absences in his campaigns. She constantly wrote to him, advising him not to enrich his companions, lest they seek his throne, and pouring out accusations against Antipater, left behind as regent of Macedonia. Alexander sent her many gifts from the spoils he took in Asia but did not allow her advice to influence his conduct of affairs. Antipater in his turn sent letters of accusation against Olympias. Alexander read them and remarked that Antipater did not realize how easily all his words could be washed out by the tears of a mother. Having made an enemy of Antipater, when Alexander died (323 B.C.), she prudently retired to Epirus once more. From there she opposed the growth of the power of Cassander, Antipater's son, but he besieged her at Pydna, and, after her capitulation, had her slain.

Opimius (ō-pim′i-us), *Lucius.* Roman consul in 121 B.C. He was put forward by the Senate to oppose the reforms of Caius Gracchus and, as the leader of the optimates, killed Gracchus and 3000 of his followers in 121 B.C. He was afterward exiled for accepting bribes from Jugurtha, king of Numidia.

Orgetorix (ôr-jet′ō-riks). Helvetian conspirator shortly before the time of Caesar's war with the Helvetians in 58 B.C. According to Caesar's account, he planned to conquer Gaul with the Helvetians, but was detected by them plotting with other chiefs to seize control of the tribe. He escaped immediate trial, but committed suicide afterward.

Oroetes (ô-rē′tēz). A Persian noble who was appointed a governor of Sardis by Cyrus the Great. He retained this post under Cambyses. He resolved to destroy Polycrates, ruler of Samos (c540–522 B.C.). Some say his hatred of Polycrates was inspired by one of his fellow Persians who reproached Oroetes because he had not conquered Samos and brought it under the dominion of Persia. Others say Polycrates had deeply offended Oroetes by his contemptuous treatment of a herald of Oroetes. Oroetes sent the herald to Polycrates on some mission and Polycrates received him as he was lying on his couch with his back to the herald. At no time during the interview did he deign to turn over and face the messenger from Oroetes, nor did he address one word to him. Whatever the reason, Oroetes, having learned that Polycrates had the mighty ambition to make himself master of the sea, sent a messenger to him. The message he bore was that Oroetes had been warned that Cambyses meant to destroy him. At the same time Oroetes said he was aware of Polycrates' great ambition, and also that Polycrates lacked the means of attaining it. If Polycrates would, therefore, come to the aid of Oroetes and save him from Cambyses, for his part Oroetes would supply Polycrates with the wealth to make himself master of the sea. However, lest Polycrates should doubt that Oroetes possessed enough wealth to make it worthwhile, he invited Polycrates to send a trusted messenger to whom he would show his treasure as a proof. Polycrates was delighted, as he was in great need of gold to build up his fleet. He sent a messenger as Oroetes had invited him to do. Oroetes filled eight great chests with stones. Over the stones he spread a layer of gold. These chests he showed to the messenger from Polycrates, who in due course reported on the vast wealth of Oroetes to his master. Polycrates decided to go to Sardis and rescue Oroetes from Cambyses and gain the promised treasure. Against the advice and warnings of his friends, soothsayers, and his own daughter, he went to Sardis with some of his followers. As soon as Polycrates came into his hands, Oroetes seized him and put him to death and hung him on a cross. Oroetes let the Samians in the train of Polycrates return to their homes but the foreigners who had come with him, including Democedes, he kept among his own slaves. Not long after this Oroetes killed the Persian who had reproached him about Samos, and during the time of the False Smerdis he did nothing to help the Persians regain the throne. When Darius became king, Oroetes showed great insolence toward him, even going so far as to kill one of his messengers. Darius longed to take vengeance on him, but since he had only recently ascended the throne and since Oroetes was very powerful in Sardis and was surrounded by a guard of 1000 men, Darius had to attack him by indirect means. He sent a volunteer to Sardis who contrived that Oroetes was murdered by his own bodyguard, whose loyalty to the king of Persia proved to be greater than that to Oroetes. After his death the treasures and slaves of Oroetes were taken to Susa.

Otanes (ọ-tā′nēz). A Persian nobleman of the 6th century B.C. According to Herodotus, when the False Smerdis ascended the throne of Persia, following the death of Cambyses, Otanes began to suspect that this Smerdis was not the true son of Cyrus because he never left the palace and never received any of the Persian noblemen. Otanes suspected that he was really a Median magus who had usurped the throne with the help of his brother, a magus who had been left in charge of Cambyses' household when the latter departed on his expedition to Egypt. Otanes sought to prove his suspicions. His daughter, Phaedima, had been one of the wives of Cambyses and was taken as a wife by Smerdis after the death of Cambyses. Otanes sent a message to her, asking if the man who shared her couch was truly Smerdis, the son of Cyrus, or some other man. Phaedima answered that she did not know because she had never seen Smerdis the son of Cyrus. Otanes then instructed her to ask Atossa if the man they both knew as their husband was truly Smerdis, for surely Atossa, the sister and wife of Cambyses and the sister of Smerdis, would know whether the man she called her husband was her own brother. Phaedima replied that she was never permitted to see the other wives of Smerdis. Otanes was now more than ever convinced that the man was not truly Smerdis. He instructed his daughter to perform the following test: When the king came to her, she was to feel his ears as he slept. If he had ears he was truly Smerdis, but if he had no ears he was the magus, for his ears had been cut off as punishment for a crime. Phaedima did as her father commanded, and reported that the man who came to her as king had no ears. Now Otanes was certain that this was an impostor. He confided his information to two other Persian nobles, who, as it happened, had already entertained the same suspicions, and the three decided to take three more loyal Persians into their confidence. At this time Darius, the son of Hystaspes, came to Susa and he was made a seventh member to plan how they should remove the false king. The names of the seven conspirators were Otanes, Aspathines, Gobryas, Intaphernes, Megabyzus, Hydarnes, and Darius. Darius urged instant action, for if so many already knew what he thought he alone knew, more would find out soon and warn Smerdis. In fact, he threatened that unless they acted at once, he himself would betray them to Smerdis rather than take the risk of being betrayed himself. Otanes would have preferred more men to aid them, and he counseled delay but was overruled. The seven set out at once for the palace, succeeded in entering it, and themselves cut down the False Smerdis and his brother. Following his death and exposure, the capital was in a ferment. The conspirators now met to decide on a government to succeed Smerdis. Otanes favored a government by the people. He pointed out the excesses of Cambyses and the insolence of Smerdis as evils attendant on a monarchy, in which the monarch can do as he likes and is answerable to no one. Otanes thought it was inevitable that the power which is customarily vested in a monarch leads to excessive pride and arrogance and promotes great envy in those who aspire to such power; thus the kingdom is continually in turmoil. He thought the excesses and unlimited power of monarchs could be avoided by a democracy, but Otanes was overruled. The conspirators decided to choose one of themselves as king. Hereupon Otanes said that as he neither wanted to rule or to be ruled, he would withdraw his name from consideration for the role on one condition: that none of them or their descendants should ever claim the right to rule over him or his descendants. The others agreed, and thenceforward the family of Otanes was the only free family in Persia. Its members submitted to the rule of the king or not, as they chose, although they were compelled to obey the laws of the land like all other Persians. Later Otanes successfully commanded an expedition for the conquest of Samos.

Otho (ō'thō), *Marcus Salvius.* Emperor of Rome (January-April, 69); born 32 A.D.; committed suicide, in April, 69. He was governor of Lusitania under Nero, whose mistress was Poppaea Sabina, Otho's wife. He overthrew Galba by a conspiracy after helping him gain the purple, and was in turn overthrown by Vitellius.

fat, fāte, fär, fåll, åsk, fãre; net, mē, hèr; pin, pīne; not, nōte, möve, nôr; up, lūte, pùll; oi, oil; ou out; (lightened) ęlect, agǫny, ŭnite;

——P——

Paches (pa'kēz). Athenian commander; fl. at the end of the 5th century B.C. He was sent to capture Lesbos, which had revolted from Athens in 428 B.C. After a winter siege the city of Mytilene, the chief Lesbian city, surrendered to him, 427 B.C., on condition that the Mytileneans would be allowed to send a delegation to Athens to plead their cause, and that Paches would not imprison, enslave, or put to death any of the inhabitants of the surrendered city. He accepted the terms and invested the city. On learning that a Peloponnesian fleet had been seen coming to the relief of Mytilene, Paches set out after it and the Peloponnesians fled. Paches went on to Ionia, seized Notium, and gave it to a faction in Colophon. Afterward, Paches was called to account for his activities by his enemies. As he was giving his account of his generalship in court he drew his sword and killed himself.

Pansa (pan'sa), ***Caius Vibius.*** Roman consul in 43 B.C. He was the colleague of Hirtius with whom he defeated Antony at Mutina, 43 B.C. He died the same year.

Papirius Cursor (pa-pir'i-us kėr'sôr, -sọr), ***Lucius.*** Roman consul five times and dictator twice, hero of the Second Samnite War. As dictator he won a victory over the Samnites in 309 B.C. His name became a byword for great strictness and severity.

Papirius Cursor, Lucius. Roman consul and general in the Third Samnite War (298–290 B.C.); son of the hero of the Second Samnite War. According to Pliny, he erected the first sun-dial at Rome.

Parmenio (pär-mē'ni-ō) or ***Parmenion*** (pär-mē'ni-ọn). Macedonian general, born c400 B.C.; executed without trial, on the orders of Alexander the Great, 330 B.C. He was the leading councilor and ablest general of Philip II of Macedon, who sometimes called him his only general. He defeated the Illyrians (356 B.C.); acted as envoy of Philip at the signing of a peace treaty with Athens, 346 B.C.; and when Philip was preparing war to liberate the Greek cities of Asia

Minor from Persian control, he crossed the Hellespont with an advance force. Philip was murdered before he could carry out his plan to drive back the Persians. Parmenio won control of the Hellespont and kept it. When Philip's successor, Alexander the Great, arrived (334 B.C.), he had a base from which to launch his expedition into Asia. Parmenio served Alexander as loyally and well as he had served Philip. He commanded the left wing at the battles of Granicus, Issus, and Arbela. Perhaps because of his experience and because he was old enough to be Alexander's father, he sometimes gave him advice, which was seldom taken. When the Macedonians came to the Granicus River, where the Persians were arrayed to meet them, Parmenio advised Alexander to wait until morning to cross the river and make his attack, before the Persians had time to draw up their line. Alexander's characteristic reply was that he would disgrace the Hellespont, which he had already crossed, if he allowed himself to be detained by a miserable stream such as the Granicus, even for a night. The Macedonians crossed and defeated the Persians (334 B.C.). Again, some time after the battle of Issus (333 B.C.) the defeated Darius sent to Alexander asking to ransom his family and proposing to cede to Alexander all of his kingdom west of the Euphrates River. Parmenio said he would accept the offer if he were Alexander. Alexander remarked, "So would I, if I were Parmenio," and proceeded to draft an imperious letter to Darius in which he refused his terms and demanded his surrender in person. On the eve of the battle of Gaugamela (331 B.C.), Parmenio advised a night attack against the vastly superior forces assembled under Darius. In this case, Alexander said, "I will not steal a victory," and ordered the attack for the morning. The Persians facing Alexander were completely routed and he would have pursued Darius who fled on horseback, but Parmenio was in difficulties in his sector and sent to Alexander for aid. Before Alexander came up the enemy was routed, thanks to the Thessalian cavalry. Some say that from this time Alexander had less confidence in Parmenio. However, he was left in charge (330 B.C.) of the enormous treasure the Macedonians had assembled at Ecbatana, the capital of Media, when Alexander at last found an opportunity to pursue Darius. Philotas, son of Parmenio, was also a general in Alexander's army. With the rich spoils taken and distributed to the Macedonians, Philotas began to lead a wildly extravagant life, and to rival Alexander himself in the rich gifts he gave his friends. Parmenio wrote to his son to be "less great," for he knew Alexander had received accusations against Philotas. Alexander became convinced that Philotas was conspiring against him, had him accused, tried, and put to death. He then sent messengers to Media with orders to kill Parmenio, against whom there was no charge; but the fact that he was the father of Philotas made him an object of danger to Alexander. The murder of Parmenio (330 B.C.), a loyal general who had rendered great service to two generations, marked a departure from Alexander's ordinarily generous and mild conduct toward his friends.

Paulus (pô'lus), *Lucius Aemilius.* Roman consul in 219 and 216 B.C. He was the colleague of Varro in the Roman defeat at Cannae, 216 B.C., where he was killed.

Paulus, Lucius Aemilius. [Surnamed *Macedonicus,* meaning "the Macedonian."] Roman general, born c229 B.C.; died 160 B.C. He was the son of Lucius Paulus, who took part in the defeat at Cannae (died 216 B.C.), and claimed descent from the philosopher Pythagoras. His sister Aemilia was the wife of Scipio Africanus. His wife Papiria was a daughter of the consul Maso. She bore him two sons, one of whom was adopted by Scipio Africanus and took the name Scipio (Publius Scipio Aemilianus). The other was Fabius Maximus. Aemilius divorced Papiria. There seemed to be no good reason for the divorce, and in explanation a story of another Roman who divorced his wife was told: This man's friends were surprised when they heard of the divorce; was his wife not discreet, was she not beautiful, did she not give him sons? In reply he held out his shoe and asked, "Is this not handsome? Is it not new? But no one of you can tell me where it pinches my foot." Afterward, Aemilius married again and had two more sons.

Aemilius was noted in Rome for his integrity and his courage. In 193 B.C. he was elected aedile over 12 competitors. He was made augur in 192 B.C. and devoted himself to the study of the ancient rituals, which he performed with the most precise regard for the forms. In military matters he was equally exact in observing the established customs and practices. He was sent to Spain (191 B.C.) as praetor and defeated the revolting barbarians, slaying about 30,000 of them and subduing 250 cities. He restored order and left the province (189 B.C.) having refused to enrich himself by as much as a penny through plunder of the province. In 182 B.C. he was elected consul and undertook an expedition against the Ligurians, whom he defeated, though their forces outnumbered his by five to one. Because the Ligurians formed a buffer between the Gauls and the Romans he did not treat them harshly. He seized their ships in which they had been making piratical raids, but restored the captives he had taken. When he returned to Rome he was not made consul again, as he expected to be, and gave himself up to his duties as augur and to the education of his sons, the elder of whom he introduced to the men of affairs in Rome.

The Romans had been successful in their wars on all fronts save that with Perseus, king of Macedonia. He defeated them in several engagements, though he was not considered an especially skillful general. The Romans felt disgraced by the defeats and sought a new commander for the war. Aemilius was urged to run as consul, but declined at first on the grounds of his age, and perhaps out of pique at not being chosen consul again when he returned from his successful Ligurian campaign. But he was at length persuaded to stand for the office and was chosen consul in 168 B.C. for the second time. Now in his sixties, he became commander of the Roman forces in the war against Perseus. It is said that when he went home after being made consul he found his little daughter in tears, and learned she wept for the death of her "little Perseus," a pet dog. Aemilius knew this for a favorable omen. Before he set out to join the army he made a speech to the Romans, in which he announced that the first time he became consul he had sought the office. This time he had become consul because the Roman people needed a general. Therefore he cherished no feelings of gratitude for the office. On the contrary, if the people had confidence in him they must not attempt to tell him what to do. All he required of them was that they vote the necessary supplies and money to carry on the war, for if they sought to command their commander his campaigns would be as ridiculous and as unsuccessful as those of his predecessors. Such frank speaking greatly impressed the

Romans. They voted what he asked for. He joined the Roman army near Mount Olympus in Greece, about which Perseus had set up his camp, and by an encircling movement prepared to attack Perseus at Pydna (168 B.C.). That night the moon changed color many times and finally disappeared. Some say the Romans, according to their custom, tried to call her light back by clashing bronze utensils and by holding up many torches toward the heavens. Others say Aemilius, a well-educated man, knew an eclipse of the moon would take place, and had forewarned his men so that they would not take it as an evil omen. But the Macedonians were terrified, and rumor spread rapidly through their ranks that it portended the eclipse of a king. Aemilius sacrificed 11 heifers to the moon. At daybreak he sacrificed 20 oxen to Hercules without getting favorable omens for the coming battle. When the twenty-first victim was sacrificed the omens were favorable, on condition that the Romans did not initiate the attack. Aemilius vowed hecatombs and games to Hercules if he should be successful. During the day he occupied himself about his camp, waiting until afternoon, when the sun would be in the eyes of the enemy and not blinding his own men. Careful not to defy the omens produced by the sacrificial victims, he did not take the offensive, but tricked the Macedonians into beginning the attack. His strategy was spectacularly successful: 25,000 Macedonians were slain, while he lost only between 80 and 100 of his own men. Perseus was routed, thus ending the Third Macedonian War. Perseus fled to Pella, later sailing to Samothrace where he took refuge in the temple of the Dioscuri with his wife and children. But his enraged Macedonians seized him and themselves gave him into the hands of Aemilius. After the victory at Pydna, Aemilius rested his army, while he traveled about Greece. One of his journeys was to Delphi, where he set up a statue of himself on the pillar Perseus had raised for a statue of himself. He visited Olympia and held games, offered sacrifices, gave feasts, and won the admiration of the Greeks. Of the plunder taken from Perseus, he kept none himself, but sent it all to Rome except for some books he allowed his sons to take from the library of Perseus. After freeing the Macedonian cities and exacting tribute from them for Rome (less than they had paid to their own king), Aemilius marched into Epirus and, on orders from the Roman Senate, allowed his soldiers to plunder it. The sack of Epirus did not satisfy them, for it yielded but little. They thought with envy of the rich treasure that had gone to Rome, and were ready to join in a vote to deny Aemilius a triumph when he returned. However, a veteran, covered with wounds, made a speech in honor of Aemilius, the soldiers changed their minds, and he was voted a triumph. It was celebrated in November, 167 B.C. Three days were required for the procession carrying the captured armor and spoils from the victory of Pydna to pass. Perseus, who had begged to be spared the humiliation of marching in the procession, was scorned by Aemilius for his cowardice. Aemilius pointed out one way in which he could avoid being exhibited as a captive, but Perseus could not bring himself to take his own life at that time. He marched in the procession with his two sons and his daughter, following his own chariot and captured armor and accompanied by many captive Macedonian nobles. At the end of the procession came Aemilius, clad in a purple robe, carrying a spray of laurel, and riding in his war charoit. His triumph was held in the midst of personal disaster. Five days before it was celebrated the elder of the two sons by his second wife died. Three days after the triumph the second son died. Aemilius took this as an evil sent by the gods to balance the good fortune he had met with in war. The Romans continued to reward him. In 164 B.C. he was made censor, a post of great honor because of its power over the senators and life of the Romans. Four years later, after a brief illness, he died, having enjoyed many honors from the Republic, and leaving to it two sons, one of whom, Scipio the Younger, destroyed Carthage (146 B.C.) and became the most influential Roman of his day.

Pausanias (pô-sā′ni-ạs). Son of the Spartan king Cleombrotus and nephew of Leonidas. He was a Spartan general. When Leonidas I, the Spartan king, died at Thermopylae, Cleombrotus, his brother, became regent for Pleistarchus, the son of Leonidas; Cleombrotus died in 480 B.C. and Pausanias became regent. At the earnest request of the Athenians, when Mardonius occupied Attica for a second time (479 B.C.), the Spartans sent out Pausanias, in command of a force of Spartans, to the aid of the Athenians. At Plataea he commanded the Spartans and Tegeans, the other Greek

fat, fāte, fär, fâll, ȧsk, fãre; net, mē, hèr; pin, pīne; not, nōte, mȯve, nôr; up, lūte, pull; oi, oil; ou out; (lightened) ḙlect, agȯny, ṳnite;

forces having withdrawn according to plan, in a battle against vastly superior numbers of Persians under the command of Mardonius. Pausanias and his Spartans and Tegeans won a glorious victory (479 B.C.). Mardonius was killed in the battle and it was suggested to Pausanias that he behead and crucify the body of Mardonius to avenge Leonidas, whose body had been mutilated in this manner by the Persians after the Battle of Thermopylae. Pausanias replied to this suggestion that such acts were more suited to barbarians than to Greeks, and even in barbarians were detestable. Moreover, he considered Leonidas to have been amply avenged by the Persian lives that were taken, not only at Plataea, but in his own battle at Thermopylae. Pausanias ordered the booty of the Persian camp to be gathered. A tenth part of it was dedicated to Apollo at Delphi. Other portions were offered to the gods at Olympia and on the Isthmus. The rest was divided among the soldiers according to their merits. Pausanias himself received ten of every kind of thing found in the Persian camp—women, horses, camels, money, vessels, etc. Herodotus says that when Pausanias came upon the rich war-tent of Mardonius, he commanded the Persian captive cooks and bakers to prepare a banquet in the Persian manner. When he saw the rich couches, covered with gold and silver, tables inlaid with the same precious metals, and the feast that was spread on them, he ordered his own men to prepare a Spartan meal. Then he called the Greek generals to see both meals. He told them he wanted them to see the folly of the barbarians who, when they had such fare as this, had come to rob the Greeks of their poverty. After Plataea Pausanias led his forces against Thebes, because the Thebans had made common cause with the Persians, and demanded the surrender of the Theban chiefs whom he held responsible for the alliance of Thebes with the Persians. The Thebans refused to give these men up and the city was attacked. Thereupon two Theban chiefs, Timagenidas and Attaginus, volunteered to surrender to Pausanias to spare the city further siege. But when agreement was made with Pausanias, Attaginus fled and escaped, and sent his children to Pausanias in his place. Pausanias, however, refused to hold them guilty for he did not consider the children responsible for their father's offense. But the other men surrendered by the Thebans he took to Corinth and slew. In 478 B.C. he continued the war against Persia, took Cyprus and, when he was besieging Byzantium (which he subsequently took, 477 B.C.), he set up a great bowl as an offering at the entrance to the Euxine Sea. Later, Pausanias seems to have nourished an ambition to become tyrant of Greece, and to this end he seems to have conducted a treasonable correspondence with Xerxes. He was recalled to Sparta for trial but was acquitted of the charges. He then returned to Byzantium and seized the Straits, but was driven out (c475 B.C.) by the Athenians under Cimon. Returning to Sparta, he plotted a revolt of the helots. This was exposed at the last moment and he was forced to flee. He took refuge in the sanctuary of Athena on the Acropolis of Sparta, and was starved to death there by order of the ephors as a punishment for his treason (c466 B.C.).

Pausanias. Spartan king, colleague of Agis I; reigned 445–426 and 408–394 B.C. He brought an end to the civil war in Attica that followed the defeat of Athens in the Peloponnesian War, and helped the Athenians to restore their democracy (403 B.C.). He was known to be an opponent of the Spartan general Lysander. In a Spartan attack on Thebes (395 B.C.) Pausanias marching from the south, was to meet Lysander marching from the north, at Haliartus. Lysander arrived first and was forced into battle by the Haliartians and was killed. By the time Pausanias arrived an Athenian force had come to the aid of the Thebans, and Pausanias felt his position was hopeless. He recovered the body of Lysander and then asked for a burial truce, thereby admitting defeat. Afterward, the Spartans accused him of betraying Lysander and of refusing to fight, and condemned him to death. However, since he did not return to Sparta, the sentence could not be carried out, and he died an exile in Tegea.

Peisistratus (pī-sis′tra-tus). See *Pisistratus.*

Pelopidas (pḙ-lop′i-dạs). Theban general, killed at Cynoscephalae, Thessaly, 364 B.C. He was the great and good friend of the Theban patriot Epaminondas, and like him hated the Spartan overlords of the city, but unlike Epaminondas, Pelopidas went to Athens as an exile. Aware that Thebes could not be freed by force, he resolved to free it by guile. With six friends, all disguised as hunters, he crossed Mount Cithaeron and mingled with the Theban peasants who returned within the city walls at nightfall. In this manner the

---

fat, fāte, fär, fåll, àsk, fãre; net, mē, hėr; pin, pīne; not, nōte, möve, nôr; up, lūte, pùll; oi, oil; ou out; (lightened) ḙlect, agǫny, ụnite;

conspirators entered the city safely. Another conspirator hid them in his house. Still another conspirator invited the Spartan polemarchs to his house for a great banquet, at which, as a special lure, he promised the presence of some beautiful women in whom the Spartans were interested. In the course of the banquet, it is said, a letter was delivered to one of the Spartan polemarchs, but he, enjoying himself, said he would tend to business the next day, and put it away unread. The letter advised him that a conspiracy was afoot. The Spartans called for the women who had been promised them. When all the attendants had left the room the women, heavily veiled, were brought in and seated themselves beside the Spartans. They were invited to lift their veils by the amorous Spartans. As they did so the "women" buried daggers in the bodies of their hated Spartan masters, for the women were Pelopidas and his six companions. Following the deaths of the polemarchs, Pelopidas and his friends went to the houses of other Spartan leaders and killed them, and freed the political prisoners. Those Theban patriots who hated the Spartans but had felt the time was not ripe for action, now joined Pelopidas and the revolution was successfully proclaimed. Athenian volunteers who had helped in securing the overthrow of Sparta were afterwards repudiated by Athens. But in this manner Thebes was liberated (379 B.C.). Later, Pelopidas was one of the Theban generals in the army of Epaminondas. The night before the battle of Leuctra, some say, a vision came to Pelopidas as he slept. Nearby his tent were the tombs of the Leuctrides, daughters of a local hero, Scedasus. Pelopidas dreamed that he saw the Leuctrides crying at their tombs and cursing the Spartans. Scedasus appeared to him and commanded him to sacrifice a maiden with auburn hair to the Leuctrides if he wished to defeat the Spartans in battle. The vision disturbed Pelopidas. Next day he related it to the generals and seers of the army. Some said such a maiden should be sacrificed at once, and cited the sacrifice of Macaria, daughter of Heracles, to bring victory against Eurystheus, and that of Menoeceus, son of Creon, for the defense of Thebes. Others held that such sacrifices would never be demanded by gods. While they were discussing the matter, a filly with a shining red coat broke away from the herd and ran through the camp. One of the soothsayers who was discussing the vision of

(obscured) errant, ardent, actor; ch, chip; g, go; th, thin; ᴛʜ, then; y, you;
(variable) ḍ as d or j, ṣ as s or sh, ṭ as t or ch, ẓ as z or zh.

Pelopidas cried out to him that here was the sacred victim,
a maiden sent by the gods to be sacrificed. All agreed to
accept the gift of the gods. They wreathed the head of the
colt with flowers, led her to the tombs of the Leuctrides,
prayed, and sacrificed her. On that same day, the Thebans
overcame the Spartans at Leuctra (371 B.C.). Pelopidas
brought Thessaly under Theban protection and arranged
an alliance with Macedonia, and took hostages, including
young Philip, who was to become the ruler of Macedonia. In
368 B.C., when he was on his way home, he stopped at the
camp of Alexander of Pherae who, without his knowledge,
had become an ally of Athens. Alexander detained him, but
he was released through the intervention of Epaminondas in
command of a Theban army. In 364 B.C. he started for
Thessaly again at the head of an expedition. Before he left
there was an eclipse of the sun, an evil omen. At Cynoscephalae (364 B.C.) he defeated the forces of Alexander of
Pherae. However, in the moment of victory he happened to
spy Alexander himself, and rashly rushed against him. Alexander escaped to his guards and Pelopidas, pursuing recklessly, was killed.

Perdiccas I (pėr-dik′as). King of Macedonia, the legendary
founder of the Macedonian kingdom, active c650 B.C.
Herodotus tells the following story concerning him: Perdiccas, a descendant of Temenus, the Heraclid who won Argos
as his share of the Peloponnesus, fled from Argos with his
brothers, Gauanes and Aeropus. They went first to Illyria,
and then to Macedonia. Arrived in Macedonia, the three
brothers hired themselves out as laborers to the king; one
tended the horses, another the cows, and Perdiccas, the
youngest, looked after the young stock. At this time even the
kings were poor, and the king's wife prepared the meals. She
noticed that each time she baked bread the loaf for Perdiccas
swelled to twice its normal size. She pointed this phenomenon out to the king, who recognized it as an omen but did
not understand what it meant. In fear he ordered the three
brothers before him and commanded them to leave his kingdom. They agreed to but first demanded to be paid their
wages. At this the king was infuriated. The sun, shining
down the chimney of the room in which they were standing,
made a patch of sunshine of the floor. Pointing to this the
king said, "There are the wages you deserve; take them."

The two older brothers were stunned at this injustice, but Perdiccas took a knife and made a mark around the patch of sunlight and said he accepted the payment. Then he took the light of the sun on his breast three times, and the brothers departed. When the king learned of this last gesture, and was warned that it must have some meaning, he sent horsemen after the brothers, to slay them. But they had crossed a river, one revered in Argos, and when the horsemen came to the river its waters rose and swelled so that the horsemen dared not cross over and thus the brothers escaped. They went to Mount Bermius, which is so cold that no one can ascend it. Some say this mountain is near the wonderful rose gardens of Midas. From this mountain Perdiccas and his brothers gradually conquered all of Macedonia, and Perdiccas became king.

Perdiccas II. King of Macedon, c450–413 B.C. He was at one time an ally of Athens, but became an adversary and stirred up a revolt of the cities of Chalcidice against Athens (433–432 B.C.). He persuaded the inhabitants of the Chalcidian cities on the coast to abandon them and retire to the strong city of Olynthus to oppose Athens. It was largely owing to the maneuvering of Perdiccas that the Chalcidians invited the Spartan general Brasidas into the region. Perdiccas helped to defray the expenses of the Spartan army, and Mende, Acanthus, and Scione were won over to Sparta. Shortly afterward Perdiccas again changed sides. He abandoned Brasidas in a perilous position and helped Athens to prevent reinforcements from coming to his aid.

Perdiccas III. King of Macedon (364–359 B.C.). He was a son of Amyntas and a brother of Philip II of Macedon. With the aid of an Athenian fleet under Iphicrates, various pretenders to the Macedonian throne were crushed and Perdiccas secured it under the regency of Ptolemy Alorus. He assassinated Ptolemy, who had killed his brother Alexander and had married Eurydice, the mother of Alexander, Perdiccas, and Philip. He then threw off the influence of Thebes and allied himself to Athens. Perdiccas was killed, 359 B.C., in battle against the Illyrians.

Perdiccas. One of the generals of Alexander the Great; assassinated in Egypt, 321 B.C. He was the son of Orontes, an independent prince of Macedonia. Before setting out to conquer Asia Alexander impoverished himself by giving away his estates, farms, and revenues to his friends so that they would have enough money and provisions to follow him in comfort. Perdiccas asked him what he had kept for himself. "My hopes," Alexander is said to have replied. Perdiccas then announced that Alexander's soldiers would be the partners in his hopes, and refused to accept the estate Alexander offered to him. After the death of Alexander (323 B.C.) Perdiccas became regent for Alexander's son who was subsequently born to Roxana. He wished to keep Alexander's empire intact, although he allied himself to Ptolemy, who wished to break it up, against Antipater and Antigonus. He set out to subdue Asia Minor and conquered Cappadocia, 322 B.C. Antigonus had refused to help him in the conquest of Asia Minor, and when Perdiccas set out against him he fled to Antipater and Craterus and asked their aid on the ground that Perdiccas intended to seize the throne. Ptolemy abandoned Perdiccas and joined them. Perdiccas moved to attack the allies but was unsuccessful in an attempt to cross the Nile at Pelusium and was defeated. His soldiers mutinied and murdered him.

Periander (per-i-an'dèr). Tyrant of Corinth (c625–585 B.C.). He was a son of Cypselus, whom he succeeded on the throne of Corinth. At first he ruled mildly, but became ever more harsh as time passed. According to Herodotus, he sent a messenger to Thrasybulus, tyrant of Miletus, to inquire how best to secure his government. Thrasybulus took the messenger to a field of wheat. Without saying a word Thrasybulus walked through the field, knocking off and throwing away the ears of wheat that grew the highest. He then, still without replying to the question Periander's messenger had asked him, sent the messenger back to Corinth. Periander, on hearing of this performance from his messenger, understood that Thrasybulus was advising him to destroy all the leading citizens. He immediately set about to follow this advice, and went at it with great energy, slaying the leading citizens. One day he stripped the clothes off all the women of Corinth whom he had ordered to go to the temple of Hera, because a message from the Thesprotian oracle said that his wife Melissa, whom he had slain, was cold. She sent word that the clothes buried with her did not keep her warm because they had not been burned. He caused the clothes he now stripped from the Corinthian women to be burned

fat, fāte, fär, fâll, àsk, fâre; net, mē, hèr; pin, pīne; not, nōte, möve, nôr; up, lūte, pùll; oi, oil; ou out; (lightened) ēlect, agǫny, ūnite;

in a pit. It was during Periander's reign, according to
Herodotus, that Arion, the musician, was set upon by the
crew of the ship in which he was returning to Corinth, and
was compelled to cast himself into the sea. A dolphin took
him on its back and bore him to Corinth. Periander dis-
believed the story Arion had to tell him when he arrived in
Corinth. When the ship on which Arion had set sail from
Italy arrived Periander questioned the crew concerning
Arion. They assured him that Arion was safe in Italy, enjoying great prosperity. Periander thereupon produced Arion,
gave them the lie, and put them to death. By his wife Melissa
Periander had two sons. When they were 17 and 18 years old
respectively they were entertained by Procles, their mother's father. He treated them with great kindness and interest, and one day asked them if they now knew who had
caused the death of their mother. The older boy, a dull
youth, paid no attention to the question and later forgot that
it had even been asked. Lycophron, the younger son, realized that it was his father who had slain his mother. When
he returned to Corinth he refused to have anything to do
with his father, and was cast out by him. Ultimately he found
refuge in Corcyra. As Periander advanced in years he wished
for the return of Lycophron. He realized that his older son
was doltish and wished Lycophron to succeed him on the
throne. Lycophron was at last persuaded to return when
Periander agreed that he would withdraw from Corinth if
Lycophron would return, but before Lycophron could depart the Corcyreans, angry at Periander because he had
abducted 300 boys from the best families and sent them to
Lydia to become eunuchs, seized Lycophron and put him to
death. Thus an oracle, pronounced before the birth of Cypselus, father of Periander, was fulfilled. It was to the effect
that Cypselus and his sons—but not his grandsons—would
rule Corinth. Despite almost universal agreement on the
despotism of Periander, he appears to have acted for the
good of Corinth, establishing colonies to the north, promoting trade, extending Corinthian influence, and developing
a program of public works. He is usually counted among the
Seven Wise Men of Greece.

Pericles (per'i-klēz). Athenian statesman, general, and orator,
born probably c495 B.C.; died 429 B.C., of the plague, at
Athens. He was a member of a powerful and influential

(obscured) errạnt, ardẹnt, actọr; ch, chip; g, go; th, thin; ᴛн, then; y, you;
(variable) ḍ as d or j, ş as s or sh, ţ as t or ch, ᶎ as z or zh.

family of Athens, of the tribe of Acamanthis. His father Xanthippus fought at the battle of Mycale (479 B.C.) and was prominent politically. His mother Agariste, a member of the Alcmaeonidae, and a niece of Clisthenes, dreamed a few days before he was born that she had given birth to a lion. He received an excellent education. He studied music and politics with Damon, heard the lectures of the Eleatic philosopher Zeno, and was chiefly instructed and strongly influenced by Anaxagoras of Clazomenae, whose rationalistic philosophy and scientific approach freed his pupil and friend to a large extent from the superstitions of his age. As an example of the methods of Anaxagoras, it was said that a ram's head, from which a single horn grew, was brought to Pericles. Soothsayers said this meant that the two factions of Athens would unite under Pericles. Anaxagoras took the specimen, dissected it, and showed that the single horn was developed owing to physical causes. In the event, both Anaxagoras and the soothsayers were honored: Anaxagoras for his science; the soothsayers because Pericles did in fact become the head of a united Athens.

As a member of a powerful family and as a leader, Pericles was not immune to personal attacks. His head was long and pointed and the comic poets gleefully spoke of him as "Onion Head." To cover up the malformation of his head, statues and pictures of Pericles always portrayed him helmeted. His critics said he was vain, proud, and supercilious. However, he was a man of great self-control and patience, and pursued his course. This was, at first, to stay out of public life, for he feared that his many advantages—good looks, wealth, oratorical gifts, and powerful connections, might draw too much envy and lead to his ostracism. (Ostracism was a means to secure the exile of any man who might be a potential source of unrest, disorder, or danger to the state; it was not necessary for a man to have committed a crime, civic or otherwise, to be ostracized.) After the disappearance of Aristides, Themistocles, and Cimon from public life, Pericles became prominent. His policy was to win the support and respect of the masses. This he did with money and by weakening the authority of the Areopagus, whose members came from the richest classes of the state. At the same time, he instituted democratic reforms. He reorganized state office-holding so that henceforth the office-holders were

fat, fāte, fär, fåll, ȧsk, fāre; net, mē, hėr; pin, pīne; not, nōte, möve, nôr; up, lūte, pùll; oi, oil; ou out; (lightened) ēlect, agǫny, ūnite;

paid, thus making it possible for all citizens to accept office, and even to seek it. His personal life was simple, with limited social connections, and he made it a point not to make many public appearances or speeches. He was a speaker of such eloquence that he was called "Olympian," but he wisely realized that his eloquence would lose its golden lustre if people heard it too frequently. His chief rival at first was Cimon, whom he caused to be ostracized (c459 B.C.), but who was recalled later. After the death of Cimon, Thucydides emerged as a rival. Pericles wooed the masses with diversions, and sent out colonies—to the Chersonese, Naxos, and Sybaris, which had been destroyed three times and was now rebuilt as Thurii. Through these colonies he siphoned off some of the excess population of Athens, and at the same time strengthened the outposts of the empire. He sent envoys throughout the Greek world, calling for the fulfillment of the sacrifices that had been promised during the Persian War and for the rebuilding of the temples that the barbarians had destroyed. However, owing to Spartan resistance to it, this Pan-Hellenic project, of which Athens would have been the leader, failed. He declared that the rebuilding of the temples was a sacred duty, in gratitude for the help the gods gave the Greeks in the Persian War. To fulfill it, Pericles set about beautifying the city. His critics claimed he used the money of the Delian League for this purpose. The funds, contributed by the allies, had been kept in the Treasury at Delos. Pericles transferred the funds to Athens (454 B.C.) and justified the transfer on the grounds that Athens must fulfill her sacred duty to the gods, that Athens had earned it by keeping the Persians at bay during and after the Persian Wars as she had undertaken to do, and on the ground that it provided employment at home. He made Phidias superintendent of all public building. Under his charge Periclean architecture was created; the Parthenon was built, a temple of Initiation at Eleusis was erected, the long walls between Athens and Piraeus were finished, a temple of Athena Nike was built on the southwestern side of the Acropolis, a temple of Hephaestus rose on the Hill of Colonus, and one of Poseidon was built at Sunium. The temples were adorned within and without by magnificent sculptured groups, as the pediments of the Parthenon, and images of the gods, notably the statue of Athena in the Parthenon, by

Phidias. During the construction of the Odeum a workman was injured. Pericles cured him, thanks to the instructions the goddess Athena gave him in a dream it is said, and in honor of this cure he caused a golden statue of the goddess, made by Phidias, to be placed near the altar on the Acropolis.

With the ostracism of his opponent Thucydides (441 B.C.), Pericles became sole master of Athens. From then on, according to Plutarch, he was a changed man. He became much sterner with the people, and controlled them through the two-edged sword of hope and fear. At the same time, he was careful of the public good, and although he had great power and opportunity, he did not add a single drachma to the estate his father had left him. He maintained himself as undisputed master of Athens through his wisdom and his eloquence, and never lost sight of the fact that his acts were subject to review by the people at the end of each year. As it was, he was chosen one of the ten generals of Athens year after year and, in fact, he was the general among generals.

His policy of increasing Athenian power and influence on the Greek mainland met with little success. Aegina remained an unwilling ally, Megara and Boeotia were lost, a revolt in Euboea was quelled, and the Thirty Years' Peace was arranged with Sparta (446–445 B.C.). In the Sacred War (448 B.C.) he had seized the temple of Delphi, which had been handed over to the Delphians by the Spartans, and restored it to the Phocians. The Spartans had engraved on the left side of the bronze wolf, by the great altar, their privilege of consulting the oracle first. Pericles caused a claim for the same privilege for the Athenians to be engraved on the wolf's right side. However, the friendship with the Phocians was short-lived. As a result of these setbacks, he turned his attention to strengthening Athens as a sea power. In 448 B.C. peace was concluded with the Persians. He pacified the Chersonese and secured the Greek cities of the Pontus.

Pericles' wife bore him two sons, Xanthippus and Paralus, but the couple was so unhappy that they separated by mutual consent. She married another and he took as his mistress Aspasia, a beautiful, intelligent Milesian, who excelled at political discussion and was a friend of some of the leading thinkers of the day. She was attacked by the comic poets as the "new Omphale," Cratinus plainly called her a

fat, fãte, fär, fåll, åsk, fãre; net, mē, hėr; pin, pīne; not, nōte, mŏve, nôr; up, lūte, pùll; oi, oil; ou out; (lightened) ĕlect, agŏny, ūnite;

prostitute, others spoke of her as Deianira and Hera. Some said she wrote Pericles' speeches. It was said that she urged Pericles to wage war on Samos, to avenge her native city of Miletus. He conquered Samos (440 B.C.), and established a democracy, then sailed off, leaving a few ships behind. The Samians revolted, seized the Greek ships and branded their Athenian prisoners on their foreheads with an owl, symbol of Athens. Pericles returned to Samos, besieged it for nine months and forced its surrender. He razed the walls and levied a fine on the Samians. On his return to Athens he celebrated a magnificent funeral for the fallen and was chosen to make the funeral oration, a speech which won him much applause.

In 433 B.C. he sent a small fleet to observe in the war between Corcyra and Corinth. The fleet was to assist the Corcyraeans defensively. This was one of the incidents that marked the prelude to the Peloponnesian War, and was an excuse for the Spartans to claim that Athens had broken the Thirty Years' Peace. Pericles offered to submit all questions in dispute between Athens and Sparta to arbitration, but Sparta refused. Embassies went back and forth. The Spartans demanded that the Athenians drive out the curse of the goddess. This was a reference to the followers of Cylon, who (c632 B.C.) were slain after having been promised safe conduct if they would come out of the temple on the Acropolis where they had fled as suppliants after an abortive attempt to win control of the city. The curse was that the family of the Alcmaeonidae should be exiled from Athens forever. The Alcmaeonidae had returned to Athens and Pericles was the most prominent member, as well as the most powerful man in Athens. The Athenians replied with a demand that the Spartans drive out the curse of Taenarus, referring to the slaying of Pausanias, and the death of some suppliants at the temple of Poseidon at Taenarus. These were pretexts. The Spartans had decided on war as the only means of arresting the growing power of Athens.

After listening to their allies and ambassadors from Athens who sought peace, the Spartans declared that the Thirty Years' Peace had been broken and decided for war (431 B.C.). Pericles' strategy was to allow the Spartans to exhaust themselves by attacks on Athens, while Athens remained inside its walls. He remained unmoved by the pleas of many to attack the Spartans. He sent out a fleet to harass the Peloponnesus and the Spartans withdrew, but returned the next year. In that year (430 B.C.), plague broke out in crowded Athens. His enemies blamed it on Pericles. He manned a fleet, and was on board, ready to sail, when there was an eclipse of the sun. In spite of the unfavorable omen he sailed, but his expedition was not very successful, and when he returned he was deprived of his command and fined. He was now attacked by many, including his son Xanthippus. But the latter died of the plague, and Pericles withdrew with dignity, only losing his composure when his younger son also succumbed to the plague. A year later he was recalled to power in Athens by the people, but soon he too fell a victim to the plague and died, in 429 B.C.

The empire of which Pericles was the leader was composed of many unwilling states; they were ruled with an autocratic hand, were deprived of all control over their policies and destinies, and were compelled to contribute to the treasury at Athens. At home, his law (451–450 B.C.) that only those whose parents were legally wedded Athenians could be citizens was most undemocratic and limiting; the law rose to plague him in his connection with Aspasia the Milesian. At the summit of power he had, naturally, many enemies. He was attacked indirectly through Phidias, who was accused of stealing the gold he was supposed to have used on his statue of Athena. This accusation was disproved, since Phidias had provided that the gold could be removed for weighing. Phidias was next accused of impiety, because he showed his own and Pericles' likenesses on the shield of the goddess. He was cast into prison and died, or as some say, he died an exile. Coming closer, the critics of Pericles attacked Aspasia as an alien, but he was able to protect her. In addition, his old friend and teacher, Anaxagoras, was accused of impiety and fled. Plutarch claims that because of these troubles Pericles was anxious for war. Other witnesses do not bear out this conclusion. Rather, war between the two most powerful states of Greece was inevitable since they could not agree, as Cimon had so devoutly hoped, on a course by which their powers would be united

The contributions of Pericles to Athens and to the western world were great. He ended the Persian Wars, confirmed Athens as the leading sea power of Greece, and

---

fat, fāte, fär, fȧll, ȧsk, fãre; net, mē, hèr; pin, pīne; not, nōte, mȯve, nôr; up, lūte, pu̇ll; oi, oil; ou out; (lightened) ḝlect, agǫny, ṵnite;

established democratic reforms that tended to strengthen Athenian democracy. He brought commercial prosperity to the city, which he so beautified that the period of his ascendancy came to be known as the Golden Age of Athens, and he encouraged art and literature. The funeral oration which he gave for the dead who first fell in the Peloponnesian War contrasts Sparta and Athens and is a testament of his ideas of and ideals for Athens. In it he describes the Athenian democracy as he sees it: an administration that favors the many rather than the few, whose laws provide equal justice for all, and whose offices are open to any one with capacity; an administration that is made possible and strengthened by public and private respect for magistrates and the law. To this is added: diversion for the spirit in the form of public games and sacrifices, beautiful buildings, and a flourishing commerce that brings the products of the world to Athens. In military affairs and foreign policy, Athens is a city open to the world, welcoming all, even at the risk of being observed by an enemy, because the native spirit of the Athenians is its greatest strength and protection. In developing these points he names Athens the school of Hellas, and proudly declares to the Athenians that we "have left imperishable monuments behind us."

Pericles the Younger. Athenian commander; executed 406 B.C. He was the son of Pericles and his mistress Aspasia. By a Decree of the People he was declared legitimate in 429 B.C. He was one of the Athenian commanders who defeated the Peloponnesians under Callicratidas in the sea fight at Arginusae (406 B.C.). In this battle, which was an Athenian victory, 25 Athenian ships and their crews were lost. For some reason, unknown, the other ships did not stop to pick up the men in the water. The Athenians felt that many of these men might have been saved, and anger over their loss raged against the commanders who had not ordered their rescue. Eight of the commanders were tried by the Athenian Assembly, rather than by constituted courts, for criminal negligence. The commanders were found guilty, their property was confiscated, and they were condemned to death. Pericles was one of six who were actually executed (406 B.C.).

Perseus (pėr'sūs, -sē-us). Last king of Macedon, son of Philip V, whom he succeeded in 179 B.C. He began war with the

Romans in 172 B.C. and defeated them in several engagements. The Romans elected Aemilius Paulus as consul and sent him to Greece to command the Roman forces against Perseus, whose army was encamped near Mount Olympus. Aemilius brought his forces up by an encircling movement and prepared to attack Perseus at Pydna (168 B.C.). On the eve of the battle an eclipse of the moon brought terror to the Macedonians, who took it as an omen of the eclipse of Perseus. Perseus had great treasure, but was so miserly he refused to pay his mercenaries and duped his allies. He kept his treasure but was soundly defeated by Aemilius Paulus at Pydna and fled to Pella. From there he sailed to Samothrace and took refuge, with his wife and children, in the temple of the Dioscuri. His gold was stolen by Cretan sailors and the Macedonians, enraged by his flight, his oppressive rule, and by their defeat which they attributed to him, seized him and turned him over to Aemilius Paulus. Perseus begged to be spared the humiliation of being exhibited as a captive in a triumphal procession. Aemilius scorned him for his cowardice, and suggested that he could avoid the humiliation by committing suicide. Perseus could not bring himself to this step. With his children, his captured chariot and armor, he was paraded as a captive before the throngs of Rome (167 B.C.). In the end, some say, Perseus starved himself to death in prison. Others say the soldiers who guarded him prevented him from sleeping so that at length, worn out, he died.

Phalaris (fal′a̲-ris). Tyrant of Acragas in Sicily from c570 to c554 B.C., notorious for his cruelty (notably his human sacrifices in a heated brazen bull). The inventor of the bull was the first victim to be roasted alive. The spuriousness of some 148 epistles which passed under his name was shown by the classical scholar Richard Bentley in his *Epistles of Phalaris* (1697).

Phalereus (fa̲-lē′rös, fa̲-lir′ē-us), **Demetrius.** See **Demetrius Phalereus.**

Pharnabazus (fär-na̲-bā′zus). Persian satrap of Phrygia; fl. c400 B.C. After the complete failure of the Athenian expedition to Sicily (415–413 B.C.), Pharnabazus, with the idea of recovering the Athenian cities of Asia Minor for Persia, made an alliance with Sparta. He was a loyal and energetic ally, aiding the Spartans with men and above all, with money, and pro-

---

fat, fāte, fär, fâll, ȧsk, fãre; net, mē, hèr; pin, pīne; not, nōte, möve, nôr; up, lūte, p·ull; oi, oil; ou out; (lightened) ḝlect, agǫny, ūnite;

viding vigorous support to them to the end of the Peloponnesian War. Though he continued as a friend of Sparta
he did not approve of the high-handed methods of the Spartan leader Lysander in Asia Minor and secured his recall.
When the Spartans waged war against the Persian king Artaxerxes they treacherously turned on Pharnabazus (399
B.C.). King Agesilaus led an army against his satrapy and
plundered it up to the walls of the city where Pharnabazus
lived (395 B.C.). Pharnabazus asked for a meeting with
Agesilaus. Agesilaus arrived first and sat down on the grass.
Members of Pharnabazus' train came and began to spread
rich rugs for their master, but when he saw that Agesilaus
sat simply on the ground he took his seat beside him and
waved away his minions with their luxurious carpets. He
addressed the Spartan king. He reminded him that he had
ever been a loyal and generous friend of Sparta, that he had
never betrayed his trust as other satraps had done, but had
throughout helped Sparta in the war against Athens. Now
the Spartans rewarded him by ravaging his province so that
he could hardly get his dinner except by picking up the
scraps the Spartans left. Was this, he asked with dignity, a
fitting reward for the services he had rendered to Sparta?
Agesilaus answered that since Sparta was at war with the
Persian king she must harass and fight against all the parts
of his empire, including the province of Pharnabazus. Agesilaus invited him to revolt against the king and to join the
Spartans as an ally. Pharnabazus displayed the same loyalty
to his king as he had shown as an ally of Sparta. If Artaxerxes, he replied, replaced him and put another in command over him as satrap, he would be glad to become the
friend and ally of Sparta. But as long as he held a post of
command under the king he would support him with all his
strength and would fight against his enemies with all his
might. Agesilaus was so impressed with his loyalty that he
agreed to withdraw from the territory of Pharnabazus at
once, and to respect it in the future. Afterward, Pharnabazus
joined the Athenian admiral Conon to his fleet, and with him
defeated the Spartans at Cnidus, 394 B.C. The following year
he accompanied Conon with a fleet and attacked the shores
of Laconia. On his return to his satrapy he left the fleet with
Conon, and gave the Athenians money to rebuild the Long
Walls and to fortify the Piraeus. He opposed the King's

(obscured) errạnt, ardẹnt, actọr; ch, chip; g, go; th, thin; ᵺн, then; y, you;
(variable) ḍ as d or j, ş as s or sh, ṭ as t or ch, ẓ as z or zh.

Peace (387 B.C.), brought about by Spartan diplomacy, but accepted it on being given a daughter of King Artaxerxes in marriage. He attempted (385 and 373 B.C.) unsuccessfully to invade Egypt.

Pharnaces I (fär'nạ-sēz). King of Pontus (c185–169 B.C.). He conquered Sinope in 183 B.C., and unsuccessfully made war on Eumenes II of Pergamum.

Pharnaces II. King of Pontus (c63–47 B.C.); son of Mithridates VI (Mithridates the Great) of Pontus. On the suicide of Mithridates in 63 B.C., he revolted and made himself master of that part of his father's dominions lying along the Cimmerian Bosporus. He afterward invaded Pontus, but was defeated by Caesar at Zela in 47 B.C. In the triumph celebrated at Rome for this victory, one of the chariots carried the inscription: "Veni, vidi, vici" (I came, I saw, I conquered).

Pheidon (fī'dọn). King of Argos; fl. probably in the middle of the 7th century B.C. He reunited the practically independent Argive cities under his strong and able rule and Argos again played a prominent part in the affairs of the Peloponnesus. He marched at the head of an army across Arcadia to Olympia, seized the management of the Olympic Games from the Eleans, and presided over the festival himself. Afterward he restored control of the games to Pisa, in whose territory the sanctuary of Zeus at Olympia was, and who had presided over the games until Elis wrested control away from them. Pheidon also introduced a system of weights and measures into Argos which was adopted also in the Peloponnesus and in Athens. He is also said to have struck the first Greek coins in Aegina.

Phidippides (fī-dip'i-dēz). Athenian herald and athlete. When the Persians landed at Marathon (490 B.C.), he was sent as a courier from Athens to Sparta, asking the latter city's help against the invader. On the way he was met by Pan, near Mount Parthenius. The god asked him why the Athenians, to whom he had always shown himself friendly, neglected him, and promised to aid them in the coming struggle with the Persians. Phidippides continued his journey to Sparta, covering the 150-miles distance in two days, according to Herodotus. In Sparta he delivered the Athenian call for aid. The Spartans, highly sympathetic, promised to go to the assistance of the Athenians, but regretted that for religious

fat, fāte, fär, fåll, àsk, fãre; net, mē, hèr; pin, pīne; not, nōte, mõve, nôr; up, lūte, pùll; oi, oil; ou out; (lightened) ẹlect, agǫny, ụnite;

reasons they could not set out until the full of the moon.
When they did arrive the battle was over; the Athenians,
with Plataean aid, had soundly beaten the Persians at Marathon. On his return to Athens Phidippides reported his conversation with Pan, and after the battle of Marathon the
Athenians raised a sanctuary to the god under the Acropolis,
for they considered that he had helped them as he promised,
and caused the Persians to withdraw in panic before the
Athenian onslaught.

Philadelphus (fil-a̯-del′fus), *Attalus.* See *Attalus II.*

Philadelphus, Ptolemy. See *Ptolemy II.*

Philip II (fil′ip). King of Macedon (359–336 B.C.), born 382
B.C.; assassinated at Aegae, the old capital of Macedonia, in
336 B.C. He was the son of Amyntas II and Eurydice, and the
father of Alexander the Great. Philip lived some years as a
youth at Thebes, whither he had been taken as a hostage
(367 B.C.), and it was from the Boeotians, under the guidance of Epaminondas whom he knew and admired, that he
received his military training. For some reason he was permitted to return to Macedonia (364 B.C.). The Macedonian
kings, from their ancient fortress capital at Aegae, had
power over all the area on the north and northwest coasts
of the Thermaic Gulf (ancient Myrtoan Sea, modern Gulf of
Salonika). Beyond this area of relatively complete control,
their power extended to the borders of the Illyrians in the
west and to those of the Paeonians in the north, but the
tribes within the region, with the active assistance of the
Illyrians and Paeonians, continually contested Macedonian
rule. King Perdiccas, older brother of Philip, was slain (359
B.C.), in one of the frequent wars with the Illyrians. His son
Amyntas, the legitimate heir, was a child. Philip became
guardian of Amyntas and immediately undertook to overcome the domestic and foreign enemies of Macedonia. His
first problem was to beat back the pretenders to the throne.
He defeated an Athenian fleet that came to the aid of one
of them. Out of respect and admiration for the Athenians,
he released without ransom those whom he had taken prisoner. His other rivals were also repulsed. The Macedonian
kings were of Greek stock and Philip's lifelong policy was to
identify himself with Greece and Greek culture. Having
secured his power at home he next subdued the Paeonians
and the Illyrians (358 B.C.), thus clearly establishing his con-

trol over his troublesome neighbors. In the same year he made a secret agreement with the Athenians by which he undertook to recapture their colony of Amphipolis on the coast of western Thrace in return for the free city of Pydna, on the west coast of the Thermaic Gulf. He took Amphipolis (358) which commanded the gold mines of Mount Pangaeus in Thrace, deceived the Athenians and kept it. As they had been perfectly willing to betray Pydna they had no just grounds to cry treachery against Philip. This did not prevent them from doing so, however. He fortified Crenides, a gold-mining settlement on the coast of Thrace opposite the island of Thasus, and renamed it Philippi for himself. The capture of Amphipolis and the fortified settlement of Philippi gave him control of a gold-mining area which made Macedonia the richest state in Greece. About this time he abandoned the old inland capital at Aegae and moved his court to Pella, somewhat nearer the sea. He took Pydna and Potidaea and handed them over to the Olynthian Confederacy. Wielding supreme authority, he now set aside his nephew and took the title of king. The next year was devoted to consolidating his power and improving his army. Men of all tribes were put under arms and had constant practice in actual warfare. The Macedonian phalanx, so skillfully and successfully used by Philip and later by his son, was organized and drilled into a mobile, effective weapon. In 357 he married Olympias, daughter of a prince of Epirus, a stormy and mystic princess who ultimately caused his death. In 356 she bore his famous son Alexander. He captured Methone (c353), the last city of Athens on the Thermaic Gulf, and on the invitation of the Thessalians, he marched into Thessaly to take part in the Sacred War against Phocis. He was forced to withdraw by the Phocians, but the following year he returned and made himself master of Thessaly, having decisively beaten the Phocians who were in temporary control there. At Thermopylae (352) he was momentarily checked by a force sent by Athens, Sparta, and Achaea to oppose his descent into Greece. In the same year he carried on successful campaigns in Thrace.

By 352 B.C. Philip had organized a formidable army and secured his treasury by control of the gold mines on the coasts of Thrace. He had subdued the rebellious tribes on his borders and won control of the lands along the north

fat, fāte, fär, fâll, ȧsk, fãre; net, mē, hėr; pin, pīne; not, nōte, mȯve; nôr; up, lūte, pu̇ll; oi, oil; ou out; (lightened) ẹlect, agǫny, ūnite;

Aegean from Thermopylae to the Propontis. His ambition
was to unite all Greece under the overlordship of Macedonia
and to bring the Greek culture which he admired, and of
which he considered himself an heir, to Macedonia. He admired Athens above all Greek states and would have preferred to win her friendship. But Athens rejected his friendly
overtures. The city that had once been the leader of the
Greek world hoped to recover her power in the Aegean and
to bring down Macedonia. At about this period Demosthenes in Athens began delivering the speeches known as
the *Philippics,* warning the Greeks that Philip would eventually conquer all Greece unless he were opposed. On the
other hand, there were some who saw in Philip a potential
uniter of the quarreling Greek states. Their view did not
prevail. Athens took every opportunity, no matter how
flimsy and dangerous to herself and her interests, to oppose
Philip. In 349 Philip marched against Chalcidice to punish
Olynthus, which had betrayed him in collusion with Athens.
Most of the cities of Chalcidice submitted without a contest.
Those that did not were taken by force and destroyed, as was
Stagira, a city which he later restored and repopulated in
honor of the philosopher Aristotle, whom he had invited to
become tutor to his son Alexander. In 348 Philip took Olynthus and destroyed it completely. The orations of Demosthenes known as the *Olynthiacs,* whose purpose was to stir
the Athenians to aid Olynthus, resulted in the sending of an
Athenian force to the rescue of Olynthus. But the Athenians
arrived too late. Olynthus had fallen; the city was razed and
its citizens sold into slavery. Philip maintained his tolerant
spirit toward Athens; envoys sent from there to Pella were
courteously received. A peace was made but, thanks to the
intransigence of Demosthenes, the terms were not so broad
as to include the alliance between Athens and Macedonia,
which Philip wanted. When, as a result of the Sacred War,
Phocis was expelled from the Amphictyonic Council (346
B.C.), Macedonia took her place, and Philip presided over
the Pythian Games held in the same year. In 342, by campaigns in Thrace, he made the Thracian kingdom a depend-
ency of Macedonia and built the city of Philippopolis there
as a center of Macedonian influence. In 340–339 he besieged Perinthus and Byzantium. Athens supported his enemies in the region, and without a fleet his sieges were

unsuccessful. In 339 the Amphictyonic Council called on him for aid against the Locrians of Amphissa in a new Sacred War. Philip at once answered the summons. He captured Amphissa, and then went into Boeotia where Athens and Thebes, alarmed at his growing influence in Greece, had united to oppose him. He completely defeated their combined forces at Chaeronea (338 B.C.). He placed a Macedonian garrison over Thebes, but true to his policy of respect and friendship for Athens (which was very shabbily rewarded on the whole), he treated Athens leniently. He released the Athenian prisoners without ransom and gave Oropus to Athens, but compelled her to surrender the Chersonesus to Macedonia. He returned the Athenians who fell in the battle of Chaeronea to Athens for burial, under a guard of honor that included his son. The Athenians set up a statue of Philip in the agora in gratitude for his generosity. After this, Philip marched into the Peloponnesus which submitted without a struggle, except for Sparta, which suffered devastation at his hands for its obstinacy.

Philip was now master of all Greece. He summoned all the Greek states to a congress at Corinth. All except Sparta sent representatives. In the following year (337 B.C.) he was elected commander of the Greek forces to liberate the Greek cities of Asia Minor from the Persians, and to avenge the barbarous acts against the Greeks and their gods committed by the Persians in the days of Xerxes. An advance expedition was sent to the Hellespont under Parmenio, but Philip was assassinated before he could take the field. Despite his genius as a conqueror and administrator he could not keep order in his own household. His wife Olympias, whose reputation was not stainless (to such a degree that it was whispered that Philip was not the father of her great son Alexander), became inflamed at the infidelities of Philip. He had conceived a profound distaste for her when he found a serpent lying beside her as she slept. He had attachments with many women, some of whom were temporarily acknowledged as wives in the polygamous Macedonian court. He fell in love with Cleopatra, niece of his general Attalus, and added to the fury of Olympias by definitely casting her aside to marry Cleopatra. At the wedding feast, Attalus proposed a toast and publicly hoped for a *legitimate* heir. Alexander dashed a cup of wine in the face of Attalus for the insult to his mother. Philip rose to slay his son with his sword, but tripped over a couch as he lunged at him. With scorn, Alexander pointed to his father as a "man who would pass from Europe to Asia but trips in passing from couch to couch." After this Alexander fled the court of Philip and went with his mother to Epirus. When a son was born to Philip and Cleopatra, Alexander feared lest his place in the succession be disturbed. The fire kindled in Olympias by her supposed wrongs had not in the least cooled. She found, with Alexander's knowledge, a tool for her longed-for vengeance. At the marriage of Philip's daughter to the king of Epirus, a pawn of Olympias named Pausanias rushed at Philip as he marched in the wedding procession and stabbed him with a Celtic dagger. Pausanias was caught and killed; Olympias, sister of the bridegroom, was avenged, as she thought, and Alexander's succession was assured. Philip's death fulfilled an oracular pronouncement. The oracle of Trophonius had warned him to beware of a chariot, and because of this Philip never entered one. But it was to no avail: on the ivory hilt of the dagger Pausanias plunged into his side was engraved the figure of a chariot. Philip had done what no Greek state was strong enough to do: he united Greece. His reign marks the end of the old city-state system in Greece and the growth of a Greek nation. By his organization of the army and his selection of generals, he prepared the way for Alexander's conquests.

Philip III (of *Macedon*). [Also: ***Philip III Arrhidaeus.***] King of Macedon 323–317 B.C.; murdered 317 B.C. He was an illegitimate son of Philip II. He was proclaimed king by the troops after Alexander's death in 323 B.C. His own death was caused by Olympias, widow of Philip II and mother of Alexander.

Philip IV (of *Macedon*). King of Macedon; son of Cassander. He reigned for a few months c297 B.C.

Philip V (of *Macedon*). King of Macedon (220–179 B.C.); born 238 B.C.; died 179 B.C. He was a son of Demetrius II. His father died while he was still a child, and the kingdom was governed by a regent, a cousin of Philip's. Philip assumed complete power when the regent died, 220 B.C. He was at war with the Aetolian League (220–217), was allied with Carthage and at war with Rome (later also with the Aetolian League) 214–205 B.C., and began the second war against

(obscured) errant, ardent, actor; ch, chip; g, go; th, thin; ᴛʜ, then; y, you; (variable) ḍ as d or j, ş as s or sh, ṭ as t or ch, ẓ as z or zh.

Rome in 200. He was defeated by Flaminius at Cynoscephalae in 197 B.C., and was thereafter at peace with the Romans, recognizing them as his masters and concentrating on his own Macedonian kingdom. Philip's reign marks the disappearance of Greece as a world power.

Philippides (fi-lip'i-dēz). See *Phidippides.*

Philomelus (fil-ọ-mē'lus). Phocian general of the 4th century B.C., who rallied his countrymen to resist the heavy fines that had been levied on them by the Amphictyonic League that charged them with impiety. He cited the Homeric verses from the *Iliad,* "Phocian warriors. . . . Those who possessed Cyparissus and likewise Pytho the rocky." These verses he made the basis of a claim that Phocis rightfully owned Delphi (Pytho), and proposed to seize it. With the rich treasures of the sanctuary in their possession the Phocians could raise levies to resist the Amphictyonic League. The Phocians took Delphi and fortified the treasury with a wall. Philomelus wished the oracle to continue its prophecies, for he did not want to alienate the rest of the Greek world, but the priestess refused. He threatened the priestess and in alarm she told him to do as he liked. Taking this as permission, he availed himself of the treasures of the sanctuary. One of those said to have been taken by him was the great golden shield given to Delphi by the Lydian king, Croesus. Philomelus and the soldiers he hired with the proceeds of the treasures held off their enemies for years but at last suffered defeat at Neon, on the slopes of Mount Parnassus. Philomelus fought bravely but, covered with wounds, was driven to the edge of a cliff. There, rather than submit to capture, he hurled himself over it to his death.

Philopoemen (fil-ọ-pē'men). General of the Achaean League, called "the Last of the Greeks" because, so it is said, Greece produced no more illustrious men after him. He was born at Megalopolis, Arcadia, Greece, c252 B.C.; drank poison at Messene, Greece, 183 B.C. His father Craugis, an aristocrat, died in Philopoemen's infancy, and he was brought up by a Mantinean exile who lived at Megalopolis. He was well educated, and from childhood showed an interest in and aptitude for the military arts. In young manhood he occupied himself with hunting, tilling his lands, studying the philosophers, reading military histories, and studying the more warlike parts of Homer. He is described as of splendid physique,

powerful, modest in dress and manner, frugal at table, and
homely. Concerning his plain features, Plutarch tells that
once, after he had become general of the Achaean League,
he arrived as a guest at a house in Megara. His hostess who
had never seen him before noted his simple dress and
homeliness and thought he was a servant. She set him to
work chopping wood, which he did without protest or explanation. When his host came home and found his distinguished guest performing the work of a servant he asked the
meaning of it. Philopoemen gravely told him he was "paying
the fine of my deformity."

In 223 B.C. Cleomenes III of Sparta made a surprise attack
on Megalopolis at night and seized the market-place.
Philopoemen escaped with a group of young men. He persuaded them not to treat with Cleomenes, as they were
willing to do, but to go back and win Megalopolis by force
of arms. He and his group joined with the Achaeans and
Arcadians, and the Macedonians under Antigonus, and met
and defeated the Spartans at Sellasia, 222 B.C. In the battle
Philopoemen, a cavalryman, saw that the infantry would
decide the battle. He voluntarily gave up his horse and
joined the foot-soldiers. He fought with great bravery and
skill. It is said that an enemy spear pierced both his thighs
and pinned his legs together. In his determination to keep
fighting, he sank to his knees and by a violent movement of
his legs broke the enemy spear. Antigonus was filled with
admiration for him and invited him to serve under him in
Macedonia. Philopoemen declined. Instead he sailed to
Crete as a leader of mercenaries and took part in a civil war
there. When he returned to Megalopolis, after 11 years, he
was named commander of the Achaean League. With authority and discipline he shaped his forces into a splendid
fighting machine. The mettle of the forces was tested at the
Larisus River (210 B.C.) when, with his allies, he defeated the
Eleans and the Aetolians and killed their commander. He
was now greatly admired and was given the opportunity to
reorganize the infantry. He replaced their short spears and
oblong wicker shields with long spears and round shields,
and gave the foot-soldiers breastplates and greaves to protect their bodies. He was insistent that the soldiers keep
their armor bright, that the glitter of shining armor might
terrify the enemy. Following the defeat of the Eleans and

Aetolians, he engaged the Spartan tyrant Machanidas at Mantinea (207 B.C.). The Achaeans seemed to have lost the battle, but Philopoemen regrouped his forces, chose new ground for his attack, and drew victory from defeat; Machanidas was slain and his severed head was exhibited to the Achaeans. Following the victory he went on and took Tegea, and marched into Laconia and pillaged it at will. After this he was so idolized that when the harpist at the Olympic Games began the ode:

Who to Greece gives the great and glorious jewel of freedom,

all eyes turned to Philopoemen, and the whole company burst into applause. His name alone inspired fear in his enemies: the Thebans withdrew from Megara when it was rumored that Philopoemen was coming to the aid of the city; Nabis, the new tyrant of Sparta, evacuated Messene (201 B.C.) on news that Philopoemen, no longer a general but a private citizen, had arrived before the city with the army; Philip V of Macedon so feared him he tried to have him assassinated. When his term as general was up Philopoemen went back to Crete. For this he was much criticized, as he left Megalopolis hard-pressed by its enemies. By request, he returned to his country some years later and again became commander of the Achaeans (altogether he was commander eight times). Philip V had been defeated by the Romans. Nabis of Sparta was at war with Rome and the Achaeans. Philopoemen defeated the Spartans, burned their camp at Gythium, compelled the Spartans to join the Achaean League (191 B.C.), and prevented the Romans from entering the city of Sparta. For this last the Spartans, having got rid of Nabis, offered him rich gifts, which he refused. In 184 B.C. the city of Messene revolted. Philopoemen sent Lycortas to quell the revolt, which was the second that had broken out in Messene, then, with a small band, he decided to go to Messene himself, unaware that Lycortas was already on his way back. In a skirmish Philopoemen was wounded in the head, taken captive, and carried off as a prisoner. According to Pausanias, the aristocrats clamored for his death, while the people, who called him the "Father of the Greeks" wanted to save him. Someone sent him poison, and rather than endure the shame of having been taken alive, he drank the poison. His bones were later returned to Megalopolis;

fat, fãte, fär, fåll, ȧsk, fãre; net, mē, hėr; pin, pīne; not, nōte, mȯve, nôr; up, lūte, pùll; oi, oil; ou out; (lightened) ẹlect, agǫny, ụnite;

many statues were set up to honor him for his successes against tyrants. One at Tegea described him as the "author of blameless freedom." Thirty-seven years after his death (146 B.C.) certain of the Romans wanted to destroy the statues. The Greek general and historian Polybius defended Philopoemen, and the Roman consul Mummius, noted for the barbarity with which he had ravaged Greece, refused to dishonor Philopoemen; the statues of the man who had reorganized the forces of the Achaean League and used them so effectively were allowed to stand.

Philotas (fil-ō′tạs). Macedonian general, killed 330 B.C., in Drangiana, C Asia. He was the son of Parmenio, general who served Philip as well as Alexander. Under Alexander, Philotas commanded the heavy cavalry of the Macedonian forces. On the successful expedition into Asia great treasures were taken as spoils and distributed among the Macedonians. Philotas made an ostentatious display in gift-giving and indulged himself in the most arrogant extravagance and luxury. He is said to have boasted to his concubine, Antigone, who had been given to him as part of his share in the spoils, that the victories for which Alexander took credit were won by his father and himself. Antigone repeated his indiscreet and boastful words to his enemies, and they came at last to the ears of Alexander. While in Drangiana, a plot to kill Alexander was uncovered; Philotas was accused. Though boastful and arrogant, no proof that he was connected with the plot was brought forward. However, he is said to have admitted that he knew of the existence of a plot but had done nothing about it. The Macedonians, before whom his case was laid by Alexander, found him guilty, pierced him with their javelins, and killed him.

Phocion (fō′shi-ọn). Athenian statesman and general; born c402 B.C.; put to death 318 B.C. He was of a good Athenian family, and in his youth was a pupil of Plato and Xenocrates. As a young man he attached himself to the Athenian general Chabrias, whose admiration he won. Chabrias advanced him, and he commanded the left wing of the Athenian fleet in the sea-fight with the Spartans off Naxos in 376 B.C. that resulted in an Athenian victory. Even after the death of Chabrias, Phocion continued to honor him and showed his loyalty by his care for Chabrias' son, Ctesippus, an intractable and capricious youth. Once on an expedition Ctesippus harried him with criticism and advice. Phocion exclaimed, "Chabrias, Chabrias, surely I make you a large return for your friendship in enduring your son." Phocion early established a reputation for unimpeachable honesty, and won the admiration of the Athenians because no amount of money could tempt him. He was devoted to the interests of the state and impervious to public criticism. Of a kind and gentle nature, he was forbidding in appearance, and never hesitated to tell the Athenians wherein lay their errors. He was a forceful speaker, capable of putting great good sense into very few words. He never sought the favor of the people. On the contrary, he invariably publicly disapproved of their actions. Once, it is said, when he delivered an opinion and it was approved by all, he turned to a friend and asked, "Can it be that I am making a bad argument without knowing it?" The great object of his civil policy was peace with Macedonia, because Athens was not in a position to oppose her. He frequently exposed those who spoke in favor of war as being either unwilling or unable to fight. Demosthenes, the most fiery advocate of war, once said to him, "The Athenians will kill you, Phocion, should they go crazy." To which he replied, "But they will kill you, should they come to their senses." Although he was an outspoken advocate of peace, and although he never sought the office, he was appointed general by the Athenians 45 times. Because of his reputation for justice and honesty, he alone of the generals sent out by Athens to the allies was welcomed by them. In 348 B.C. he was sent to put down a revolt in Eretria, in the island of Euboea. The victory he won there consisted mainly in avoiding defeat. In 339 B.C. he was sent to the Hellespont to the relief of Byzantium, which was undergoing siege by Philip II. Chares, the Athenian who had preceded him, had accomplished little since the Byzantians so distrusted him they refused to allow him in their city, but for Phocion they threw open their gates. Philip was forced to withdraw and Phocion recovered some cities he had taken. Then, having sustained a wound, he returned to Athens. In 344–343 B.C. he answered an appeal from Megara for aid, and helped to build the long walls from Megara to her port. His immutable policy was peace, and he tried to persuade Athens to accept Philip's terms. Demosthenes urged war, but recommended that it be waged as far from Attica as possible. "My good

sir," said Phocion, "let us not ask where we can fight, but
how we shall be victorious. For in that case the war will be
far away; but wherever men are defeated every terror is close
at hand." The Athenians followed Demosthenes, and were
disastrously defeated by Philip at Chaeronea (338 B.C.).
Phocion recommended that the kindly overtures of Philip
after the defeat be accepted. Philip trusted and admired
him; Athens was granted peace on moderate terms and
Philip returned the Athenian dead with a guard of honor.
Phocion disapproved of the sacrifices of rejoicing that were
proclaimed by the Athenians when Philip was murdered
(336 B.C.), for, said he, the force that had defeated them at
Chaeronea was diminished now by only one man. He opposed Demosthenes' speeches against Alexander, and after
the destruction of Thebes (335 B.C.) strongly advised the
Athenians to surrender the leaders of the war party, including Demosthenes, demanded by Alexander, because in Phocion's view they were responsible for bringing Athens low
by their fiery speeches and their violent policies. Phocion
was one of the envoys sent to Alexander. He advised him to
end the war in Greece and, if he sought glory, to fight the
barbarians. Alexander made him his guest and friend, and
when he returned to Athens Alexander sent him a gift of 100
talents because, "Alexander judges that you alone are a man
of honor and worth." Phocion refused to accept the gift.
Alexander was angered because he would not accept anything from him. Thereupon Phocion asked for the release of
four men who had been taken. Alexander released them.
Later (324 B.C.), Alexander offered him the revenues of any
one of four cities. Phocion again refused the gift. When the
Athenians murmured against Alexander he told them,
"Either be superior in arms or be friends with those who are
superior." After the death of Alexander and the defeat of
the Athenians at Crannon (322 B.C.) by Antipater, Phocion
went to Antipater at Thebes as an envoy of Athens. The
terms imposed by Antipater were harsh, but Athens had no
choice but to accept them. Phocion won the confidence of
Antipater as he had of Philip and Alexander, and became
virtual ruler of Athens under him. Antipater said he had two
friends at Athens: Phocion, whom he could not persuade to
take anything, and Demades, to whom he could never give
enough. On the death of Antipater, Philip Arrhidaeus, the

imbecile half-brother of Alexander, was king under the control of Polysperchon. Polysperchon was an opponent of Cassander, son of Antipater. He persuaded the Athenians to try Phocion, now a very old man, on a false charge of treason. In a frenzy of madness, as Demosthenes had predicted, the Athenians refused to hear his defense and condemned him. He drank the hemlock in May, 318 B.C. As an added indignity, he was at first denied burial, but a friend took his body and burned it. His wife gathered his bones and buried them under his own hearth. Very soon the Athenians regretted their madness. They gave his bones public burial and raised a statue to him in the market-place.

Phormio (fôr'mi-ō). Athenian admiral; fl. last half of the 5th century B.C.; died probably c428 B.C. He went with reinforcements to the blockade of Potidaea (432) and helped to surround the city. In 430 B.C. he commanded a fleet of 30 ships that captured Amphilochian Argos on the Ambracian Gulf, sold the Ambraciots, who had taken the city, into slavery, and restored the Amphilochian inhabitants. He then went to Naupactus and guarded the western entrance to the Gulf of Corinth. The following year he twice defeated superior Spartan fleets sent against him in the Gulf of Corinth.

Phyllidas (fil'i-das). Theban patriot; fl. in the first half of the 4th century B.C. He plotted with the Theban exile Pelopidas to overthrow the pro-Spartan polemarchs of Thebes who were sustained by a garrison of 1500 Spartans in the Theban citadel. Phyllidas was the secretary of the polemarchs. He arranged a great banquet, supposedly in honor of the polemarchs, for the day following the secret entry into the city of Pelopidas and his six fellow conspirators. Phyllidas lured the polemarchs to his banquet by promising them the company of some beautiful noblewomen whom they desired. In the course of the feast the polemarchs asked for the promised women. Phyllidas said they would come only when the polemarchs were alone. The attendants were dismissed and the women entered, heavily veiled. When the polemarchs requested them to raise their veils and expose their beauty the "ladies" plunged daggers into the bodies of the polemarchs and the few friends who had remained with them, for according to plan, the "beautiful women" were Pelopidas and his six colleagues in the plot to free Thebes. As a result of the deaths of the polemarchs and other political murders

fat, fāte, fär, fâll, àsk, fāre; net, mē, hèr; pin, pīne; not, nōte, möve, nôr; up, lūte, pùll; oi, oil; ou out; (lightened) ḝlect, agǫny, ūnite;

which immediately followed, the Spartan garrison withdrew from the citadel (378 B.C.) and the Thebans regained control of their city.

Pisistratus (pī-sis′trạ-tus). [Also: *Peisistratus*.] Tyrant of Athens, 561–527 B.C. (with intervals). He was born c605 B.C., the son of Hippocrates, a descendant of Neleus, and was named for Nestor's son Pisistratus. He was a relative of Solon with whom, in spite of political differences, he remained on friendly terms to the end of Solon's life. At a time of civil strife between two factions in Athens Pisistratus seized the opportunity, at the head of a third party of agricultural followers whose support he won by the promise of liberal land laws, to gain power for himself (c561 B.C.). According to Herodotus, he achieved power in the following manner: He gashed himself and his mules, then drove his chariot into the market place of Athens. Displaying his wounds, he asked for a guard to protect him, reminding the Athenians of his brave exploits when he led an army against the Megareans (c570 B.C.) and recovered Salamis for the Athenians and captured the Megarean port of Nisaea as well. The Athenians granted him a guard armed with clubs. With this, Pisistratus revolted, captured the citadel, and secured power in Athens. Having established himself in power, however, he made no upsetting changes in the laws or offices but administered the government according to the established usages and was a wise ruler. Only a short time passed before the leaders of the other two factions, the aristocratic parties, Megacles and Lycurgus, composed their differences and drove Pisistratus out (c560 B.C.). He went into exile. The harmony between Megacles and Lycurgus was short-lived. Megacles sent a herald to Pisistratus and offered to restore him to power on condition that Pisistratus marry his daughter. He agreed. But the problem of how his restoration was to be accomplished had to be overcome. The device used was, according to Herodotus, extremely silly in view of the fact that the Athenians were reputed to be the cleverest of the Greeks, but it worked. Pisistratus found an unusually tall and beautiful woman, dressed her in armor, and drove her in a cart to the city. Heralds preceding the procession proclaimed that this was the goddess Athena, and that it was her wish that the Athenians restore Pisistratus. The Athenians accepted the hoax and he regained

power (c559 B.C.), and then married the daughter of Megacles. Pisistratus already had grown sons, and as the Alcmaeonidae, of which family Megacles was a member, were under
a curse for breaking their oath in regard to the followers of
Cylon, Pisistratus resolved not to have any children by his
new wife. Megacles learned that the childlessness of his
daughter was deliberate and was roused to anger against
Pisistratus. He again composed his differences with the
party of Lycurgus and plotted to expel Pisistratus, but he,
learning of the plot, fled to Eretria (c556 B.C.). He spent the
next ten years scheming how to regain power in Athens. He
and his sons Hippias and Hipparchus collected money,
armed mercenaries and allies who were in their debt, and set
out to return to Athens. They landed near Marathon and
were joined by many who, as Herodotus says, "loved tyranny better than freedom." But others says the rule of Pisistratus was not unpopular, and that it was on the whole
beneficial. At first the Athenians ignored the movements of
Pisistratus, but when they realized he had left Marathon and
was approaching the city with an army they gathered forces
to resist him. The two forces encamped opposite each other.
An Acarnanian soothsayer announced to Pisistratus:

Now has the cast been made, the net is out-spread in the
water,
Through the moonshiny night the tunnies will enter the
meshes.

Pisistratus understood the saying and instantly acted on it.
He fell upon the Athenian army just after they had finished
their midday meal and were relaxing in their camp, and put
them to rout. He now became ruler of Athens for the third
time (c544 or 541 B.C.), and this time he took vigorous
measures to secure his power. The Alcmaeonidae fled the
country. Pisistratus took land from his enemies and gave it
to his agricultural followers. He made peace with the neighboring states. He oriented Athenian diplomacy towards
Ionia in an effort to make the Aegean Sea the area of
Athenian hegemony. He took the city of Sigeum from the
Mytilenaeans by force of arms and established his bastard
son Hegesistratus as tyrant there. He beautified the city of
Athens, gave his support to the art of poetry, encouraged
the dramatic representations that were given at the festivals
of Dionysus, and changed the character of the Panathenaean

fat, fāte, fär, fäll, àsk, fãre; net, mē, hèr; pin, pīne; not, nōte, möve,
nôr; up, lūte, pùll; oi, oil; ou out; (lightened) ĕlect, agǫny, ūnite;

festival to give it a national rather than a local flavor. In the latter years of his rule he commissioned a learned body to establish a definitive text of the *Iliad* and the *Odyssey*. This version, which collated and set in order the many bits and sections recited by the rhapsodists, is the one from which all subsequent texts of Homer are derived. Under his just and beneficent rule Athens was strong, prosperous, and at peace. At his death (527 B.C.), Pisistratus left his sons Hippias and Hipparchus in control of the city.

Piso (pī'sō), *Calpurnius.* Name of a family of the Gens Calpurnia distinguished in Roman history. Among the members were the following: Lucius, a censor, consul (133 B.C.), and author; Lucius, a politican, father-in-law of Julius Caesar, consul in 58 B.C., and later a member of the party of Mark Antony; Cnaeus, governor of Syria under Tiberius—according to some accounts he poisoned Germanicus at the request of Tiberius, but when he returned to Rome and showed documents as evidence of Tiberius' complicity, Tiberius destroyed the documents and disavowed him, and he was sentenced to death by the Senate; Caius, the leader of an unsuccessful conspiracy against Nero in 65 A.D. who committed suicide when the plan fell through; and Lucius, the successor of Galba for four days, put to death by Otho (69 A.D.).

Pittacus (pit'ạ-kus). Greek politician and poet, born c650 B.C., in Lesbos; died c569B.C. He was chiefly responsible for the overthrow of the tyrant of Mytilene (c611 B.C.). He won the confidence of the people and was elected by them to be their ruler for a term of ten years. He restored order in Mytilene by banishing the nobles who resisted his power, among them the poets Alcaeus and Sappho, and he secured domestic peace by the enactment of wise laws and a firm rule. At the end of the ten years for which he had been chosen he voluntarily relinquished his power. After his death he was enrolled as one of the Seven Wise Men of ancient Greece.

Pius (pī'us), *Metellus.* See *Metellus, Quintus Caecilius* (died c64 B.C.).

Plancus (plang'kus), *Lucius Munatius.* Roman soldier, orator, and consul (42 B.C.). He served under Julius Caesar in the Gallic and civil wars, and attached himself successively to Brutus, Anthony, and Octavian (it was he who proposed in the Senate that the title of Augustus should be bestowed on

---

(obscured) errạnt, ardẹnt, actọr; ch, chip; g, go; th, thin; ᴛH, then; y, you;
(variable) ḍ as d or j, ş as s or sh, ṭ as t or ch, ẓ as z or zh.

the last-named). Horace addressed to him Ode vii, Book I.

Poliorcetes (pol"i-ôr-sē′tēz), *Demetrius*. See *Demetrius I* (of *Macedonia*).

Pollio (pol′i-ō), *Caius Asinius*. Roman politician, military commander, orator, author, critic and patron of literature. He was born c76 B.C.; died at Tusculum, Italy, 5 A.D. He was an adherent of Julius Caesar, took part in the battle of Pharsalus (48 B.C.), and later commanded against Pompey's son in Spain. After the assassination of Caesar he became a partisan of Mark Antony, and was named governor of Transpadane Gaul. In 40 B.C. he was consul and helped to reconcile Octavian and Antony. He defeated the Parthians in Illyria in 39 B.C. For this victory he was honored with a triumph at Rome, and with the booty taken from the Parthians he caused a public library, the first such, to be erected in Rome. Henceforth he retired from public life and devoted himself to literature. He was a patron of Vergil and Horace. When he was governor of Transpadane Gaul he withdrew Vergil's estate from the lands being distributed to the veterans and thus saved it for the poet. Vergil addressed one of his eclogues to him. Of his own works—tragedies, a history of the civil wars of his own day, and speeches—only a few fragments of the speeches are extant.

Polycrates (pō-lik′rạ-tēz). He was a son of Aeaces. By an insurrection he made himself master of Samos and was tyrant of the island from c540 to 522 B.C. In the beginning he shared control with his two brothers, but then killed one, banished the other, and made himself sole ruler. He had an alliance of friendship with Amasis, king of Egypt. He built a fleet and waged war throughout the eastern Mediterranean, plundering friend and foe alike on the theory that friends are much more pleased if what has been taken from them is restored than they are to be spared in the first place. Polycrates overcame the Lesbians at sea when they came to the aid of Miletus, and forced his Lesbian captives to dig a vast moat around his palace at Samos. Good fortune attended all his endeavors. He lived in a magnificent style and was a patron of literature and the arts. He enjoyed such great prosperity and good luck that his friend and ally, Amasis of Egypt, became uneasy. He wrote to Polycrates to this effect: The uninterrupted good fortune of Polycrates disturbs him, because he knows that the gods are envious and will bring him down. Amasis is more pleased when the good fortune of his friends is mingled with an occasional setback, for in that way the gods are appeased. He has never known a man whose extreme good luck did not end in calamity. He therefore suggests to Polycrates that, to distract the gods from too close a scrutiny of his prosperity, he take the thing that is dearest to him and cast it away where it can never be found. In this way he will suffer a grievous loss and, in the eyes of the gods, his good fortune will have been tempered. Polycrates read the message from Amasis and found his advice good. He considered which of his treasures it would grieve him most to lose and decided on a signet ring, an emerald set in gold. He put to sea in a 50-oared ship and when he was well out, he hurled the ring into the sea. Then he returned home and grieved for his loss. Shortly thereafter a fisherman caught a splendid fish. It was such a superb specimen that he decided to give it to Polycrates. He took it to the palace and presented it to him. Polycrates was pleased with the gift and asked the fisherman to dine with him. In preparing the fish servants cut it open; within it they found Polycrates' ring. With joy they restored it to their master. Polycrates immediately sent word to Amasis and told him the whole story. Whereupon Amasis concluded that it was not given to man to divert fate from its destined path on his fellow men. He was so certain that Polycrates would end in disaster that he straightway dissolved his alliance of friendship with him, that he might be spared having to grieve over a friend when disaster inevitably overcame Polycrates. This, at any rate, is the reason that Herodotus gives for the end of the alliance between Polycrates and Amasis. When Cambyses was preparing war against Egypt (c525 B.C.), Polycrates offered him assistance and sent him a number of ships manned with those whom Polycrates thought were the most likely to rebel against his rule. These ships he gave to Cambyses with instructions never to allow the men to return home. However, some of this crew escaped, or deserted, or never got to Egypt at all. They returned to Samos and defeated Polycrates in a sea-fight, but were defeated by him when they attacked him on land. They then appealed to the Spartans for aid against Polycrates. In the meantime Polycrates imprisoned the wives and children of his loyal subjects so that they would not go over to the rebels. He threatened to burn the prisoners if his subjects joined the exiles. The Samian rebels succeeded in gaining the assistance of Sparta. Some say the Spartans agreed to help the Samian exiles out of gratitude. Others say it was to punish Samos for stealing a bowl Croesus had sent them, and an embroidered linen corselet sent them by Amasis. The Corinthians also joined the Samian exiles in their war against Polycrates, to avenge an old insult. The Spartans brought a strong force and attacked Samos. For 40 days they besieged the island. Then, finding they were making no headway, they lifted the siege and sailed away. Polycrates now conceived the ambition to become master of the sea. Oroetes, a Persian who had been made governor of Sardis by Cyrus, aware of Polycrates' ambition and determined to destroy him, sent him a message in which he avowed that Cambyses, Cyrus' successor, was seeking Oroetes' life. He offered Polycrates all his wealth to enable him to become lord of the sea if Polycrates would come to his rescue and carry him away from Sardis. In the meantime, he invited Polycrates to send a trusted messenger to whom he would show all the wealth which he would give to Polycrates. Polycrates sent his messenger. The wily Oroetes filled eight chests with stones, and covered these with a layer of gold. These he showed to the messenger from Polycrates, who in his turn reported to his master. Hearing of this great store of gold, Polycrates, despite many warnings from seers and from his friends, decided to go to Oroetes in person. His daughter dreamed that she saw Polycrates hanging in the air, washed by Zeus and anointed by the sun. Even this dream did not deter him. On the contrary, he threatened to keep his daughter unwed if she did not cease her entreaties to him to remain at home. Accompanied by many friends he sailed off to Oroetes. In Sardis Oroetes set upon him and killed him in a manner which (according to Herodotus who tells these events) was too horrible to describe. Oroetes crucified the dead body of Polycrates, rains sent by Zeus washed it, and the sun's rays anointed it. Thus the dream of Polycrates' daughter was fulfilled. His end also confirmed the gloomy predictions which his friend Amasis of Egypt had entertained concerning the disasters which were certain to befall any man whose good fortune was uninterrupted.

Polysperchon (pol-i-spėr′kon) or *Polyperchon* (pol-i-pėr′kon).

fat, fāte, fär, fâll, àsk, fāre; net, mē, hėr; pin, pīne; not, nōte, mŏve, nôr; up, lūte, pùll; oi, oil; ou out; (lightened) ēlect, agǫny, ūnite;

Macedonian general in the service of Alexander the Great; born c380 B.C.; died after 303 B.C. He succeeded Antipater as regent in 319 B.C. He was superseded by Cassander, son of Antipater.

Polyzelus (pol-i-zē'lus). Brother of Gelon, tyrant of Gela and Syracuse; fl. in the early part of the 5th century B.C. He succeeded Gelon as general of the Syracusan army and tyrant of Syracuse. He sent his race horses and chariots to compete in the Olympic and Pythian games, as did other tyrants of Sicily. A fragmentary inscription found at Delphi, in association with fragments of the monumental four-horse chariot group of which the famous bronze *Charioteer* is the principal surviving piece, suggests that Polyzelus may have been the dedicant.

Pompeia (pom-pē'ạ). Second wife of Julius Caesar, and a granddaughter of Sulla. Her marriage to Caesar, which took place in 67 B.C., was terminated in 61 B.C. She was charged with misconduct during the ceremonies of the Bona Dea. These rites were extremely sacred, and men were rigorously excluded from them. During one performance of the rites, a male intruder dressed in woman's clothing was detected in the house. He was found to be Publius Clodius, a notorious scoundrel reputed to be the lover of Pompeia. This was a colossal scandal and it was charged that Pompeia had arranged or connived at his presence there. Neither the charge of impiety nor of infidelity with Clodius was ever proved. This being so, it was asked of Caesar why he divorced her. The future master of Rome answered that "Caesar's wife must be above suspicion."

Pompeius Magnus (pom-pā'us mag'nus), *Cnaeus*. Roman general, elder son of Pompey the triumvir; put to death, 45 B.C. Some time after the defeat of his father at Pharsalus (48 B.C.) by Caesar, Cnaeus Pompeius joined his brother Sextus in Spain. The brothers were defeated by Caesar at Munda, in Spain, 45 B.C. Cnaeus escaped but was captured shortly afterward and put to death.

Pompeius Magnus, Sextus. [English, *Pompey;* called *Pompey the Younger.*] Roman soldier; younger son of Pompey (Cnaeus Pompeius) the Great; born 75 B.C.; killed at Miletus, 35 B.C. His forces were defeated by Julius Caesar at Munda in 45 B.C. He became powerful as commander of a fleet on the coasts of Sicily and Italy, and by cutting off Rome's grain supply from Africa, hoped to starve the Romans into receiving him again. He was defeated in a naval battle by Agrippa in 36 B.C., and fled to Asia Minor, where he was captured and executed.

Pompey (pom'pi). [Called *Pompey the Great;* full Latin name, *Cnaeus Pompeius Magnus.*] Roman general, born 106 B.C.; murdered in Egypt, Sept. 28, 48 B.C. He was the son of Cnaeus Pompeius Strabo, a Roman general, under whom he served (89 B.C.) in the Social War. As a youth Pompey was noted for his temperate manner of living, for his skill in war, his honorable character, and his availability to those who sought his favors. Strabo was hated for his avarice, and his soldiers mutinied against him, but such was the respect and affection they had for Pompey that he was able to persuade them to return to their general. After his father Strabo died he was accused of misappropriation of the public funds. Pompey defended him so brilliantly that the praetor in charge of the case offered him his daughter Antistia in marriage. Lucius Cornelius Cinna, a leader of the popular party, supporter of Marius and opponent of Sulla, seized control of Rome during Sulla's absence. He was slain in 84 B.C. and was succeeded by Carbo, another leader of the popular party. Pompey resolved to join the conservative party of Sulla, but not before he had collected an army. In a short time he had gathered three legions with all their equipment in Picenum, forced the followers of Carbo to give way, and defeated a combined force of three generals sent against him (83 B.C.). When he at last met Sulla he arrived as a young general of proven abilities. Sulla greeted him as *Imperator* and, wishing to reward him, persuaded him to divorce Antistia and to marry a connection of his, one Aemilia, who was at the time married and about to bear a child. Pompey divorced Antistia and married Aemilia, who subsequently died in childbirth. Pompey now went to Sicily and successfully cleared the island of Sulla's Marian enemies. Carbo was seized on the island of Pantelleria, dragged before a tribunal in chains, and condemned to death. From Sicily Pompey crossed over to Africa where, within 40 days, he had conquered the followers of Marius, subdued Numidia, and once more made the name of Rome respected in Africa. When he returned to Rome (81 B.C.), Sulla came to greet him and gave him the title *Magnus* (Great), which

fat, fāte, fär, fåll, åsk, fāre; net, mē, hėr; pin, pīne; not, nōte, möve, nôr; up, lūte, pùll; oi, oil; ou out; (lightened) ėlect, agǫny, ūnite;

Pompey kept and handed down to his sons. However, Sulla opposed Pompey's demand for a triumph because, he said, the laws did not permit a triumph to one who had been neither praetor nor consul, and moreover, Pompey was too young—24—to be a senator and was still a knight. Pompey pointedly remarked that "more [people] worship the rising than the setting sun," and when Sulla saw how popular he was he allowed him his triumph, regardless of the laws. Pompey's obvious popularity and power soon made Sulla uneasy, and relations between them became less warm. After Sulla's death (78 B.C.), Marcus Aemilius Lepidus (father of the triumvir) sought to change Sulla's constitution, gathered an army, and made himself master of Cisalpine Gaul and part of Italy. Pompey was named general, and with the consul Caius Lutatius Catulus he marched against Lepidus. He went to Mutina, where Marcus Junius Brutus (father of Caesar's chief assassin) commanded the forces of Lepidus and compelled his surrender. Brutus was permitted to retire, but after he had withdrawn Pompey treacherously sent men after him to slay him (c77 B.C.). Lepidus was driven out of Italy. Pompey next had himself named proconsul and went to Spain to help Metellus Pius in the war against Sertorius. He was in Spain from 76 to 71 B.C. and, after the death of Sertorius, defeated his successor Perpenna and ended the war. He returned to Rome at the time of the revolt of Spartacus, the so-called Servile War, and went to assist Crassus. Crassus defeated the main body of the forces of Spartacus (71 B.C.), but Pompey, marching up, came upon those fleeing after the defeat by Crassus and wiped them out and received much of the credit for ending the Servile War. He demanded a triumph for his victories in Spain and asked permission to stand for the consulship. The Senate opposed him because he had not held the required offices, but he joined with Crassus, and since each had an army poised at the gates of Rome the Senate withdrew its opposition. He had his triumph, his second, and became consul with Crassus (70 B.C.). During their term, in which they publicly disagreed, the tribunes and censors were restored, and the Senate was compelled to share the administration of justice with the knights.

While Rome had been preoccupied with wars and civil wars, the pirates who ever infested the Mediterranean had

(obscured) errạnt, ardẹnt, actọr; ch, chip; g, go; th, thin; ᴛʜ, then; y, you;
(variable) ḍ as d or j, ş as s or sh, ṭ as t or ch, ẓ as z or zh.

become increasingly powerful and bold. They had 1000 ships, had taken 400 cities, plundered temples, and so interfered with the grain supply on which Rome depended that the city was in great distress. Gabinius, a friend of Pompey, proposed a decree by which Pompey was to be given enormous power for the purpose of clearing the seas of the pirates. When the decree was read there were many who saw the dangers in the great power it would give to one man and they opposed it. But the Gabinian Law was passed (67 B.C.), and Pompey was granted power to take what money he needed, to equip a large fleet, and to enroll crews and fighters at his discretion. In three months he drove the pirates from the sea. He took 20,000 prisoners, most of whom were humanely allowed to settle in small towns in Cilicia and Greece. To reward him, Manilius proposed that the provinces of Lucullus, other territory, and command of the Mithridatic War be given to him. This law was also opposed by some senators. Catulus, renowned for honor and virtue, spoke against it as he had against the Gabinian Law. Cicero supported it, for reasons of personal policy. The law was passed (66 B.C.), and its effect, in conjunction with the Gabinian Law, was to give Pompey unlimited power on land and sea. Opponents of the law were well aware of its effect. "We have at last then, a sovereign," they said, "The Republic is changed into a monarchy." Having received command of the war against Mithridates, thus publicly humiliating Lucullus and denying the services he had already rendered, Pompey set out for the East. He defeated Mithridates at the Euphrates, but Mithridates escaped. Tigranes, king of Armenia, surrendered to Pompey, who fined him 6000 talents and restored certain of his lands. Pompey surged through the East with his army, defeated the Iberians, went into Colchis, marched back to quell a revolt of the Albanians, converted Syria into a Roman province (64 B.C.), reduced Judaea (63 B.C.), founded cities, administered justice, settled disputes between cities, and with imperial power restored order. As he was returning to Rome after his splendid victories he learned what all Rome knew: that his third wife, Mucia, had betrayed him with Caesar. He called Caesar "my Aegisthus," and sent Mucia a divorce. When he later married Caesar's daughter Julia (59 B.C.) he was heavily criticized. On his arrival in Rome he voluntarily disbanded his

fat, fāte, fär, fâll, åsk, fãre; net, mē, hėr; pin, pīne; not, nōte, mŏve, nôr; up, lūte, pŭli; oi, oil; ou out; (lightened) ĕlect, agǫny, ūnite;

army. The triumph he was awarded (61 B.C.) for the conquest of Asia was the most magnificent Rome had ever seen. This was the apex of his career. From this time, as Plutarch says, "he was insensibly ruined by the weight of his own power." He had as little talent for politics as he had greatness as a general and soon frittered away the great popularity he had won. He turned away from the conservative party and allied himself with Publius Clodius, a renegade patrician, at whose demand he abandoned his old friend Cicero. He allowed Caesar to reconcile him with Crassus, formed with them the First Triumvirate (60 B.C.), and filled the city with his loyal soldiers to secure the command of Gaul for Caesar for five years. But he could not control the street mobs of Clodius, who openly scorned him, and he had lost the respect of the Senate when he abandoned Cicero. He secured the restoration of Cicero, who reconciled him with the Senate, and then was given the task of supplying Rome with grain. In this position he was again master at Rome, and he carried out his task with great success. Meantime, Caesar was tremendously successful in Gaul, and was intriguing against Pompey. He crossed the Alps and wintered at Luca. Pompey and Crassus met him there (56 B.C.), renewed the triumvirate, agreed to seek the consulship again, and to procure another five-year term for Caesar in Gaul. By means of bribery and street mobs, Crassus and Pompey won the consulate (55 B.C.) and Caesar got his command in Gaul. In the division of the provinces between the consuls, Pompey took Africa and Spain; Crassus got Syria and command of a war against the Parthians. Pompey did not set out for his provinces. He was severely criticized for jaunting about Italy with his young wife, Julia, and leaving the administration of his territories to his lieutenants. Crassus was killed in his war with the Parthians (53 B.C.), and the year before that Julia had died. The links, always fragile, between Caesar and Pompey were now broken, and their rivalry for control of Rome came out in the open. The city was in a ferment. It was proposed that Pompey be made dictator, but Cato successfully opposed this. However, the disorder was so great that Cato later endorsed the proposal that he be named sole consul, and this was done (52 B.C.). In the midst of the political confusion Pompey married Cornelia, the widow of Crassus' son,

(obscured) errạnt, ardẹnt, actọr; ch, chip; g, go; th, thin; ᴛʜ, then; y, you;
(variable) ḍ as d or j, ş as s or sh, ṭ as t or ch, ẓ as z or zh.

and allied himself to the conservative party. He served as sole consul for five years, and in this time restored order and embarked on a policy of legislation designed to curb Caesar. He felt so secure in his power that he scorned Caesar and refused to gather an army against him. Caesar's agents circulated freely in Rome, armed with booty that they liberally distributed in bribes to win opponents of Pompey. When at last Caesar crossed the Alps with an army, Pompey had no force with which to oppose him. Before he could collect one he learned that Caesar had crossed the Rubicon. Pompey hesitated, bewildered by the sudden collapse of his influence, and unable to decide on any of the conflicting plans offered him. Italy was in a ferment; Rome was in a state of wildest confusion. Those outside the city flocked in, while those in it were making all haste to leave. As the uncertainty and confusion reached a climax, Pompey declared that he would consider all who stayed in Rome as enemies. With many prominent men he left the city to Caesar, and when the latter pursued him he took ship at Brundisium and sailed to Macedonia. Caesar was now master of Italy, but Pompey still controlled the sea. Many eminent men, looking to him to save the Republic, joined him; among them was Labienus, who had been greatly honored by Caesar, and Marcus Junius Brutus, whose father Pompey had caused to be murdered, as well as Cicero. Caesar did not follow him immediately. First he went to Spain, conquered Pompey's troops there, and added them to his own army. Then he went to Macedonia and asked Pompey for a conference. Pompey refused to meet him, seized all the ports, and cut off Caesar's supplies, forcing him to withdraw to Thessaly. Pompey's plan, a sound one, was to exhaust Caesar, but his followers were eager to give battle. They claimed Caesar's withdrawal to Thessaly was a sign of weakness, and urged Pompey to return to Rome. He did not want to appear to flee before Caesar a second time (as he had at Brundisium), and hoped to defeat him in Thessaly. He yielded to the demands of his subordinates, for nothing that had happened in his life had prepared him to accept the abuse and criticism they now heaped on him for refusing to fight. A council of war was held at Pharsalus, in Thessaly, at which it was decided to engage Caesar. Caesar was relieved, "At last," he said, "we shall fight men and not famine." In the battle that followed

fat, fāte, fär, fåll, åsk, fāre; net, mē, hėr; pin, pīne; not, nōte, mŏve, nôr; up, lūte, pŭll; oi, oil; ou out; (lightened) ḙlect, agǫny, ṵnite;

on Aug. 9, 48 B.C., Pompey, with a force of 45,000 legionaries and 7000 cavalry, was utterly routed by Caesar, with 22,000 legionaries and 1000 cavalry. For the first time in his life Pompey knew what it was to be defeated and to flee. In a small boat he went to Mytilene to fetch his wife Cornelia and his son. He sailed to Egypt and sent to the young king, Ptolemy XIII, to ask for asylum. Ptolemy's advisers persuaded him to kill Pompey, some say, for "dead men don't bite." Pompey was waiting in his boat off shore for the king's decision. A few men came to him in a small and humble boat. He suspected from their lack of ceremony and the insignificance of their equipage that Ptolemy did not mean to welcome him with honor. Nevertheless, he got into their boat. When they neared the beach his freedman Philip leaped out to help him ashore. He stretched out his hand to Philip, and as he did so was stabbed in the back. Some say it was one of his former centurions who killed him for Ptolemy. Others in the boat set on him and killed him with many blows. They cut off his head, stripped his body, and left it naked on the shore. Philip washed it in sea water, wrapped it in one of his own garments and, using an abandoned fishing boat as a pyre, burned it. When Caesar reached Egypt and learned of his murder he ordered the assassins executed; the ashes of his fallen rival were restored to Cornelia, who buried them on his estate near Alba.

Ponticus (pon′ti-kus). See *Lucullus, Lucius Licinius.*

Poppaea Sabina (po-pē′ạ sạ-bī′nạ). Wife of Otho, and mistress, and subsequently wife, of Nero. She was divorced from the former and married the latter in 62 A.D. She is usually blamed as the person who chiefly influenced Nero in his murder of his wife Octavia, her sister Antonia, his mother Agrippina, the philosopher Seneca, and others. He is said to have kicked her so severely, in a fit of rage, that she died (65 A.D.).

Porsena (pôr′sẹ-nạ), *Lars.* [Also: *Porsenna.*] In Roman legend, a king of Clusium in Etruria, who gained power over Rome in the 6th century B.C. He was allied with the banished Tarquins against Rome.

Porus (pō′rus). Indian king who governed the land between the Hydaspes and Acesines rivers (in what is now the northern Punjab); killed c318 B.C. When Alexander the Great advanced to the Hydaspes River (326 B.C.), some of the reigning princes of the lands through which he passed voluntarily submitted to him and kept much of their powers. Porus, a powerful prince, prepared to resist and gathered an army on the farther bank of the Hydaspes to prevent Alexander from crossing it. His most formidable weapon was a large corps of elephants, the sight and smell of which drove Alexander's horses into a frenzy. The river was swollen by seasonal rains and for a time the two armies faced each other from opposite banks. Alexander made many feints, as if to put his army in motion, but in the end he marched 16 miles up the river with part of his army, crossed, and attacked Porus from his own side. Porus, mounted on a magnificent elephant, was in the thick of the fighting, and was wounded. His elephants, so formidable when met head on, were maddened by attacks from all sides, threw their riders in many cases, and raged about trampling friend and foe alike. According to Plutarch, Porus' own elephant maneuvered him tenderly through the strife, and when it felt Porus weakened by arrow wounds, the elephant knelt down for Porus to dismount and plucked the arrow from his body with its trunk. When Porus saw his army routed he did not flee, but turned his elephant and rode off. Messengers from Alexander persuaded him to return. Alexander asked him how he expected to be treated. Porus replied, "Like a king." He was. Alexander treated him royally and gave him back his kingdom, somewhat enlarged in area, which he was to govern as a dependent of Macedonia. After the death of Alexander, Porus was treacherously slain (c318 B.C.) by the Macedonian general Eudemus.

Prexaspes (prek-sas'pēz). A faithful Persian attendant of Cambyses II (King of Persia, 529–c521 B.C.). Cambyses ordered him to slay his brother Smerdis (Bardiya), because while Cambyses was in Egypt he dreamed Smerdis sat on the royal throne and his head touched the heavens. Prexaspes returned to Susa and killed Smerdis, either by drowning him or during a hunting expedition. He then returned to Cambyses and reported that he had carried out his orders. On one occasion Cambyses asked Prexaspes what the Persians were saying about him. Prexaspes answered that they praised him greatly but said that he was overfond of wine. Cambyses was furious. He said he would shoot an arrow at the son of Prexaspes; if he hit the child in the heart the Persians who said he was overfond of wine and mad were liars; if he failed to hit the child in the heart, they were speaking the truth. Straightway he carried out his threat. He shot the son of Prexaspes with an arrow, had the body cut open and showed Prexaspes that his arrow had pierced his son's heart. Prexaspes, seeing that he was mad, agreed that the Persians who said Cambyses was mad were liars. Some time later two brothers, Median magi, planned a revolt against Cambyses. One of them looked very much like Cambyses' murdered brother Smerdis, and assumed the same name. While Cambyses was still in Egypt he set himself on the throne, stated that he was Smerdis, son of Cyrus, and declared himself king. Cambyses, hearing of this, thought Prexaspes had betrayed him, and had not slain Smerdis after all. He charged him with betrayal, but Prexaspes assured him his brother was dead. He helped him to learn that it was another Smerdis, a magus, who had rebelled and seized the throne. Thus it was that Cambyses' dream that Smerdis sat upon the royal throne and his head touched the heavens was fulfilled, but it was not his brother Smerdis, but another, and he had caused his brother's murder for nothing. In a rage Cambyses sought to mount his horse, wounded himself on his sword, and shortly thereafter died. Smerdis the rebel magus being still on the throne, Prexaspes now swore that he was the real Smerdis, brother of Cambyses, and also swore that he had not killed him, since it was unsafe to acknowledge the truth after the death of Cambyses. Later Smerdis the magus enlisted the aid of Prexaspes. To quiet rumors that were springing up he asked Prexaspes to go to the top of a tower and announce that the Persians were ruled by Smerdis the son of Cyrus, and no other. He knew that Prexaspes was the man most likely to be believed in this matter. Prexaspes agreed. He went to the tower, recited the genealogy of the Persian kings from the time of Achaemenes, said that he himself, at the command of Cambyses, had killed Smerdis the son of Cyrus, and that the present Smerdis was a magus and an impostor. Then Prexaspes hurled himself head first from the tower and perished.

Ptolemy I (tol'e̯-mi) (of *Egypt*). [Surnamed **Soter,** meaning "Savior" or "Preserver," and **Lagi,** "Son of Lagus;" Latin, **Ptolemaeus.**] King of Egypt (306–285 B.C.), founder of the Greek dynasty in that country. He was born c367 B.C.; died 283 B.C. He was the alleged son of Lagus, a Macedonian of ignoble birth, and Arsinoë; but as Arsinoë had been the concubine of Philip II of Macedon, he was commonly supposed by his contemporaries to be the son of that monarch. He was one of Alexander the Great's most trusted generals, serving as one of those who guarded the king's person, and holding a place of high command. He accompanied Alexander throughout the Asiatic campaigns, of which he wrote a history. On the journey of Alexander to the oracle of Zeus Ammon in Libya, Ptolemy records as evidence of divine interest in Alexander that two snakes slithered along in front of the Macedonians to guide them through the trackless desert to the shrine, where the priest addressed Alexander as a son of Zeus. Ptolemy was one of those given a Persian princess, Artacama, for a bride at the great marriage festival celebrated by Alexander at Susa (324 B.C.), but after the event the princess seems to have disappeared from Ptolemy's history. In the distribution of the provinces on the death of Alexander in 323 B.C. Ptolemy obtained the government of Egypt. He managed to gain possession of Alexander's body and carried it off to Memphis until a suitably magnificent burial could be arranged. In so doing he incurred the enmity of Perdiccas, who had become regent of Asia. Ptolemy formed an alliance with Antipater against Perdiccas. He married Eurydice, daughter of Antipater, to strengthen the alliance but later put her aside in favor of his own half-sister Berenice. Perdiccas invaded Egypt in 321 B.C. but was murdered by his own troops. In the involved struggles of the Diadochi (the "successors" of Alexander) Ptolemy periodically invaded, won, and lost part of Syria; won, lost, and won Cyprus; subdued Cyrene; took Corinth, Megara, and Sicyon in Greece, but did not retain them. He afterward concluded an alliance with Cassander, Seleucus, and Lysimachus against Antigonus, who fell in the battle of Ipsus in 301 B.C. He assumed the title of king in 306 or 304. In 304 B.C. his efficient support of the Rhodians against Demetrius enabled them to repel his formidable attack, whence he received the surname Soter or Preserver from the Rhodians, who thereafter awarded him divine honors. During his reign Alexandria became the Egyptian capital; the library was founded by him and he made the city a place where scholars could work. He abdicated in 285 B.C., in favor of Ptolemy II, his son by Berenice.

Ptolemy II (of *Egypt*). [Surnamed ***Philadelphus;*** Latin, ***Ptolemaeus.***] King of Egypt (285–246 B.C.); son of Ptolemy I. He was born in the island of Cos, 309 B.C., and died 246 B.C. He annexed Phoenicia and Coele-Syria, encouraged commerce, literature, science, and art, and raised the Alexandrian Museum and Library, founded by his father, to importance. He completed the lighthouse on Pharos, one of the seven wonders of the world, and is credited by ancient writers with authorizing the Bible translation known as the Septuagint, and the Egyptian history of Manetho.

Ptolemy III (of *Egypt*). [Surnamed ***Euergetes,*** meaning "Benefactor"; Latin, ***Ptolemaeus.***] King of Egypt (246–221 B.C.); son of Ptolemy II, whom he succeeded in 246 B.C. He was born c282 B.C., and died 221 B.C. To avenge the murder of his sister Berenice in a dynastic intrigue, he invaded (c245) Syria and captured Babylon, but was recalled in 243 B.C. by a revolt in Egypt. He expanded the Egyptian fleet and gained control of the eastern Mediterranean, and further extended his domain by his marriage to Berenice of Cyrene.

Ptolemy IV (of *Egypt*). [Surnamed ***Philopator,*** meaning "Father-loving"; Latin, ***Ptolemaeus.***] King of Egypt (221–203 B.C.); son of Ptolemy III. He was born c244 B.C., and died 203 B.C. He defeated Antiochus the Great at Raphia in 217 B.C., but in general he was an ineffective ruler; he held his throne by murdering several near relatives.

Ptolemy V (of *Egypt*). [Surnamed ***Epiphanes,*** meaning "Illustrious"; Latin, ***Ptolemaeus.***] King of Egypt (203–181 B.C.); son of Ptolemy IV. He was born c210 B.C., and died 181 B.C. His dominions were overrun by Antiochus III, who had agreed to divide the Egyptian possessions with Philip V of Macedon, and saved only by the interference of Rome. He married Cleopatra, daughter of Antiochus, in the winter of 193–192 B.C., in accordance with a treaty of peace concluded with Antiochus some years previously. The Rosetta Stone commemorates his assumption of his majority in 196 B.C.

Ptolemy VI (of *Egypt*). [Surnamed ***Philometor,*** meaning "Mother-loving"; Latin, ***Ptolemaeus.***] King of Egypt (181–145 B.C.); son of Ptolemy V. He was born c186 B.C., and died 145 B.C. The early years of his reign were a regency under his mother. He was captured during an invasion of Egypt by Antiochus IV, King of Syria, in 170 B.C., whereupon his younger brother Ptolemy VIII proclaimed himself king. He was presently released by Antiochus, and for a time reigned conjointly with his brother. Expelled by his brother, he sought relief in person at Rome in 164 B.C., and was reinstated at Alexandria, his brother being forced to retire to Cyrene, which he was allowed to hold as a separate kingdom. He supported Demetrius II in the struggle in Syria against Alexander Balas and was killed in the battle near Antioch that saw Demetrius' final triumph.

Ptolemy VIII (of *Egypt*). [Surnamed *Euergetes* (and called *Ptolemy Euergetes II*) or *Physcon,* meaning "Potbelly"; Latin, *Ptolemaeus.*] King of Egypt (170–116 B.C.). He was born c184 B.C.; and died 116 B.C. He was a younger brother of Ptolemy VI, on whose death in 145 B.C. he usurped the throne, putting to death the legitimate heir Ptolemy VII (surnamed Neos Philopator), and marrying the widowed queen, his sister. (For history previous to this event, see Ptolemy VI). He was expelled from Alexandria by the populace, who supported his wife, in 130 B.C. but recovered his capital in 127. His very evil reputation is probably due to his usurpation of the throne, the murder of the prince, and his later murder of his son by his sister, who would have succeeded him, and thus is well-founded. He married (c130 B.C.) his wife's daughter by her first husband, Ptolemy VI.

Ptolemy IX (of *Egypt*). [Surnamed *Lathyrus* or *Soter,* meaning "Savior," "Preserver"; called also *Ptolemy Soter II*; Latin *Ptolemaeus.*] King of Egypt (116–81 B.C.); son of Ptolemy VIII. He died in 81 B.C. On the death of his father he ascended the throne conjointly with his mother, Cleopatra. He was, in 108 B.C., expelled from Egypt by Cleopatra. He succeeded, however, in maintaining himself in Cyprus, which he held as an independent kingdom until the death of his mother in 88 B.C., when he was recalled by the Alexandrians. They had in the meantime expelled his brother, who had reigned as Ptolemy X.

Ptolemy X (of *Egypt*). [Called *Ptolemy Alexander I*; Latin, *Ptolemaeus.*] King of Egypt (108–88 B.C.); brother of Ptolemy IX; died 88 B.C. He was made joint ruler with his brother, and after his expulsion (108 B.C.) ruled alone. After his mother's death, he was attacked and deposed by Ptolemy IX, and was killed fighting against his brother in Cyprus.

Ptolemy XI (of *Egypt*). [Called *Ptolemy Alexander II*; Latin,

Ptolemaeus.] King of Egypt (80 B.C.); son of Ptolemy X. He ruled after the death of his uncle, Ptolemy IX, having married the widow of his predecessor through the offices of the Roman Sulla. Ptolemy very shortly thereafter killed her and was murdered himself by an outraged mob (80 B.C.).

Ptolemy XII (of *Egypt*). [Surnamed *Neos Dionysus* or *Auletes,* meaning "Flute-player"; Latin, ***Ptolemaeus.***] King of Egypt (80–51 B.C.); illegitimate son of Ptolemy IX. He died 51 B.C. He succeeded to the throne on the extinction of the legitimate line of the Ptolemies in 80 B.C. He was expelled by the populace in 58, but was restored by the Romans in 55 B.C.

Ptolemy XIII (of *Egypt*). [Latin, ***Ptolemaeus.***] King of Egypt (51–47 B.C.); son of Ptolemy XII; died 47 B.C. He ascended the throne conjointly with his sister Cleopatra, whom he expelled in 49 B.C. The reinstatement of Cleopatra by Caesar in 48 B.C. gave rise to war. Ptolemy was defeated on the Nile, and was drowned in the flight.

Ptolemy XIV (of *Egypt*). King of Egypt (47–44 B.C.); brother of Cleopatra; died 44 B.C. For political reasons Julius Caesar had Cleopatra marry her adolescent younger brother, but she had him killed in order that her son by Caesar, Caesarion, might reign as Ptolemy XV.

Ptolemy (of *Mauretania*). King of Mauretania and last of the Ptolemaic line; son of Juba II and grandson of Antony and Cleopatra. He was summoned to Rome and put to death by Caligula (40 A.D.), whose cupidity had been excited by his great wealth.

Publicola (pub-lik′ō-lạ). Name given to Publius Valerius, legendary Roman statesman and general of the 6th century B.C., who was renowned for his eloquence and his generosity. He was one of several prominent citizens who sought to throw off the harsh rule of the Tarquins, and helped Lucius Junius Brutus to drive them out following the rape of Lucretia, wife of Tarquinius Collatinus, by the son of Tarquin the Proud. Following their expulsion, the Romans decided not to entrust their affairs to one leader but to divide the rule between two consuls. Valerius fully expected to be chosen as one of the consuls for his aid in driving out the Tarquins, and withdrew from public affairs in disappointment when Collatinus was chosen instead as the colleague of Brutus. However, he was one of the first of the senators to take the oath against the Tarquins, and

---

(obscured) errạnt, ardẹnt, actọr; ch, chip; g, go; th, thin; ᵺн, then; y, you; (variable) ḍ as d or j, ş as s or sh, ṭ as t or ch, ẓ as z or zh.

swore to defend Roman liberty with his sword.

Tarquin sent envoys from Gabii, whither he had gone for refuge, to treat with the Romans, but Valerius barred their admission to the city. Next, Tarquin sent to say he resigned all claim to the throne, and asked only that his treasure be sent to him, that he and his dependents might not be in want. The Romans decided to cast out the treasure with the tyrant and admitted envoys to collect and dispose of his effects. The envoys used their time in Rome to conspire against the Republic. They met with members of the Aquilii and Vitelii families and wrote letters to Tarquin outlining a plot to kill the consuls and restore him as ruler of Rome. Some say they bound themselves to secrecy by drinking the blood of a human sacrifice. By chance, Vindicius, a slave in the house of the Aquilii, overheard their plot. Fearing that the consuls, both of whom were related to members of these two houses, would not believe him, he chose to go to Valerius, who was noted for his availability and for his justice. When Valerius heard of the plot he rushed to the house of the Aquilii with trusted aides and found the letters of which Vindicius had informed him. While he was still in the house the Aquilii returned and set upon him, but he successfully fought them, twisted their gowns around their necks, and dragged them to the Forum. Valerius produced Vindicius, an accusation was lodged, and the letters of the plotters were read. Among the conspirators were two sons of Brutus. Brutus handed them over to the lictors who put them to death for their crime against Rome; then Brutus withdrew from the Forum. Collatinus, the other consul, would have restored Vindicius to his masters and allowed the conspirators to depart from Rome. Valerius opposed him. He sent for Brutus, who returned to the Forum and called on the Roman people to pass judgment on the other conspirators; for, he said, he had already passed judgment on his own sons. The people put the matter to a vote and condemned the conspirators, and they were executed on the spot. Collatinus resigned the consulship and withdrew from the city. Valerius was elected consul in his place (509 B.C.). Vindicius was freed and made a citizen, the palace of Tarquin was razed and the Campus Martius, on which it stood, was rededicated to the god Mars.

However, Tarquin had not given up his intention of re-

fat, fāte, fär, fâll, ȧsk, fãre; net, mē, hėr; pin, pīne; not, nōte, mȯve, nôr; up, lūte, pu̇ll; oi, oil; ou out; (lightened) ęlect, agǫny, ūnite;

gaining power in Rome. He received aid from the Tuscans
and approached Rome with a great force. The consuls led
the Roman troops against them. Brutus and Aruns, son of
Tarquin, killed each other in the battle; both sides sustained
such losses that each thought itself defeated. The Romans
were thoroughly disheartened. Valerius was uncertain what
to do. In the night a divine voice issued from a nearby grove
and proclaimed, "The Tuscans have lost one more man than
the Romans." This inspirited the Romans and discouraged
the Tuscans, most of whom thereupon withdrew; those who
remained were taken prisoner by the Romans. When the
dead were counted, it was found that there was one more
Tuscan corpse than Roman. Valerius returned to Rome in
a chariot drawn by four horses, pronounced the funeral
oration of Brutus and buried him with honor, and was himself honored with a triumph. With the death of Brutus,
Valerius was the sole ruler, and soon the Romans complained that he exercised kingly power and lived royally in
a palace on the hill. Informed of these criticisms, he hired
workmen and ordered them to demolish his palace during
the night. The Romans were pleased that he heeded their
criticisms, but were saddened by the loss of so fine a palace;
and they were ashamed that Valerius had no place to live but
was compelled to go about from house to house among his
friends. They gave him a piece of ground and built him a
new, less magnificent, house. Sensible of their fear of tyrants, he gave up many of the trappings of power, but such
was the force and charm of his personality that the people
obeyed him without question and he actually increased his
personal power. To strengthen the Republic he brought the
Senate, reduced in numbers by the Tarquins, up to strength.
He promulgated liberal laws and revised the tax laws to
make them more equitable and less onerous. To guarantee
the public funds, he made the temple of Saturn the treasury
and gave the people the right to elect two treasurers, or
quaestors. And lastly, he ceased to rule alone: Marcus
Horatius became his fellow consul. For his justice, his service to the Republic and to the Roman people, he was
named Publicola, "The People's Respectful Friend."

Before Tarquin's second war against Rome, a prodigy
occurred that greatly heartened the Romans. While still king
he had begun the temple of Capitoline Jupiter, and had

ordered artists of Veii to make a terra-cotta chariot to be placed atop it. Although he was driven out of Rome before the temple was completed, the artists went ahead and molded the chariot and set it in the fire to harden, whereupon it swelled to such a size that they could hardly withdraw it from the kiln. Soothsayers said this meant success for the people who possessed the chariot, and the Tuscans refused to give it to the Romans. Shortly afterward, in the course of games at Veii, the winner of the chariot-race was driving out of the arena. Suddenly his horses bolted, and in spite of his efforts to control them, they carried him off to Rome. The people of Veii were alarmed at this, and ordered the Tuscan artists to give up their earthen chariot to the Romans. Meanwhile, Tarquin had found assistance with Lars Porsena of Clusium, the most eminent and the most powerful ruler of Italy. He declared war on Rome and marched toward the city. Publicola, who was consul again, marched out to meet him. In the following battle Publicola received so many wounds he had to be carried from the field. The Romans retreated in dismay within their walls, leaving Horatius Cocles, with Titus Herminius and Spurius Lartius, to resist the Etruscans at the bridgehead. Horatius valiantly held back the Etruscans until the bridge behind him was destroyed, then leaped into the Tiber and swam to the city. The Etruscans laid siege to Rome. Publicola was eager to treat with the Etruscans but Tarquin arrogantly refused to have anything to do with him. This angered Lars Porsena. The Etruscan leader, it is said, was impressed by Mucius Scaevola, who secretly entered the Etruscan camp and, when caught, held his hand in the fire to demonstrate the valor of the Romans. Lars Porsena agreed to a parley with the Romans and peace was made. The Romans gave ten young men and ten virgins to the Etruscans as hostages; among the latter was Valeria, daughter of Publicola. One day the maidens were bathing in the river. Cloelia, one of them, swam across to freedom and urged the others to do the same. When his daughter appeared to him, Publicola was angry at the violation of the Roman pledge, and immediately returned her and the other maidens to the Etruscan camp. In the peace treaty, Lars Porsena showed great magnanimity to the Romans, who sent him a throne decorated with ivory as a token of their gratitude.

At a later time, many women of Rome were afflicted by a strange disorder; their children were either still-born or born deformed. Publicola consulted the Sibylline Books, sacrificed to Pluto, restored certain games, and, the gods being thus appeased, the unusual births no longer occurred.

Altogether, Publicola was consul four times. He won Appius Claudius, a powerful Sabine ruler, to the side of Rome. He gave him, and the 5000 men he brought with him, land in Rome, made them citizens, and gave Appius a seat in the Senate. The other Sabines considered Appius a traitor. They marched to Fidenae and prepared an ambush against the Romans. Publicola learned of it and put the Sabines to rout, and was honored with a triumph. He died soon afterward, full of years, greatly honored and loved, and having seen his work for the establishment of the Republic prosper. He was buried at the public expense in the city, an honor awarded only to those who had performed great services for their country, and was mourned by the women of Rome for a year.

Publius Aelius Hadrianus (pub'li-us ē'li-us hā-dri-ā'nus). Full Latin name of ***Hadrian.***

Publius Cornelius Dolabella (kôr-nēl'yus dol-a̧-bel'a̧). See ***Dolabella, Publius Cornelius.***

Pyrrhus (pir'us). King of Epirus, and one of the greatest generals of antiquity; born c318 B.C.; killed at Argos, Greece, 272 B.C. He was the son of Aeacides, king of Epirus, and Phthia. His father claimed descent from Neoptolemus (also called Pyrrhus), son of Achilles. While Pyrrhus was still an infant the Molossians revolted, overthrew Aeacides, and killed his family and his friends. Pyrrhus was saved and carried off by loyal friends of his family. According to Plutarch, as the party fled before the Molossians they came to a raging river and had no means of crossing it. The people they saw on the other side could not understand their shouts over the roar of the flood. In desperation one of the party inscribed the name of the royal fugitive on a piece of bark, weighted it with a stone, and hurled it across the river. The men on the other side read it, understood the urgent need of the party to cross, hastily constructed a raft, and came over to fetch them. The first man who touched the bank happened to be named Achilles. He took young Pyrrhus in his arms and conveyed him to safety across the river. Pyrrhus was taken to the court of Glaucias, king of Illyria. King Glaucias hesitated to give him asylum, out of fear of Cassander, an enemy of Aeacides. As he pondered, so the story goes, the child crept to him and pulled himself to his knees by grasping the king's robe. Glaucias was moved to compassion and took the child into his own household and brought him up with his own sons until he was 12 years old. At that time Glaucias sent him back to Epirus at the head of an army and restored him to his throne. Some say, however, that Glaucias did not restore him with an army, but that he was recalled by the Epirotes. At the age of 17 he went to Illyria to attend the marriage of one of the sons of Glaucias. While he was gone the Molossians revolted again and set his cousin Neoptolemus on the throne. Pyrrhus went to Demetrius Poliorcetes, son of Alexander's general Antigonus, who was related to him by marriage. The successors of Alexander the Great were still struggling for control of his empire. Pyrrhus joined Demetrius and Antigonus against Lysimachus, Seleucus, Ptolemy, and Cassander, and fought bravely at the battle of Ipsus, 301 B.C. Demetrius and Antigonus were defeated, and Pyrrhus went as a hostage to Ptolemy in Egypt. There he noted that Berenice, wife of Ptolemy, exercised great influence. He courted her and won her good will, and made such a splendid impression on Ptolemy that he was given his stepdaughter Antigone in marriage. Out of gratitude, he later named his first son Ptolemy, and named a city he founded in Epirus Bereniceïs. Antigone secured men and money for him, and helped him to win back his kingdom (295 B.C.), the government of which he at first shared with the usurper, his cousin Neoptolemus. However, the divided rule was highly unsatisfactory to both parties. Partisans of Neoptolemus plotted to kill Pyrrhus. He was informed of the plot and forestalled the conspirators by killing Neoptolemus and making himself sole ruler. He was now in position to pursue his own ambitious plans. He first interfered in the affairs of Macedon, still at the mercy of those struggling to win control, and then seized the coast of Macedon and the regions of Ambracia, Acarnania, and Amphilochia. He was persuaded to meet his opponents to discuss peace. When sacrifices were to be made preparatory to swearing to the peace, a boar, a bull, and a ram were brought forth as victims. The ram dropped dead. Soothsayers pre-

dicted that one of the three kings negotiating the peace
would die, whereupon Pyrrhus refused to swear to the articles. Shortly after this Alexander, king of Macedon at the
peace negotiations, was murdered by Demetrius, thus fulfilling the prediction. Demetrius made himself king of Macedon, and thus a rival of Pyrrhus who had resolved to win
control of the unhappy country. Pyrrhus won victories, great
renown for himself by his bravery, skill, and daring, and the
admiration of the Macedonians he defeated, who compared
him to Alexander the Great. In the meantime, Demetrius
had gone into Epirus and was ravaging it. Pyrrhus returned,
and under a truce kept much of the Macedonian territory he
had won.

Pyrrhus devoted himself exclusively to military affairs.
After the death of Antigone he took several wives, for political reasons, and did all he could to foster the warlike natures
of their various sons. It is said that when one of the latter
asked him to which of them he would leave his kingdom, he
replied, "To the one who has the sharpest sword." He won
great fame and devotion from the Epirotes, who called him
"the Eagle." "If I am an eagle," he said, "you have made me
one; for it is on your arms, as upon wings, that I have risen
so high." He was noted as a beneficent prince, who was
quick to forgive an injury and even quicker to repay a kindness. In 286 B.C. he embarked on a plundering raid into
Macedon. Meeting no resistance, he advanced as far as
Edessa (Aegae). Then Demetrius raised a force and he withdrew, losing a considerable number of his men to the harassing attacks of Demetrius on the way. Demetrius planned to
win back Asia, but was unwilling to leave so dangerous an
enemy as Pyrrhus behind him. For this reason he made
peace with him. Seleucus, Ptolemy, Lysimachus, kings respectively of Asia, Egypt, and Thrace, became alarmed at
the preparations of Demetrius for war. They took up arms
against him and urged Pyrrhus to do the same. Encouraged
by a vision of Alexander the Great that came to him in a
dream, Pyrrhus marched against Demetrius. He took Beroea
on the Haliacmon River. Demetrius returned to drive him
out, but the Macedonians went over to Pyrrhus; Demetrius,
deserted by his army, disguised himself and fled. Pyrrhus
won his camp without striking a blow. Lysimachus now arrived and demanded half the kingdom. Pyrrhus did not feel

(obscured) errạnt, ardẹnt, actọr; ch, chip; g, go; th, thin; ᴛʜ, then; y, you;
(variable) ḍ as d or j, ṣ as s or sh, ṭ as t or ch, ẕ as z or zh.

strong enough to defeat him and yielded to his demand. When Demetrius had been driven from Athens by Pyrrhus, Lysimachus felt strong enough to attack Pyrrhus. He attacked his camp at Edessa, cut off his supplies, and compelled him, through hunger, to retire to Epirus, thus ending his influence and power in Macedonia in the same year in which he had won it (286 B.C.). Now, says Plutarch, Pyrrhus might have enjoyed the peaceful possession of his own kingdom, but he had no talent for peace. The people of Tarentum, engaged in a war with the Romans, asked him to come and command them. He immediately envisioned a conquest of the western world and gathered his host. Plutarch quotes a supposed conversation between Pyrrhus and one of his most trusted lieutenants, Cineas. "Suppose," said Cineas, "that you conquer the Romans, what then?" He would go and conquer Sicily. "And supposing a successful conquest of Sicily." Next he would win Africa. "And after that?" He would settle back and enjoy peace and prosperity. "But," persisted Cineas, "you have that now. Why risk men, treasure, and the horrors of war for what you already have?" Pyrrhus could give no answer, which made him somewhat discontented with Cineas but in no way changed his mind. He set out for Italy with 3000 horse, 20,000 foot, 20 elephants, 2000 archers, and 500 slingers. On the way his fleet was scattered by a great storm. He reached Italy with a small number of horse, 2000 foot, and two elephants. At Tarentum he found the people frivolously dissipating their time and strength; he immediately and sternly organized them for the war they had asked him to command. He learned that the Roman consul, Laevinus, was approaching with a large army, and sent word to him that he would act as mediator between the Romans and the Greeks in Italy. Laevinus replied that he "neither accepted Pyrrhus as a mediator nor feared him as an enemy," and continued his march. Although all his forces had not yet arrived, Pyrrhus resolved to act. He rode out to observe the Roman camp, and remarked with admiration that "the disposition of these barbarians has nothing of the barbarian in it." In the battle that followed at Heraclea (280 B.C.) Pyrrhus defeated the Romans, but lost many of his best men. He took the Roman camp and won many cities that had been allied to Rome. He advanced toward Rome itself and sent an embassy to the

Senate, offering generous terms of peace. As the Senate considered whether to accept, Appius Claudius, who had built the Appian Way and had brought water from the Anio to Rome, had himself led into the Senate. He was blind, and now, he said, he wished he were deaf as well, so that he would not hear the Romans, who boasted that they could have defeated Alexander the Great, trembling before Pyrrhus who could not even hold Macedon. When he finished speaking the Senate voted for war, and sent word to Pyrrhus that when he had left Italy they would be glad to make a treaty of friendship with him; otherwise they would continue to fight him. The Roman Fabricius came to discuss ransom for the Roman prisoners and made a deep impression on Pyrrhus by his absolute refusal to accept any of the gifts offered him. Fabricius learned of a plot to poison Pyrrhus, and warned him of it. In gratitude, Pyrrhus freed the prisoners without ransom. When the Romans again rejected his peace offers he attacked at Asculum in Apulia, on the slopes of the Apennines. A fierce battle raged, which was ended by the coming of night. The next day on ground suitable for effective operation by his elephants, Pyrrhus drove the Romans back and defeated them (279 B.C.). In the two days Pyrrhus lost all his best officers and many men whom he could not replace. When he was congratulated on his victory he said, "Another such victory and we are done!" (Whence the expression "Pyrrhic victory.")

Following his victories in Italy, Pyrrhus was invited by the Greeks of Sicily to drive out the Carthaginians. He went to Sicily, drove back the Carthaginians, took the strongly fortified city of Eryx (Lilybaeum), and offered splendid sacrifices to Heracles and held games in his honor. The Carthaginians offered to make peace, but he sent the reply he had received from Rome: that he would make peace with them when they had withdrawn from the island. His ambition was to conquer Africa, and in a very high-handed way he began to levy men and ships, and lost the good will of the Sicilians. His plans misfired; Rome and Carthage joined to oppose him; he decided to go back to Italy (276 B.C.). On the way he lost part of his fleet to Carthaginian attacks, and when he landed in Italy he was harassed by the Mamertines. In an engagement he was wounded in the head. One of the Mamertines tauntingly called for Pyrrhus to come forth. He

(obscured) errant, ardent, actor; ch, chip; g, go; th, thin; ŦH, then; y, you;
(variable) d̡ as d or j, ş as s or sh, ţ as t or ch, z̧ as z or zh.

strode through his army, his head streaming with blood, faced the man who had taunted him, and clove his skull with his sword. The Mamertines were dazzled with admiration, and henceforward left him alone. Returning to Tarentum, he attacked the Romans at Beneventum and was defeated (275 B.C.). He now returned to Epirus, marched into Macedon and took all before him, winning Aegae, and the admiration of the Macedonians, many of whom flocked to his standard. At the request of a Spartan dissident he marched into the Peloponnesus, plundered Laconia, and prepared to take the city of Sparta, but failed and withdrew. However, his "hopes grew as fast as they were cut off" and he marched to Argos, harassed as he went by the Spartans. By treachery he entered Argos at night. In the darkness and confusion his soldiers scattered and fought to little purpose. At daybreak Pyrrhus was greatly disturbed to see an image of a bronze bull and a wolf fighting, for an oracle had said he would die when he saw a wolf encountering a bull. As he observed the turmoil in the city, and the fact that his elephants could not operate in the confined space, he decided to withdraw, and sent orders to his son Helenus to break down a part of the wall of the city to facilitate his exit. His order was misunderstood. Helenus drove into the city with his forces. The streets were jammed, those trying to get out were blocked by those forcing their way in. The elephants went mad and added terror to the confusion. One elephant, searching for his fallen master, trod frantically on all before him until he found his master's body. This he took up in his trunk and placed on his tusks, then bellowing furiously he trampled on all around him. Pyrrhus saw his position was hopeless. He removed his plumed helmet and gave it to a friend, then wheeled his horse and charged in among the enemy. He received a slight wound in the breast and turned to engage the man who had accidentally made the thrust. This man's mother was watching the battle from a nearby roof. Seeing her son in great peril she seized a tile from the roof, threw it with all her might, and struck Pyrrhus on the head. He fell from his horse unconscious. Argives who did not recognize him dragged him to a nearby porch. There one who had served under Antigonus recognized him and drew his sword to cut off his head, but as he raised his arm Pyrrhus opened his eyes and gave him such a fierce look that he wavered, and succeeded in only wounding the fallen general on the face. After many blows, he hacked off his head. Alcyoneus, son of Antigonus, rode up and asked for Pyrrhus' head. He took it to his father and flung it at his feet. Antigonus struck him for an impious barbarian and then, grieving for the changes Fortune brings to men, wept for his grandfather Antigonus, killed at Ipsus, 301 B.C., and for his father Demetrius, who had died in prison. He clothed the body of Pyrrhus in rich garments and put it, with the head, on a funeral pyre and burned it with due honor. The life of Pyrrhus was studded with possibilities. He might have made Epirus a formidable kingdom. He might have arrested the expansion of Rome and won Sicily from the Carthaginians. Instead, when he left Italy he remarked prophetically, "What a battleground I am leaving to Rome and Carthage." Hannibal is said to have ranked Alexander the Great as the world's greatest general, and Pyrrhus next to him.

Quintius (kwin'shi-us, -shus) or *Quinctius* (kwingk'shi-us, -shus), *Flamininus*. See *Flamininus, Titus Quintius* or *Quinctius*.

Quintus Fabius Maximus (fā'bi-us mak'si-mus). See *Fabius Maximus, Quintus*.

Rabirius (ra̧-bē'ri-us), *Caius*. Roman senator, fl. 1st century B.C. In 63 B.C., at the instigation of Julius Caesar, he was accused by the tribune Titus Labienus of the murder of Lucius Appuleius Saturninus, which had taken place in 100 B.C. Caesar revived an obsolete procedure and acted, with Lucius Caesar, as judge in the trial of Rabirius, who was defended by Cicero. Rabirius was condemned, but before the decision could be ratified by the people, Quintus Metellus Celer, the praetor, dissolved the assembly.

Rabirius, Caius Postumus. Nephew and adopted son of Caius Rabirius. He was defended successfully by Cicero (54 B.C.) when Gabinius brought charges of extortion against him. Cicero's speech *(Pro Rabirio Postumo),* used for his defense, survives.

Regulus (reg′ū-lus), *Marcus Atilius.* Roman general; died c250 B.C. He was consul in 267 B.C., and as consul again in 256 during the First Punic War, he defeated the Carthaginian fleet of Ecnomus, invaded Africa, and defeated the Carthaginian army. The Carthaginians asked for peace, but Regulus laid down such harsh terms that they could not accept them and resolved to continue the war. In 255 B.C. the Carthaginians under the Spartan general Xanthippus defeated Regulus and took him prisoner. According to Roman tradition, after the Carthaginian defeat at Panormus by the Roman proconsul Metellus (250 B.C.), the Carthaginians sent Regulus, who had been held in captivity for five years, with an embassy to Rome to ask for peace or an exchange of prisoners. Regulus is said to have given his word that he would return to Carthage. When his embassy produced no results because he himself strongly advised the Senate not to accept the Carthaginian terms, he refused to follow the advice of friends who urged him to stay in Rome. Instead, he went back to Africa and was tortured to death. Later, Carthaginian prisoners who were handed over to his family were put to death with most cruel tortures. Some say the story of Regulus was afterward invented to justify the torture which his family had inflicted on the Carthaginian prisoners. In any case, the story of the honor and bravery of Regulus became a favorite with the Romans.

Roxana (rok-san′ạ, -sā′nạ). [Also: *Roxane.*] Wife of Alexander the Great; murdered at Amphipolis, Macedonia, 311 B.C. She was a Bactrian princess, the daughter of King Oxyartes, and was married to Alexander in 327 B.C. Alexander took other wives, according to the Oriental custom he increasingly followed, perhaps with the view to linking the Barbarians more closely with their Macedonian conquerors. In 324 B.C. he married Statira, daughter of Darius III, at Susa. After his death Roxana, then carrying his child, sent for Statira, who did not know Alexander had died. With the help of

Perdiccas Roxana killed Statira and her sister, threw their bodies into a well, and filled it up with earth. At Babylon she bore Alexander's posthumous son, who was accepted by the Diadochi (Alexander's generals and successors) as co-king with Alexander's half-brother Arrhidaeus. Roxana went to Macedonia, where she sided with Olympias, Alexander's mother, against Cassander, and was put to death with her son by order of Cassander, 311 B.C.

Rufus (rö′fus), *Marcus Caelius.* See *Caelius.*

Rufus, Publius Sulpicius. See *Sulpicius Rufus, Publius.*

Rullianus (rul-i-ā′nus). See *Fabius Maximus, Quintus.*

Rullus (rul′us), *Publius Servilius.* Roman tribune of the people (63 B.C.). He sponsored a law for redistribution of lands to the advantage of the poorer citizens. Cicero made four speeches (three extant) against the measure, which was withdrawn, being obviously an attempt on the part of the party of Caesar to lay the onus of oppression on the aristocratic party.

Rupilius (rö-pil′i-us), *Publius.* Roman politician, consul in 132 B.C. He is noted for the severity with which he prosecuted the followers of Tiberius Gracchus. He was subsequently brought to trial and condemned for persecuting them. In the meantime, he had suppressed a slave war on the island of Sicily in 131 B.C., and had organized the island as a Roman province.

S

Sandrocottus (san-drō-kot′us) or *Sandrokottos* (-os). [Also: *Chandragupta.*] The founder of the Maurya or Magadha kingdom in India (capital, Patna). He died c286 B.C. He reigned c322–c298 B.C. According to the Greek tradition he was an Indian king who in the time of Seleucus I (Seleucus Nicator) ruled over the Gangaridae and Prasii on the banks of the Ganges. He was of humble origin, and was the leader of a band of robbers before obtaining the supreme power. In the troubles following the death of Alexander, he extended his sway over the greater part of N India, conquering the Macedonians left by Alexander in the Punjab. Seleucus invaded his dominions, but did not succeed, and, concluding a peace, ceded to Sandrocottus his conquests in the Punjab and the country of the Paropamisus, receiving in return 500 war elephants. For many years afterward Seleucus had as his ambassador at the court of Sandrocottus, Megasthenes, to whose work entitled *Indica* later Greek writers were chiefly indebted for their accounts of India. The king is supposed to have abdicated and later to have committed suicide. The identification of Chandragupta with Sandrocottus admits of no reasonable doubt. This identification is of the utmost importance to Indian chronology, in which everything depends upon the date of Chandragupta as ascertained from that of Sandrocottus as given by the classical writers. Hindu and Buddhist writers are entirely silent as to Alexander, but show that Chandragupta overthrew the dynasty of the Nandas and "established freedom in India by the help of robbers." His capital was Pataliputra (in Greek, Palibothra), the modern Patna. The dynasty of the Nandas is often spoken of as the "nine Nandas," meaning "nine descents," or according to some, "the last king Mahapadma and eight sons." Mahapadma Nanda was the son of a Sudra (the lowest of the four castes of India), and so by law a Sudra himself. He was a tyrant. The Brahman Chanakya is represented as having brought about his fall. Chandragupta was then raised to the throne and founded the Mauryan dynasty, of which the great Asoka was the third king. The commentator on the Vishnupurana says that he was a son of Nanda by a low-caste woman named Mura (whence he and his descendants were called Mauryas). The Buddhists claim that the Mauryas were of the same family with Buddha, the Sakyas.

Saturninus (sa-tėr-nī′nus), **Lucius Appuleius.** Roman demagogue. He was quaestor in 104 B.C. and tribune of the people in 103 and 100 B.C. Politically he was a supporter of Marius and ardently sought the favor of the popular party. With the aid of his personal bodyguard, bribery, and murder, he helped Marius to be elected consul for the sixth time, 100 B.C., and was himself made tribune of the plebs for the second time. As tribune he proposed that land north of the Po, won from the Cimbri by Marius, be distributed to Marius' veterans, and that colonies be founded in Sicily,

Greece, and Macedonia. Furthermore, he demanded that
the Senate should swear to approve the laws proposed by
the tribunes. Only Metellus Numidicus refused to be in-
timidated by Saturninus and his unruly band. He refused to
swear the required oath and was banished. Saturninus
secured the passage of his agrarian laws following a period
of great disorder. At the end of the year (100 B.C.) he was
elected tribune again for the following year. At the same
time his lawless ally, Glaucia, sought to become consul. The
senatorial candidate for the consulship was Memmius. Partisans of Saturninus and Glaucia murdered Memmius. The
tide of public feeling turned against Saturninus and Glaucia,
and though Marius was greatly indebted to them he was
ordered by the Senate to take up arms against Saturninus.
Saturninus was defeated in the Forum, and was slain by a
mob who removed tiles from the building where he had
been imprisoned and pelted him to death with them.

Scaevola (sē'vō̱-la̱, sev'ō̱-). *Caius Mucius.* Roman hero. According to legend, when Lars Porsena was besieging Rome in
509 B.C., Scaevola, concealing a dagger about his person,
went to the king's camp with the intention of putting him to
death, but killed instead a royal secretary whom he mistook
for Porsena. He was threatened with death by fire unless he
revealed the details of a conspiracy which he said had been
formed at Rome for the purpose of assassinating Porsena,
whereupon he thrust his right hand into a sacrificial fire
burning on an altar hard by, and permitted the flames utterly to consume the flesh and bones. This extraordinary
demonstration of disregard for physical pain so excited the
admiration of Porsena that he ordered Scaevola to be
released. The story, which is perhaps as widely known as the
one about the Spartan boy who remained impassive while a
fox devoured his entrails, probably stems from an etiologi-
cal legend hinging upon the name Scaevola, which means
"left-handed."

Scipio (sip'i-ō). [Called *Scipio the Elder;* full name, *Publius Cornelius Scipio Africanus.*] Roman general; son of Publius Cornelius Scipio; born c236 B.C.; died probably 183 B.C. He
served at the battle of the Ticinus (Ticino) River (218 B.C.),
where he is said to have saved his father's life, and also at
Cannae (216 B.C.) where he was one of the few Roman
officers to survive. He became aedile in 212, and was ap-

(obscured) errant, ardent, actor; ch, chip; g, go; th, thin; ᵮʜ, then; y, you;
(variable) ḏ as d or j, ş as s or sh, ţ as t or ch, ᶎ as z or zh.

pointed to the chief command in Spain as proconsul in 210 B.C. He landed at the mouth of the Iberus (Ebro) River and captured Carthago Nova (Cartagena), the Carthaginian port and headquarters in Spain, and with it took a rich store of war supplies. In 209 B.C. he defeated Hasdrubal, Hannibal's brother, but could not prevent him from marching to Italy to aid Hannibal. Scipio won over many of the Spanish chiefs to his side, and in 206 B.C. decisively defeated the Carthaginians at Ilipa and completed the conquest of Spain. The following year he was elected consul and was given Sicily as his province. Hannibal was at this time operating in southern Italy. Scipio was an ardent advocate of carrying the war to Africa. Over the objections of the Roman nobles he invaded Africa, 204 B.C., and the following year defeated Scyphax, the Numidian ally of Carthage, and a Carthaginian army under Hasdrubal (son of Gisco). The Carthaginians refused to accept his peace terms, although they were moderate, the war was continued, and in 202 B.C. he defeated Hannibal, who had been recalled from Italy to defend Carthage, at the battle of Zama. Carthage was compelled to submit, accepted the reasonable terms that Scipio offered for peace, and the Second Punic War was brought to a conclusion (201 B.C.). When Scipio returned to Rome he was welcomed with the greatest enthusiasm. He accepted the surname Africanus but disclaimed the other honors the grateful Romans would have given him. In 199 B.C. he was censor, but otherwise for the next few years after the end of the war he lived quietly, withdrawn from the political scene. In 194 B.C. he was consul for the second time, and in 193 he went to Africa to mediate a dispute between the Numidian king, Massinissa, and Carthage. In 190 B.C. his brother Lucius was given chief command in the war against Antiochus III of Syria. Scipio accompanied him as legate and between them they decisively defeated Antiochus. On their return to Rome, however, Lucius, who had taken the name Asiaticus, was accused of diverting to his own use some of the money paid by Antiochus to Rome, was tried, condemned, and fined. In 187 B.C. enemies of Scipio brought a charge against him of having accepted a bribe from Antiochus. On the day of the trial he completely reversed the popular mood and won their enthusiastic acclaim by reminding them that it was the anniversary of his victory

fat, fāte, fär, fâll, ȧsk, fãre; net, mē, hèr; pin, pīne; not, nōte, möve, nôr; up, lūte, pùll; oi, oil; ou out; (lightened) ẹlect, agǫny, ụnite;

of Zama. In the end the crowd marched to the Capitol with him to give thanks to the gods for such a noble citizen and to pray for more like him. After this Scipio retired to his country estate at Liternum, on the coast of Campania, where he remained until his death. Scipio was the father of Cornelia, who became the mother of the Gracchi.

Scipio. [Called *Scipio the Younger;* full name, ***Publius Cornelius Scipio Aemilianus Africanus Numantinus.***] Roman general; born c185 B.C.; died 129 B.C. He was the second son of Aemilius Paulus Macedonicus (c299–160 B.C.) and Papiria, daughter of the consul Maso. His father's sister was Aemilia, wife of Scipio Africanus the Elder. When he was a young man he was adopted by Scipio Africanus, the elder son of Scipio Africanus the Elder, whence his name. He accompanied his father on the campaign against Perseus, king of Macedonia, and took part in the battle of Pydna (168 B.C.). When the battle ended in Roman victory, young Scipio was missing. His father grieved, and the men in the army, who admired the young soldier's bravery, set out to look for him. However, he soon returned to the camp with several companions, covered with blood but glowing with enthusiasm, and announced that he had been pursuing the enemy. On his return to Rome he pursued his studies, with special attention to literature. Lucilius and Terence the poets, and Panaetius the philosopher were among his friends. Polybius, the Greek general and historian who had been brought to Rome as a hostage, with 1000 other prominent Achaeans, became his intimate friend and adviser. Scipio secured (151 B.C.) the release of the Achaean hostages and they returned home. In the same year he went as military tribune to Spain where he served with distinction and won the respect of the Spanish tribes. In 149 B.C., on the outbreak of the Third Punic War, he went as military tribune to Africa, and by his personal bravery and skill saved the army of the consul Manilius from destruction. In 147 B.C., although he was under the legal age, he was appointed consul with Africa as his province. He besieged Carthage with great vigor, skill, and bravery, and despite the heroic resistance of the defenders of the citadel took it, 146 B.C. Polybius, who accompanied him, describes the war in his *History.* In accordance with instructions from Rome he leveled Carthage to the ground. Some say the land on which it stood was plowed and sowed with salt so that no city could ever rise on it again. When he returned to Rome he was given a splendid triumph. He acted as censor, 142 B.C., and in his term attempted to raise the moral level of the age by removing some of the more notorious men from the ranks of the senators. One who had been degraded brought charges of high treason against him (139 B.C.), but he defended himself brilliantly in speeches which were greatly admired in his time but are now lost; he was acquitted. In 134 B.C. he was again elected consul, with Spain as his province. He reorganized the Roman army that had been vainly trying to take Numantia there, and in 133 B.C. captured the city and established Roman power in Hither Spain. For his success in the capture of Numantia he was given the surname Numantinus. On his return to Rome, 132 B.C., he allied himself with the aristocratic party against the popular party, although the latter was led by his brothers-in-law the Gracchi. He appears to have been a moderate, not so much attracted by the conservatism of the aristocratic party as he was repelled by the extremism of the popular party. He was found dead in his room one morning after a tempestuous day in the forum, and was commonly supposed to have been assassinated. Scipio the Younger was one of the outstanding examples of all that was best in the Roman character in the waning days of the Republic. He was a brave and brilliant soldier, and a cultivated man of public honor and private virtue.

Scipio, Publius Cornelius. Roman general; killed 212 or 211 B.C. He was consul in 218 B.C., when he attempted unsuccessfully to prevent Hannibal's passage of the Rhodanus (Rhône), and was defeated at the Ticinus (Ticino) River and (with Sempronius, his co-consul, who insisted on fighting against his advice) at the Trebia (Trebbia) River. In 217 B.C. he defeated the Carthaginian fleet at the mouth of the Iberus (Ebro), whereby he gained for the Romans the supremacy of the sea. With his brother, Cnaeus Cornelius Scipio, he gained several victories over the Carthaginians in Spain, but was defeated and slain with his brother, possibly due to the desertion of native tribes who had been wooed away by Carthaginian gold. He was the father of Scipio Africanus the Elder.

Scipio, Quintus Caecilius Metellus Pius. See *Metellus Pius Scipio, Quintus Caecilius.*

fat, fāte, fär, fåll, ȧsk, fāre; net, mē, hėr; pin, pīne; not, nōte, möve, nôr; up, lūte, pŭll; oi, oil; ou out; (lightened) ḝlect, agǫny, ụnite;

Seleucids (sē-lö′sidz). [Also: **Seleucidae.**] Royal dynasty in Syria which reigned from 312 B.C. to c64 B.C.; descended from Seleucus I (Seleucus Nicator).

Seleucus I (sē-lö′kus). [Surnamed **Nicator,** meaning "Conqueror."] King of Syria; born 358 B.C.; died 280 B.C. He was the father of Antiochus I. Following the sudden death of Alexander the Great in 323 B.C. his chief generals, including Perdiccas, Seleucus, Antipater, Antigonus, Ptolemy, Eumenes, Craterus, and Lysimachus, being men equally of ambition and of violence, began without delay to contend among themselves for power and dominion. Perdiccas became regent for the dead conqueror's posthumous son but Antipater also claimed the regency and was supported by Ptolemy, Antigonus, and Craterus. Thus began the intermittent struggles known as the Wars of the Diadochi (Successors), which continued until 281 B.C. Seleucus was Perdiccas' chief supporter, but following the latter's defeat by Ptolemy, he engaged in the conspiracy which led to the assassination of Perdiccas in 321 B.C. In 312 B.C. he secured control of Babylonia. The city of Seleucia was built as the capital of this realm, superseding Babylon. Ambitious more than any of the others of the Diadochi to reëstablish Alexander's empire in its fullness, he invaded India, but after a defeat at Pataliputra (now Patna) in 305 B.C. he made peace with the Indian monarch Chandragupta on terms, including a gift by the latter of 500 elephants. In 306 or 305 B.C., following the example of Antigonus, he assumed the title of king. In 301 B.C. he joined with Lysimachus, Ptolemy, and Cassander, son of Antipater (who died in 319 B.C.), to defeat and kill Antigonus, whose ambition threatened all the other surviving Diadochi, at the battle of Ipsus. In the division of spoils following this victory, Seleucus received Syria. Thereafter he extended his rule over a large part of Asia Minor, and his power reached its height with the defeat and death of Lysimachus in 281 B.C. Following this his ambition overreached itself, as the sequel showed. Aspiring to dominate the original seat of Alexander's power, he invaded Macedonia, where in 280 B.C. he was assassinated at the instigation of Ptolemy II. Seleucus I instituted the tight, efficient system of administration, modeled on Persian absolutism, which characterized the rule of the Seleucids.

Seleucus II. [Surnamed **Callinicus,** meaning "Gloriously Vic-

(obscured) errạnt, ardẹnt, actọr; ch, chip; g, go; th, thin; ᵺH, then; y, you; (variable) ḍ as d or j, ṣ as s or sh, ṭ as t or ch, ẓ as z or zh.

torious."] King of Syria; died 226 B.C. He was the eldest son of Antiochus II and the father of Antiochus III. This monarch of the Seleucid dynasty hardly deserved his surname; his story is more interesting for what was done with, for, and to him, than for any achievement of his own. His mother was Laodice, whom his father, in the course of diplomacy, put aside to marry Berenice, daughter of Ptolemy II and sister of Ptolemy III of Egypt. These formalities completed, Antiochus returned to live with Laodice, but presently she poisoned him and proclaimed their son Seleucus king (247 B.C.). Berenice summoned Ptolemy III to support the claim of her infant son to the throne, but before Egyptian aid could arrive, Seleucus procured the murder of Berenice and his rival. Ptolemy wrested parts of Syria and Asia Minor from Seleucus, who later recovered some of the lost territory. His redoubtable mother, however, backed a revolt by his younger brother Antiochus Hierax, to whom Seleucus was constrained to yield a portion of his kingdom in Asia Minor, after a battle at Ancyra (modern Ankara) in 235 B.C. His death a few years later was due to accidental causes.

Seleucus III. [Surnamed *Soter,* meaning "Savior."] King of Syria (226–223 B.C.); eldest son of Seleucus II. He tried to retake Asia Minor from Attalus of Pergamum but failed. He was killed in a conspiracy.

Seleucus IV. [Surnamed *Philopator,* meaning "Father-loving."] King of Syria (187–175 B.C.). He inherited a diminished empire from his father, Antiochus III. He was assassinated in a plot led by Heliodorus and was succeeded by his brother Antiochus IV.

Seleucus V. King of Syria (125 B.C.). He was killed in a plot directed by his mother, Cleopatra Thea.

Seleucus VI. King of Syria (96–95 B.C.).

Sertorius (sẽr-tō'ri-us), *Quintus.* Roman general; assassinated 72 B.C. He served under Marius in the wars against the Cimbri and the Teutones, served in Spain in 97 B.C., and was quaestor in 91 B.C. When civil war broke out (88 B.C.) in Rome, he opposed the aristocratic party that was headed by Sulla and became commander of one of the armies that besieged Rome under Marius and Cinna. He was not, however, in favor of the bloodshed that followed Marius' success in gaining control of Rome. He was praetor in 83 and went to Spain as Marian commander either in the same or the following year. When Sulla gained control of Rome, Sertorius was proscribed and fled to Mauretania, where he captured Tingis (Tangier), and waged war, generally with success, against the Sullan commanders. At the request of the Lusitanians, he returned to Spain and became their leader against the Romans. He was opposed by Quintus Caecilius Metellus Pius after 79, and also by Pompey after 77 B.C. Following the death of Sulla, he was joined by Marcus Perpenna (or Perperna) and other Romans (77 B.C.). Neither Pius nor Pompey could defeat him. However, Perpenna grew jealous of his power, and intrigued with other Roman officers against him, and assassinated him, 72 B.C.

Servius Sulpicius Galba (sèr'vi-us sul-pish'us gal'ba̧). See *Galba, Servius Sulpicius.*

Smerdis (smèr'dis). [Also: *Bardiya.*] A son of Cyrus the Great, and the younger brother of Cambyses. Cyrus made him governor of the provinces in the east before he died. He accompanied Cambyses on his campaign against Egypt, but was sent back to Persia by his jealous brother because, according to Herodotus, Smerdis was the only one of all the Persians able to bend a bow that the Aethiopians had sent to Cambyses. Cambyses then dreamed that Smerdis sat on the royal throne and that his head touched the heavens. He interpreted this to mean that Smerdis would seize his throne. To prevent this, Cambyses ordered his trusted aide Prexaspes to return to Persia and secretly to slay Smerdis. Prexaspes successfully carried out this command (c523 B.C.), but the death of Smerdis was not generally known, and a false Smerdis arose and assumed his place and name.

Smerdis, False. [Original name, *Gaumata.*] A Median *magus* (priest). His brother Patizeithes was left in charge of the king's household when Cambyses, son of Cyrus the Great, left Susa to attack Egypt. Patizeithes conceived a bold plan to rebel against Cambyses and seize the throne. He knew that Smerdis, son of Cyrus, had been secretly slain at Cambyses' order. His brother Gaumata bore a strong resemblance to Smerdis. Patizeithes engineered a revolt, which consisted in setting Guamata on the throne, announcing that he was Smerdis, son of Cyrus, and sending heralds throughout the land and beyond its borders to proclaim that Smerdis, not Cambyses, was the true king. When this news reached Cambyses he concluded that Prexaspes, the trusted aide whom he had ordered to slay Smerdis, had betrayed him and had not carried out his orders. He charged Prexaspes with treachery. Prexaspes assured Cambyses that he had carried out his orders and had buried Smerdis with his own hands, and that the man who had sent out the heralds proclaiming Smerdis was king could not be Smerdis, son of Cyrus, unless the dead could return to life. Prexaspes called the herald who had brought the news before him and questioned him; he learned that the herald had never seen Smerdis but had received his orders from Patizeithes, the magus left in charge by Cambyses. Prexaspes immediately divined what had happened: that Gaumata, the brother of Patizeithes, had set himself up as Smerdis and seized the throne. Cambyses determined to return to Susa and expose the impostor, but as he leaped to his horse he was wounded by his own sword. The wound did not heal. When he realized that his end was near he called the chief Persians to him and related to them that because of a false dream he had caused his brother Smerdis to be slain. He assured them that the Smerdis now occupying the throne was an impostor. He charged his chiefs not to allow the throne of Persia to remain in the hands of the Medes, but to recover it, taking whatever means were necessary. After the death of Cambyses Prexaspes swore that he had not killed Smerdis, as it was unsafe for him to admit it now that a Smerdis was on the throne. The chiefs who had heard the words of dying Cambyses thought he had invented his tale out of hatred of his brother and in the hope of causing his downfall, so Smerdis the magus was undisturbed in his reign. He ruled for seven months, and in this time freed all the nations under his sway from war service. But in the eighth month there were some who began to suspect he was not truly Smerdis, for he never left the palace and no one was allowed to see him. One of those whose suspicions were aroused was Otanes, a Persian nobleman. His daughter Phaedima had been among the wives of Cambyses, and on his death she was taken over, with the other wives, by Smerdis. Otanes sent word asking his daughter if the man who shared her couch was actually Smerdis, the son of Cyrus, or some other man. She replied that she did not know, as she had never seen Smerdis, and furthermore, she could not ask because all the wives had been separated by the new king and were forbidden to communicate with each other. Otanes was now sure that this king was an impostor. He instructed his daughter, when the king came to her bed, to feel his ears while he slept. If he had ears it was truly Smerdis, the son of Cyrus, but if he had no ears it was Gaumata the magus, because during the lifetime of Cyrus, Gaumata the magus had had his ears cut off as a punishment for a crime. Phaedima, in spite of the risk, agreed to do as her father commanded. She subsequently reported that the man who came to her as the king had no ears. Otanes knew now that this man was Gaumata, an impostor. He shared his information with five others whose suspicions had been aroused, and when Darius the son of Hystaspes came to Susa on official business, they took him also into their confidence. Darius urged instant action lest, since so many already knew the king was an impostor, others take action instead. He threatened to reveal their conspiracy to Smerdis himself if they did not act at once. The six others agreed to make an immediate attack on the king in his palace and set out. Meantime the false Smerdis had decided to make a friend of Prexaspes, since he alone knew for certain of the death of Smerdis. Prexaspes was won by his bribes and agreed to go to the tóp of a tower and proclaim to the people that the Persians were ruled by Smerdis, son of Cyrus, and none other. When he had mounted the tower, however, Prexaspes, a loyal Persian, recited the genealogy of the Persian kings and ended by saying that he had, at the command of Cambyses, killed Smerdis son of Cyrus; that the present ruler was an impostor, a Median magus. Then calling down curses on the Persians if they did not regain the throne from the Medes, he leaped from the tower to his death. Darius, Otanes, and the other conspirators learned of these events as they were on their way to attack Smerdis. All except Darius favored postponing the attack because of the turmoil into which Prexaspes' statements and death had thrown the capitol. As they argued with Darius two pairs of vultures, pursued by seven hawks, flew over. The hawks overtook the vultures and clawed them with their talons and goaded them with their beaks. This omen convinced them that they should immediately carry out their plan. They proceeded to the palace. As prominent Persian nobles they were admitted without question, but being accosted by eunuchs in the courtyard, they forced their way past and en-

(obscured) errạnt, ardẹnt, actǫr; ch, chip; g, go; th, thin; ᴛʜ, then; y, you;
(variable) ḍ as d or j, ṣ as s or sh, ṭ as t or ch, ẓ as z or zh.

tered the palace. They found the two brother magi within, discussing the revelations of Prexaspes, set upon them and killed them (521 B.C.). Darius and the others decapitated them, mounted their heads on pikes, and went out of the palace, exhibiting the heads and shouting that the impostor was dead. When the Persians realized how they had been hoodwinked they turned on all the other magi and killed every one they could lay their hands on. Ever after, the anniversary of the day was celebrated by a great festival called the Slaughter of the Magi, and no magus dared to show his face abroad on that day.

Solon (sō'lon). Athenian law-giver (born c638 B.C.; died, c559 B.C.). He was the son of Execestides, who claimed descent from the last Athenian king, Codrus. The family had been a wealthy as well as a noble one, but because his father had dissipated his fortune Solon was obliged to engage in trade. His business activity caused him to travel widely, especially in Ionia, and gave him contacts with and knowledge of foreign lands and rulers, as well as a wide experience of affairs. He built up his own fortune, not that he was an admirer of wealth, but he thought there was no odium attached to it if it were gained justly. His own comment on wealth was:

"For often evil men are rich, and good men poor;
But we will not exchange with them
Our virtue for their wealth, since one abides alway,
While riches change their owners every day."

He was a cultivated man, and by his own account, a persistent seeker of wisdom, who grew old "ever learning new things." He wrote poetry, in the Ionic dialect, at first for his own amusement, but later and principally as a means of teaching and exhorting his fellow Athenians to pursue the course he thought they should follow, a course determined by Justice. Fragments of his poetry, the earliest surviving Athenian writings, are extant, and Athenian school-boys for generations after him learned his poems by heart. He early turned his attention to political ethics and to a consideration of improvement in the laws governing the Athenians. Plutarch mentions a conversation between Solon and one Anacharsis. The latter scoffed at Solon for his belief that injustice could be eliminated by law, for the laws, he said, are like spiders' webs: they entangle the weak but are torn to pieces by the strong. Solon replied that men would keep

fat, fāte, fär, fåll, åsk, fāre; net, mē, hėr; pin, pīne; not, nōte, mŏve, nôr; up, lūte, pull; oi, oil; ou out; (lightened) ĕlect, agǫny, ūnite;

their agreements when they were convinced that it was to their advantage to do so.

As a statesman Solon realized that control of the island of Salamis, lying opposite the port of Athens, was essential for the safety of the city. Because previous attempts to win it from Megara had ended in failure and the Athenians were tired of the war, a law was passed in Athens forbidding the mention of the name Salamis. Solon considered this disgraceful. He composed a poem inciting the Athenians to "recover" Salamis and, pretending madness to evade the law, recited the poem in the agora and so aroused the ardor of the populace that an expedition was undertaken under his leadership. Some say that in obedience to a command of the oracle at Delphi he rowed across to the island at night and made sacrifices to propitiate the heroes of Salamis—Cychreus and Periphemus. He returned to Attica, gathered a force of 500 men and sailed against Salamis and captured the city (c600 B.C.), and erected a temple to Euryalius (Ares) on the promontory where he had landed. This, however, did not end the dispute between the people of Megara and Athens over control of Salamis, and the matter was submitted to a board of Spartan judges for arbitration. The Spartans awarded it to Athens, some say on the basis of these verses from the *Iliad:*

Ajax from Salamis led his warships; twelve was the number
(Led them and stationed them where the Athenians stood in battalions).

And some say they awarded Salamis to Athens because Solon proved to them that Eurysaces, son of Ajax, had become a citizen of Athens and had brought the island with him. In any case, Solon now became prominent in public affairs. In later times his defense of the temple of Apollo at Delphi against the people of Cirrha (c590? B.C.), added to his prestige. Many urged him to make himself tyrant but he refused, saying, "a tyranny is a lovely place but there is no way down from it."

In his time there was great social and political unrest in Athens. The three main parties were the Hill, that favored a democracy, the Plain, that favored an oligarchy, and the Shore, that fell somewhere in between. Solon was well aware of the strife in the city and the reasons for it. Driven by greed, he exclaimed, the leaders enrich themselves unjustly, sparing neither the wealth of the state nor the temple treasures, and undermining the ancient foundations of justice. But, he declared, Justice, though silent, knows all the past and present, and never fails to come in time to punish. In 594 B.C. he became archon and was given broad powers to correct the abuses existing between the very rich and the very poor, and which were causing such unrest that civil war was threatened. These abuses, and the conflicts between classes, arose out of the impoverishment of the small landowners and the miserable condition of the free laborers. The small landowners were forced to pay such ruinous rates on money they borrowed that they were crushed, and, as Solon said, the black earth itself was enslaved. The free laborers received only one-sixth of what they produced as wages, and fell into debt in order to live. At this time a debtor who could not pay could be taken as a slave by his creditor. When Solon assumed office he immediately declared that debts which entailed slavery were annulled, and declared free those who had been enslaved according to previous contracts. This act, which freed many, was celebrated by a public feast. He made other reforms. He limited the area of land that could be owned by one person in order to curtail the growth of large estates; he forbade the exportation of Attic products, save for olive oil, because so much grain was exported by large proprietors for high prices that not enough remained to feed the population; and he made laws for the encouragement of trade and manufactures. In this time there were four tribes in Athens, named for the four sons of Ion: Geleon, Aegicores, Argades, and Hoples. Solon divided the people of the four tribes into four classes according to wealth, and assigned taxes and civic responsibility to each class in accordance with its ability to pay or participate. He reformed the constitution, the so-called constitution of Draco, retaining those features he considered good and changing others. By his reforms some political rights were granted to the peasants, who prior to this had been citizens with no rights; and he reconstituted the courts to give all four classes of citizens, chosen by lot, a share in the administration of justice. For this last alone he may be called the founder of Athenian democracy, for by it he gave the citizens some control over the administration which gov-

---

fat, fāte, fär, fâll, àsk, fãre; net, mē, hėr; pin, pīne; not, nōte, möve, nôr; up, lūte, pùll; oi, oil; ou out; (lightened) ĕlect, agǫny, ūnite;

erned them, as public officials were answerable to the courts. He established the Council of 400, consisting of representatives from the three upper classes of the four tribes of Athens, to prepare the business of the Assembly; and he changed the function of the Council of the Areopagus, henceforth to be composed of former archons, to lessen its power. Public officers were to be chosen by lot and by election. Choosing by lot left the decision to the gods; it also insured that no class would have a monopoly. In some cases, a certain number of names were drawn and those so chosen in turn elected one of their number to office. In addition, a law was adopted that would disfranchise a citizen who refused to take sides in times of disagreement. The purpose of it was to compel the citizens to accept their civic responsibilities. Laws concerning the marriages of heiresses, wills, the dress of women, burial and mourning, were also adopted; all were designed to remove inequities or to eradicate excesses that had arisen, as in dress and mourning customs. Solon's laws were inscribed on wooden panels. Every citizen was required to swear to obey them, and they were to remain in force for 100 years.

Solon's reforms, based on his ideas of justice, satisfied no one. They antagonized the rich, who lost some of their property and power, and failed to satisfy the poor, who had hoped for the redistribution of the large estates and for the cancellation of their debts. Solon seems to have decided that there would be less pressure to tamper with his new laws if he were not there to be pressured. He therefore asked permission to leave Athens for ten years. In this time he traveled widely, visiting Egypt, Cyprus and probably Asia Minor. At Cyprus he helped the king to lay out a new city, which was called Soli in his honor. According to a story of Herodotus, in the course of his travels he visited Croesus, king of Lydia, who was at that time one of the richest and most powerful monarchs of the known world. Croesus thought the traveling Athenian, whose reputation for wisdom had preceded him, would surely be impressed by the wealth and power of the Lydian king. He therefore asked Solon to name the happiest man in the world, certain that his own name would be given in answer. Solon named an obscure Athenian, Tellus. To the shocked question of Croesus as to why this man was happiest, Solon replied it was because he had lived an honorable life, had children whom he lived to see grow up and have children of their own, and died a glorious death fighting for his country, for which he was given a public funeral and paid the highest honors by the Athenians. Croesus recovered his poise and asked Solon to name the second happiest man, thinking this time he would surely be named. Solon named Cleobis and Biton, because they had honored their mother and were rewarded with a peaceful death by the goddess Hera. Croesus now became angry; did Solon put so little value on his wealth and power that he rated Croesus even below ordinary men? Solon's reply was that no man can be called happy until his life has ended happily, for the gods are jealous of their power and will seek to bring misfortune to him who enjoys too great prosperity. Riches above the needs of man do not necessarily bring happiness, but a healthy man who has no misfortunes, who sees his children grow up, and who ends his life well, can be called happy. For, added Solon, "in every matter we must mark well the end; for oftentimes God gives men a gleam of happiness, and then plunges them into ruin." This story of Herodotus is undoubtedly apocryphal, for Solon left Athens shortly after he had been archon and was away only ten years. Croesus did not succeed to the throne of Lydia until 560 B.C. However, true or not, it illustrates an ethical and religious principle of the Greeks of the time and for some generations thereafter.

All of Solon's reforms had been made with the object of forestalling a tyranny and of restoring peace to Athens. In his last days he saw the city he had set on the road to democracy fall into the power of a tyrant in spite of his efforts. Pisistratus, a friend of Solon, seized control and established a tyranny (561 B.C.). The aged Solon, so it is said, went into the agora and urged the citizens to throw off the tyranny. The city, he cried, would not perish by the will of the gods but by the folly of her citizens. His words were not heeded. He went to his house and placed his arms before the door, saying he had done all he could for his country and its citizens must now do likewise. His friends feared for his life because of his open opposition to Pisistratus. They urged him to leave Athens and when he refused asked him on what he relied to protect him from the tyrant. "On my old age," he is said to have answered. He was in no danger however. Although their political views were opposed, Pisistratus retained his friendship and respect for Solon. He lived a full and enjoyable life in Athens, and ultimately was inscribed as one of the Seven Sages of Greece. When he died, c559 B.C., his body was burned and the ashes were scattered over the island of Salamis. His name has passed into the English language as a synonym for a legislator or a wise official.

Spartacus (spär′tạ-kus). Thracian who became a Roman slave and gladiator at Capua. He headed an insurrection of slaves (Servile War) in Italy in 73 B.C., and routed several Roman armies, but was ultimately defeated by Crassus on the Silarus River and slain (71 B.C.).

Sperthias (spėr′thi-ạs) and *Bulis* (bū′lis). Two Spartans. According to Herodotus, Darius the Great sent heralds to Sparta demanding earth and water from the Spartans as a token that they submitted to him. The Spartans cast the heralds into a well and told them to fetch their own earth and water. This was a violation of the immemorial sanctity, recognized by all nations, of the persons of heralds. The descendants of Talthybius, Agamemnon's herald, who held the hereditary right to the office of herald in Sparta, went to the temple of Talthybius there and called down his wrath on the Spartans. Thenceforth victims at sacrifices failed to give good omens. After this had gone on a long time the Spartans were extremely troubled. They called for two Spartans willing to give their lives for their country. Sperthias and Bulis, Spartan noblemen, offered themselves. They volunteered to go to Xerxes, son of Darius and present ruler of Persia, and submit to death at his hands to atone for the deaths of the Persian heralds at the hands of the Spartans. On their way to Susa they were received by the satrap Hydarnes. He pointed out to them many evidences of the advantages accruing to the friends of the Persian ruler, and asked them why they would not consent to become friends with Xerxes. They replied that he knew only half the story. Having always been a slave he was pleased to live in comfort, but if he had ever tasted liberty, such as they knew, he would urge them to fight to the death to retain it. Leaving Hydarnes, they went to Susa. There they refused to bow their heads before Xerxes, claiming that they worshiped no man, that this was not why they had come to Susa, and repelling with force

(obscured) errạnt, ardẹnt, actọr; ch, chip; g, go; th, thin; ᵺ, then; y, you; (variable) ḍ as d or j, ṣ as s or sh, ṭ as t or ch, ẓ as z or zh.

those who sought to compel them to make obeisance to Xerxes. They addressed him, telling him they had come to give their lives to atone for the Persian heralds slain by the Spartans. Xerxes, "with true greatness of soul," according to Herodotus, answered that he would not do as the Spartans had done. He would not break the laws honored by men of all nations regarding the persons of heralds. He allowed Sperthias and Bulis to return home, and because of their noble willingness to die the anger of Talthybius was temporarily appeased, only to rise up again and visit itself on the sons of Sperthias and Bulis 60 years later.

Stolo (stō'lō), **Caius Licinius Calvus.** See **Licinius** (fl. 377–361 B.C.).

Strabo (strä'bō), **Cnaeus Pompeius.** Roman statesman; killed by lightning, 87 B.C. He served Rome as quaestor in Sardinia (103 B.C.), praetor (94), propraetor in Sicily (93), and consul (89 B.C.). He took part in the Social War and was sponsor of the law that granted to the inhabitants of Transpadane Gaul the same privileges as were enjoyed by the Latin colonies. He was the father of Pompey the triumvir.

Sulla (sul'ạ), **Lucius Cornelius.** [Surnamed *Felix.*] Roman general and dictator; born c138 B.C.; died 78 B.C. He was the son of an obscure and impoverished patrician family, and as a young man was compelled to live in lodgings for lack of his own estate. This fact was remembered by his enemies when he subsequently became wealthy in the service of the state. Towards the end of his life he took the surname Felix *(Fortunate)* in grateful acknowledgment to the gods, who always smiled on his undertakings as will presently appear. According to Plutarch, he loved a wealthy woman of plebeian birth and so charmed her that when she presently died she left him all her fortune. His stepmother also left him her property. He thus arrived at a fairly comfortable financial state and prepared to enter public life. In 107 B.C. he was appointed as quaestor to the consul Marius, and went to Libya to serve in the war against Jugurtha (107–106 B.C.). Sulla made friends with the Numidian king, Bocchus, who was also the father-in-law of Jugurtha. Bocchus plotted with Sulla to surrender Jugurtha to him. At some risk to himself Sulla put himself in Bocchus' power for the purpose of executing the plot. Bocchus secured the presence of Jugurtha by trickery and, though he wavered as to whether it would

fat, fāte, fär, fâll, àsk, fāre; net, mē, hėr; pin, pīne; not, nōte, möve, nôr; up, lūte, pùll; oi, oil; ou out; (lightened) ẹlect, agǫny, ụnite;

be more to his advantage to seize Sulla, decided Jugurtha was more of a danger to him and surrendered him to Sulla and ended the war. Marius, as consul, was honored with a triumph for the war, but Sulla was publicly credited with the seizure of Jugurtha. For his pride's sake he had a seal ring made, on which was engraved a figure of Bocchus surrendering Jugurtha to him. The prominence Sulla won in the Numidian war was not pleasing to Marius. Nevertheless, he concealed his jealousy and used Sulla to good advantage in subsequent campaigns. Sulla served under him during his second and third consulships (104 and 103 B.C.), and won the friendship of the Marsi for Rome. Becoming aware that Marius was acting to halt his advancement, he attached himself to Catulus, co-consul with Marius. Catulus, less ambitious or more indolent than Marius, gave Sulla free rein. He subdued the Cimbri and Teutones (104–101 B.C.) in the Alps and returned to Rome. In 93 B.C. he became praetor as the result of lavish expenditures, and in 92 B.C. as propraetor of Cilicia he defeated the general of Mithridates VI and restored Ariobarzanes to the throne of Cappadocia. In this war, carried on with the help of Roman allies, he slew many Cappadocians and Armenians, and received an envoy of the Parthian king Arsaces, who asked for friendship and alliance with Rome. He then returned to Rome, where the breach with Marius became open rivalry when Bocchus dedicated some images at Rome that portrayed Sulla accepting the surrender of Jugurtha. The rivalry between Marius and Sulla to control Rome was submerged by the outbreak of the Social War, 90 B.C. The war was so-called because it was a war between Rome and her Italian allies (*socii* meaning allies). Sulla achieved great fame by his exploits in the war, which included the defeat of the Samnites and the capture of Bovianum (89 B.C.). In 88 B.C. he became consul with Pompey. He brought the Social War to an end by the capture of Nola, and then by lot was chosen commander of the war against Mithridates, which had been renewed by the latter in attacking Rome's allies. Marius wanted the command of this war and his attempts to get it brought on civil war in Rome. Many omens are said to have foretold the civil conflict. Mice gnawed at the sacred gold in the temple; keepers caught one of them in a trap. It produced five young and immediately ate three of them. A trumpet rang out in a shrill

(obscured) errạnt, ardẹnt, actọr; ch, chip; g, go; th, thin; ᴛʜ, then; y, you;
(variable) ḍ as d or j, ṣ as s or sh, ṭ as t or ch, ẓ as z or zh.

and dismal tone and amazed and terrified the people. Seers said this foretold a change in conditions at Rome and a new age of man. While the Senate sat to consider these prodigies a sparrow flew into their chamber with a grasshopper in its mouth. The bird threw part of the insect on the Senate floor and flew off with the rest of its body. Seers interpreted this gloomily as a sign of trouble among the Romans. Marius allied himself to Sulpicius Rufus, an unscrupulous and dangerous popular leader who was tribune of the plebs. He proposed that Marius be made general in command of the Mithridatic War, and when the Senate refused to act he roused a mob against them. In the mêlée Pompey's son was killed. Sulla fled to the house of Marius, who might have killed him, but allowed him to escape. He fled to his army at Nola. In the meantime Sulpicius had deposed Pompey as consul and secured command of the Mithridatic War for Marius. But when the tribunes arrived at Nola to take over the army for Marius they were stoned by Sulla's troops, whose loyalty he had won by his flattery, his military successes, and the plunder he helped them to secure. When Marius learned of his defiance of the tribunes he attacked Sulla's partisans in Rome, slew many of them, and seized their property. Thus the civil war began.

It is said that a vision came to Sulla at this time. He dreamed a goddess stood beside him and gave him a thunderbolt. She named his enemies and invited him to strike them with the thunderbolt. He did so and they at once vanished. Encouraged by this omen, he marched on Rome; the first Roman ever to lead a Roman army against Rome. When he entered the gates of the city some of the people showered his army with rocks and tiles hurled from the roof tops. He ordered the houses fired, friend and foe alike. Marius could not stop him from entering the city. He fled to a temple for refuge, and then left the city. Sulla was now master. He called the Senate together and had Marius and Sulpicius condemned to death in absentia. He had won a political and military but not a popular victory. The people distrusted him as an arrogant aristocrat and feared him because he had shown his scorn of their tribunes. Nevertheless, he was the master. In 87 B.C. he set out to command the war against Mithridates. He went to Athens, which sided with Mithridates and was the center of his activity in the west, and laid siege to the city. When he needed timber for his siege engines he ruthlessly cut down the sacred groves of the Academy and the Lyceum. When he needed money for his operations he sent to Epidaurus, Olympia, and Delphi and removed the treasures from their temples. At Delphi the priests thought to frighten away his envoys by causing a musician to play the flute in an inner chamber and informing them that the music came from the god, who forbade them to harm his shrine. The envoys were fearful and relayed the message to Sulla. He sent back word that the music had been misinterpreted: the god was playing to welcome a friend; the envoys were ordered to proceed with the pillaging of the shrine. Among the treasures taken from Delphi was the great silver bowl dedicated there by the Lydian king Croesus. Sulla promised that he would replace the treasures necessity compelled him to seize from the temples. He took Athens (86 B.C.) by treachery, marched into the city at night and gave it over to his men to plunder. The streets ran with blood. But thanks to the pleas of some Roman senators in his train he did not destroy the city. He went on to take the Piraeus and burned it. From here he took his forces into Boeotia, met the forces of Mithridates' general Archelaus at Chaeronea and defeated them (86 B.C.). In the following year reinforcements came to Archelaus. An enemy charge inflicted damage on Sulla's troops and they fell back. As they retreated Sulla jumped from his horse and pushed toward the enemy on foot, crying, "For me, O Romans, an honorable death here; but you, when men ask you where you betrayed your commander, remember to tell them, at Orchomenus." His men rallied and next day defeated Archelaus at Orchomenus (85 B.C.). In 84 B.C. he went into Asia and defeated Fimbria, a Marian leader who sought to take his command, and compelled Mithridates to come to terms with him. Mithridates and Sulla met at Dardanus in the Troad. Mithridates agreed to give up Asia (Asia Minor) and Paphlagonia; to restore the kings of Bithynia and Cappadocia, whose thrones he had seized; to pay an idemnity to Rome; and to contribute 70 ships to the Roman fleet. Sulla for his part guaranteed Mithridates in the territory that was left him and made him an ally of Rome.

In the meantime, terrible news had reached him from Rome. Marius had returned (87 B.C.) and captured the control of the city. Sulla's wife had come to him in Athens and told him of the destruction of his property in Rome and of the wholesale slaughter of his friends. Having concluded peace with Mithridates he now prepared to return to Rome. His soldiers, who had taken enormous booty while in his service, voluntarily swore allegiance to him. He sailed across to Italy (83 B.C.) and landed at Brundisium. By this time Marius had died (86 B.C.) and the opposition to Sulla was led by Cinna, Carbo, and the Younger Marius. Sulla defeated the forces sent against him by Marius the Younger and the consul Norbanus, then defeated Marius at Signia, near Praeneste. Marius escaped to Praeneste, but arrived after the gate had been closed. He was hauled up over the walls by a rope to safety. Sulla's generals, Pompey, Crassus, Metellus, and Servilius, were equally victorious in their areas. At last Carbo, the remaining leader of the opposition, fled to Libya (82 B.C.). The Samnites had taken advantage of the civil war to march on Rome. Sulla defeated them at the Colline Gate and was again master of Rome. He issued a sweeping proscription against his enemies. By the proscription any one who wished could kill with impunity anyone whose name appeared on the proscribed list. Many on the list were Sulla's enemies. Others were the owners of fine properties Sulla wished to take, for himself or for his friends. The sons and grandsons of those who were proscribed lost their civil rights. This was the first time in Roman history, but not the last, that a reign of terror was inaugurated by means of a proscription. Marius the Younger committed suicide. Sulla caused to be slain all those in the city of Praeneste who had helped Marius—to the number of 12,000.

Sulla now made himself dictator, thus reviving an office that had lapsed 120 years earlier, celebrated a magnificent triumph for the Mithridatic War, and took the surname Felix (*Fortunate*) to acknowledge his debt to the gods. In 80 B.C. he became consul. His activities had resulted in the crushing of all opposition and the expropriation of the property of Marius' followers to the advantage of Sulla's. As master of Rome he made various constitutional reforms. He reorganized and restored the power of the Senate and weakened the power of the tribunes. He established a system of courts of justice. To support the political system he established military colonies on large grants of land throughout Italy. One

fat, fāte, fär, fåll, àsk, fāre; net, mē, hėr; pin, pīne; not, nōte, möve, nôr; up, lūte, pull; oi, oil; ou out; (lightened) ẹlect, agǫny, ụnite;

of Sulla's enemies was Julius Caesar. He pursued the latter to such an extent that he was forced to change his lodging nightly. Finally, Sulla yielded to the pleas of the aristocratic party *(optimates)* to forgive Caesar. As he did so he warned those who pleaded in Caesar's behalf that the man they pleaded for would one day destroy their party. In this he was an excellent prophet. The personal life of Sulla was as vigorous and ruthless as his military life. In his hours of relaxation he enjoyed the company of actors and jesters, drank deep, and gave himself to every form of voluptuousness. He could show the most benign patience with his friends, or the most brutal anger. Of himself he said he never failed to reward his friends' kindnesses or to punish his enemies' wrongs, and this was inscribed on his monument. However, frequently the kindnesses of friends were transformed in his eyes into the wrongs of enemies. He was married at least four times. One of his wives was Caecilia, daughter of the pontifex maximus Metellus. He married her when he was 50 years old, having put aside previous wives, and always showed her the greatest deference. Yet when at last she was dying he divorced her and had her removed to another place so as not to pollute his house with her death. This however, was in accordance with the custom, and did not at all hinder him from giving her a magnificent funeral. He resigned the dictatorship in 79 B.C. and retired to Puteoli, where he amused himself with his actor friends and finished his *Memoirs.* He died quietly in 78 B.C., was given a splendid public funeral, and was buried in the Campus Martius.

Sulpicius Galba (sul-pish′us gal′ba), *Servius.* See *Galba, Servius Sulpicius.*

Sulpicius Rufus (rö′fus), *Publius.* Roman politician and orator; born c121 B.C.; killed 88 B.C. Prior to his tribunate in 88 B.C. he had been a member of the aristocratic party *(optimates)* but upon becoming a tribune of the plebs he switched his allegiance to the popular party *(populares).* It is said that he had a personal bodyguard of 3000 young men who kept Rome in a turmoil and Sulpicius powerful, and that he bought popularity by selling the Roman citizenship for a price. He was a partisan of Marius, the leader of the popular party, and proposed that he be made general in command of the war against Mithridates (88 B.C.). The consuls, Sulla and Pompey, refused to let the matter come to a vote. Sulpicius used his bodyguard to stir up a riot against them. Both fled. Sulpicius deposed Pompey from his consulship and took the command of the Mithridatic War away from Sulla, who had won it by lot, and gave it to Marius. However, the tribunes who went to Nola to take over Sulla's army were stoned by his loyal troops. Sulla led them against Rome, made himself master of the city, and condemned Sulpicius and Marius, who had fled, to death in absentia. Sulpicius was killed by a slave Sulla had freed for the express purpose of killing him. Afterward, Sulla caused the slave to be hurled to his death from the Tarpeian Rock.

Syennesis (si-en'ẹ-sis). Name common to all the kings of Cilicia mentioned in history, especially that of a vassal of Persia, at the time of the expedition of Cyrus the Younger (401 B.C.).

T

Tarquinius Collatinus (tär-kwin'i-us kol-ạ-tī-nus). In Roman legend, the husband of Lucretia, and a kinsman of Tarquinius Superbus. His wife was ravished by Tarquinius Sextus, son of Tarquinius Superbus. The outrage precipitated revolt against the Tarquins and they were driven out of Rome (509 B.C.). The kings of Rome were succeeded by two consuls. Lucius Junius Brutus who led the revolt was one, and Tarquinius Collatinus as the man who had most reason to hate Tarquinius Superbus and his family was the other. Some say that Tarquinius resigned his consulship and withdrew from Rome because he had appeared too mild in punishing the conspirators who sought to restore Tarquinius Superbus, and thus he earned the distrust of the Romans. Others say the Romans hated the very name Tarquinius and had no confidence in Collatinus because of his family connections. Their uneasiness reached such proportions that Brutus sought to quiet them by asking Collatinus to leave Rome. "Depart, our friend . . ." he is said to have urged, "the people are persuaded that with the family of Tarquinius the kingship will vanish from among us." Collatinus

fat, fāte, fär, fâll, àsk, fāre; net, mē, hėr; pin, pīne; not, nōte, mȯve, nôr; up, lūte, pu̇ll; oi, oil; ou out; (lightened) ẹlect, agọny, ụnite;

was astonished at the evidence of distrust. However, since Brutus promised that he could take his possessions with him and would even add to them if they were insufficient, Collatinus decided it was better to go before the temper of the people became dangerous and forced him to flee empty-handed. He resigned his consulship and retired to Lavinium.

Tarquinius, Sextus. Youngest son of Tarquinius Superbus. He was sent to Gabii by his father, who had failed to take that city by storm. According to some accounts, he told the Gabini he was fleeing the harshness of his father, and so won their confidence that they awarded him a position of great power in their councils. He continually urged the Gabini to make forays against Rome, and in these he was the leader. According to plan, the Gabini were successful in these raids and the reputation of Sextus became so great that his was the most influential voice in the city. He sent an envoy to his father, so the story goes, telling him he was now in control of Gabii and asking his father for instructions. In a procedure reminiscent of that Thrasybulus, tyrant of Miletus, replying to Periander (c625–585 B.C.), tyrant of Corinth, Tarquinius is said to have refused to utter a word to the envoy of Sextus. Instead he walked about his garden with him, knocking off the heads of the tallest poppies that grew there. When the envoy returned and described his actions, Sextus knew he was to get rid of the leading men in Gabii. This he did by means of false charges, murders, and exile. Thereupon he delivered an unresisting city to Tarquinius. Later, when the Romans were besieging the Rutulian city of Ardea, Sextus and other young nobles fell to discussing the virtues of their wives. On the suggestion of Tarquinius Collatinus they agreed to ride to Rome and surprise their wives. Lucretia, wife of Collatinus, was found to be industriously engaged with her maids in household tasks. The other wives were feasting and amusing themselves. Lucretia easily won the palm for being the most virtuous of the wives. Sextus was aroused not only by her beauty but also by her reputation for chastity. He returned to her house in Collatia some nights later by himself. Lucretia received him graciously as a colleague and kinsman of her husband. During the night he entered her chamber and ravished her, after threatening that if she did not submit, he would kill her and lay the naked body of a slave beside her so that she would appear convicted of adultery in its vilest form. When Sextus left her, she sent for her husband and her father, revealed what had happened and, adjuring them to avenge her, committed suicide. This deed of Sextus precipitated the revolt against the Tarquins and resulted in their expulsion from Rome (509 B.C.). Sextus fled to Gabii, but there, because of his former cruelties and betrayals, he was put to death by the outraged Gabini.

Tarquinius Superbus (sö-pėr'bus), **Lucius.** In Roman tradition, the seventh and last king of Rome (534–510 B.C.); son of Tarquinius Priscus, and son-in-law of Servius Tullius. In the traditional account he was married to Tullia, daughter of Servius Tullius. His brother Aruns was also married to a daughter of Servius Tullius, who was also named Tullia. According to some accounts, Tullia, wife of Aruns, was ruthless and ambitious; her husband was neither. Tullia, wife of Lucius Tarquinius, was of the same mild disposition as Aruns. Tullia, wife of Aruns, contrived the murder of her husband and of her sister, and married her brother-in-law, Lucius Tarquinius. Some say she continually urged him to seek the throne which, she claimed, her own father occupied unjustly. Lucius Tarquinius was of the same mind. He won many young Romans to his side by extravagant promises and with this backing went to the Senate House and seated himself on the throne. When Servius, now an old man, hurried to the Senate and challenged him, he seized the aged king, carried him out of the chamber, and flung him into the street. In the confusion, the aides of Servius were scattered or fled. At Tullia's suggestion, some say, Tarquinius sent agents to pursue Servius as he made his way alone through the streets and slay him. Later Tullia, on her way home, drove her chariot over her dead father's body. With the supporters he won to his side, Tarquinius made himself master of Rome. He immediately showed his cruelty by refusing to permit the burial of his father-in-law's body. One of his first acts was to demand a bodyguard, lest another attempt to seize power, as he had successfully done. To consolidate his power he tried capital offenses himself without the assistance of advisers. Thus he assumed the power of life and death over his enemies. He reduced the Senate by bringing charges against many of its members, sentencing some to death and others to exile, and seizing their property in either case. He broke with the tradition that the king consult the Senate, and he made war, signed treaties, and concluded peace without referring to that body. In order to strengthen himself outside Rome he made friends with the cities of the Latin peoples. By bribery and fraud he secured the death of the one Latin leader who dared speak against him, Turnus Herdonius. For his arrogant flaunting of traditional Roman forms and his tyrannical acts, Tarquinius was given the name Superbus, "the Proud." Tarquinius began the wars against the Volsci, which continued intermittently for the next 200 years. He seized Pometia from them. He waged war on Gabii, but when he could not storm the city, according to Livy, he resorted to guile. He sent his youngest son, Sextus, as his agent. Sextus went to Gabii as a suppliant, claiming that his father was as harsh to his children as he was to his subjects, and asked asylum of the Gabini. The Gabini were completely taken in by his words, admitted him to their city, and gradually gave him such power that he was able to deliver the city to Tarquinius without a struggle. Tarquinius also made peace with the Aequi, made an alliance with the Etruscans, and sent out colonists from Rome to Signia and Circeii. In Rome he engaged on a vast program of public works, among which was a temple of Jupiter which he proposed to raise with the plunder from the Volscian city of Pometia. All the ancient shrines, except that of Terminus, on the Capitol were moved, so that the place would clearly belong to Jupiter. The Romans became restless under the harsh rule of Tarquinius. In the palace a prodigy occurred when a snake glided out of a wooden pillar. Tarquinius dared not entrust the interpretation of such a prodigy to the Etruscan soothsayers who usually performed this service, and sent his sons Titus and Aruns to Delphi. According to legend, the priestess told them he who first kissed his mother would become king of Rome. Lucius Junius Brutus, their cousin who accompanied them, on hearing this pretended to stumble, fell, and kissed the earth, the Great Mother. During a siege of Ardea, a city of the Rutulians, Sextus, the youngest son of Tarquinius Superbus, rode to Collatia and there ravished Lucretia, wife of Tarquinius Collatinus. She called her husband and her father to her, revealed what had happened, asked them to punish the criminal, and then plunged a dagger into her breast. Lucius Junius Brutus, who was present, lifted the dagger, dripping with Lucretia's blood, and swore to pursue and drive out of Rome Tarquinus Superbus, his wife, and his evil children. A similar oath was sworn by the others present. They carried the corpse of Lucretia to the market-place in Collatia. A great crowd gathered, and all who saw Lucretia's body remembered some evil Tarquinius Superbus had brought to him. Brutus urged them to take up arms and march on Rome. They did so, and a crowd gathered in the Forum. Brutus, who had always appeared slow-witted, amazed the assemblage with an impassioned speech calling for the expulsion of the Tarquins. Meanwhile, Tarquinius Superbus, at Ardea, learned what was going forward. He hurriedly set out for Rome but found the gates barred against him on arrival. He went into exile at Caere but by no means gave up his hopes of returning to Rome as king. A plot to kill the consuls who succeeded him as rulers of Rome failed. He appealed for aid to the people of Tarquinii and Veii. They sent forces to help him but they were defeated by the Romans under the consul Publius Valerius (Publicola), in a battle in which Brutus, the first consul, was killed. Tarquinius next sought aid from Lars Porsena of Clusium, the most powerful of the Etruscan kings. The forces of Lars Porsena besieged Rome. This action ended after some months in a peace treaty between Rome and Lars Porsena. Tarquinius again appealed to Lars Porsena, but this time, after parley with eminent Romans, Lars Porsena refused him aid, and said he would no longer give him asylum. Tarquinius Superbus went to the Latin city of Tusculum to live with his son-in-law. About 500 B.C., in a war between the Romans and Latins, he took part and was wounded at Lake Regillus. He never regained power in Rome, and died, some say, at Cumae, 495 B.C.

Taxiles (tak′si-lēz). Indian king in the Punjab who received Alexander the Great, 326 B.C., on his march into India. His real name was Omphis, but he was called Taxiles after his city, Taxila.

Teutobod (tū′tō-bod). King of the Teutones, defeated by Marius at the battle of Aquae Sextiae (modern Aix), 102 B.C.

Theagenes (thē-aj′e-nēz). Tyrant of Megara; fl. 7th century B.C. He obtained a bodyguard, overthrew the wealthy nobles of

Megara, and made himself tyrant (c640 B.C.). His daughter
was married to the Athenian Cylon, whom Theagenes encouraged to attempt to win control of Athens. The attempt
ended in failure. Theagenes constructed an aqueduct for
Megara during his rule. He was at length overthrown and
banished from Megara.

Themistocles (thē-mis′tō-klēz). Athenian statesman and commander, born c528 B.C.; died, in Asia, c462 B.C. He became
a political leader in opposition to Aristides, who was ostracized in 483 B.C., and recognizing the continued Persian
threat, was instrumental in increasing the naval resources of
Athens. He persuaded the Athenians to use the money in
their treasury to build up the fleet to 200 ships. When
Xerxes made ready to invade Greece, the Athenians consulted the oracle at Delphi. The priestess predicted utter
destruction for the Athenians and urged them to fly. The
Athenians again sought the priestess as suppliants, and said
they would not leave the precinct until they received a more
favorable response. The priestess answered them thus:

> When the foe shall have taken whatever the limit of Ce-
> crops
> Holds within it, . . .
> Then far-seeing Zeus grants this to the prayers of Athena:
> Safe shall the wooden wall continue for thee and thy chil-
> dren.
>
> .   .   .   .   .   .
>
> Yet shall a day arrive when ye shall meet him in battle.
> Holy Salamis, thou shalt destroy the offspring of women,
> When men scatter the seed, or when they gather the har-
> vest.

Though this seemed somewhat more hopeful, it was open
to various interpretations. Some thought "the wooden wall"
referred to the Citadel of Athens, which had originally been
of wood. Others thought "the wooden wall" meant the
ships, but those who took this view were disturbed by the
reference to Salamis and thought it meant that the fleet
would be defeated there. Themistocles now came forward.
According to his interpretation, "the wooden wall" meant
the ships, and the inclusion of "Holy Salamis" indicated a
victory there. The Athenians, determined to preserve their
liberty at any cost, adopted his view and prepared to defend
themselves with their fleet. Themistocles went as one of the

(obscured) errạnt, ardẹnt, actọr; ch, chip; g, go; th, thin; ᴛʜ, then; y, you;
(variable) ḍ as d or j, ṣ as s or sh, ṭ as t or ch, ẓ as z or zh.

commanders of a Greek expedition to Thessaly while Xerxes was preparing to pass into Europe from Asia, but the expedition withdrew on the advice of messengers from Macedonia. Later, at Artemisium, he is said to have accepted a bribe from the Euboeans to make a stand at Artemisium and protect the Euboeans. He used part of the money to bribe other commanders, who wished to withdraw, and the remainder he kept for himself, unknown to anyone. The battle fought at Artemisium, at the same time as the land battle at Thermopylae, was inconclusive, but the Persians suffered great losses through storms at sea. When Athens was at length overrun by the Persians, the Athenian fleet withdrew to Salamis. Themistocles wanted to engage the Persian fleet there, but had great difficulty persuading the other captains to do so, particularly the most important of the allies, the Spartans, who wished to retire to the Isthmus, build a wall across it, and defend the Peloponnesus. Themistocles understood that the Greek fleet, because of its superior maneuverability, could do great damage to the Persian fleet in the enclosed area of Salamis, whereas in the open sea the Persians would have the advantage. To force the hand of his unwilling allies, Themistocles sent a messenger to the Persian fleet. The burden of his message, which was true, was that the Greeks, in fear of the Persians, were on the point of flight; that they were at odds with each other; and that now was the time for the Persians to strike. The Persians took cognizance of the message and redeployed their land and sea forces to surround the Greeks at Salamis. While the Greek captains argued, Aristides, the old enemy of Themistocles, but one with him in his desire to preserve Greek liberty, came to them and told them their arguments were now academic, as they were surrounded. Thus, thanks to Themistocles, the matter was taken out of their hands; they had no option but to fight on the site Themistocles had chosen, and won a magnificent victory at Salamis (480 B.C.). After the victory and the flight of the Persians, Themistocles was out-voted in his desire to pursue the Persians to the Hellespont and destroy the bridges which they must use to return their land forces to Asia. Seeing that the allies would not go, he prevailed on the Athenians to give up the pursuit. At the end of the war all Greece rang with the fame of Themistocles, but through the jealousy and rivalry of the

fat, fāte, fär, fâll, ȧsk, fāre; net, mē, hėr; pin, pīne; not, nōte, möve, nôr; up, lūte, pŭll; oi, oil; ou out; (lightened) ĕlect, agŏny, ūnite;

commanders, the Athenians withheld the honor that was his due to him—the crown of victory. He went to Sparta and was received and honored as no other stranger had ever been honored by the Spartans. When the Persians had withdrawn, the Athenians returned to rebuild their ruined city. Themistocles urged them to drop everything and rebuild the walls of the city, and also to build a walled way between Athens and her port, Piraeus, so that they would always have access to their fleet. The Athenians did as he advised, but after the dangers of the war had passed, there were many in Athens who were bitterly jealous of Themistocles. The story of his bribe to remain and fight at Artemisium came out, and he was ostracized (c471 B.C.). He lived in exile in Argos and elsewhere. He was charged with complicity in the treason of the Spartan Pausanias, who planned to rule Greece with Persian aid; learning that the Athenians planned to seize him, as the Spartans had seized Pausanias, he fled. He went to Corcyra, and ultimately to Asia, where he sent a message to King Artaxerxes. He made a claim on the friendship of Artaxerxes, son of Xerxes, because, he said, he had prevented the Athenians from sailing to the Hellespont and destroying the bridges by which the Persian army of his father returned to Asia. He asked to be allowed to stay in Asia one year, at the end of which time he promised to present himself to the king. Artaxerxes granted his request. Themistocles spent his year of grace learning the Persian language and customs of the country. At the end of the year he arrived at the court of Artaxerxes and was received with every evidence of respect and honor. He put his genius at the service of Artaxerxes and was rewarded by being named governor of the district of Asiatic Magnesia. Thucydides speaks of Themistocles as a man who exhibited "the most indubitable signs of genius," one who had an extraordinary and unparalleled claim on Greek admiration because of his native capacity, his ability to meet any emergency, and his wisdom as to present courses and future prospects. Though there was a story that he committed suicide, because he failed in his promises to the Persian king, Thucydides says he died of disease. A monument to him was set up in Magnesia. Because he was charged with treason, he could not lawfully be buried in Athens, but relatives secretly took up his bones and buried them in his native soil.

(obscured) errạnt, ardẹnt, actọr; ch, chip; g, go; th, thin; ᵺ, then; y, you;
(variable) ḍ as d or j, ş as s or sh, ṭ as t or ch, ẕ as z or zh.

Theramenes (thĕ-ram′ĕ-nēz). Athenian politician and military commander; executed 404 B.C. He was one of the leaders in the establishment (411 B.C.) of the oligarchic rule of the Four Hundred, which he later opposed for its extremity. He served at Cyzicus, Arginusae, and elsewhere, and was instrumental in procuring the condemnation of the Athenian generals after Arginusae. He was one of the negotiators (405–404 B.C.) for peace with Sparta, became one of the Thirty Tyrants, and through the influence of Critias was forced to drink poison.

Theron (thĕ′rŏn). Tyrant of Acragas in Sicily (488–472 B.C.). His daughter Damareta was married to Gelon, tyrant of Syracuse, with whom Theron had close political ties. Under Theron, whose rule is said to have been mild and just, Acragas prospered and became second only to Syracuse in wealth. A quarrel between Theron and Terillus, tyrant of Himera, gave the Carthaginians an opportunity to interfere in Sicily. Theron united with Gelon to drive them out (480 B.C.), and as a result he won control of Himera. After the war he devoted himself to the enlargement and beautification of Acragas. In his time the foundations were laid for the row of temples along the south wall of the city that were brought to magnificent completion only long after his death.

Thrasybulus (thras-i-bū′lus, thrạ-sib′ụ-lus). A 6th century B.C. tyrant of Miletus under whose rule the city prospered greatly, and who planted colonies of Miletus on the Euxine Sea. He successfully resisted the threats of the kings of Lydia. According to Herodotus, in the 12th year of a war with Alyattes, king of Lydia who had inherited the war from his father, Alyattes invaded Milesia and set the grain afire, as he had been doing annually. A gale of wind swept the fire to the temple of Athena at Assesus and burned it to the ground. Afterward, Alyattes fell sick and sent to inquire of the oracle at Delphi how he might be cured. His messengers were told by the priestess that she would not answer his inquiries until the temple of Athena at Assesus was rebuilt. Periander of Corinth, a friend of Thrasybulus, heard of the oracle and sent word of it to Thrasybulus, that he might be prepared. Therefore, when Ayattes sent heralds to Thrasybulus to arrange a truce during which the temple could be rebuilt, the heralds were met by a startling sight. Thrasybulus, foreseeing that Alyattes would send to him as

fat, fāte, fär, fåll, åsk, fāre; net, mē, hėr; pin, pīne; not, nōte, mȯve, nôr; up, lūte, pu̇ll; oi, oil; ou out; (lightened) ĕlect, agǫny, ụnite;

a consequence of the oracle, had caused all the grain that was in the city to be brought into the market-place, and had ordered the people to set to feasting and revelry when he gave the signal. When the heralds arrived, they found the Milesians enjoying themselves as if there had never been any war at all, and amusing themselves in the market-place, surrounded by an abundance of grain. The heralds immediately reported this to Alyattes and he, who had thought that by this time the Milesians would have exhausted their supplies and be glad of a truce, on learning of the plenty they still enjoyed, instead of offering a truce made peace with Thrasybulus and ended the long war. After this Alyattes rebuilt the temple of Athena and recovered from his sickness. One of the reasons for the friendship of Thrasybulus and Periander was advice he had given Periander when the latter became ruler of Corinth. Periander sent a messenger to him, to ask what sort of government he should establish. Thrasybulus took the messenger into a wheat field, and as he talked, kept breaking off the heads of the tallest stalks and throwing the ears on the ground, but he never answered the question the messenger had brought from Periander. On his return to Corinth the messenger reported that he had no answer from Thrasybulus, and described his strange conduct in the wheat field. But Periander understood the meaning of his actions, and immediately sought out the leading men of his realm and destroyed them.

Thrasybulus. Athenian commander and statesman; killed 388 B.C. In 411 B.C. he was at Samos with the Athenian navy, and persuaded the sailors there to rise against the oligarchy of the Four Hundred that was governing at Athens, and to proclaim their allegiance to the democracy. Under his direction the Assembly that had been abolished at Athens was revived at Samos. He secured the return to Samos of Alcibiades and had him elected general. In 410 B.C. he commanded one division of the fleet that defeated the Spartans at Cyzicus. Following this, and other Spartan defeats, the Four Hundred at Athens were overthrown. Athens enjoyed some successes in its war with Sparta, but was ultimately defeated at Aegospotami (405 B.C.). Under the protection of the Spartan general Lysander, an interim body of 30, later known as the Thirty Tyrants, was chosen to govern Athens. Thrasybulus was driven into exile with other democrats.

The exiles took refuge at the fortress of Phyle in Attica and resisted an army sent against them by Athens. In 403 B.C. Thrasybulus burst out of Phyle with the exiles and seized Munychia at the Piraeus. This led to the overthrow of the Thirty Tyrants and the reëstablishment of Athenian democracy. Thrasybulus aided Thebes against Sparta in 395 B.C., and commanded with great success in the Aegean Sea in 390 B.C. He was killed in his tent at Aspendus in Pamphylia by natives who were outraged by the violence of his soldiers.

Thrasyllus (thra-sil'us). Athenian commander in the Peloponnesian War; put to death 406 B.C. He opposed the oligarchs in 411 B.C., and helped to overthrow them. He was one of the commanders at Cynossema in 411 B.C., and was a general at Arginusae in 406 B.C. and one of those who was executed for permitting the crews of sunken ships to drown rather than breaking off the pursuit of the enemy to rescue them.

Tiberius (tī-bir'i-us). [Full name, *Tiberius Claudius Nero Caesar.*] Second Roman emperor, born Nov. 16, 42 B.C.; died March 16, 37 A.D. He was a member of the ancient patrician Claudian family whose ancestors, according to some accounts, had come from the Sabine country to Rome in the time of Romulus. Others say the Claudians came to Rome in the 6th century B.C. His father was Tiberius Nero, who had been a quaestor and had been a commander of Caesar's fleet. His mother was Livia Drusilla, a woman of great force and ambition, and the intelligence to pursue it. Some say Tiberius was born at Fundi, but most say he was born on the Palatine Hill. His birth took place during the disorders that followed the assassination of Caesar, when Octavian, the future Augustus, had not yet consolidated his power. According to a tale told by Suetonius, Livia sought to foretell the sex of her unborn child by warming an egg in her hands. She and her handmaids kept the egg warm until it hatched; a strong cock with a spectacular comb emerged from the shell and foretold the greatness of her as yet unborn son. In his youth an astrologer was similarly encouraging, saying he would be a king without a crown. The childhood of Tiberius was extremely unsettled, as his parents were continually fleeing before the displeasure of Octavian. Tiberius Nero had turned against Caesar, even proposing that his assassins should be rewarded, and he sided with Mark Antony in his early bid for power. When Antony was reconciled with Octavian, Tiberius Nero returned to Rome (39 B.C.) with his family, and his mistaken enthusiasm for republican government was forgiven by Octavian. This forgiveness may have been prompted by the fact that Octavian saw Livia and fell in love with her. Though she had borne one child, Tiberius, and was about to produce another, Octavian compelled Tiberius Nero to divorce her and immediately made her his own wife (38 B.C.).

The young Tiberius began to appear before the public at an early age. He delivered his father's funeral oration at the age of nine. He was quaestor, praetor, and consul, each time before he was old enough legally to occupy the offices. He appeared as an advocate and as prosecutor before the Senate, fought against the Cantabrians in Spain, led an army to Armenia (20 B.C.), where he restored the king as a vassal of Rome, and served as governor of Transalpine Gaul (19 B.C.). In 15 B.C. he went with his brother Drusus to subjugate the Germans at the source of the Rhenus (Rhine) and the Ister (Danube). In 11 B.C. he carried on a successful campaign against the Pannonians. This was followed by other successes in Germany. Augustus appointed him tribune for five years in 6 B.C. Suddenly he decided to retire from public life. He gave as his reason his unwillingness to appear to compete for popular favor with Caius and Lucius, the grandsons of Augustus, who had now come of age. Livia, to whom no children had been born of her union with Augustus, tried to persuade him not to retire. Augustus refused to consent to his retirement, for following the death of Drusus, Tiberius was the most capable commander of the Roman armies. Tiberius went on a hunger strike in order to gain his wish, and at the end of four days Augustus reluctantly gave him leave to depart. He went to Rhodes, which he remembered from a previous visit as an idyllic spot. Some say his ardent wish for self-imposed exile came from his bitterly unpleasant marriage. He had first married Vipsania Agrippina, the daughter of Augustus' good friend and military commander, Marcus Vipsanius Agrippa. With her he was happy; she bore him a son, Drusus. When she was about to bear their second child, Augustus ordered Tiberius to divorce his beloved wife and marry his daughter Julia (12 B.C.). It was said that when afterward Tiberius happened to see

Vipsania in the street, tears came into his eyes and he followed her with such a look of unhappiness on his face that
Augustus arranged it so that he would never lay eyes on her
again. After his forced marriage to Julia her licentiousness
became increasingly flagrant, and since he could not divorce
her, Tiberius at last got off to Rhodes leaving Julia and his
son Drusus behind. In Rhodes he lived quietly. When he
learned that Julia had been banished by her father for her
adulteries, he asked permission to return to Rome. Augustus now refused it, and as his influence waned alarmingly,
Tiberius came to be known as "the Exile." He continued to
make application to Augustus for his return. Livia added her
pleas, and Augustus was persuaded to change his mind. The
message that he could return having been received, Tiberius
set out for Rome (c2 A.D.), after an absence of seven years.
Within three years of his return Caius and Lucius, natural
heirs of Augustus, had died. Augustus adopted him and
Agrippa Postumus (his last remaining grandson) as his sons
(4 A.D.). Agrippa Postumus was accused of plotting against
Augustus and was banished. Tiberius became the heir apparent.

For the next years he led the armies. He pacified Germany. Next he went to Illyria to suppress a revolt. The war
was hard-fought and long. After three years he was victorious. This success was particularly important to Tiberius and
to Rome, for it came at the time (9 A.D.) when the loss of
Varus with three legions in Germany had plunged all Rome
into mourning. From Illyria he went to Germany to salvage
what he could from the defeat of Varus. On his return from
Germany he celebrated a belated triumph for his Illyrian
victory. He gave a great banquet with 1000 tables laid for his
guests, and gave each man present three pieces of gold.
Under customary procedure, Bato, the defeated Illyrian
leader, would have been strangled. In a rare instance of
magnanimity, Tiberius made him rich presents and gave
him a house in Ravenna, because once during the war Bato
had had the Romans trapped in a gorge and allowed them
to escape rather than defeat them in an unequal fight.
Tiberius used the spoils of the Illyrian war to restore the
Temples of Concord and of the Heavenly Twins (Castor and
Pollux). When Augustus was in his last brief illness, he summoned Tiberius to his side. Some said Augustus made

fat, fāte, fär, fåll, åsk, fāre; net, mē, hėr; pin, pīne; not, nōte, möve,
nôr; up, lūte, půll; oi, oil; ou out; (lightened) ĕlect, agǫny, ūnite;

Tiberius his heir partly at the insistence of Livia, but mostly because all his natural heirs, save Agrippa Postumus, were dead. And some say among Augustus' last words were these, "Alas, poor Rome, doomed to be chewed by those slow-moving jaws." Tiberius' enemies said Augustus never liked him. On the other hand, it appears that Augustus admired his military skill, and felt that he would be able to protect Rome from her enemies.

Tiberius did not immediately reveal the death of Augustus. First, Agrippa Postumus must be disposed of. Whether Livia or Tiberius gave the order for his death is not known, but when it was announced to him, Tiberius had the man who had carried out the order executed. He then went to the Senate to announce the death of Augustus. He asked for the protection of a Praetorian Guard for his person and assumed imperial powers, although he did not take the title of emperor. His assumption of power did not take place with unanimous approval. The soldiers in Germany clamored for Germanicus, their general, to take power, but he rebuked them and honorably refused to take advantage of their enthusiasm and affection. Other abortive plots against Tiberius were easily crushed. Tiberius conducted himself modestly as supreme ruler, although there was never any doubt as to who held the power. He refused to allow his followers to dedicate temples and priests to him as a divine being. He restored the authority and dignity of the consuls, and preserved the forms of republican government. He made some attempt to elevate the moral tone of life among the upper classes of Rome, which had become increasingly dissolute. He tried to control high prices with price ceilings, and limited to some extent the expense of public shows. An ardent student of Greek and Roman literature himself, he encouraged literature. He undertook tax reforms that greatly strengthened the financial condition of Rome. He abolished the ancient right of sanctuary and temples and also abolished foreign cults, especially those of the Egyptians and the Jews; it was in his reign that Christ was crucified. Remaining in Rome, he yet kept his generals and governors in the outposts on the alert by his frequent announcements that he was about to visit them, even going so far as to order transportation and food for his train. Then he would cancel the journey. He did this so many times he was given the nickname "Callipedes," from an actor whose specialty it was to give an imitation of a runner while never moving from one spot.

In 26 A.D. Tiberius left Rome to dedicate a Temple to Capitoline Jupiter at Capua and one to Augustus at Nola. From there he went to the island of Capreae (Capri), and remained there almost uninterruptedly until his death. Tiberius had never been popular at Rome. He was harsh and often cruel, as were his immediate predecessors, but unlike them, he apparently had no avenue to the affections of the people. In his days at Capreae he acquired a hideous reputation for the most grossly immoral practices and for savage cruelty, according to the Roman biographers who exaggerated and preserved his reputation for evil. He seemed to become indifferent to affairs of state, and carried them out by correspondence. He had always been considered stingy. He now became rapacious, confiscating estates at will and with almost no excuse. He was relentless toward his ex-wife Julia, and refused to ameliorate the harsh conditions of her exile. He quarreled with his mother, did not attend her funeral, refused to allow her to be deified, and annulled her will. He cared so little when his son Drusus died, so it is said, that when a delegation from Troy came, a month or so later, and offered him condolences, he replied by offering them condolences for the loss of their own eminent citizen, Hector. Some say he arranged to have Germanicus, his nephew and adopted son, and a very popular general, poisoned. He exiled Agrippina, wife of Germanicus, and had her flogged so severely she lost an eye, but he could not prevent her from starving herself to death. He accused the sons of Germanicus, his adoptive grandsons, of plotting against him and ordered them starved to death. The youngest son of Germanicus, Caius, called "Caligula," he spared. When apprised of the hatred and contempt in which he was held by the Romans, he said, "Let them hate me, so long as they fear me." He made his favorite, Sejanus, commander of the Praetorian Guard, and gave him unlimited power to punish his enemies, but when Sejanus began to acquire a following in his own right, Tiberius had him killed (31 A.D.). He rewarded informers and inflicted punishments indiscriminately. His reign, according to unfriendly Roman writers, was one of terror, and he was as much terrified as anyone, fully aware of his many enemies. He kept himself barricaded on Capreae. Suetonius tells that once he left the island and started for Rome. On the journey a pet serpent that he fed with his own hand was found nearly devoured by ants. Soothsayers told him it was a sign he must "beware the power of the mob." He started back to Capreae at once. He dreamed (still according to Suetonius), that a statue of Apollo he was planning to dedicate in the library of a temple of Augustus appeared to him and said, "Tiberius will never dedicate me." A few days before he died, the lighthouse at Capreae was struck by lightning. These signs of imminent death were fulfilled on March 16, 37 A.D., when he died at Misenum. News of his death, which some said was caused by poison administered on the order of Caius Caligula, provoked an outburst of joy. He was succeeded by Caius.

Tiberius Claudius Drusus Nero (klô'di-us drö'-sus nir'ō). Full name of *Claudius,* emperor of Rome 41–54 A.D.

Tigranes (tī-grā'nēz). King of Armenia; died after 56 B.C. He was a son-in-law of Mithridates the Great. He conquered Syria and part of Asia Minor, but was defeated by Lucullus in 69 B.C., surrendered to Pompey, and was deprived of his conquest.

Timoleon (ti-mō'lē̱-o̱n, tī-). Greek general and statesman, born at Corinth; died 337 or 336 B.C., at Syracuse. He was the son of Timodemus, of an illustrious Corinthian family. Timoleon was noted as a great patriot, for his mild and gentle disposition, for his hatred of tyrants, and for his personal courage. To illustrate his various characteristics— once in battle his brother, pierced by many wounds, fell and was in imminent danger of death. Timoleon rushed to his side, held his shield over his brother to protect him, and warded off the enemy until help arrived. This same brother afterwards got command of a body of mercenaries and threatened to make himself tyrant. Timoleon tried to reason with him and to persuade him not to attempt despotic power but failed to deter him and was mocked for his pains. Timoleon went with two companions to his brother's house, withdrew to a corner of the room, covered his head and wept while his companions, according to plan, assassinated his brother. Those who admired Timoleon credited him with putting his country before his family. His mother, however, did not take this view. Her anger at Timoleon so depressed him that he was only with difficulty persuaded not to starve himself to death, and he withdrew from public life. For the next 20 years he lived in obscurity.

When Dionysius the Younger, exiled tyrant of Syracuse, returned after ten years and reestablished himself as tyrant, the Carthaginians threatened Syracuse. The Syracusans sent to Corinth, their mother-city, for help. As the Corinthians, having decided to send help to their colony, debated who should be put in command of the expeditionary force, some one proposed that Timoleon be named. He was given the appointment and had begun collecting his forces when a letter from Hicetas, tyrant of Leontini, arrived, saying there was no need to send forces to aid Syracuse as he had been appointed general by the Syracusans. His letter angered the Corinthians, who suspected a design to make himself tyrant of Syracuse, and made them more than ever eager to send Timoleon. A force was outfitted. When they were ready to sail, the priestess of Persephone dreamed that the goddess and her mother were preparing for a journey and said they were going to sail with Timoleon. Because of this favorable omen the Corinthians equipped a sacred trireme and named it for the goddesses. Timoleon went to sacrifice at Delphi before his departure. As he did so a crown that had been presented as a votive offering slipped from its place and fell on his head, indicating that he had been crowned by the god himself. These were the first of many omens, noted by Plutarch, that showed Timoleon to be under divine protection. He set sail (344 B.C.) with ten ships to relieve Syracuse. Before Timoleon reached his destination, he learned that Hicetas had besieged Dionysius in the citadel of Syracuse and had made a treacherous agreement with the Carthaginians to prevent Timoleon from coming to the aid of Syracuse. Envoys of Hicetas met him at Rhegium, which, having thrown off its tyrant, welcomed him warmly. But 20 Carthaginian ships, sent thither by Hicetas, lay at anchor in the harbor. Timoleon understood that this was a threat, and realized that Hicetas and the Carthaginians meant to divide Sicily between them. As he could not pass by the Carthaginian fleet, he asked the envoys from Hicetas, who carried orders to him to return to Corinth, to present their proposals to him in a public meeting within the gates of Rhegium. The envoys agreed; the Carthaginians, the envoys, and the people of Rhegium went into the market-place. The gates were closed and speeches were begun. Timoleon, with the help of the Rhegines, delayed the proceedings with many speeches and counter-proposals. While he did so, nine of his ships quietly sailed past the unattended Carthaginian fleet. When word was brought to him of their escape, Timoleon slipped through the crowd, boarded the last of his ships, and sailed away. The Carthaginians, noted for their duplicity, were deeply chagrined at the trick Timoleon had played on them, and the people of Rhegium were delighted that the Carthaginians had been beaten at their own game.

Timoleon and his fleet put in at Tauromenium, whose ruler, Andromachus, hated tyranny and allowed him to use the city as a base. Hicetas sent the Carthaginian ships to Syracuse. Timoleon set out for Adranum where he met the forces of Hicetas that had come to meet him. While the ranks of Hicetas were still coming up, Timoleon attacked and routed them, though they were vastly superior in numbers. The people of Adranum came streaming out of the city to welcome Timoleon, of whose success they had had divine warning: the doors of the temple of Adranus, the Sicilian fire-god, had flown open of themselves, the spear of the god trembled, and sweat poured off the face of the image, all of which portended wonderful victories. After this victory the other Greek cities of Sicily, which had hitherto distrusted him and feared he wanted to make himself tyrant, flocked to Timoleon's side, and his forces were greatly increased. Dionysius, still shut up in the citadel at Syracuse, sent a message offering to surrender to him. Timoleon secretly sent 400 of his soldiers, all he could safely get through the enemy lines, to accept his surrender and take him off the island citadel. Timoleon shipped him to Corinth and his men took possession of all the stores, horses, and men that Dionysius had left in the citadel. Now the situation at Syracuse was this: Timoleon's men occupied the citadel; the forces of Hicetas occupied the mainland city and territory of Syracuse; and the Carthaginian fleet was in the harbor. Timoleon himself was at Adranum. Hicetas sent two men to assassinate him as he made a sacrifice at the altar. As they were about to attack him, a man in the crowd leaped at one of the would-be assassins and killed him, crying out that he

(obscured) errạnt, ardẹnt, actọr; ch, chip; g, go; th, thin; ŦH, then; y, you; (variable) ḍ as d or j, ṣ as s or sh, ṭ as t or ch, ẓ as z or zh.

had just recognized him as the man who had slain his father. The other assassin confessed the plot and all marveled at the manner in which the gods protected Timoleon. After the failure of the plot, Hicetas invited Mago, the Carthaginian commander, with 60,000 troops into the city of Syracuse, which had never fallen to Carthaginian attack but was now handed over to them. Hicetas continued to besiege Timoleon's men in the citadel. In an attempt to prevent the besieged from receiving supplies, he went with Mago to take Catana, which was sending food to the citadel by small boat. Timoleon's commander in the citadel sallied out in their absence and seized the strongest part of the city as well as stores of supplies and arms. On the accomplishment of this, and perhaps because he feared that the Greeks might unite against him, Mago decided to leave Sicily and abandoned Hicetas. Timoleon jeered at the cowardice of the Carthaginians, attacked Hicetas, and took the city by storm without losing a man. He destroyed the island citadel that had been the refuge of tyrants, and on its site raised courts of justice. Italy and Greece rang with his fame and the glory of his success. After the wars and sieges, Syracuse was sadly depopulated. Timoleon sent to Corinth to ask for colonists. Many came, and the city began to revive.

The Carthaginians, smarting under the cowardice of Mago, now sent a force of 70,000 under Hasdrubal and Hamilcar to attack Timoleon. With his force of 5000 foot-soldiers and 1000 horse, he marched to meet the enemy. Some of his mercenaries deserted on the way because they had not been paid and because they thought it was folly to attack such an overwhelmingly superior force, but others joined him. On the march his army met some mules loaded with parsley. His soldiers were made uneasy by this because of the association of parsley with the dead. Timoleon heartened them by saying the material of victory crowns had come to them of its own accord, for victors at the Isthmian Games at that time were crowned with parsley. He took some of it and made a wreath for his own head, and his men followed his example. Coming up to the Crimisus River, he saw that the Carthaginians were crossing it. A torrential rain and hail storm, with flashes of lightning and peals of thunder, greatly impeded the Carthaginians with their heavy armor. As they crossed the river Timoleon fell on them and slaughtered them by the hundreds (341 B.C.). Some say 10,000 were killed. The spoils were so great it took his men three days to collect them all and raise their victory trophy. The most beautiful of the captured armor was sent to Corinth to be dedicated in the temple of Poseidon. The defeated Carthaginians sailed away under command of Gisco. Timoleon pursued Hicetas and captured him alive in the land of Leontini. Hicetas and his sons were put to death. The wives and daughters of Hicetas and his friends were brought to trial in Syracuse and, with no opposition from Timoleon, they also were put to death. The Carthaginians sued for peace, and now for a time the sieges and wars ended. Timoleon freed the other Greek cities from their tyrants; Greek Sicily was restored to order, its lands were repeopled, and its cities revived. Timoleon, having accomplished what he had set out to do, voluntarily laid aside the great powers that he had exercised. He remained in Syracuse, where he was honored as a common father by the Syracusans. In his old age he went blind, but the Syracusans did not falter in their gratitude to him and their affection and honor for him. Occasionally he was brought into their assembly to hear a debate. After listening carefully he would pronounce his opinion on the proper course to follow and the Syracusans took his advice. After a brief illness, he died (337 or 336 B.C.), was given a great public funeral, and his ashes were buried in the market-place. Timoleon, of excellent character, unusual capacity, and incorruptible patriotism, was one of very few whose ventures were so unfailingly rewarded with success that it was commonly believed that the gods had a special love for him and protected him.

Timotheus (ti-mō′thȩ̄-us, -moth′ȩ̄-us; tī-). Athenian naval commander; son of Conon; died, 354 B.C. He was an able commander who did much to restore the power of Athens after the Peloponnesian War. He made an expedition around the Peloponnesus in 376 B.C., and achieved some successes, the most important of which was to win Corcyra for Athens. He was ordered back to Athens on the conclusion of a peace with Sparta, 374 B.C. In his next command he was hampered by lack of money. The Athenians had voted certain measures to relieve Corcyra, which had been attacked by Sparta after Timotheus left, but had not voted the money to carry them out. Timotheus was compelled to lose valuable time collecting money and ships. When he returned from a cruise about the Aegean for this purpose he was accused of fraud, was relieved of his command and subjected to trial. Thanks to the intervention of Alcetas, king of Epirus, and Jason of Pherae, whom he had persuaded to join the second Athenian Confederacy, he was acquitted. But he was discredited in Athens and left to enter the service of the king of Persia. He later returned to Athens and was sent as leader of an expedition against Samos, which he captured, 365 B.C. He next was given command of the fleet that was operating off Macedonia and won great success in the area; he compelled Methone and Pydna to join the Athenian Confederacy, and won Potidaea, Torone, and other cities, but was unsuccessful in two attempts to take Amphipolis. In 356 B.C. he was one of three commanders sent to subdue rebellious Chios. He and Iphicrates, a co-commander, decided not to press the attack because of a violent storm. Chares, the third commander, attacked against their advice and without their support and was driven off with great loss. He accused Timotheus and Iphicrates of treachery. They were brought to trial on a charge of having accepted bribes from the Chians. Iphicrates was acquitted but Timotheus, who had made enemies by his arrogant manner, was fined 100 talents. Unable to pay such a large sum, he withdrew to Chalcis and died soon after. Afterward the Athenians regretted their harsh treatment of Timotheus and allowed his son to settle the fine for 10 talents. Timotheus was buried in the Ceramicus; statues in his honor were set up in the market-place and on the Acropolis.

Tissaphernes (tis-a̯-fèr′nēz). Persian satrap; executed c395 B.C. He became satrap in Asia Minor (413 B.C.). As an enemy of Athens, he stirred up revolt (412 B.C.) of the Athenian cities of Asia Minor and made an alliance with Sparta. He was hostile to Cyrus the Younger, and discovered and disclosed the latter's plans to Artaxerxes II. He took part in the battle of Cunaxa (401 B.C.), in which Cyrus was killed, and acted as guide to the Ten Thousand Greeks during the early part of their return journey from Cunaxa. In the course of the march Tissaphernes gathered the Greek generals and captains of the Ten Thousand in his tent, treacherously had the captains slain and sent the generals in chains to the Persian court, where they were put to death. He was appointed chief ruler in W Asia by Artaxerxes, was defeated by Agesilaus of Sparta in 395 B.C., and was put to death through the influence of Parysatis, who blamed Tissaphernes for the death of her son Cyrus.

Titus (tī'tus). [Full name, *Titus Flavius Sabinus Vespasianus.*] Roman emperor; born 39 A.D.; died September, 81 A.D. He was the son of Vespasian. He was called "the delight of mankind" because of his free distribution of gifts to his people. He was educated with Britannicus, served in the army, conducted the Jewish war after the departure of his father, and in 70 A.D. captured Jerusalem, for which he was given a triumph at Rome and in honor of which his brother Domitian erected the Arch of Titus. He was associated with Vespasian in the government, and succeeded to the throne on Vespasian's death, June, 79 A.D. Though dissipated in his habits before he became emperor, he devoted himself thereafter to bettering the lot of the Romans. He finished the Flavian Amphitheater ("Colosseum") and built the Baths of Titus. The eruption of Vesuvius that buried Pompeii, and a fire at Rome, occurred in his reign. On his death he was succeeded by his brother, the cruel and tyrannous Domitian.

Tomyris (tom'i-ris). Queen of the Massagetae, a large tribe dwelling in the plain beyond the Aral and Caspian Seas. Cyrus the Great, wishing to become lord of the tribe, sent an embassy to Tomyris inviting her to become his wife. Tomyris recognized, according to Herodotus, that his true purpose was to gain control of her kingdom and rejected his suit. Cyrus then prepared to conquer her kingdom by force, as guile had failed. He built boats to ferry his army across the river into her country. Tomyris sent an ambassador to him, and advised him to cease from making war, for he could not be sure that he would profit by the outcome. She counseled Cyrus to be content to rule over his own and allow her to rule her own. However, if Cyrus was unwilling to take her advice, she proposed that she would withdraw her forces three days' march within her frontier, or, if Cyrus preferred, he could withdraw his forces three days' march into his country; the withdrawing army would then wait until the other army caught up with it, whereupon they would engage in battle. Cyrus took council with the chief Persians. They advised him to let Tomyris invade his country. But Croesus, Lydian king who had been captured by Cyrus, objected; he said that if Cyrus let the Massagetae in and they defeated the Persians, the Massagetae would not withdraw and Cyrus would lose his country. On the other hand, if Cyrus defeated them, he would gain nothing but his own country. Moreover, it would be shameful to withdraw before a woman. Cyrus took his advice and sent word to Tomyris to withdraw, which she did. Cyrus now advanced against Tomyris. After three days' march he left one-third of his army, as Croesus had advised him to. This portion was the weakest third and he instructed them to make camp, to serve up a rich banquet, to drink wine and make merry. Meanwhile Cyrus withdrew with the rest of his army. The Massagetae attacked the forces in camp with one-third of their forces, and although the Persians resisted, they were overcome by the Massagetae. Then, as Croesus had foretold, the Massagetae fell on the feast which the Persians had been enjoying, and being unused to wine, drank of it until they were sated and fell into a stupor. Cyrus now returned and slew many of them and took Spargapises, son of Tomyris, captive. Tomyris sent Cyrus a message, chiding him for overcoming the Massagetae with wine and not with arms. She warned him to restore her son and retire, or she would glut him with blood. Spargapises, restored to sobriety and finding himself a captive, begged to be freed from his bonds. Cyrus released him, and instantly he took his own life. Tomyris, learning his fate, regrouped her forces and attacked. In fierce, desperate hand-to-hand fighting, the Massagetae prevailed, hacked the Persian army to pieces and killed Cyrus himself. Tomyris filled a skin with human blood, found the corpse of Cyrus, decapitated it, and flung the head into the skinful of blood. She maltreated the body and apostrophized it, saying that even though she had conquered Cyrus in battle, he had conquered her through the death of her son, but, as she had sworn, she had glutted him with blood. This, according to Herodotus, is how Cyrus met his death at the hands of a woman.

Torquatus (tôr-kwā′tus), **Titus Manlius.** See **Manlius Torquatus, Titus.**

Trajan (trā′jạn). [Full Latin name, **Marcus Ulpius Trajanus;** surnamed **Dacicus** and **Parthicus.**] Roman emperor (98–117 A.D.); born in Italica, Spain, 53 A.D.; died at Selinus, Cilicia, July or August, 117. He entered the army at an early age, served as military tribune in various provinces, marched from Spain to Germany (c88), was made consul (91) and by Nerva consular legate in Germany, and was adopted by Nerva, and succeeded him on the latter's death in January, 98. He developed the defenses of the empire on the northeastern frontier, built many roads and other improvements, founded the institution of *alimenta* (for rearing poor children in Italy), and encouraged various reforms. He conducted (c101–106) a successful war against the Dacians under Decebalus, and annexed Dacia to the empire; the Column of Trajan at Rome commemorates this conquest. He incorporated (114) Damascus, and part of Arabia, into the empire, and carried on an indecisive war with the Parthians (114–116). There were revolts in the eastern part of the empire and among the Jews in the last part of his reign, but he died before he could organize a campaign to put down the rebels.

Tritantaechmes (trī″tan̦-tēk′mēz). A son of Artabanus and nephew of Darius the Great of Persia. He was a Persian captain under Xerxes in the invasion of Greece, 480 B.C. According to Herodotus, when he heard that the prize for which men contested at the Olympic Games was not money but a crown of olive leaves he said, "Alas, Mardonius, what manner of men hast thou brought us to fight against, who contend not for money, but for honor."

V

Valerius (va̦-lir′i-us), **Marcus.** [Surnamed *Corvus.*] Roman general; born c371 B.C.; died c270 B.C. He distinguished himself in the First Samnite War. He is said to have won his surname when, having accepted single combat with a giant Gaul, he was aided by a raven that flew in the face of his opponent and enabled Valerius to win.

Valerius, Publius. Real name of *Publicola;* (q.v.).

Varro (var′ō), **Caius Terentius.** Roman politician; died after 200 B.C. He became consul, with Lucius Aemilius Paulus, in 216 B.C., and loudly criticized the harrying tactics of Fabius in the war against Hannibal. He boasted that he would defeat the enemy in a day, collected a force of 80,000–90,000 men and, in defiance of all advice, sought the enemy. He engaged Hannibal at Cannae in Apulia, and suffered a catastrophic defeat. According to some accounts, 50,000 Romans fell and 10,000–20,000 were taken captive. It was the most terrible defeat the Romans had ever sustained.

Varus (vär'us), *Publius Quintilius.* Roman general. He was consul (13 B.C.), governor in Syria (6–4 B.C.), and commander in Germany (6–9 A.D.). His rigorous measures led to a German alliance against him, and he was totally defeated by Arminius in the famous battle in the Teutoburger Wald (9 A.D.). When he saw that the battle was lost, he fell upon his sword. The three legions under his command were massacred to a man. This defeat profoundly affected the Romans; henceforth they abandoned the idea of a frontier on the Albis (Elbe). Augustus bitterly mourned the loss of the three legions, and the anniversary of the loss was observed in Rome as a day of mourning.

Vercingetorix (vėr-sin-jet'ọ-riks). Chief of the Arverni in Gaul, the leader of the great rebellion against the Romans in 52 B.C. He gained various successes against Caesar, but was besieged by him at Alesia and surrendered in 52 B.C. He was exhibited in Caesar's triumph at Rome in 46 B.C., and then by Caesar's order beheaded (c45 B.C.).

Verres (ver'ēz), *Caius.* Roman official; put to death under a proscription of Mark Antony, 43 B.C. He was praetor in 74 B.C., and later, as governor of Sicily (73–70 B.C.), plundered the island of property, art treasures, and the like. The Sicilians brought him to trial (70 B.C.) for his extortions. Cicero, who had offered his services to the Sicilians, undertook his prosecution. Verres was defended by Hortensius, who tried unsuccessfully to delay the trial to the following year when he would be consul. Cicero presented his evidence and Hortensius, unprepared, abandoned his client. Verres went into exile at Massilia (Marseilles) taking much of the loot from Sicily with him. Of the six orations against Verres composed by Cicero, only the first was actually delivered.

Verrucosus (ver-ụ-kō'sus), *Quintus Fabius Maximus.* See *Fabius Maximus, Quintus.*

Vespasian (ves-pā'zhạn). [Full Latin name, *Titus Flavius Sabinus Vespasianus.*] Roman emperor (69–79 A.D.); born near

Reate, Italy, Nov. 17, 9 A.D.; died June 24, 79 A.D. He was
of humble origin, but rose to distinction in the army, and
became consul in 51. He was afterward governor of Africa,
and in 67 was appointed commander-in-chief against the
insurgent Jews. He was proclaimed emperor in 69. His general Antonius Primus overthrew Vitellius in the same year,
and Vespasian arrived at Rome in 70, leaving his son Titus
to continue the Jewish war. The chief events of his reign
were the destruction of Jerusalem by Titus (70), the victories
of Agricola in Britain, and the suppression (70) of the revolting Batavians under Civilis. He restored discipline in the
army and order in the finances, and expended large sums on
public works, including the Flavian Amphitheater ("Colosseum"), which, however, he did not live to finish. On his
death he was succeeded by his sons Titus (79–81 A.D.) and
the unspeakable Domitian (81–96 A.D.).

Vitellius (vi-tel′i-us), *Aulus.* Roman emperor (69 A.D.); born 15
A.D.; killed at Rome, in December, 69 A.D. To say that he was
a favorite of Tiberius, Caligula, Claudius, and Nero is to give
eloquent testimony of his adaptability, servility, and profound knowledge of all forms of debauchery. He was appointed governor in lower Germany by Galba in 68, and was
proclaimed emperor by the army at the beginning of 69. His
generals Caecina and Valens defeated Otho, and he entered
Rome in the middle of 69. His brief reign was marked by a
rise in debauchery and license, but when the forces of Vespasian marched on Rome his followers dwindled. The Romans are said to have insisted that he keep the purple. His
forces were defeated by those of Vespasian under Antonius
Primus, and he was taken from hiding and murdered.

Xanthippus (zan-thip′us, -tip′-). Father of Pericles. He was of
democratic tendencies, though of aristocratic family, and
was partly responsible for the ostracism of Hipparchus (not
Hipparchus the son of Pisistratus, but a kinsman) and Megacles. A few years later (484 B.C.) he was himself ostracized

---

(obscured) errạnt, ardẹnt, actọr; ch, chip; g, go; th, thin; ꟻн, then; y, you;
(variable) ḏ as d or j, ş as s or sh, ṭ as t or ch, ẓ as z or zh.

at the instigation of his opponents. However, when Athens
was threatened by the Persian invasion under Xerxes he was
recalled (480 B.C.), and named as one of the Athenian commanders in the war. Following the victory of the Greeks over
the Persians at Mycale (479 B.C.), in which he commanded
the Athenian fleet, he sailed to the Hellespont (478 B.C.) and
captured the fortress of Sestos. After the Persian War he
shared the direction of the affairs of Athens with Aristides
and Themistocles. About 472 B.C. he joined with Aristides
and others to bring about the ostracism of Themistocles.

Xenophon (zen'ō-fon). Greek soldier, historian, and essayist;
born at Athens, c430 B.C.; died after 357 B.C. He was a son
of Gryllus, of aristocratic background and sympathies. He
was a disciple of Socrates. This came about, according to a
popular story, in the following manner. In his youth Xenophon was walking in the streets of Athens and was stopped
by the philosopher. Socrates asked him where various goods
might be secured. The youth answered politely. Then Socrates asked, "And where can you get high-minded men?"
Xenophon was unable to answer. "Then follow me," said
Socrates. Xenophon did as he was bid, and remained ever
after an admirer and defender of Socrates. However, his
contact with him must have been of short duration. Prox-
enus, a Boeotian friend of Xenophon, invited him to join
him in an expedition with Cyrus the Younger, brother of
Artaxerxes II, the Great King of Persia. Socrates advised
him to consult the oracle of Delphi, because he disapproved
of the plan. Xenophon did so, but since he had made up his
mind to secure the wealth and honor the expedition seemed
to promise, he agreed to go on the expedition as a mercenary. At the outset the 10,000 Greeks in Cyrus' army did not
know the true destination of their march, and when they
learned that they were to fight the Great King it was too late
to turn back. The battle was fought at Cunaxa, in Babylonia,
401 B.C. Cyrus was killed, and his oriental troops were defeated, but the Greeks were victorious in their sector. Artaxerxes wished only to rid himself of the 10,000 well-trained,
menacing mercenaries. He offered them a guide for the
journey to the sea. On the way the generals of the Greeks,
as well as their captains, were treacherously slain on the
order of their Persian guide Tissaphernes. The Greeks
found themselves alone and leaderless in the heart of hostile

fat, fāte, fär, fâll, àsk, fāre; net, mē, hèr; pin, pīne; not, nōte, möve,
nôr; up, lūte, pùll; oi, oil; ou out; (lightened) ēlect, agōny, ūnite;

country, over a thousand miles from Greece. With great
presence of mind Xenophon, who had been serving without
rank, rallied their spirits, scorned surrender, and proposed
the election of new officers to lead them to the sea. He was
elected one of the generals and thereafter guided their
march, through unknown and dangerous lands, in the face
of barbarous enemies, until the glorious day early in 400 B.C.
when those in the vanguard raised the joyous cry, "Tha-
lassa!" (The sea!). From the heights above Trapezus they
looked down on the Euxine Sea. Here Xenophon gave up
his command of the 10,000. He thought of establishing a
colony on the Phasis River but abandoned the idea when his
life was threatened by those who opposed it. The whole
heroic and incredible journey of the 10,000 was described
by Xenophon in the *Anabasis* (the Up-going, i.e., the expedition up from the coast). Simple and direct, in parts almost
a day-to-day record of events, the work has great immediacy
as a description of stirring events by one of the chief participants. It was written much later, after he had served various
Spartan harmosts and the Spartan king Agesilaus, who became his great friend. In 394 B.C. Athens declared war on
Sparta. Xenophon was accused of "Laconism" and condemned. Thereafter he accompanied Agesilaus at Coronea
in the same year. Afterward he retired to an estate at Scillus
near Olympia, given to him by the Spartans, and spent the
next 20 years in retirement.

In this period he wrote the *Anabasis;* the *Cyropaedia,* an
idealized biography of Cyrus the Great in which Xenophon,
sacrificing the truth, expressed his ideas on the education of
a ruler; the *Memorabilia,* a defense and description of the life
of Socrates as he remembered it, which evolves as a portrait
of a man rather than a study of a philosopher. Other works
were a *Symposium,* in which he sought perhaps to correct
certain details and atmospheres of Plato's work of the same
name; *Ways and Means,* concerning means of raising money
for Athens without resorting to tribute; *Hiero,* a dialogue on
government between Hiero of Syracuse and the poet Simonides; *Agesilaus,* a eulogy of his friend; *Hellenica,* a history
in which he continues the history of Thucydides, though
without that writer's lack of bias and without his accuracy,
from 411 B.C. to the end of the Peloponnesian Wars, and on
to the battle of Mantinea (362 B.C.). In this work Xenophon

(obscured) errạnt, ardẹnt, actọr; ch, chip; g, go; th, thin; ᴛʜ, then; y, you;
(variable) ḍ as d or j, ṣ as s or sh, ṭ as t or ch, ẓ as z or zh.

criticizes Sparta, which he had always admired greatly, for arrogance, and noted that punishment follows injustice. He also wrote *The Oeconomicus* which gives advice on household management and outlines the duties of husband and wife; essays on hunting and horsemanship, and other works. After Sparta's defeat by Thebes at Leuctra, 371 B.C., he was forced to leave Scillus and went to Corinth, where he spent his last years. In the meantime he had educated his sons, Gryllus and Diodorus, in the finest tradition. An alliance between Sparta and Athens against Thebes removed the old stigma of "Laconism"; the sons joined the Athenian army, and Gryllus fell at Mantinea, lauded for his courage. The image of Xenophon that comes to us across the centuries is of a noble, honest, heroic, and somehow endearing man, who did what he thought just without ambition, and who left in the *Anabasis* a stirring record of one of the most thrilling Greek exploits outside the proper history of Greece.

Xerxes I (zẽrk'sēz). [Old Persian, *Khsayarsha;* in the Bible, *Ahasuerus.*] Son of Darius the Great and Atossa, born c519 B.C.; assassinated 465 B.C. Before Darius became king of Persia he had a wife and several sons. On his accession to the throne, following the death of Cambyses and the murder of the False Smerdis, Darius also took as part of his kingly possessions the wives of Cambyses who had fallen to Smerdis. Atossa was one of these, and came to be one of the most influential of the wives of Darius. To her and Darius, Xerxes was born as their first son and, according to Herodotus, Atossa was determined that he should be the heir rather than his older half-brothers, born before Darius was king and to another wife. It was finally decided, on the advice of the Greek exile Demaratus, that the sons born before the father was king or heir apparent, had no claim to the throne as they were the children of a private person; only the sons born to the king and the wife he had after he became king were legitimate heirs. Demaratus cited a similar instance in Spartan history in support of his point, which he had every wish of making in order to please the queen. Thus it was, that when Darius was preparing a punitive expedition against Greece after the battle of Marathon, he appointed Xerxes as his heir. But Herodotus, who tells this story, adds the comment that with or without the suggestion of Demaratus Xerxes would have been named heir, because of the great influence of Atossa. On the death of Darius, Xerxes duly succeeded him (485 B.C.). At this time revolt had broken out in Egypt, and it seemed to Xerxes more important to put it down than to make an expedition into Greece. In the year following therefore, he marched against Egypt, subdued the country, and crushed it under a more tyrannical rule than that under which it had existed in the time of Darius. In the meantime, Mardonius, cousin of Xerxes, was aflame to win glory for himself, and to this end continually pressed on Xerxes the necessity to punish the Greeks, and at the same time he pointed out the advantages to Persia of extending her sway over Greece. To add to these persuasions, the Pisistratidae came as exiles from Athens to the Persian court and urged Xerxes to march against Greece, in the hope that they would be restored to power in Athens; and envoys from Thessaly also came and invited him into Greece and promised him all assistance should he do so. Xerxes consulted with his generals, and all save his uncle Artabanus agreed that a punitive expedition should be undertaken. They did so out of fear, according to Herodotus. Artabanus advised caution; he pointed out the difficulties; he reminded Xerxes that the lightning strikes the tallest tree, that the gods smite the most powerful men. Moreover, he advised him not to underestimate the Greeks. Xerxes scornfully rejected his advice as cowardly, and in his turn reminded Artabanus of the great deeds his forbears had accomplished with boldness. The decision to make war was made. But on thinking it over Xerxes decided that the advice of Artabanus was good, and he changed his plans. Next day he announced the cancellation of the expedition. All the generals were delighted, save Mardonius. However, according to Herodotus, a vision appeared to Xerxes in a dream and seemed to threaten him with destruction if he did not proceed against the Greeks. He discussed his dream with Artabanus, who tried to explain it away, but when the figure of the dream appeared to Artabanus himself, and threatened him for persuading Xerxes to abandon the expedition, Xerxes and Artabanus concluded that the war on Greece was demanded by the gods.

Preparation now went forward with vigor in the following years. Four years were spent in gathering the host, the largest that had ever been assembled. In addition to a huge land

(obscured) errạnt, ardẹnt, actọr; ch, chip; g, go; th, thin; ᵺ, then; y, you; (variable) ḍ as d or j, ş as s or sh, ţ as t or ch, ᶎ as z or zh.

army a fleet was gathered. At last all was in readiness, provisions were stored at strategic points on the route, beasts of burden were collected, cables for bridges were prepared, and the armies were gathered at Sardis. Xerxes sent heralds throughout Greece, except to Athens and Sparta, demanding earth and water as tokens of submission to his rule, for he thought surely they would send the tokens through fear of his overwhelming force. He then (Spring, 480 B.C.) proceeded toward Abydos on the Hellespont, where he had caused a bridge of boats to be constructed so that his vast army could the more easily cross into Europe. Some say that when he set out from Sardis for Abydos there was an eclipse of the sun, a token of ill omen for the Persians. Others say this omen occurred on his departure from Susa for Sardis. In either case, his priests, when called on to interpret the omen, said it foretold destruction for the Greeks, for the sun was the oracle of the Greeks, but the moon was the oracle of the Persians. Xerxes rode forth with his baggage bearers, beasts of burden, polyglot army and their camp followers, spearmen, sacred horses, and an empty chariot of the Persian god Ormazd drawn by eight milk-white steeds. The chariot was empty because it would have been impious for a mortal to ride in the god's car. On the way to Abydos the army passed through Troy, where Xerxes sacrificed 1000 oxen to Trojan Athena and poured libations to the heroes who fell in the Trojan War. At Abydos he reviewed his army from a white marble throne that he caused to be set on a hill outside the city. As he saw the whole plain and the strait filled with his army and his ships, he first congratulated himself and then wept. To the question of Artabanus as to why he wept he replied that it was out of pity for the shortness of man's life, for he suddenly realized (so says Herodotus) that of all his tremendous host not one would be alive in a hundred years. Artabanus was still full of fears as to the outcome of the venture, and warned Xerxes of two great dangers: the land, that would not support the needs of the great army; and the sea, which had no harbors big enough to protect such a fleet in case of storms. Herodotus, who gives these conversations, could invent them after the fact, for it did indeed turn out that Xerxes' army, as other armies in later times that pushed too far from their base of supplies, suffered from lack of food and water; and parts of the great

---

fat, fāte, fär, fâll, ȧsk, fãre; net, mē, hėr; pin, pīne; not, nōte, möve, nôr; up, lūte, pull; oi, oil; ou out; (lightened) ĕlect, agǫny, ūnite;

fleet were destroyed by storms. But that was in the future, and Xerxes was unmoved by his fears. After offering a libation from a golden goblet to the Hellespontine waters, or perhaps to the sun, he ordered his host to cross at Abydos. The crossing lasted seven uninterrupted days and nights. When the whole army was across a prodigy occurred: a mare gave birth to a hare. This could only mean, says Herodotus, that Xerxes would lead a great host against Greece but would have to run for his life to regain the point from which he had set out. But this omen as well as others was disregarded.

According to Herodotus, the number in the Persian train, including non-combatants and camp-followers, was 1,700,-000. Later scholars estimate the number of fighting men at 180,000. Soldiers from all parts of the Persian empire and their allies made up the army. In the fleet, it was said, were 1207 ships furnished by the Phoenicians, Egyptians, Cyprians, Ionians, Lycians, and many others. Of these, those of the Phoenicians were superior in quality and numbers. Demaratus the exiled Spartan king accompanied Xerxes on the expedition, and was questioned concerning the valor of the Greeks, and whether they would resist the Persians. Xerxes thought they would not. Demaratus assured him on more than one occasion that the Spartans, at least, would never submit, and that if there were only 1000 Spartans they would nevertheless take the field. Xerxes laughed at what he considered to be wild words, and continued his march along the coast of Thrace, crossing the Strymon River and forcing the nations along the way to join his march. Near the promontory of Athos, across which a ditch had been cut for the passage of his ships, Xerxes separated from the fleet, and the army continued to Pieria, where the heralds he had sent out to demand earth and water from the Greek cities returned. They brought back tokens of submission from many, among them the Thessalians, Locrians, Achaeans of Phthiotis, Thebans, and all the Boeotians except the Plataeans and Thespians. According to Herodotus, the Greeks who did not give tokens of submission took the following oath: "From all those of Greek blood who delivered themselves up to the Persians without necessity, when their affairs were in good condition, we will take a tithe of their goods, and give it to the god at Delphi." Xerxes had

(obscured) errant, ardent, actor; ch, chip; g, go; th, thin; ᴛʜ, then; y, you;
(variable) ḍ as d or j, ṣ as s or sh, ṭ as t or ch, ẓ as z or zh.

sent no heralds to Athens and Sparta, for when his father Darius had done so his heralds to those cities were slain in defiance of the sacred law protecting the persons of heralds. Although the Persian force was directed in name against the Athenians, the Greeks understood that it was in truth directed against them all, and it was for this reason that many determined to resist the Persian advance. But now that the Persian force was near, the hearts of many failed. Oracles predicted doom and allies deserted, but some of the Greeks maintained their courage. The Persian army reached Thermopylae and the fleet reached Cape Sepias off Euboea without suffering any battle losses. At Cape Sepias a violent storm, caused, the Athenians said, by their prayers to their kinsman Boreas, rose and destroyed 400 of the Persian ships, unnumbered men, and rich treasure. At Thermopylae Xerxes learned the truth of Demaratus' statements concerning the valor of the Spartans, for although the forces of Xerxes won the pass, it was only after the loss of thousands of Persians in the face of the resistance offered by Leonidas and his 300 Spartans and 700 Thespians. After the battle at Thermopylae and an inconclusive sea fight at Artemisium, the Persian army marched down the valley of the Cephissus River and on to Athens. At the approach of the Persians most of the Athenians withdrew with their families to the island of Salamis. A few took refuge on the citadel (Acropolis) and prepared to resist the Persians. They attacked the citadel, took it, massacred the defenders, and set fire to the temples on the Acropolis and burned Athens. Thus Xerxes had made himself master of Athens and carried out the vengeance his father had intended. But the war was not over. Themistocles, the Athenian general, by a stratagem compelled the Greek allies who still had the will to resist to meet the Persian fleet at Salamis. As Xerxes watched from a hill overlooking the bay, he saw his fleet suffer disastrous defeat (480 B.C.). He now feared his restless Ionian subjects would break down his bridges and prevent his return into Asia if he did not fly at once, but to cover up his plans he continued warlike preparations against Salamis. However, he consulted his generals as to whether he should stay and conquer Greece or return to Persia. Only Artemisia the female admiral, of all his advisers, advised him to return to Persia and allay the fears of his people that would arise when

---

fat, fāte, fär, fåll, àsk, fãre; net, mē, hèr; pin, pīne; not, nōte, möve, nôr; up, lūte, pùll; oi, oil; ou out; (lightened) ĕlect, agǫny, ūnite;

they learned of the defeat at Salamis. On her advice and at the urging of Mardonius, he left the latter in charge of a large land force and hurriedly set out for the Hellespont. Arrived there, he found that storms had destroyed his bridges of boats, but his force was now so small that he was able to embark in ships and so return to Asia. On his return to Susa, weakened by the losses his arms had suffered and later by the defeat of the forces he left behind, at Plataea and Mycale (479 B.C.), he became involved with court intrigues. The power of Persia had been so severely weakened that it never fully recovered. Xerxes was assassinated in 465 B.C. in a palace conspiracy. Ahasuerus, the king of Persia who appears in the Book of Esther in the Old Testament, is identified with Xerxes I.

(obscured) errant, ardent, actor; ch, chip; g, go; th, thin; ŦH, then; y, you;
(variable) ḍ as d or j, ş as s or sh, ţ as t or ch, ẓ as z or zh.

DATE DUE